APOPHORETA
ΑΠΟΦΟΡΗΤΑ

LATIN AND GREEK STUDIES
IN HONOR OF
GRACE L. BEEDE

GRACE L. BEEDE

ΑΠΟΦΟΡΗΤΑ

APOPHORETA

LATIN AND GREEK STUDIES IN HONOR OF
GRACE L. BEEDE

EDITED BY JEREMIAH REEDY

BOLCHAZY-CARDUCCI PUBLISHERS

CHICAGO, 1985

©Bolchazy-Carducci Publishers
8 South Michigan Avenue
Chicago, Illinois 60603

INTERNATIONAL STANDARD BOOK NUMBER 0-86516-059-7
LIBRARY OF CONGRESS CATALOG CARD NUMBER 84-72745

PRINTED IN THE UNITED STATES OF AMERICA

CONTENTS

Editor's Introduction — vi

Grace Lucile Beede - *Curriculum Vitae* — viii

Tabula Gratulatoria — x

†GERALD F. ELSE - Persuasion and the Work of Tragedy — 1

DANIEL L. ARNAUD - An Aspect of Wit in Ovid's *Metamorphoses* — 9

CARRIE COWHERD - Ciceronian Precepts and Humor in Persius — 41

GERTRUDE C. DRAKE - Mythopoeic Fortune in Apuleius, Boethius, Dante and Chaucer — 59

BRENT M. FROBERG - Food and the Comic Spirit in the Plays of Plautus — 75

JUDITH LYNN SEBESTA - Carl Orff and the *Carmina Burana: Cantiones Profanae* — 85

HERBERT W. BENARIO - Tacitus and Suetonius Paullinus — 103

DIONYSIUS A. KOUNAS - Profiles and Policies of Athenian Conservatives in the Early Fourth Century B.C. (403-378) — 118

RICHARD LUMAN - In the Fulness of Times — 152

JAMES E. SPAULDING - Germano-Roman Numismatic Art — 177

WINTON U. SOLBERG - Cotton Mather, *The Christian Philosopher*, and the Classics — 213

RAYMOND V. SCHODER, S.J. - Theodoros of Samos: An Ancient Greek Artistic Genius — 247

CLARENCE A. FORBES - The Greeks and Their Feats — 259

JOHN FRANCIS LATIMER - Acts of the Apostles 26: 4-5: Are All the Translations Wrong? — 271

EDGAR C. REINKE - Classical Education and the Western Tradition — 301

JEREMIAH REEDY - *Logos, Mythos* and *Urdummheit* — 321

Notes on Contributors — 345

INTRODUCTION

When Grace Beede was chair of the Classics Department at U.S.D., we used to celebrate the Saturnalia every other year or so. She must have spent weeks making fudge, taffy and brownies, baking cookies, cakes and other treats in addition to preparing the necessary decorations, costumes, games, etc. After feasting on the results of her culinary skills, we were always given more food—*apophoreta*—to take with us "in the folds of our togas." The Greek dictionary defines *apophoreta* as "presents which guests receive at table to take home." Though the word is Greek, the custom is Roman. Thus it seemed that *Apophoreta* would be a not inappropriate title for this collection of essays in honor of Grace Beede. These studies are literally gifts which will be presented to her at a banquet. In another sense, of course, the articles of those of us who studied with her are the fruits of gifts we received as a result of our association with her. Everyone who associates with Grace Beede comes away a richer and better person; the number of those who have been recipients of her *apophoreta* is legion.

This *Festschrift* consists of sixteen essays: six on literary topics and four on historical ones. The remaining six deal with numismatics, art history, ancient athletics, the Bible, education and myth. While it would not be possible in a single volume to do justice to Grace's many interests, the diversity of the essays reflects the broad range of her professional interests. She has taught at one time or another, in one class or another, all of the subjects of these essays. What unity this volume has is provided by the desire many people felt to honor an outstanding scholar, teacher and person.

The *curriculum vitae* given below lists but a small fraction of the societies and organizations Grace belongs to and only a few of the offices she has held and still holds, but she has never been simply a nominal member of a group. Every organization has enjoyed the benefits of her enthusiasm, loyalty and willingness to "pitch in" and get things done. Many a dean learned quickly that if you wanted to get something done at U.S.D., you asked Grace Beede. Her involvements, however, have extended far beyond the field of Classics and far beyond academia. She is a member of the American Harp Society and the Annie D. Tallent Club; she is an honorary member of the National Collegiate Players, and she has been president of the U.S.D. Danforth Meditation Chapel Foundation since its inception. She served as Worthy Grand Matron of the Order of the Eastern Star in 1946 and 1947. Her service to the larger community beyond the campus has brought her countless honors; for example, she was honored by the South Dakota Bicentennial Commission and the American Revolution Bicentennial Administration for serving as chair for Vermillion of the American Revolution Bicentennial observance. In 1975 the Vermillion Chamber of Commerce presented her with a "Distinguished Citizen Award," and in 1978 she was inducted into the Western Heritage Hall of Fame. One can only exclaim with Vergil, *"Mirabile dictu."* For generations of students and colleagues Grace has served as a model in the three areas American universities have sought to promote: scholarship, teaching and service to others.

Editing is never an easy task, but this was a labor of love, and it was made easier by the enthusiastic cooperation of all the authors of essays. They answered their mail promptly and were diligent about meeting deadlines—evidence of their eagerness to honor Grace. I wish to thank them and everyone listed in the *Tabula Gratulatoria*. Without their assistance and encouragement this volume would never have seen the light of day.

I conclude with a statement from John Henry Cardinal Newman, a statement I never tire of quoting, *viz.* that the "teacher's main duty is to inspire." Teachers cannot learn for students, and they cannot force students to learn. It is by their scholarship, enthusiasm, love of learning, love of teaching and love of students that great teachers inspire others so they want to learn. This is what makes Grace a great teacher, and it is the inspiration that she as a loving teacher and loving person gave us that puts us in her debt. We offer these studies to her with gratitude and affection in partial payment of our indebtedness.

Rome
July, 1984   J.R.

GRACE LUCILE BEEDE—*Curriculum Vitae*

1905	Born August 22, Meckling, South Dakota
1926	B.A. *summa cum laude,* University of South Dakota
1926-27	Student, Smith College
1927-28	Professor of Latin, Hiwassee College
1928-70	Professor of Classics, U.S.D.
1928-69	Member of Executive Committee, Classical Association of the Middle West and South, representing South Dakota
1930	Vergilian Bimillennial Pilgrimage and *Aeneid* Cruise
1930	Author of numerus reviews in *The Classical Journal* and *The Classical Outlook*
1936	Ph.D., University of Chicago
1936	*Vergil and Aratus: A Study in the Art of Translation* published by University of Chicago Press
1940-68	Member of Triennial Council, Phi Beta Kappa
1942-56	Associate Editor of *The Classical Journal*
1942-52	Lecturer in Art, U.S.D.
1943	National Vice President, Classical Association of the Middle West and South
1943	"Proverbial Expressions in Plautus," *Classical Journal*
1944	"The Price of Leadership," *Mortar Board Quarterly*
1945	"Today is Ours," *The Eleusis of Chi Omega*
1946-60	Editor of Phi Beta Kappa's *Index: A Handbook for New Members*
1947-70	Chair, Classics Department, U.S.D.

GRACE LUCILE BEEDE

1951	National Vice President, Classical Association of the Middle West and South (second time)
1952-70	Professor of Art, U.S.D.
1958	College Lecture: "The Classics in the Geophysical Year" (first woman so honored)
1960-69	Editor of *Inter Nos*, South Dakota Latin Newsletter
1961	"The Humane Element: An Ariadne's Thread for our Time,"*Kentucky Journal of Humanities*
1964	Recipient of *Ovatio*, C.A.M.W.S., Toledo, Ohio
1967	Editor of *Classical Greek Drama: A Collection of Festival Papers* (first imprint of The Dakota Press, U.S.D.)
1967	Grace L. Beede Women's Dormitory dedicated, U.S.D.
1970	Two "Grace L. Beede Scholarships" established by College of Arts and Sciences, U.S.D. and South Dakota's Alpha of Phi Beta Kappa
1970	Professor of Classics and Art, *Emerita*
1970-	Director of Independent Study in Classics, U.S.D.
1971	Honorary D. Litt., Sioux Falls College
1972	Contributor to *The First Score: The Harrington Lectures, 1953-72*
1974	Homeric Seminar and Greek Tour
1974-76	American Revolution Bicentennial Observance chairman for Vermillion, Clay County and U.S.D.
1975	"Distinguished Citizen Award" from Vermillion Development Co. and Chamber of Commerce
1976	Bicentennial Fellow of Phi Beta Kappa
1978	Charter Inductee, Western Heritage Hall of Fame, Pierre, South Dakota
1979-	Honorary Editor of *Nuntius*
1981	U.S.D. Commencement Speaker (first woman so honored)

TABULA GRATULATORIA

Usher and Edith Barnes Abell	Vermillion, South Dakota
Daniel L. Arnaud	Groton, Massachusetts
Dr. Marjorie H. Beaty	Vermillion, South Dakota
Herbert W. Benario	Atlanta, Georgia
Raphael H. Block	Vermillion, South Dakota
Joseph H. and Margaret H. Cash	Vermillion, South Dakota
Henry V. Cobb	Chapel Hill, North Carolina
Carrie Cowherd	Washington, D.C.
Gertrude C. Drake	Edwardsville, Illinois
Mr. and Mrs. William E. Ekman	Vermillion, South Dakota
†Gerald F. Else	Ann Arbor, Michigan
Clarence A. Forbes	Columbus, Ohio
Brent Froberg	Vermillion, South Dakota
Elbert W. Harrington	Vermillion, South Dakota
Mrs. Harold Jordan	Vermillion, South Dakota
Dr. and Mrs. Robert H. Knapp	Vermillion, South Dakota
Wayne S. and Esther M. Knutson	Vermillion, South Dakota
Dionysius A. Kounas	Lawrence, Kansas
Andre P. and Linda S. Hansen Larson	Vermillion, South Dakota
John Francis and Helen B. Latimer	Washington, D.C.
Anthony O. Lennon	Fort Dodge, Iowa
Richard Luman	Ardmore, Pennsylvania
Nancy Hoy McCahren	Vermillion, South Dakota
E. Jay Michelson	Pierre, South Dakota
John and Lynn Milton	Vermillion, South Dakota
General and Mrs. Lloyd R. Moses	Vermillion, South Dakota
Les Parry	Vermillion, South Dakota
Jeremiah and Dolores Reedy	Saint Paul, Minnesota
Edgar C. Reinke	Oviedo, Florida
Dean and Mrs. Herbert S. Schell	Vermillion, South Dakota
Raymond V. Schoder, S.J.	Chicago, Illinois
Judith Lynn Sebesta	Vermillion, South Dakota
Winton U. Solberg	Urbana, Illinois
James E. Spaulding	Vermillion, South Dakota

PERSUASION AND THE WORK OF TRAGEDY
†Gerald F. Else

My thesis in this paper will be that rhetoric and poetry were even more closely interconnected in Aristotle's thought than has been realized, and in particular that persuasion plays a major role in both his rhetorical and his poetic theory.

A key point in the whole argument is the chronology. It is essential to recognize that the basic stock of both the *Rhetoric* and the *Poetics* belongs to Aristotle's early period in the Akademy, in the 350's, rather than to his second sojourn in Athens, after 335. Acceptance of this early dating has been gaining ground with respect to the *Rhetoric*; it is just beginning to be established for the *Poetics*. Yet it is of major importance for our evaluation of that work to see it not as the ripe fruit of a lifetime of meditation on literature, but as a series of brilliant *aperçus* tossed off by a young genius on his first—or possibly his second—passage through the subject. It was a passage negotiated in closest contact, both written and oral, with Plato, and fired by the intense intellectual excitement of life in the Akademy around 360, when new horizons were being opened up and explored in every direction.

In Books 2 and 3 of the *Republic*, published around 370, and again in Book 10, around 360, Plato recorded his opposition to the poets, especially Homer and the tragedians, as misrepresenters of gods and men and corrupters of youth. Meanwhile, in the *Phaidros* (around 365?) he made a partial about-face in his attitude toward rhetoric, which he had previously (in the *Gorgias*, about 390) attacked even more savagely than poetry. He was now prepared not only to admit that a "true" rhetoric was possible, but to lay down some of the scientific principles which it must follow. And this change of stance was not of merely theoretical import, for within a decade or less, not later than 355, Aristotle was actually teaching such a course of rhetoric in the Akademy—surely with Plato's approval—and codifying its principles in the rhetorical treatises which we still possess.

Aristotle was just 24 years old in 360, and deeply involved in all the various explorations that were going on in the Akademy. In the two fields that interest us here he was playing apparently contradictory roles: he was carrying out and extending the master's ideas in rhetoric while stoutly opposing them in poetry. But I suggest that from Aristotle's own point of view he was playing not contradictory but *complementary* roles: he was out to show that rhetorical and poetic art, though both involve substantial commitments to feeling, can both be rational forms of activity.

Plato had laid down in the *Phaidros* three main principles for a new rhetoric: 1) a speech must be an organic unified whole, 2) the orator must know what he is talking about, and 3) he must know what kinds of discourses there are and which kinds of people will respond to which ones. Requirement no. 1 is not explicitly mentioned in our *Rhetoric*; it appears to all the more effect in the *Poetics*, of which more shortly. Requirement no. 2 is dealt with in Book 1 of the *Rhetoric*, which states that rhetoric is a counterpart or offshoot (*antistrophos*, *Rhet.* 1 *init.*; *paraphyés ti*, 1356a25) of dialectic, and that the orator must command the appropriate forms of argumentation, especially the "rhetorical syllogism," the enthymeme. Book 1 also distinguishes (no. 3) the three species of oratory: deliberative, forensic (judicial), and epideictic, and analyzes the great common *topoi* with which they deal: the goals of human action, the various kinds of polity, the virtues and vices, pleasure, etc. (It was of course during this same period that Aristotle was working out the rules and procedures of logic, in the *Topics* and *Analytics*, and one of his main concerns was the close affiliations between rhetoric, dialectic, and ethics. No other writer on rhetoric in antiquity shared this broad range of interests.)

The other part of requirement no. 3, concerning the audience, is already partly involved in Book 1, but the main discussion, speaking to the question *how the listener is to be put in a certain mood or frame of mind*, is in Book 2 (Chapters 2-11, on the feelings). These discussions offer a rich phenomenology—one of the richest in Aristotle's works—of the human psyche and its typical behavior. Here Aristotle is responding to one part of Plato's demand for a scientific rhetoric; but we observe a fundamental difference between his view of the psyche and Plato's. Plato (cf. esp. *Rep.* 10, 602c-606c) saw the appetitive and emotional side of our nature as wholly irrational; Aristotle saw it as comporting an element of reason, calculation. We fear someone, for example, because we are persuaded that he has power to harm us and is likely to do so. Fear arises from an "expectation of imminent evil." Without that calculation, the emotion would not be felt.

It must be admitted on the other side that Aristotle appears, basically, to take a dim view of human nature. He is aware of the importance of appeals to ordinary human beliefs and feelings but would prefer, if it were possible, that the orator speak only of facts. Similarly, when all is said and done he has a low opinion of style: it is all "meant for the listener." "Nobody teaches geometry that way."

Book 3, where the principles of style are discussed, has the closest possible ties with the corresponding parts of the *Poetics*; indeed it could be argued that Aristotle first took serious note of style in connection with oratory (hence, e.g., *clarity* as the prime virtue of style) and only then transferred his ideas to poetry.

Aristotle's task vis-à-vis poetry, namely to defend it, appeared to differ from that in rhetoric, but he undertook it in the same spirit of cheerful confidence, and in the course of it he pressed into service certain key ideas borrowed from rhetoric, the *Phaidros*, and the Athenian jury-courts.

Plato in the *Phaidros* had called for unity in speeches, *logoi*—but *logos* in Plato's language denotes any verbal communication, including poems. In any case Aristotle did not apply the idea to speeches (why, is not clear), but he did apply it to poems, namely to the poetic *action*. The unified poetic action, says Aristotle, has to be built out of 'universals', and 'universals' are defined here (*Poet.* 9. 1351b 8-9) as "what kind of person it logically befalls, according to either probability (*to eikos*) or necessity, to say or do what kinds of thing." In other words, only speeches or actions typical of human behavior in general can be woven into a unified poetic plot.

I need only add that the "probability" Aristotle talks about here is the same *eikos* which had been the master-principle of rhetoric from the beginning: that which is *or can be made* persuasive to a listener—not a philosopher, but an average man acting as listener, e.g. in a jury-court.

Aristotle's coördinate concepts of unity and the universal are meant to answer one part of Plato's original charge against the poets. The poets do not misrepresent men; they present a true picture of the tendencies of human nature. (The gods, to be sure, are ignored.)

The second part of Plato's original indictment was that the poets, Homer above all, delude and mislead us by playing multiple roles as 'imitators'. *Mimesis* was used here in a new sense, to mean specifically the employment of direct speech in tragedy and epic. But it is not simply a question of syntax. Homer, the master deceiver, lurks behind the speeches in the *Iliad*, pretending that he is the old priest, Agamemnon, and the rest in turn, so that we are lured into giving up real simplicity of character for these false patterns of diversity.

Aristotle's response to this is to retain the term *mimesis* but to invert its meaning. Instead of a sly, intensely personal effort by the poet to deceive us by pretending to be someone else, *mimesis* now denotes the objective representation of a poetic *mythos*, a unified nexus of action woven out of 'universals'. Far from being a menace to established norms, the poet is almost (not quite) a philosopher. He is a phenomenologist of human character.

Aristotle argues further that imitation is a basic human impulse, and an *intellectual* one, stemming from the desire to know. This basis, and its connection with the 'universal', are the things which enable *mimesis* to become a really objective concept and serve as the corner-stone of Aristotle's doctrine.

So much for the general theory of the poetic plot, the *systasis tôn pragmatôn*. The more difficult part remains, concerning the tragic, emotional side: pity and fear and all that. These emotions are discussed at length in Book 2 of the *Rhetoric*, chapters 5 and 8, and in a way obviously affiliated with what is said about them in the *Poetics*. Thus here again we find the two arts closely linked; but this time the decisive inspiration for the doctrine in the *Poetics* came neither from the *Phaidros* nor from the rhetorical art *per se* but from the operation of homicide trials in Athens.

In his second formulation of the emotional charge against poetry, in *Republic* 10, Plato alleges that we are helpless prey to the emotional impact of tragic drama, and especially to the tendency to *pity* (*eleos, oiktos*). Aristotle does not deny the importance of pity and fear; on the contrary, he puts them at the center of his theory of tragedy. The eliciting of these emotions, and the production of the pleasure that stems from them, is even more a function of the poet than of the orator. How is he to do it? By constructing an action which has the general virtues of unity, coherence, etc., and also puts a *certain kind of man* through a *certain kind of change* from good to bad fortune. What is required is a heinous and horrible deed like that of Oidipous, but one which we are persuaded was committed by a good rather than a bad man and *out of ignorance* (*di'hamartian*).

The point of these carefully adjusted requirements is that we do not need to be saved from our emotions; on the contrary, the unaided good sense and healthy emotional endowment of the ordinary theater-goer, *functioning as a judge of action*, will pronounce a sound verdict: he will acquit Oidipous of *adikia*, will feel due commiseration for him, and will derive from the whole experience an *oikeia hêdonê*, a special, emotionally tinged pleasure. I do not speak of 'katharsis' here, because I am not convinced that it belongs to the Aristotelian "package"; but I do point out that this whole emotional mechanism depends integrally upon persuasion; for Aristotle, unlike Plato, believes that the emotions have a rational component and are therefore open to persuasion. If we ask *how* the persuasion is worked in the case of Oidipous, the answer appears to be Oidipous works it himself by what he does and says after he discovers the fearful truth: that is, by the expression of his profound revulsion and remorse. That is the proof of his goodness of character and the proof that ignorance was indeed the cause of his heinous acts.[1]

Such is Aristotle's theory of the tragic plot and the tragic emotions. It is a brilliant effort, but when all is said and done its scope is restricted to a relatively small number of plots (as Aristotle himself admits), and it does not speak to Plato's deeper objections.

In *Republic* 10 Plato makes a startling confession: that in reprehending Homer and the tragic poets he was not merely concerned for the spiritual welfare of an imaginary set of young 'Guardians', but feels deeply threatened in his own soul. Until somebody who is "not a poet himself but a poet-lover"—i.e., Aristotle—steps forward and shows that poetry is not merely pleasurable but useful to the individual *and* the commonwealth, he, Plato, will continue to sing incantations to exorcise it from his own spirit.

There is a division here that goes very deep. Plato feels in his bones the power of a *tragic vision of life*, beginning with Homer—the Homer of the *Iliad*—and culminating in tragic drama. He, the disciple of Socrates, cannot admit that there is any truth in that vision. If there were, the whole rationale of his own life would be destroyed. He must fight the alien message with all the force at his command—and yet, the enemy, Homer, is so incredibly seductive; he snuggles up to Plato with the most insidiously persuasive images of the evil that men (*and* gods) do and suffer—it is a never-ending struggle on the battlefield of the soul.

Aristotle—the young Aristotle—has no eyes or ears for that struggle, and he does not believe that tragedy has any tragic message to convey. His vision is resolutely reductive and reasonable. Tragic drama is just a highly competent and instructive representation of the things that human beings do and say under great pressure, structured in such a way as to exercise our judicial faculties and provide a harmless pleasure based on the emotions of pity and fear.

Yet that formulation is not quite complete and not quite fair. Aristotle wanted to vindicate the treasures of Greece's national literature against Plato's one-sided attack, and he wanted to do it for the average citizen, not for members of an intellectual elite. He therefore—and because he was a fourth-century Greek—put his defense of tragedy in terms compatible with the other art that reached deepest into the civic life of fourth-century Athens: the reasoned art of speech.

NOTES

1. This points is further stated with all possible emphasis by Oidipous himself in the *Oidipous at Kolonos*, 258-274.

AN ASPECT OF WIT IN OVID'S *METAMORPHOSES*

Daniel L. Arnaud

palam mutuandi, hoc animo ut vellet agnosci.
(Seneca, *Suas.* 3.7)

A form of wit which is, perhaps, most characteristic of Ovid himself is sustained literary wit. Surprisingly, scholars have paid little attention to this aspect of wit in the *Metamorphoses*. I say surprisingly, for this is the very type of humor that E. K. Rand in 1912 singled out in the *Amores* and *Ars Amatoria* as particularly indicative of the character of the *Metamorphoses*.[1] Many scholars since the publication of Rand's paper have amplified his comments and substantiated his conclusions about the *Amores* and *Ars Amatoria*, but none has really followed his cue to examine this aspect of the *Metamorphoses* itself—even though many have made happy observations in the course of discussions of other matters which would seem strongly to indicate that this type of wit is at work in the *Metamorphoses*.

The type of wit which Rand saw in the *Amores* and *Ars Amatoria* is essentially based in literary allusion—allusion either to a specific passage or, more generally, to a genre or a particular convention within a genre. In Rand's main example (*Am.* 1.6, the song of the locked-out lover) the fun lies in recognizing that Ovid is winking at a literary convention. The convention itself is primary in the poem—it itself inspired the poem; it was not just the vehicle used to express the poet's thoughts. As Rand saw, the poem—indeed the majority of the

Amores and, on at least one level, the *Ars Amatoria*—is an intellectual, literary *jeu d'esprit*.

For literary allusion to be fully effective as wit, the audience must, of course, be informed; it must be familiar with that to which the allusion is made. Some 'modern' examples will make this quite clear. Here is T. S. Eliot describing Macavity, The Mystery Cat, "the Napoleon of crime":

> Macavity's a ginger cat, he's very tall and thin;
> You would know him if you saw him, for his eyes are sunken in.
> His brow is deeply lined with thought, his head is highly domed;
> His coat is dusty from neglect, his whiskers are uncombed.
> He sways his head from side to side, with movements like a snake;
> And when you think he's half asleep, he's always wide awake.[2]

It is a delightful stanza. But here now is Sherlock Holmes telling Watson about "Ex-professor Moriarty, of mathematical celebrity":

> "He is the Napoleon of crime, Watson... His appearance was quite familiar to me. He is extremely tall and thin, his forehead domes out in a white curve, and his eyes are deeply sunken in his head. He is clean-shaven, pale and ascetic-looking, retaining something of the professor in his features. His shoulders are rounded from much study, and his face protrudes forward and is forever slowly oscillating from side to side in a curiously reptilian fashion."[3]

That a knowledge of the description of Moriarty adds a dimension to one's enjoyment of the Eliot needs no elaboation. (Indeed the portrait of Macavity also resembles that of Moriarty in a number of other particulars.)

Sometimes, of course, the 'allusion' is more broadly done and more generally based. But the essential effect is the same: the reader who recognizes what the author has done receives an extra helping of enjoyment, the passage takes on another dimension for him. Here is a statement by Henry Fielding from the preface to *Joseph Andrews* which states it plainly: "In the diction, I think, burlesque itself may be admitted; of which many instances will occur in this work, as in the description of the battles, and some other places, not necessary to be pointed out to the classical reader, for whose entertainment those parodies or burlesque imitations are chiefly calculated."[4] And now an excerpt from one of the scenes to which he refers:

> No sooner did Joseph Andrews perceive the distress of his friend, when first the quick-scented dogs attacked him, then he grasped his cudgel in his right hand, a cudgel which his father had of his grandfather, to whom a mighty strong man of Kent had given it for a present in that day when he broke three heads on the stage. It was a cudgel of mighty strength and art, made by one of Mr. Deard's best workmen, whom no other artificer can equal, and who hath made all those sticks which the beaus . . .
>
> No sooner had Joseph grasped his cudgel in his hands than lightning darted from his eyes; and the heroic youth, swift of foot, ran with the utmost speed to his friend's assistance.[5]

The effect of the allusion needs not be pointed out to the classical reader.

The result of the "imitation" need not, of course, be broad comedy. Our response may be nothing more than the gentle pleasure of recognition, of knowing that although the author has not told us openly, we know what he is about. Portions of Byron's *Don Juan*; the consummately esoteric section of *Ulysses* in which Joyce changes his style each page or so to present a capsule history of the English language; Max Beerbohm's Ovidian *A Defence of Cosmetics* (which, incidentally, was taken seriously when it appeared in *The Yellow Book* and set off an inordinate furor); Nabokov's *Pale Fire*; Pope's *The Rape of the Lock*—though they vary one from another, each displays essentially the same kind of intellectual literary wit. Nor indeed is this type of intellectual wit the exclusive province of literature. The final allegro movement of Shostakovitch's *Piano Concerto No. 2 (op. 101)*—written for his pianist son, Maxim—contains a series of Hanon's five-finger exercises—a feature surely included for, or at least only capable of being enjoyed by, the "pianoed" listener. On the level of allusion to an entire genre, Prokofieff's *Classical Symphony* is itself a satire or parody of the general classical symphonic form. Though they differ in degree, these are all examples of *wit*. And it is a type of wit which is intended for (and depends on) an audience which is both informed and intellectually alert to the craftsmanship, the technique, of the author—precisely the sophisticated audience for which Ovid wrote (yet to which, unfortunately for Ovid, Augustus apparently did not belong).

One further observation: all these allusions (whether we call them parody, satire or burlesque) are based in the author's affection and respect for the thing to which he alludes. There is no bitterness, no malice, no derision, no scorn. The fun is not at the *expense* of anyone. Eliot clearly likes and respects Doyle; Fielding writes for the *entertainment* of the classical reader who shares with him a common (and clearly cherished) background; Shostakovitch does not belittle the importance of Hanon's exercises. Similarly, when Ovid plays with the conventions of poetry and poetic form, he plays respectfully with a craftsman's respect for his craft. The old charge against him that he was "insincere" and did not "care deeply" about anything (stemming, no doubt, from the light-hearted way in which he treated elegiac love and based on the more than dubious assumption that levity and sincerity are mutually exclusive) can be answered quite simply by saying that Ovid did indeed care deeply about something. He cared about *poetry*—its forms and its conventions—and about his craft as a poet. This serious concern is evidenced, if in no other way, by the very fact that he "parodied" literary convention, that he went to poetic convention for his inspiration. His obvious concern for the form of poetry comes out again and again in his work and shines through any facade of levity. The introductory poem to the *Amores*, for example, puts his decision to write elegy in terms of literary form: he was about to write an epic but Cupid stole a foot from the second line and left him with elegiac couplet! Again, in *Am*. 3.1 he has the muses of Tragedy and Elegy debate the benefits of their respective genres. And throughout the *Tristia* he talks about literary genre and form.

A prime example of extended literary wit in the *Metamorphoses* is the storm in the Ceyx-Alcyone episode of Book XI.

"The Storm" had long been a standard literary piece (especially in epic, yet also in elegiac poetry) but it will come clear, I think, that in the *Metamorphoses* storm Ovid is not just writing *within* the tradition of the convention, he is writing *about* it. His subject, almost more than the storm which kills Ceyx, is the *conventional literary* storm itself. Setting out to write the Conventional Storm, he openly alludes to former literary storms: he expands, he reverses, he combines—all for the entertainment of his audience. He himself is patently aware of the tradition and makes us, his audience, aware of his awareness.

I must at the outset make one very important point. The presence of literary wit in the passage does not of itself negate completely the seriousness or the pathos of the episode (just as the presence of elements usually associated with elegiac poetry does not negate the fact that the tone of the passage is in large part epic). "Wit" and "seriousness" are not mutually exclusive.[6] The effect of the literary wit in the Ceyx-Alcyone story is to keep us intellectually aware of Ovid; it inhibits our involvement in the story. Through it Ovid *controls the intensity* of pathos and seriousness. He does not eliminate pathos and seriousness; he keeps it at a moderate level.[7]

* * *

The literary sea-storm tradition begins, of course, with Homer. There are three major sea-storms in the *Odyssey*. The first (5.291 ff.) strikes Odysseus after he has finally been sent on his way from the island of Calypso equipped with wine, water, and other provisions. He sails for seventeen days without incident, but on the eighteenth, as he draws near Phaeacia, Poseidon sees him and, deciding that he has not suffered enough, gathers the clouds for a storm. Darkness covers land and sea. The four winds all blow at once and roll up huge waves. Odysseus is gripped by fear and blames Zeus for the storm. He envies those who have died on land at Troy and received honors and funeral rites. A huge wave strikes the raft from above, whirling it around and stripping it of its mast and Odysseus, who is hurled into the raging sea. When he comes to the surface he manages to grab the raft and cling to it as it is tossed about. Help arrives in the shape of Ino who gives him a magic cloth and some good advice—to abandon the raft, strip off his heavy wet clothes, and to swim for shore with the aid of the magic cloth. While he is pondering her suggestions, Poseidon hurls up a tremendous wave which shatters what is left of the raft. Catching hold of a bit of timber, Odysseus decides to follow Ino's advice. He is finally saved when Athena takes pity on him and checks the storm winds.

The second storm of the *Odyssey* (12.403 ff.) strikes Odysseus' ship after his men had foolishly slaughtered some of the cattle of the Sun. This storm is sent by Zeus. He envelops the ship in a heavy black cloud. The west wind blows violently and snaps off the mast and its rigging. The falling mast strikes the pilot on the head and kills him. Zeus then hurls a thunderbolt against the ship. The sailors are tossed overboard by the bolt and all drown, but Odysseus somehow manages to stay with the remains of the ship until the west wind finally abates and the south wind blows him back towards Scylla and Charybdis for further adventure.

At *Odyssey* 14.301 ff. Odysseus is received by his swineherd, Eumaeus, and learns from him about the behavior of the suitors during his absence. Keeping his true identity hidden from the old man, Odysseus tells him a long, fictitious tale about his adventures. He tells of an encounter with a grasping Phoenician merchant who had lured him on a voyage to Libya in order to sell him on the slave market. Zeus planned destruction for the ship. When it left Crete and was out at sea, he put a black cloud over it. He thundered and lightninged, striking it with a firebolt. The crew was dashed overboard. 'Odysseus' despaired, but Zeus came to his aid and put into his hands the ship's mast to which he clung for nine days until finally on the tenth he was washed ashore at the land of the Thesprotians where he was received by King Pheidon.

Here, then, at the outset, are the basic features of the literary storm (epic) which will appear in varying degrees in subsequent storms: initiation of the storm by some god; great darkness and heavy clouds; violent winds; thunder and lightning; huge waves and one especially large one which crashes down upon the ship; a terrified hero who pleads for help from the gods and envies those who have died on dry land; the ship loses its mast and later disintegrates; and the sailors with the exception of at least the hero (who must continue on to greater things) lose their lives.

By the time of the publication of the *Aeneid*, the storm was well established as a set literary piece.[8] It will be helpful here to reproduce a portion of one of Saint-Denis' many valuable comparative tables. He notes the relative density of stock elements (having selected a base of twenty) in the storms of *Aen.* 1 and 3, *Met.* 11, and *Fasti* 3. Saint-Denis seems to have virtually disregarded the storm in *Aeneid* 5 which contains the great majority of these elements.

Stock Elements	*Aeneid*	*Met. 11*	*Fasti 3*
Winds from all directions	1.81-86	490	—
Battle of winds	1.82	491	—
Cries of sailors	1.87	495	—
Whistling of rigging	1.87	495	—
Crashing waves	—	496, 529	—
Claps of thunder	1.90	496	—
Height of waves which seem to reach the sky, enormous mountains	1.103, 3.421-3, 3.564-7	497-8	—
Color of water mixed with sand, silt and foam	1.107, 3.557	499-501	—
Watery valleys touch the bottom of the abyss	1.106-7, 3.564-5	502-6	591 (?)
Pounding of waves compared to pounding of ballista	—	507-9	—
Breaking up of ship	1.122-3	514-15	592 (?)
Torrential rains	3.194, 5.10	516-19	—
Collapse of sky and upheaval of sea	1.84, 1.129, 3.564	517-18	(591-2)
Darkness	1.88-9, 3.198	520-21	—
Lightning	1.90, 3.199	522-23	—
Force of the Tenth Wave	—	530	—

Impotence of human skill	3.201-2	537-38	593
Forebodings of death	1.91	538	—
Envy of those who died on dry land	1.94-101	539-40	597-98
Pleas for divine assistance	1.93	540-42	594

Aeneas is battered by three storms in the *Aeneid*—once each in the First, Second, and Fifth Books.[10] At the beginning of Book Five, Aeneas and his men are sailing from Carthage and the fires of Dido's funeral pyre when (5.8 ff.) a black rain cloud appears over their heads bringing with it darkness and storm. Palinurus laments the situation and assumes that Neptune is responsible for it. As he then explains to Aeneas, the havoc is being caused by the west wind. They turn the ships with the wind to ride out the storm and in a short while arrive safely at the shores of Sicily. This is really not a full-blown storm; but some of the stock features are here, primarily the darkness and the pilot's lament.

In Book Three Aeneas tells Dido's court of his trip from Crete after an abortive attempt at founding a settlement there. They had no sooner gotten out to sea when a dark cloud appeared, bringing on a storm.[11] The winds roll up great waves and the ship is tossed about by the sea. Lightning flashes through the clouds. Palinurus confesses that he is at a loss and does not know their position. They wander for three dark days and nights before finally sighting what proves to be the Strophades, the land of the Harpies. The storm is strikingly similar to the one in Book Five—just a bit more elaborate. There are the same dark clouds, winds, and confused Palinurus (albeit less articulate here than in Book Five), plus lightning and larger waves.

The *locus classicus* for the Latin epic storm is *Aen.* 1.81 ff. Juno, peeved at her inability to harass Aeneas sufficiently, enlists the aid of Aeolus, persuading him to let loose the full fury of the winds on the Trojan fleet as it makes its way from Sicily towards Italy. Aeolus responds with a courtly, "Your wish, my lady, is my command" (*tuus, o regina, quid optes,/ explorare labor; mihi iussa capessere fas est.* 1.76-77) and, plunging his sword into the mountain side, releases the winds. Like an army prepared for battle they rush upon the sea, heaving up huge waves. All the winds blow at the same time. Men shout; ropes creak. The clouds bring darkness. Aeneas trembles with fear and envies those who died in battle on dry land. The waves surge towards heaven. Oars snap, leaving the ship at the mercy of the sea. A mountainous wave (*aquae mons*) smashes down upon the ship. As the sea is hurled up into towering waves the sandy ocean floor lies exposed. Some ships are hurled onto the rocks, some onto sand bars. One is struck by a huge wave which tosses the pilot overboard. The ship itself is sucked down by the swirling waters. The sea is dotted with floudering sailors and bits of debris as one by one the ships come apart at the seams. Finally, Neptune, rising from the depths to discover the devastation, scatters the winds and clouds, brings back the sun, and aids in salvaging what remains of the fleet.

That Virgil's storms were "literary" was recognized in antiquity. Macrobius, speaking of the many Homeric reminiscences in the *Aeneid* says:

> (Sat. 5.2.13)
> quid quod et omne opus Vergilianum velut de quodam
> Homerici operis speculo formatum est? nam et
> tempestas mira imitatione descripta est—versus
> utrius que qui volet conferat—

Elsewhere, however, he says that the storm in *Aen.* 1 is modeled after the scene in Book I of Naevius' *Punic Wars*:

> (Sat. 6.2.30)
> in primo Aeneidos tempestas describitur, et Venus
> apud Iovem queritur de periculis filii, et Iuppiter
> eam de futurorum properitate solatur, hic locus
> totus sumptus a Naevio est ex primo libro belli
> Punici.

But regardless of the apparent inconsistency, the important point is clear: Virgil's storm was recognized as having *literary* antecedents. The storm was clearly considered part of the furniture of epic, one of its stock features. Juvenal, complaining about hack practitioners of the epic art, says how familiar he is with the stock themes:

(*Sat.* 1.7)
nota magis nulli domus est sua quam mihi lucus
Martis et Aeoliis vicinum rupibus antrum
Vulcani. Quid agant venti, quas torqueat umbras
Aeacus . . .

No one knows his own house so well as I know the
groves of Mars, and the cave of Vulcan near the
cliffs of Aeolus. What the winds are brewing;
whose souls Aeacus has on the rack . . .
(G. G. Ramsay)[12]

Saint-Denis provides nautical evidence for the literary quality of Virgil's storms. He notes that Homer's storm in *Od.* 5 is a cyclone—the winds all blowing together at the same time—as distinct from a hurricane in which only a single wind blows with great force. Citing Bérard[13] he makes the interesting point that whereas cyclones do occur where Homer has his occur, they are for the most part rare in the Mediterranean. And that thus, when Virgil describes a cyclone off the coast of Sicily—where they do not in fact occur—he reveals that he has done his research in the library rather than in the field.[14] "... *plus ou moins maladroits, tous les bons élèves d'Homére et d'Ennius—Virgile en tête—conçoive la tempête comme un cyclone, ce qui fait surire les marins.*" He makes the same point in two comments on Plautus (whose storm description he admires for its accuracy), the first comparing him with Ennius, the second with Virgil.[15]

... chez Ennius, la poésie de la mer est extérieure
et littéraire; chez Plaute, intérieure et populaire.
Ennius a lu Homére, Plaute a observé les marins.
Les gens de métier n'hésiteraient pas à trouver
que Plaute est le plus vrai, le plus attachant.

Entre la tempête de *Rudens* et celle de l'*Enéide*,
un marin n'hésiterait pas: il préféreait la première.
Mais c'est l'influence de Naevius, Ennius et Virgile
qui a prévalu: on peut le regretter.[16]

But the point is clear, regardless of the way in which Saint-Denis makes it: the epic storm even early in its history was a literary convention, not an attempt at technical accuracy.

With the publication of the *Aeneid* we have the finest statement of the Latin literary epic storm. Though the storm tradition has had many contributors—from Homer, its founder, through the many poets both Latin and Greek who followed him—any Latin storm written after 19 B.C. must of necessity be indebted to those of the *Aeneid*.

The storm as it appears in elegy is essentially the same storm as we have noted in epic, but there is a difference in focus. Where the epic storm emphasizes the strength of a hero (it is an epic clash between him and super-human forces—the forces of nature or the force of the gods[17]—from which he emerges battered but yet intact and heroic), the storm of elegy emphasizes the weakness of a victim who is powerless against the force of the storm and by which he is generally destroyed. This comes out in Propertius 3.7 where the poet envisions the death at sea of his friend, Paetus. There are stock elements—the shrieking winds, Paetus grasping a bit of wreckage, etc.—but the emphasis is not the same.

> (3.7.47)
> non tulit haec Paetus, stridorum audire procellae
>   et duro teneras laedere fune manus;

> Paetus could not bear to hear the shrieking winds
> or to wound his delicate hand with the rough rope.

> (3.7.53)
> hunc parvo ferri vidit nox improba ligno:
>   Paetus et occideret, tot coiere mala.

> The harsh night saw him borne on a tiny plank:
> so many evils conspired that Paetus should die.
>
>   (H. E. Butler)

The stock features are there but the focus is constantly on Paetus, the pitiful victim. "Paetus could not bear to hear..." "The harsh night saw him borne..." Even the night watches *him*. The greatest emphasis of the passage is on the death scene: Paetus' torn hands; his gulping down sea water; his final pitiful lament and prayer that his body be borne to his mother for burial. Here there is no epic struggle, no violent grandeur; rather there is annihilation and personal pathos.

One other observation. As in the storm scenes in Homer and Virgil, we see the epic storm begin and end. A god generally summons the winds into action and then, after the fury of the storm itself, we see the winds dispersed. Here, when Paetus has sunk beneath the waves for the last time we hear no more of the storm itself. Propertius does not feel compelled to tell us that the storm ended and that the sea eventually calmed. His interest was in Paetus, in what the storm did *to him*. And when Paetus ceased to be, Propertius' interest in the storm ceased.

Ovid wrote five storm scenes: one in the *Fasti*, one in the *Metamorphoses*, and three in the *Tristia*.[18] The last three, as their publication followed that of the *Metamorphoses*, will not be of major concern to us here.[19] The first of these, in point of time, is *Fasti* 3.583 ff. Anna, Dido's sister, is forced to flee from her haven with King Battus in order to avoid the wrath of her brother Pygmalion. She takes to the sea. But just as she is approaching her destination, a storm comes up. Before the ship's crew can furl the sails and row to the harbor's safety, the south wind blows them out into open water and into the fury of the storm. The sailors can do nothing. The ship is helpless. All— the pilot included—pray for help; Anna weeps and envies Dido's death on dry land. The ship is finally blown towards shore and, although it does sink, everyone manages to reach safety.

This short passage (only seventeen lines) clearly establishes that Ovid is aware of the literary tradition. A number of the stock features are here: the helpless sailors, the disintegrating ship, the prayers for help, envy of those who have died a terrestial death. Many, however, are missing: darkness, thunder and lightning, rains, battling winds, huge waves, etc.—those which pertain to the storm itself. Those which he has included are those which describe the effect of the storm on the ship. In *Aen.* 1 the storm itself is an active character, blowing, crashing, and thundering. (The verbs of the passage are predominantly in the active voice.) One senses that an epic, heroic struggle is going on between Aeneas and the divinely unleashed forces of nature. The winds and waves lash and toss Aeneas; yet, though properly terrified, he manages to hold his own. Here, however, there is no heroic struggle. There is no worthy opponent for the storm, just Anna, a poor frightened girl. And our attention is almost totally on her. The storm is described in terms of her and her ship, indirectly and with passive verbs. The waves do not toss her, she *is tossed* (*iactatur* 3.594); the wind does not overcome the sailor's skill, their skill *is overcome* (*vincitur* 3.593). The most vivid image of the passage is not a crashing wave; it is that of Anna, distraught, hiding her tears in her robe. It is the pathetic helplessness of the woman in distress which impresses one, not the force of the storm. Though definitely part of the literary tradition, this storm is clearmly more akin to the storm of Propertius 3.7 than that of *Aeneid* 1.

* * *

In Book XI of the *Metamorphoses*, Ceyx is destroyed by the most colossal storm hitherto unleashed in the pages of Latin literature. Most of the main points about the storm of the *Metamorphoses* have been made above, at least by implication. It is a set literary piece. Its indebtedness to the storm of *Aen.* 1 is clear and has long been acknowledged.[20] Yet one can see from a quick glance at Saint-Denis' table that Ovid does not restrict himself solely to *Aen.* 1 or even to Virgil. Rather he combines distinctive features from many places—associated primarily but not exclusively with epic—into a single, super-colossal, amalgamated tempest.

There would seem to be two major ways to explain his obvious references to Virgil (and, as we shall see, Homer). (1) He was attempting to do what Virgil had done just two decades before, namely to write a storm within the literary tradition. Following this view, one concludes that Ovid was essentially competing with Virgil, making his own storm mightier and larger, attempting to heighten a truly pathetic story with a truly dramatic storm. (2) Rather than seeing himself within the tradition, he saw himself outside it, looking back, commenting on it, saying to himself (much as Fielding said to himself about the epic battle and Byron about the epic tradition as a whole): "*I* know what is expected in a storm and *you*, my learned audience, know what is expected. Here then, for your intellectual entertainment, is the Compleat Storm." Given Ovid's absorption with literary form and convention; given Rand's observation about the nature of the literary paraody in *Am.* 1.6 and in the *Ars Amatoria*; given Seneca's comment (through Gallio) that Ovid was fond of alluding to Virgil—not with the intent of literary theft but in the hope that the allusions would be recognized (*Suas.* 3.7); given direct allusions to Virgil and others, and the conscious manipulation of those allusions; given all these, the second possibility—that Ovid's *Metamorphoses* storm is essentially a technical display piece, inspired by the convention itself—in short, that it is a bit of intellectual literary wit—seems the more likely.

Once again, I must stress that the presence of this kind of literary wit does not at all mean that the story in which the storm is set is thus 'comic.' As Traenkle notes,[21] the Ceyx-Alcyone episode is heavily 'elegiac.' It is a story grounded in human pathos—a lover separated from his beloved wife by a death which, through divine mercy, proves ultimately to reunite them eternally.[22] Even though both Ceyx and Alcyone are in part divine (she the daughter of Aeolus, he the son of Lucifer) Ovid emphasizes their humanity. We are to see them as human beings in love and their story as a human love story. Thus, the framework of the story is surely pathetic, elegiac, if you will. And this very elegiac quality—maintained until the storm is actually underway—makes the literary display piece, laced as it is with allusions to the decidedly heroic epic *Aeneid*, all the more effective.

Yet again, however, the term 'literary wit' can cover a wide range which varies from simple parody to the kind of estoric allusion we shall find in the storm piece. That the storm is "witty" does not mean that it is thus necessarily "funny." The story of Ceyx and Alcyone is not a humerous one. It is indeed grounded in pathos. The literary wit of the storm serves not to eliminate the pathos but rather to control it, to decrease its intensity by turning our attention in part away from the events of the story towards the technique of the poet.

The Decision and Departure of Ceyx (410-474)

Ceyx, king of Trachis, announces that he must travel to Claros to consult the oracle about the fate of his brother Daedalion (just recently turned into a hawk, as Ceyx himself has told Peleus at 11.344).[23] Alcyone, his loving and devoted wife, is fearful for his safety if he should take a sea voyage and tearfully pleads that he at least travel by land, saying that even being the son-in-law of Aeolus offers him no assurance of safety at sea (430 ff.). Moved by her pleas, but even more by the obligation he feels is his, Ceyx reluctantly (*quaerente moras*, 461) boards his ship for the journey, promising that he will return to her within two months. She, however, despite his promise, has further teary forebodings of tragedy. She swoons, reviving in time to see Ceyx waving from the departing ship. It is a tender scene. Lovers, tearful and reluctant to part, saying what proves to be their final farewell. As he describes the ship making its way out from the harbor, Ceyx waving from the stern, Alcyone waving from the shore, Ovid underlines their mutual devotion with a subtle psychological touch. In the *Fasti* passage discussed above (3.583 ff.) our vantage is clearly with Anna, with her on board her ship, as she departs. Along with her we see the land fade away as the ship makes its way out to sea: *ex oculis visa refugit huius* (*Fast.* 3.590). Here in the *Metamorphoses*, however, using the same receding shore motif, Ovid presents us with a poignant ambiguity. As the ship sails off, we are with *both* Ceyx and Alcyone at the same time. The land recedes (his point of view from on board ship) but so does the ship (her's from the shore).

(11.466)
>... ubi terra recessit
longius atque oculi nequeunt cognoscere vultus,
dum licet, insequitur fugientem lumine pinum.

> When the shore receded and she could no longer
> make out his face and features, she followed the
> fleeing ship with her gaze as long as she could.
>   (R. Humphries)

It is a lovely expression of the couple's closeness, each psychologically with the other.[24] Alcyone, after watching the ship until the tip of its sails has disappeared over the horizon, returns to her lonely couch where she cries herself to sleep. It is a most tender scene; human, pathetic, non-epic.

The Storm

Section I (479-479)

The voyage starts well. The breeze is fresh so they bring in the oars and sail with the wind. But then as evening comes on, conditions change. The wind becomes stronger; the sea, rougher. The captain turns to shout orders to trim the sails, but the wind and sea have risen so quickly that his words can not be heard above the roar. Even so, the sailors scurry automatically to try to do what must be done. They pull in the oars and plug the oar holes, get the sails down, secure what can be secured, bail water.[25]

In keeping with the elegiac tone of the decision and departure scenes, the storm just arises (as did those in Propertius 3.7 and *Fasti* 3). The gods are conspicuously absent. There is no attempt to explain the origin of the storm in divine terms (as we noted was the case in the epic tradition). Ceyx is not a superhuman upon whom the gods rain retribution for past sins (his or his ancestors'), nor is he a member of that heroic elite whose strength is tested against super-human forces. He has been presented as a human, devoted husband and loyal brother who, taking his chances with the sea, has tragic bad luck.

But at line 490 there is a marked shift. What has been *"vue, précise, technique"* becomes clearly literary; what has been strongly elegiac in tone becomes steeped in allusions to epic. The winds crash in from all directions and we find ourselves in the midst of a literary storm piece which will rage unabated for eighty-two lines.[26]

Section II (490-506)

The winds crash in from all directions; the captain is terrified and admits that he is helpless; the men shout, the rigging rattles, the sea roars, the heavens thunder; the waves seem to reach up to the sky and are now sandy yellow, now black, now frothy white; the ship is one moment tossed on high, the next dropped down to the very ocean floor.

The conventional tone of these lines is unmistakable. They contain nine of Saint-Denis' twenty stock elements. Even more, they are unmistakably Virgilian, particularly reminiscent of the strom in *Aen.* 1.

(*Met.* 11.495)
quippe sonant clamore viri, stridore rudentes.
The men sound with shouting, the ropes with hissing.
(R. Humphries)

(Aen. 1.87)
insequitur clamorque virum stridorque rudentum
There follows the shouting of men, the hissing of ropes.

Note especially the way in which the last four words of Ovid's line correspond exactly in rhythm and sound (*-e* substituting for *-que*) to those in Virgil's line. This is surely no accident. The closest other parallel in the extant literary tradition is from Pacuvius' *Teucer: strepitus fremitus clamor tonitruum et rudentum sibilus.*[27] It is clear that Ovid purposely is calling our attention to the *Aeneid*; that he means us to see his storm in relation to Virgil's.

But even more than including verbal allusions to Virgil of the type Zingerle sought out,[28] Ovid plays with the images of the *Aeneid* storm. Virgil likens the winds to the soldiers of an army: they swoop down upon the sea like a martialed army, *velut agmine facto* (1.82). Ovid introduces the theme openly. His winds wage war plain and simple: *bella gerunt venti* (11.491). This is clearly a nod to Virgil. And, as we shall see, Ovid will go yet further to include similes from Homeric battle scenes as well.

One of the most vivid pictures in the storm scene of *Aen.* 1 is that of the ships being struck by a towering wave; some of the men are lofted up on high and hang on the crest, others see the exposed sea bottom.

(Aen. 1.105)
... insequitur cumulo praeruptus aquae mons.
hi summo in fluctu pendent; his unda dehiscens
terram inter fluctus aperit; furit astus harenis

... a wall of water, a mountain
Looms up, comes pouring down; some ride the crest,
Some, in the trough, can see the boil of the sand.

Here is *Met.* 11.502 ff.:

ipsa quoque his agitur vicibus Trachinia puppis
et nunc sublimis veluti de vertice montis
despicere in valles imumque Acheronta videtur,
nunc, ubi demissam curvum circumstetit aequor,
suspicere inferno summum de gurgite caelum.

> ... The ship
> Had only chance as master; now she rode
> high on the mountain-top and saw below her
> Valleys and the pit of Hell, or now she sank
> Deep in the trough and from the infernal pool
> Looked up at Heaven's mountain.
>
> (R. Humphries)

Again, the similarity to Virgil is too close to be explained by saying that they are both writing within the same tradition, using the same conventions. Ovid is clearly *alluding* to Virgil with the expectation that his audience will see (and enjoy) what he has done. He expands and enlarges. Virgil's sailors hang from above on the mountain of water and look down into the depths; Ovid's ship *both* goes up and looks down as if from the peak of a mountain into Hell and sinks down and looks up at the heights of heaven from the infernal water.[29]

On occasion Ovid subtly corrects Virgil. The storms of both *Aen.* 1 and *Aen.* 3 have their fair share of thunder and lightning yet in each the waves reach up "to the stars": *fluctus ad sidera tollit* (1.103), *sidera verberat unda* (3.423). Ovid, quite precisely even if literarily, takes into account the fact that such a storm would most likely produce low clouds: *videtur/ pontus et inductas adspergine tangere nubes* (11.497-498). Or when, at 11.185, Ovid tells us that the voice of the captain can not be heard above the roar of the sea, one is tempted to see a wink at *Aen.* 5.14 ff. where, under somewhat similar conditions Palinurus manages to hold a fourteen line conversation with Aeneas.

Section III (507-536)

The waves crashing onto the ship are compared first to the smashing of a battering ram against the walls of a fortress, then to the charge of fierce lions heedless of the hunters' spears. The ship springs leaks and begins to come apart. Rain pours down, merging sea and sky. Dark clouds blot out the stars and flash with lightning. The waves attack again. A mighty wave, the Tenth Wave, likened to an eager soldier who first leaps a besieged city's walls, engulfs the ship. The confusion on board the doomed ship is compared to the confusion of a city in the throes of falling to the enemy.

Although there are more of Saint-Denis' stock features here—the gaping seams of the ship, the rains, the darkness, the lightning[30]—this section is notable particularly for its similes, a feature mostly absent from the literary storms which preceded Ovid. There are only two extended similes in the storms of Homer, both of which liken the storm-tossed ship to something light blown about by the wind. At *Od.* 5.327 ff. the ship is compared to thistles borne hither and yon by the north wind; at *Od.* 5.368 ff. the bits of the raft are scattered by the waves as a strong wind blows dry straw. There are also two short (identical) similes in which the men thrown from the ship dot the sea like sea birds (*Od.* 12.418-419 and 14.308-309). There are no similes in the storm of the *Argonautica*, nor again in the storms of the *Aeneid* with the possible exception of *Aen.* 1.82 (*velut agmine facto*).[31] Here, in the space of twenty-four lines Ovid introduces four vivid similes (and will add a fifth and sixth at lines 553-554). lines 553-554).

We have already noted the way in which Ovid took Virgil's indirect warfare image (*velut agmine facto*) and turned it into a direct statement (*bella gerunt venti*). He takes the battle image further: the waves crash against the ship as a battering ram crashes against a fortress—clearly a battle image. But then in comparing the attacking waves to savage lions Ovid shows again his delight in playing with literary convention. The savage lion charging his foe was a standard comparison for a mighty hero in battle: Hector charges the Greeks like a baneful lion (*Il.* 12.41 ff.); again, Hector charges like a lion (*Il.* 15. 630 ff.); Helenor charges the spears of Turnus' army as a lion charges those of the hunters who have surrounded him (*Aen.* 9.551 ff.).

> (*Met.* 11.510)
> utque solent sumptis incursus viribus ire
> pectore in arma feri protentaque tela leones,
> sic, ubi se ventis admiserat unda coortis,
> ibat in arma ratis multoque erat altior illis,
>
> Even as savage lions gain new fury
> As they come charging on to breast the weapons,
> The arms held out against them, so the billows,
> Lashed by the rising winds, rush at the vessel,
> And tower high,
>
> (R. Humphries)

When Ovid's winds wage epic war, they wage it with all the epic trappings.

After a brief 'interlude' of nine lines in which there appear five more stock elements—the breaking up of the ship, torrential rains, the collapse of sky and upheaval of the sea, darkness and lightning—the waves are back again, this time compared to an eager soldier leaping first over the wall of a besieged city.

(*Met.* 11.525)
... et ut miles, numero praestantior omni,
cum saepe adsiluit defensae moenibus urbis,
spe potitur tandem laudisque accensus amore
inter mille viros murum tamen occupat unus,
sic ubi pulsarunt noviens latera ardua fluctus,
vastius insurgens decimae ruit impetus undae
nec prius absistit fessam oppugnare carinam
quam velut in captae descendat moenia navis.

... You may have seen a soldier,
More daring than the others, in his effort
To scale the walls until at last, triumphant,
Burning for praise, he leaps the wall and stands
One man among a thousand; so, when the waves
Nine times have battered at the ship's tall sides,
The tenth one, leaping higher, comes on with a rush,
Climbs over, and goes down inside the vessel.
                                             (R. Humphries)

It seems undeniable that Ovid is here deliberately playing with Homer. And the previous simile of the lion takes on new meaning. Homer's soldier, Hector, is compared first to a wave and then to a lion (*Il.* 15.623 ff.; 630 ff.); Ovid's waves are compared first to a lion and then to a soldier.[32]

But Ovid does not even leave it with that. The simile at *Il.* 15.623 comparing Hector to a wave goes on to describe the terror which the wave instills in the hearts of the sailors (and that which Hector instills in the hearts of the Achaeans). Ovid, having compared the wave to a soldier, goes on to compare the confusion and terror in the hearts of the sailors to the terrified confusion of a city in the last throes of falling to the enemy.

(*Met.* 11.534)
... trepidant haud segnius omnes
quam solet urbs aliis murum fodientibus extra
atque aliis murum trepidare tenentibus intus.

All are in terrified confusion, just as a city
is confused when some from without seek to undermine
its walls and some hold the walls within.

(F. J. Miller)

There can be no doubt that just as Ovid was alluding specifically to Virgil (and expanding) when he had Ceyx's ship swept up to look down into Hell and then sucked down to look up into heaven, here he is specifically alluding to Homer, transferring (and reversing) similes which Homer used in battle to his own truly epic battle of the winds—for the intellectual entertainment of his sophisticated and literate audience.

One final observation about the simile comparing the Tenth Wave to an eager soldier. Saint-Denis credits Ovid with having originated the image of the Tenth Wave, the enormous, climactic wave which follows a number of smaller waves.[33] Plato (*Rep.* 472 a) mentions the same phenomenon—the huge wave larger than those which come before it—as an accepted figure of speech, calling it the Third Wave (τρικυμία). The number three was popular with the ancients, especially with the writers of epic.[34] One is tempted to see in Ovid's expansion from three to "three times three plus one" more of Ovid's obvious delight in epic exaggeration. If the Third Wave is mighty, then the Tenth Wave must be three and a third times mightier. "Three" is good enough for an every day, run-of-the-mill storm, but not for Ovid's storm of storms.[35] All these alterations and exaggerations must have been made with the expectation that they would be recognized as deliberate—and as such that they would delight his readers.

Section IV (537-548)

The sailors are terrified. One cries; another is speechless; yet another envies those who will receive proper terrestrial burial; one lifts his hands to the gods in a prayer for help; each thinks of what he has left behind—brothers, fathers, home, children. Ceyx thinks of Alcyone, wanting to be near her, yet glad that she is not just then at his side. He wishes that he could die looking at the last towards his homeland, but, alas, does not know in which direction to look.

In the first six lines of this passage Ovid makes as many bows to the epic tradition as he can, assembling all the features associated with the stock 'terror speech.' Yet he does not have any speech proper. He spreads the elements of the speech around, one to a sailor.

Fear and despair (cf. *Od.* 5.297-299; *Argo.* 2.1106-1107; *Aen.* 1.92):

> (11.537)
> deficit ars, animique cadunt
>
> ... skill fails. Nerve falters.
>
> (R. Humphries)

Envy of those who have died on land (cf. *Od.* 5.306-307; *Aen.* 1.94-96):

> (11.539)
> ... vocat ille beatos
> funera quos maneat ...
>
> ... one envies the dead
> On land, who may be buried ...
>
> (R. Humphries)

Prayers to the gods (cf. *Argo.* 2.1123-1124; *Aen.* 1.93-94):

> (11.540)
> ... hic votis numen adorat
> bracchiaque ad caelum, quod non videt, inrita tollens poscit opem;
>
> ... and another
> Calls on the gods in prayer and lifts his arms
> In vain to skies he cannot see.[36]
>
> (R. Humphries)

Ovid even adds two features of his own, the tears of one sailor[37] and the speechlessness of another.

The rapid fire way in which all these features are presented gives the impression, in the light of the traditional terror speech, that Ovid just wants to get them in, to show that he knows that his grandly epic storm would not be complete without them. His major technique, as we have seen, has been one of expansion, of elaboration. He makes the violent more violent, the colossal super-collossal; his winds are windier, his rains rainier, his darkness darker, his waves larger; to Virgil's sandy water (*furit aestus harenis: Aen.* 1.107) he adds both frothy whiteness and sinister blackness, etc. Here, then, when he tosses off the terror speech in a series of quick, almost off-hand allusions (even managing to add a couple of new features) it comes as a delightful surprise. It is almost as if he were saying, "You thought that I was going to leave out all that about people praying to the gods and wishing they had died on dry land, didn't you? How foolish to think that I might be so careless."

Thus far Ovid has been describing the outward reactions of the men to their predicament; their tears, their silence, their prayers, their cries. These are all observations of overt actions. He now takes us inside the minds of the sailors. He tells us their *thoughts*. They *think* about their family and their homes. Ceyx *thinks* about Alcyone, *wishing* (not out loud) that he could be with her.

Section V (548-562)

The sea boils in whirlpools; dark clouds double the darkness of the black night. The mast and rudder are snapped off by the wind. One last wave, likened to a victorious soldier, delivers the *coup de grâce* to the foundering ship, falling upon it as if it were a mountain (actually, two mountains) dropped into the middle of the sea. Most of the sailors drown, but some manage to cling to bits of the shattered ship which have been strewn about over the waves. Ceyx is one of the (temporarily) lucky few and, clinging, cries to Aeolus, his father-in-law, for help.

This is Ovid's final volley. To the sea, already wind-whipped and immense, he now adds swirling whirlpools *à la* Charybdis.[38] He doubles the 'ordinary' inky darkness of 11.521.

(11.549)
>... et inducta piceis e nubibus umbra
omne latet caelum, duplicataque noctis imago est.

> ... shadows
> Of pitch-black cloud hide all the sky; the darkness
> Is double night.[39]
>
> (R. Humphries)

Both the mast and rudder are snapped off by the rushing wind. In the three storms of the Odyssey only the mast is ever torn off,[40] and that in each of them. (In *Od.* 5 Odysseus drops the steering oar as he is pitched overboard, but it is not ripped off by the wind.) Aeneas' ship loses only its oars. Ovid outdoes them all.

He brings in two final similes, comparing the wave which delivers the final blow first to a victorious soldier and then to the crash of two uprooted mountains. There does not seem to be any exact precedent for either of these figures in the storm tradition. There may possibly be a slight hint of the victor in the picture of the victorious Pyrrhus of *Aen.* 2.492 ff. crashing through Priam's palace gate. The Greeks who rush in behind him are compared to the waters of a rampaging river. There might also be a trace of the uprooted mountains at *Aen.* 9.710 ff. where the falling Bitias is compared to the crash of a rock-slide off the coast of Baiae which stirs up the sea. But the similarities, if there at all, are not striking enough to be terribly significant. It would not seem far wrong to say that these are original with Ovid.

The mountains settle once and for all any question that might have remained about the size of Ovid's storm. It is superspectacular. For a finale he explodes Virgil's *aquae mons* (*Aen.* 1.105) into *two actual* mountains. Athos and Pindus, uprooted and dropped entire on poor Ceyx's ship.

> (11.554)
> Nec levius, quam siquis Athon Pindumve revulsos
> sede sua totos in apertum everterit aequor,
> praecipitata cadit pariterque et pondere et ictu
> mergit in ima ratem;
>
> ... Athos and Pindus
> Could do no worse, if torn from their foundations
> And hurled into the open sea. The final wave
> Came toppling down and under its great weight
> The ship went to the bottom.
>
> (R. Humphries)

But Ceyx manages to survive the impact. The picture of him clinging to his bit of wreckage is reminiscent of any number of storm victims—Odysseus astride the plank at *Od.* 5.370 or clutching the severed mast at *Od.* 14.311; the sons of Phrixus at *Argo.* 2.1110 ff. grabbing a beam that has been torn from their ship; or even Paetus at Propertius 3.7.53 clinging to an elegiacly pitiful sliver.

Section VI (562-573)

Ceyx thinks of Alcyone and prays that his body may be washed to her by the waves and that thus she herself may bury him. With her name on his lips, he sinks beneath the surface. Lucifer, his father, unable to leave his post in heaven, mourns by covering his face the next morning in dark clouds. Ceyx dies thinking of his Alcyone.

Ceyx dies, calling the name of his Alcyone until the end.

(11.563)
>   ... illam meminitque refertque,
> illius ante oculos ut agant sua corpora fluctus,
> optat et exanimis manibus tumuletur amicis.

>   ... Over and over
> The swimmer calls her name, prays that the waves
> May wash his body to her over the waters,
> That in his death, her hands, so dear to him,
> May tend his funeral offices.
>   (R. Humphries)

His final wish that his body be washed to her by the waves is a theme found twice in Propertius, but not at all in epic.[41] The tone is clearly elegiac. The story ends with the same tone with which it began in the departure scene. Our attention is fixed on Ceyx, the husband and lover. As he disappears beneath the waves, the storm itself disappears. What was just recently raging so furiously is now nothing. It does not really end; we are just told nothing more about it. The poet is concerned with Ceyx and when he is gone there is nothing more.

(11.568)
> ecce super medios fluctus niger arcus aquarum
> frangitur et rupta mersum caput obruit unda.

Lucifer obscurus ...

At last a huge black arc of water, swinging
Up, over, and down, plunges him fathoms under.
The Morning Star was dim that day ...
(R. Humphries)

It is the same in Propertius

(3.7.65)
subtrahit haec fantem torta vertigine fluctus;
　ultima quae Paeto voxque diesque fuit.
O centum aequoreae Nereo ...

Even as he spoke these words the wave
with twisting eddy dragged him down;
thus passed from Paetus speech and life
together.
　Ye hundred daughters of Nereus ...
(H. B. Butler)

With Paetus' death, Propertius has no more interest in the storm. It ceases to exist. Compare, however, all the storms from epic. In each there is a specific attempt to describe, or at least acknowledge, the calming of the sea, the scattering of the winds, etc.

The scene ends with the delightful Ovidian conceit of Lucifer, unable to leave his post in heaven to be at his son's side, donning the mourning garb of dark clouds, the remants, perhaps, of the storm which went we know not where.

(11.570)
Lucifer obscurus nec quem cognoscere posses
illa luce fuit, quoniamque excedere caelo
non licuit, densis texit sua nubibus ora.

The Morning Star was dim that day; you could not
Tell him at all, mourning behind the clouds,
Unable to quit his station in the heavens.[42]
(R. Humphries)

Otis notes the absence of the gods and the deliberate contrast with the storm of *Aen.* 1, concluding that "Ovid only uses Virgil to emphasize his own point of view";[43] whereas, "Virgil's storm is sort of a divine-human action sequence and reflects or symbolizes the deeper forces of *pietas* and *furor* in which Aeneas is involved."[44] Ovid's storm, lacking divine origin emphasizes the duel between the crew and the waves and winds, the duel between man and the blind malevolence of nature. All this is undeniably true.[45] But this is not *all* that the comparison accomplishes. The very fact that we are asked, through direct allusions, consciously to compare Ovid's storm with those which have gone before—most specifically the by then justly famous storm of *Aen.* 1—introduces the aspect of literary wit; the conscious play of the intellect which controls our involvement in the story itself.

Yet as we can see from a quick glance at Saint-Denis' table and from the obvious allusions to Homer, Ovid does not limit himself to *Aen.* 1 as a source for his storm. He gathers together distinctive features from many places and combines them into a single spectacular storm—larger, wilder, more dramatic and pathetic than any that had gone before. It is the Compleat Literary Storm. His inspiration is ultimately the literary convention itself. He is showing the literary world that he is well aware of the tradition in general and Virgil's handling of it in particular. His will be a storm that will out-storm all storms that had ever raged on the pages of previous literature. And he does it all the more audaciously by putting a convention most recently associated with the very epic *Aeneid* into a decidedly non-epic framework.

FOOTNOTES

1. E. K. Rand, "Ovid and the Spirit of Metamorphosis." *Harvard Essays on Classical Subjects*, 1912, pp. 209-38.

2. From T. S. Eliot, "Old Possum's Book of Practical Cats," included in *The Complete Poems and Plays 1909-1950* (New York, 1952), p. 163.

3. From Arthur Conan Doyle, "The Final Problem," included in *The Complete Sherlock Holmes* (Garden City, 1930), pp. 471 and 472. Special thanks to Prof. Richard Luman for pointing out this wonderful example.

4. Henry Fielding, *The Adventures of Joseph Andrews* (Boston, 1961), p. 8.

5. *Ibid.*, p. 202.

6. See, for example, *Am.* 3.9, the elegy on the death of Tibullus. In addition to obvious references to Tibullus' life, there are also *allusions* to his poetry, and witty conceits (Elegy herself mourning, Cupid with bow broken and quiver reversed, etc.). This is surely not comic here, but it *is* wit. The tone is one of controlled pathos—a deep grief which yet has not destroyed the poet's rationality and intellectual faculties. (Note also how Ovid has personalized the genre Elegy.)

7. Although I can not go into the matter of the overall structue of the poem here, I would like to make one observation. Heinze's division of literary elements into the categories of Epic and Elegiac has perhaps led to a tendency to think about the *Metamorphoses* in strict terms of "either-or." (R. Heinze, "Ovids elegische Erzählung." Berichte über die Verhandlungen der Sächsischen Gesellschaft der Wissenschaften zu Leipzig: Philogogisch-historische Klasse, 71 (7), Leipzig, 1919. Reprinted in: R. Heinze, *Vom Geist der Römertums.* Darmstadt, 1960, pp. 338-403.) The poem has consistently resisted this kind of classification. A good example of the chaos produced by this tendency to polarize is Von Albrecht's attempt to divide the poem into sections which are either serious or humorous, allowing no middle ground. (M. Von Albrecht, "Ovids Humor—ein Schlüssel zur Interpretation der Metamorphosen." *Der Altsprachliche Unterricht*, 6 (2), 1963, pp. 47-72.) The result is an embarrassing patchwork of "exceptions." It is especially interesting to note that many of the passages which he labels 'Serious' are those in which literary wit is most surely at work: for example, the Ceyx-Alcyone episode, the battle scene of Book V, and that of Book XII.

8. The basic work for the storm in Latin literature is E. Saint-Denis, *La Rôle de la Mer dans la Poésie Latine* (Paris, 1935). J. Landowski also treats the storm in "La Tempête des Nostoi dans le Tragedie Romaine," *Tragica I*, XLI (1952), pp. 131-151; as does M. P. O. Morford in *Some Aspects of Lucan's Rhetoric*, Dissertation, (University of London, 1963).

9. Saint-Denis, *Ibid.*, p. 354 (translation and parentheses mine).

10. There are, of course, a number of storms (preserved in varying degrees) between Homer and Virgil. At Aeschylus, *Agamemnon* 649 ff., for example, the herald tells of the storm which destroyed the Greek fleet; Sophocles is said to have had an impressive storm in his *Teucer*; in Euripides' *Trojan Women* (77 ff.) Athena speaks of the storm sent on the Greek fleet as a punishment for Ajax's attack on Cassandra; in the *Argonautica* (2.1108 ff.) a storm strikes the sons of Phrixus as they draw near Orchomenus. In Latin literature, one line survives of Livius Andronicus' translation of the *Odyssey* (5.297) (*Remains of Old Latin*, ed. and trans. E. H. Warmington (Cambridge, 1936), II, frg. 18); two lines remain from his *Aegisthus* which may deal with Agamemnon's joyful departure—a prelude to the storm (frgs. 5-6); Macrobius (*Sat.* 6.2.32) refers to the storm in Book I of Naevius' *Bellum Punicum*; there remain two fragments from Naevius about lightning flashes (frgs. 8-9), and one which seems to come from a simile dealing with winds (unassigned frg. no. 40); fragments of Ennius' *Annales* yeild a nice three-line simile dealing with the winds converging to churn up the sea (*Remains of Old Latin*, I, frg. 430-432); a

fragment from Ennius' *Achilles* is part of a simile about huge waves (frg. 18); Pacuvius' *Teucer* provides us with the first full-fledged storm in Latin literature (frgs. 341, 350-365). Four fragments from Accius' *Clytemnestra* deal with the storm which beset the Greek fleet (frgs. 237-238, 239-240, 241-242). In Accius' *Medea* (or *Argonauts*) a shepherd who had never before seen a ship, compares the Argo's wake to the effect of a storm on the sea (frgs. 381-394). Three other fragments from his work refer to hurricanes and thunder (frgs. 183-185, 401-402, 659-660); the theme of the storm runs throughout Plautus' *Rudens*; although there are no set storm scenes in Lucretius, natural phenomena play an important part in *De Rerum Natura* and really deserve to be considered part of the storm tradition. See, for instance, 1.271 ff., 2.552 ff., 5.1126 ff., 6.197 ff., 6.250 ff., 6.443 ff.

11. Notice the similarity, the almost formulaic quality, of *Aen.* 5.8-11 and *Aen.* 3.192-195.

    (5.8)
    Ut pelagus tenuere rates nec iam amplius ulla
    occurrit tellus, maria undique et undique caelum,
    olli caeruleus supra caput adstitit imber,
    noctem hiememque ferens, et in horruit unda tenebris.

    They were out of sight of land, with only sea
    Around them on all sides, alone with ocean,
    Ocean and sky, when a cloud, black-blue, loomed over
    With night and tempest in it; the water roughened
    In shadow ...

    (3.192)
    postquam altum tenuere rates nec iam amplius ullae
    apparent terrae, caelum undique et undique pontus,
    tum mihi caeruleus supra caput adsititit imber,
    noctem hiememque ferens, et in horruit unda tenebris.

    We were in deep water, and the land no longer
    Was visible, sky and ocean everywhere
    A cloud, black-blue, loomed overhead, with night
    And tempest in it, and the water roughened
    In shadow ...

    Compare also *Od.* 12.403-406 and *Od.* 14.301-304.

12. Note also Byron's comment in *Don Juan* (*The Poetical Works of Lord Byron* (London, 1928), 1. 200 ff.):

    My poem's epic, and is meant to be
    Divided in twelve books; each book containing,
    With love, and war, a heavy gale at sea,
    A list of ships, and captains, and kings reigning, ...

13. Victor Bérard, *Les Phéniciens et l'Odyssée* (Paris, 1902), I, pp. 481-482.

14. *Ibid.*, p. 50.

15. *Ibid.*, p. 82.

16. pp. 225-226. Essentially the same technical observation was made by Seneca, even if parenthetically. Speaking about the four winds, he cites Ovid's six-line description of them in *Met.* 1.61-66 and then continues, introducing *Aen.* 1.85-86 (*Quaest. Nat.* 5.2): *Vel, si brevius illos complecti mavis, in unam tempestatem, quod fieri nullo modo potest, congregentur: Una urusque notusque ruunt* ...

17. See Otis' comments on the storm of *Aen.* 1 in *Virgil: A Study in Civilized Poetry.* Oxford: Clarendon Press, 1964, p. 233 and in *Ovid as an Epic Poet.* Cambridge: University Press, Second Edition, 1970, p. 245.

18. Although a stormy sea is certainly central to the situation of *Heroides* 18 and 19 (the letters of Hero and Leander) and is indeed mentioned a number of times, there is nothing in either poem which I would call a storm scene.

19. It is of interest to note, however, in support of Ovid's fascination with literary form and stylistic convention that the storm of *Tr.* 1.2 which purports to having been written from personal experience—indeed written right on board ship in mid-storm (see *Tr.* 1.2.1 ff. and also the final poem of Book 1, *Tr.* 1.11.1-8 and 39-40)—is nonetheless patently literary. Of the twenty stock features listed on Saint-Denis' chart more than half are here, in amongst assorted autobiographical tidbits and pleas to Augustus for reprieve.

20. Saint-Denis: "*Il (Ovid) recourt ensuite dans la déscription du sinistre, à un amplification laborieuse de la tempête virgilienne.*" (*op. cit.*, p. 347.)

21. Hermann Traenkle, "Elegisches in Ovids Metamorphosen," *Hermes*, XCI (1963), pp. 459-476.

22. Otis, I think, insists too much on the "epic" quality of the story. "It is essentially an epic." ". . . and furthermore, the epic gods are still on hand." (*Ovid, op. cit.*, p. 233.) The gods are indeed there, but as he himself notes, they behave in a non-epic way: there is a "sharp and deliberate" contrast with Virgil and Homer; the storm "is not attributed to some deity; the metamorphosis is only divine by 'courtesy,' so to speak." (p. 233.)

23. Note the direct address of Alcyone at 416: *certam / te fecit, Alcyone.*

24. Somewhat the same effect is conveyed after the storm by the way in which Ovid shifts the time back at 1.573. (*Aeolis interea tantorum ignara malorum*). We have been with Ceyx during the storm. Now we come back again to the time just after the departure to be with Alcyone during the same time. The time dovetails so that we are with both of them throughout the entire span of the story. As a devoted couple in a love story, they are both equally important.

25. These details of the crew's preparations for the storm have no real precedents in the tradition (except, perhaps, at *Aen.* 5.15-16). The passage finds favor with Saint-Denis: "*Toute cette partie est vue, précise, technique.*" (*op. cit.*, p. 347).

26. The full storm, from Ceyx's departure until his death, is ninety-seven lines. Virgil's storm in *Aen.* 1 at its longest (to include Neptune's lecture to the winds and the rescue operation) is seventy-six; the storm proper is forty-three.

27. *Remains, op. cit.,* II, frg. 365.

28. Anton Zingerle, *Ovidius und sein Verhältniss zu den vorangegangenen und gleichzeitigen römischen Dichtern* (Innsbruck, 1869-71).

29. Brunner notes the contrast and alternation of Height and Depth motifs throughout the passage. T. F. Brunner, "The Simile in Ovid's Metamorphses," *CJ* LXI (May, 1966), pp. 354-363.

30. Saint-Denis credits Ovid with *"une notation heureuse"* (p. 349) at line 532 where the lightning makes the waves glow red. Rightly so. Virgil's lightning lights the heavens (1.90); Ovid goes him one better.

31. I am not considering the wonderful simile at *Aen.* 1.148 ff. comparing Neptune to the stateman as part of the storm proper.

32. Wilkins says of the "eager soldier" simile that "As Washietl indicates, Ovid is evidently consciously reversing Homer's simile in *Iliad* 15.381-83." (Eliza Gregory Wilkins, "A Classification of the Similes of Ovid," *The Classical Weekly,* XXV (1932), pp. 73-78, 81-86.) The Trojans rushing the Greek wall are here compared to a wave crashing on a ship. But the similarity to *Il.* 15.623 where *both* the wave and lion similes are used is even more striking.

33. Saint-Denis, *op. cit.,* p. 347, especially n. 23.

34. In Virgil, for instance, see among others: *Aen.* 1.110, 1.116, 3.203, 3.421, 3.566.

35. The Tenth Wave first appears in this passage. At *Tristia* 1.2.49 Ovid seems to be borrowing from himself, using the Tenth Wave and also comparing the pounding of the waves to the pounding of a ballista.

36. Here again Ovid chides Virgil with a mild correction of *Aen.* 1.93. Since the darkness is so dense, one of course can not see the stars to lift one's hands to them.

37. This might be an expansion of Virgil's *ingemit* (*Aen.* 1.93).

38. See also *Aen.* 1.115-116 where Orontes' ship is whirled around by the sea three times and then sucked down.

39. See Pacuvius frg. 356: *tenebrae conduplicantur, noctisque et nimbum obcaecat nigror;*

40. In the storm of *Od.* 14.311 ff. one assumes that it has been torn off, as Odysseus grabs it as he flounders in the sea.

41. See also *Heroides* 2.135; 18.197 for the same tender sentiment.

42. Aeolus, after the couple's tranformation into sea birds, calms the waters once each winter for seven days as a gesture of love and compassion for them and their aviary offspring.

> (11.745) perque dies placidos hiberno tempore septem
> incubat Alcyone pendentibus aequore nidis.
> tunc iacet unda maris: ventos custodit et arcet
> Aeolus egressu praestatque nepotibus aequor.

> For seven days of calm, Alcyone
> Broods over her nest on the surface of the waters
> While the sea-waves are quiet. Through this time
> Aeolus keeps his winds at home, and ocean
> Is smooth for his descendants' sake.
>
> (R. Humphries)

These two passages balance each other nicely. Each father makes a gentle gesture of mourning directly following the death of his child. But neither renders assistance at the time of their crisis.

43. Otis, *Ovid*, p. 246.

44. *Ibid.*, p. 245.

45. He might also have noted in this connection (as he brings out in another context) that the similes of the passage—unlike the two in Homer which describes the *boat* being tossed by the waves—describe the waves themselves, making them active agents.

CICERONIAN PRECEPTS AND HUMOR IN PERSIUS

Carrie Cowherd

I

Critical evaluation of Persius condemns him for lacking the *felicitas* of Horace and the *indignatio* of Juvenal. As the solemn, serious poet of Stoicism, he is said to lack humor most of all. The most recent commentator, R. A. Harvey, summarizes the consensus in his assessment: "Persius' intense preoccupation with Stoicism leaves little scope for the amusing treatment of themes found, for example, in Horace. To be sure, humor is present in the pictures of the disappointed *nummus* (2.50-51), the boorish centurion (3.78-85), and the miserly Vettidius (4.29-32); there are jocular touches in Persius' metaphors and his bizarre collocations. But the poet's main concern is the urgent development of serious moral arguments."[1] Moreover, the language of Persius is an obstacle. In his Loeb edition, G. G. Ramsay judges him precious, sometimes crabbed and tortuous, too compressed, elliptical, abrupt, and difficult to follow. The language presents a further problem in that it is so very Horatian, tempting commentators to concentrate more on the line of Horace from which each word comes than on the flow of thought. *Quellenforschung*, difficulty of language, and Stoicism have combined to deny humor to Persius. Yet humor pervades his satires and was among his goals of composition.

Persius' allusions to his humor are found in the programmatic first satire and in the famous three lines of Satire 5,14-16:

> verba togae sequeris iunctura callidus acri,
> ore teres modico, pallentis radere mores
> doctus et ingenuo culpam defigere ludo.

These lines present several problems of interpretation, some caused by the tendency to take them out of context, the others, by the difficulty of ascertaining the meaning within the context. The most elusive phrases are *verba togae, iunctura acri,* and *ingenuo ludo.* By way of illustration, Cynthia Dessen understands *iunctura acris* to refer to Persius' "peculiar use of metaphor whereby he boldly unites very disparate ideas to shock his reader into a new perspective."[2] For Harvey, on the other hand, the *iunctura acris* is simply an "abrasive" or "bizarre collocation" of familiar words, "arguably the most remarkable single feature of P.'s poetry."[3] *Pallentis . . . ludo* refers to his satiric genre, his Stoic mission, and his humor. From here, *ingenuo ludo* is most important for establishing Persius' conception of humor. This conception is best seen against a Ciceronian background.

Cicero discusses humor for the orator in *De Oratore* 2.216-90 and *Orator* 87-90, and in relation to propriety in *De Officiis* 1.103-104.[4] All three are relevant to Persius. *De Officiis* 1.103-104:

> nec enim ita generati a natura sumus, ut ad *ludum* et *iocum* facti esse videamur, ad severitatem potius et ad quaedam studia graviora atque maiora. *ludo* autem et *ioco* uti illo quidem licet, sed sicut somno et quietibus ceteris tum, cum gravibus seriisque rebus satis fecerimus. ipsumque genus iocandi non profusum nec immodestum, sed *ingenuum* et facetum esse debet .... duplex omnino est iocandi genus, unum *illiberale, petulans,* flagitiosum, *obscenum,* alterum elegans, urbanum, ingeniosum, facetum. quo genere non modo Plautus noster et Atticorum antiqua comoedia, sed etiam philosophorum Socraticorum libri referti sunt .... facilis igitur est distinctio *ingenui* et *illiberalis* ioci. alter est, si tempore fit, ut si remisso animo, gravissimo homine dignus, alter ne libero quidem, si rerum turpitudini adhibetur verborum obscenitas.

Orator 87-89 recommends the use of *sales,* which is also of two kinds:

huic generi orationis aspergentur etiam sales, qui in dicendo nimium quantum valent; quorum duo genera sunt, unum facetiarum, alterum dicacitatis: utetur utroque; sed altero in narrando aliquid venuste, altero in iaciendo mittendoque ridiculo, cuius genera plura sunt; sed nunc aliud agimus. illud admonemus tamen, ridiculo sic usurum oratorem, ut nec nimis frequenti, ne scurrile sit, nec *subobsceno*, ne mimicum, nec *petulanti*, ne improbum, nec in calamitatem, ne inhumanum, nec in facinus, ne odi locum risus occupet, neque aut sua persona aut iudicum aut tempore alienum; haec enim ad illud indecorum referuntur. vitabit etiam quaesita nec ex tempore ficta, sed domo adlata, quae plerumque sunt frigida; parcet et amicitiis et dignitatibus, vitabit insanabilis contumelias, tantummodo *adversarios figet* nec eos tamen semper nec omnis nec omni modo; quibus exceptis sic utetur sale et facetiis, ut ego ex istis novis Atticis talem cognoverim neminem, cum id certe sit vel maxime Atticum.

J. E. Sandys translates *facetiae* as "humor" and *dicacitas* as "wit;" humor is used in narration; wit, in "darting forth the shafts of raillery."[5] The caveats on the use of *ridiculum* show that the danger is that it may seem *illiberale*; *subobsceno* and *petulanti* repeat *obscenum* and *petulans* from *De Officiis*.

De Oratore 2.216-90 expands on *Orator* 87-90. The subject is divided into five parts: *unum, quid sit; alterum, unde sit; tertium sitne oratoris, velle risum movere; quartum, quatenus; quintum, quae sint genera ridiculi* (235). Cicero disclaims knowledge of *quid sit risus* and its source (235).[6] The *locus ridiculi* is found *turpitudine et deformitate quadem ... haec enim ridentur vel sola, vel maxime, quae notant et designant turpitudinem aliquam non turpiter* (236). Causing laughter is appropriate for the orator since it earns good will and admiration, puts the opponent at a disadvantage, and especially *quod tristitiam ac severitatem mitigat et relaxat* (236). The limits resemble those of *Orator* 88-89: *ea facillime luduntur, quae neque odio magno, neque misericordia maxima digna sunt . . . . vitandum est oratori utrumque, ne aut scurrillis iocus sit, aut mimicus* (238-39).

The bulk of the discussion, 240-90, concerns *genera ridi-*

culi. Two separate divisions are made, first *cavillatio* and *dicacitas*, then *re* and *dicto* (240) or *verbo* (248). As Grant has shown, *cavillatio* is identical with *ridiculum in re positum* (243) and *dicacitas* with *dicto* and *verbo*; further, *cavillatio* and *re* are the *facetiae* of *Orator* 87, "humor," and *dicacitas* is (still) "wit."[7] A combination of the two is the most delightful (248). Wit is *id quod verbi aut sententiae quodam acumine movetur* (244); humor is more sustained and is found in continuous narrative. 2.243:

> ergo haec duo genera sunt eius ridiculi quod in re positum est, quae sunt propria perpetuarum facetiarum, in quibus describuntur hominum mores et ita effinguntur, ut aut re narrata aliqua, quales sint, intellegantur, aut, imitatione brevi iniecta, in aliquo insigni ad irridendum vitio reperiantur.

2.264:

> ac verborum quidem genera, quae essent faceta, dixisse me puto; rerum plura sunt, eaque magis, ut dixi ante, ridentur; in quibus est narratio, res sane difficilis; exprimenda enim sunt et ponenda ante oculos ea quae videantur et verisimilia, quod est proprium narrationis, et quae sint, quod ridiculi proprium est, subturpia.

Most promient among the examples of wit is ambiguity, of which there are many kinds, but ambiguity usually produces admiration more than laughter. Other examples are *para prosdokian*, *paronomasia*, quotation or misquotation of verse and proverbs, words taken literally but not *ad sententiam*, antitheses, allegory, metaphor, and irony. Irony as wit is saying the opposite of what is meant.

Humor depends more on thought than specific words. Examples of humor other than caricature and anecdote include simile, understatement and overstatement, pretending not to understand, hint of ridicule, *discrepantia* "unexpected turns," concession and irony. Irony as humor is defined as saying something other than what is meant, *cum toto genere orationis severe ludas, cum aliter sentias ac loquare* (269).

The humor of the orator displays his *ingenuitas* (242); obscenity and excessive use of caricature belong to the mime; excessive indulgence in wit belongs to the *scurra* "wag" or "jester." Both the mime and the *scurra* typify *iocandi genus illiberale*. The *scurra* has no regard for occasion but is witty at every opportunity (244); he attacks unprovoked, as an incident involving a certain Appius illustrates. 2.246:

> ut iste qui se vult dicacem, et mehercule est, Appius, sed nonnumquam in hoc vitium delabitur. 'cenabo,' inquit, 'apud te,' huic lusco . . . 'uni enim locum esse video.' est hoc scurrile, et quod sine causa lacessivit, et tamen id dixit quod in omnis luscos conveniret; ea quia meditata putantur esse, minus ridentur.

His joke was *frigidum* as well as *scurrile*.

Against this Ciceronian background both the fact and the method of humor in Persius become clearer. The extra-contextual meaning of 5.16, *doctus et ingenuo culpam defigere ludo*, can be established with certainty.[8] *Ingenuo ludo* should be referred directly to *De Officiis* 1.103-104, where *ludus* and *iocus* are synonymous and the *iocus* or *ludus ingenuus* is contrasted with *iocandi genus illiberale*. There can be no real doubt that by *ingenuo ludo*, Persius asserts that his satires are humorous, and that the humor is worthy of a gentleman.[9] Further, *culpam defigere* reproduces the substance of *Orator* 89, *tantummodo adversarios figet*.

Although he lays claim to *ludus ingenuus*, by his use of *petulans*, one of the code words for illiberal humor present in both *De Officiis* 1.104 and *Orator* 88, he indicates a concern with the latter kind also. In 1.12, he describes himself as *petulanti splene*. Like *ingenuo ludo*, *petulanti splene* has meaning both within and apart from the context. Within the context it is part of the frame of the joke that Satire 1 is proclaimed to be, *hoc ridere meum* (122). 1.7-12:

> . . . nec te quaesiveris extra.
> nam Romae quis non—a, si fas dicere—sed fas
> tum cum ad canitiem et nostrum istud vivere triste
> aspexi ac nucibus facimus quaecumque relictis
> cum sapimus patruos. tunc tunc—ignoscite (nolo,
> quid faciam?) sed sum petulanti splene—cachinno.

Ignoscite (nolo, quid faciam) sed sum petulanti splene constitutes an explanation and apology for the illiberal *cachinnare*. This impulse to guffaw is irresistible but momentary; hence *petulanti splene* does not contradict *ingenuo ludo*.

The conclusion of the joke stretches from 114-34, with the completion of 8, *nam Romae quis non—*, coming in 121, *auriculas asini quis non habet?* 114-18 associates Persius with his predecessors Lucilius and Horace in attacking faults and arousing laughter.[10] After 121, he designates the kind of reader he wants and does not want, and these in terms of humor. Those who study (*palles* "turn pale over," 124) Cratinus, Eupolis, and Aristophanes should look at him. As we have seen, *De Officiis* 1.104 identifies Attic Old Comedy as *iocandi genus . . . elegans, urbanum, ingeniosum, facetum*, that is, *ingenuum*. On the other hand, the readers he does not want are those whose humor is illiberal. That their humor is illiberal is most obvious in the case of the one *lusco qui possit dicere 'lusce'* (128). This man is another Appius whose wit was *scurrile* in *De Oratore* 2.246.[11] *Callirhoen* (134) most probably represents a mime, the other extreme in illiberal humor. Finally, 131-33 foreshadows the centurions of Satires 3 and 5:

> nec qui numeros secto in pulvere metas
> scit risisse vafer, multum gaudere paratus
> si Cynico barbam *petulans* nonaria vellat.

Persius introduces the centurions to put an abrupt end to philosophical sermonizing. The centurion's caricatures of philosophers in 3.78-85 is one of the two developed illustrations of illiberal humor. It is illiberal because the centurion is interested only in raising laughter, which is immediately forthcoming. 3.86-87:

> his populus ridet, multumque torosa iuventus
> ingeminat tremulos naso crispante cachinnos.

The laughter of the youth is the ill-mannered *cachinnus* for which Persius feels compelled to apologize in 1.11-12. The brevity of the description of the centurion's laughter in 5.189-91 shows that Persius is alluding to his former, longer account of 3.78-85. The other illustration of illiberal humor belongs to the stranger in 4.33-41. His caricature of Alcibiades qualifies because of its obscenity. While the speeches of both the stranger and the centurion are illiberal, they are, nevertheless, funny.

As with *duplex iocandi genus, ingenuum et illiberale*, so Cicero's discussion of *genera ridiculi, cavillatio (facetiae, in re)* and *dicacitas (in verbo)* is pertinent to Persius. Since Persius aims for the best course, the combination of humor and wit, comparison of Cicero with the satires can reveal where his humor and wit lie.[12]

According to Cicero, wit can not be learned but comes "by nature." Wit is useful in attacking or responding to attacks. *Ex ambiguo dicta vel argutissima putantur, sed non semper in ioco, saepe etiam in gravitate versantur* (*De Oratore* 2.250). Ambiguities are characteristic of both the serious and humorous in Persius. From the other examples of wit, *para prosdokian*, allegory, metaphor, the irony are frequently found. From the examples of humor, Persius favors caricature, understatement and overstatement, *discrepantia*, and, again, irony *cum . . . severe ludas*. He is fond of deflation of elevated language, a device not specifically mentioned by Cicero but able to be included under *discrepantia*. Most of Persius' humor, however, derives from his skilful scene painting in narration. The Ciceronian definition of humorous narration, quoted above, relates to Persius' skill and is worth repeating. 2.264:

> . . . narratio, res sane difficilis; exprimenda enim sunt et ponenda ante oculos ea quae videantur et verisimilia, quod est proprium narrationis, et quae sint, quod ridiculi proprium est, subturpia.

This visual aspect of Persius' art has been recognized in other contexts; however, since he has seldom been considered funny, no connection has been made between his scene painting and his humor.[13] He describes scenes of varying lengths, some extended, some mere snapshots. Each requires visualization, for the resulting picture is more humorous than the words themselves. Although Persius shows almost all of Cicero's examples of humor and wit, discussion of the satires will concentrate on the combinations of deflation of elevated language, the two classes of irony, verbal ambiguities, and scene painting.

II

My emphasis on the humor of Persius does not deny the serious intent of the satires. All except Satire 1 are explications of Stoic doctrine. The topic of Satire 2 is the proper nature and object of prayer; Satire 3 is a general exhortation to virtue with indications of the Stoic paradox that all fools are mad. Satire 4 recommends attention to internal rather than external standards and counsels knowledge of self. Satire 5 is an investigation of the definition of freedom and of the paradox that only the wise man is free. Satire 6 treats *quid asper utile nummus habet, patriae carisque propinquis quantum elargiri deceat* (3.69-71). Satire 1 is an extended joke whose subject is Roman authors and audiences and whose purpose is to separate Persius from his milieu and establish his own place in the satiric tradition. Persius' humorous wit (or witty humor) in Cicero's words, *tristitiam ac severitatem mitigat et relaxat*.

The fact that Persius calls Satire 1 a joke, *hoc ridere meum* (122), does not, of course, guarantee that it is funny; however, the humor begins immediately, with the pomposity of the first line deflated by the second: *o curas hominum! o quantum est in rebus inane!/ "quis leget haec?"*[14] Along with irony, deflation also ends the discussion of the contemporary literary scene. 1.110-14:

> ... per me equidem sint omnia protinus alba;
> nil moror. euge omnes, omnes bene, mirae eritis res.
> hoc iuvat? 'hic' inquis, 'veto quisquam faxit oletum.'
> pingue duos anguis. 'pueri, sacer est locus, extra
> meiite.' discedo.

Between the lines of the actual joke, *nam Romae quis non*—(8) and *auriculas asini quis non habet?* (121), Persius uses *auriculae* four times, as a tease for his joke and, through the repetition in 22 and 23, in establishing the ambiguities of the first scene on which most of the humor of the rest of the satire depends.[15] The scene is one of recitation. 1.15-23:

> scilicet haec populo pexusque togaque recenti
> et natalicia tandem cum sardonyche albus
> sed leges celsa, liquido cum plasmate guttur
> mobile conlueris, patranti fractus ocello.
> tunc neque more probo videas nec voce serena
> ingentis trepidare Titos, cum carmina lumbum
> intrant et tremulo scalpuntur ubi intima versu.
> tun, vetule, auriculis alienis colligis escas,
> auriculis quibus et dicas cute perditus 'ohe'?[16]

Lumbum is *para prosdokian* for *auriculas*. *Auriculis* in 22 and 23 is, in a sense, a substitute for *lumbum*. Persius uses each part of the word, *auri*-and the diminutive suffix *-cula*, separately; especially at 22 and 23, *auri-* equals *-culis*. Concomitant with the play on *auriculis* is the additional thought that if ears can be thirsty, as they are in 4.50 (*bibulas aures*), they can be hungry too. In 22-23, Persius manages to have both jokes at the same time. *Escae* are food for the ears, and on the joke of *auri-* equals *-culus*, neither the *aures* of the reciter nor his *culus* would be able to take in much more. *Cute* must refer to the skin not of the foreskin, as some would have it, but of the rear end.[17]

The adversary's response, 24-25, extends the ambiguity and adds incongruity of images:

'quo didicisse, nisi hoc fermentum et quae semel intus
  innata est rupto iecore exierit caprificus.'

Since this comes immediately after *carmina lumbum intrant et tremulo scalpuntur ubi intima versu*, it is impossible not to hear or see *semel intus innata est rupto iecore* first as repetition of that image, with the obvious pun of *innata* and with *iecore* as one of the *intima*. The combination of *fermentum* with *caprificus* is odd and amusing, regardless of the connotation of *caprificus*.[18] Even if *caprificus* does not mean "penis" but refers to the tree's often-mentioned habit of bursting through rocks in graveyards, the images are of rising and swelling and irresistible force; and the surface meaning still matches *carmina lumbum* and the rest, above. The language is sufficiently ambiguous to allow two interpretations: Why shall I have learned except to arouse my audience? or Why, except to perform? The continuity of the conversation requires the latter.

Poetry as food is used alone in the second scene of recitation, 30-40, where the recitation is a course at a banquet. Irony produces the humorous effect. That humor is intended is confirmed by the adversary's reaction, *rides* (40). Another banquet develops in 51-62, introduced by reference to *crudi* aristocrats, composition on citron dining couches, and *calidum scis ponere sumen* (53). *Ponere* is ambiguous and what is expected to be a poem turns out to be a sow's udder.

Reverting to the combination of ideas established in 22-23, Persius shows another scene with the asses and the ears mixed up, 79-88:

> hos pueris monitus patres infundere lippos
> cum videas, quaerisne unde haec sartago loquendi
> venerit in linguas, unde istud dedecus in quo
> trossulus exultat tibi per subsellia levis?
> nilne pudet capiti non posse pericula cano
> pellere quin tepidum hoc optes audire 'decenter'?
> 'fur es,' ait Pedio. Pedius quid? crimina rasis
> librat in antithetis, doctas posuisse figuras
> laudatur: 'bellum hoc.' hoc bellum? an, Romule, ceves?
> men moveat?

Sartago loquendi venerit in linguas refers to poetry as food. *Trossulus exultat* recalls *trepidare Titos* (20) and prefigures, *para prosdokian*, *ceves*. *Cevere* is the motion of the *cinaedus*, Greek *kinaidos*.[19] The etymology of *kinaidos* is supposed to be *kinei aidoia*. Following the verbs of motion *ceves*, *men moveat* is both literal and figurative. The juxtaposition of *an . . . ceves* with *men moveat* is really very funny.

The last complaint against contemporary poetry, *tenerum et laxa cervice legendum* (98), through ambiguity, also suggests equations of *auri-* and *-culis* and poetry as food. 1.103-106:

> haec fierent si testiculi vena ulla paterni
> viveret in nobis? summa delumbe saliva
> hoc natat in labris et in udo est Maenas et Attis
> nec pluteum caedit nec demorsos sapit unguis.

Delumbe, *natat*, and *sapit* are the words admitting of ambiguity. *Delumbe* is generally understood to mean "weak"; however, it is impossible here not to remember 20-21, *carmina lumbum/intrant*, especially with the sound of *natat*, and impossible not to try to take *delumbe* literally. Moreover, *sapere* is one of Persius' words of which one must be wary. Although the surface meaning makes perfect sense, *demorsos sapit unguis* reminds of 11, *cum sapimus patruos*. Whatever Persius means there can not be expressed except by long paraphrase while the potentially humorous idea of "tasting our uncles" is what sticks.

In most of the other satires, the humor is more *sales* than substance. In Satire 2, lines 8-30 and 31-40 are humorous, the latter by reason of the preparation for and ridiculousness of the requests. The former is introduced with a solemn prayer which is immediately deflated. It presents another scene whose humor lies in visualizing it; in addition, it contains one of the funniest lines in Latin literature. Imagine the scene, 8-14:

> 'mens bona, fama, fides,' haec clare et ut audiat hospes;
> illa sibi introrsum et sub lingua murmurat: 'o si
> ebulliat patruus, praeclarum funus!' et 'o si
> sub rastro crepet argenti mihi seria dextro
> Hercule! pupillumve utinam, quem proximus heres
> inpello, expungam; nam et est scabiosus et acri
> bile tumet. Nerio iam tertia conditur uxor.'

Persius beckons him over to the side, 17-18: *heus age, responde (minimum est quod scire laboro)/ de Iove quid sentis?* While *ebulliat* is a funny word and the rest of the scene is generally funny, within its context *de Iove quid sentis?* is hilarious.[20]

The whole of Satire 3 is ironic, with the only signal being *tibi luditur* (20). The attribution of voices is still a subject of controversy; however, the simplest is also the best. Persius sets the scene, speaks near the beginning and end, and falls asleep in the middle.[21] The premise of the poem is that Persius has overslept after drinking too much the night before and for that reason, he is lectured by a friend. Many of the difficulties stem from the refusal of commentators to believe that Persius, *morum lenissimorum, verecundiae virginalis*, would carouse.[22] Therein lies the irony. The friend takes the drinking as the first step on the way to moral degradation. His lecture most resembles that given by the worried parent of a college student under the same circumstances. The points made are about the same:

> 1. One day you'll be sorry—appeal to his sense of guilt (31-43);
> 2. I didn't have all the advantage you had—comparison with the friend (44-62);
> 3. You're going to end up like such-and-such—appeal to negative example (88-106);
> 4. What's to become of you? (106-18).

Most of the humor of the poem comes in imagining the scene and is at Persius' expense. The bright morning light comes through the shutters; he is snoring, *stertimus* (3). After being awakened, he calls for his work; he feels like vomiting but breaks wind loudly. Someone brings him his work, and he can not get his ink the right consistency, finally whining, *an tali studeam calamo?* (19). The next indication of his actions are in 58-59:

> stertis adhuc laxumque caput conpage soluta
> oscitat hesternum dissutis undique malis.

He is sitting up asleep, snoring, with his mouth open and his head jerking down and then back up. That is, Persius is making fun of himself.

The premise of the satire allows for a presentation of Stoic teaching. Most of what there is, is couched in medical metaphor, but 66-72 is straightforward Stoicism. It is this call to virtue which the centurion's speech interrupts.[23] The centurion has no regard for nice distinctions, as his naming Solon as a typical philosopher shows. The caricature of the philosopher is apt, occasions laughter, and is funny. 3.77-85:

> hic aliquis de gente hircosa centurionum
> dicat: 'quod sapio satis est mihi. non ego curo
> esse quod Arcesilas aerumnosique Solones
> obstipo capite et figentes lumine terram,
> murmura cum secum et rabiosa silentia rodunt
> atque exporrecto trutinantur verba labello,
> aegroti veteris meditantes somnia: gigni
> de nihilo nihilum, in nihilum nil posse reverti.
> hoc est quod palles? cur quis non prandeat hoc est?'

The satire ends with the proposal that Persius is afflicted by the disturbing passions of avarice, lust, fear, and anger such that mad Orestes would judge him mad. The reference to madness carries us back to the *insana canicula* of line 5 and *elleborum* of 63 and suggests that the whole satire illustrates the Stoic paradox that all fools are mad.

In Satire 4, the level of irony and ambiguity is such that Dessen can say that "the dominant metaphor . . . compares the politician to a male prostitute . . . the first eight lines . . . imply a homosexual relationship between Alcibiades and the *populi*."[24] Except for the description of the miser Vettidius and the stranger's illiberal tirade against Alcibiades, the whole satire is full of seemingly innocent and straightforward words which have also straightforward sexual or, at least, genital connotations.[25] Good illustrations are the first words, *rem populi tractas*, and *dum ne deterius sapiat pannucia Baucis* (21). The problem in concentrating on the double meanings is that on the sexual level the poem is not coherent; nevertheless, so extensive a collocation can not be accidental. The solution is recourse to Persius' *ingenuo ludo* and to accept that Persius is simply teasing his reader, *severe ludit*.

The message of the satire is serious: Know yourself; have internal standards before applying external ones; see your own faults before criticizing others.[26] The tone, however, is much lighter, even apart from the sexual ambiguities. The satire is structured in terms of sucking and spitting: Socrates sucked hemlock, Alcibiades should suck hellebore, the miser sucks flat vinegar; the stranger spits out his abuse against Alcibiades, Alcibiade should spit out what he is not. The carefully constructed image of Alcibiades the precocious politician is destroyed by line 15, *blando caudam iactare popello*, where within the complexities of the poem, the only "tail" with any point is his own frontal one.[27]

Lines 25-41 are illustrations of 23-24, that no one tries to get into himself but each looks at the pack on the back in front, and of 42, that we strike and offer ourselves to injury in turn. Alcibiades prompts the ridicule of Vettidius, but if he should sun himself, some stranger would make fun of him. The humor of both characterizations results from exaggeration. There is no more reason to believe that Alcibiades really is weeding *penem arcanaque lumbi* (35) than that Vettidius considers onion a holiday meal.[28] In fact, the characterization of Vettidius is the ancient equivalent of the joke: "He's so cheap." "How cheap is he?" "He's so cheap he saves dirt; he's so cheap he eats the skin of the onion" and so forth.[29] The tirade against Alcibiades is illiberal because it is so obscene; it is exaggerated; and it is funny.

The satire ends with allusions to the passions of avarice, lust, and ambition. If Alcibiades is influenced by these, *nequiquam populo bibulas donaveris aures* (50). The last line is memorable: *tecum habita: noris quam sit tibi curta supellex*.

Most of the humor in Satire 5 is in the introduction. His topic is serious, a discussion of what freedom is. For this he needs a serious style and so begins, 1-2,

> vatibus hic mos est, centum sibi poscere voces,
> centum ora et linguas optare in carmina centum,

but Persius can not sustain the level, and so it promptly deteriorates, 3-4:

> fabula seu maesto ponatur hianda tragoedo
> volnera seu Parthi ducentis ab inguine ferrum.

The contribution of Cornutus (5-18) is to reduce the conceit to absurdity, especially in *cornicaris* (12) and *nec scloppo tumidas intendis rumpere buccas* (13). The description of his proper style, discussed above, precedes the final absurdity, 17-18:

> hinc trahe quae dicis mensasque relinque Mycenis
> cum capite et pedibus plebeiaque prandia noris.

Persius chooses to ease into his subject.[30] *Verba togae*, attributed to him by Cornutus, symbolizes not only Latin but also freedom, since the toga was the dress of the free Roman. His devotion to Cornutus is expressed in the "toga words," *excutienda* (22) and *sinuosa (27)*. *Ingenuo* (16) also emphasizes that he is freeborn. The license granted to his youth is described in terms relating to the dress and ornament of free boys and the ceremony marking his enrollment as a free citizen. But as a free citizen, he subjected himself to Cornutus. His subjection to Cornutus is subjection to reason: *et premitur ratione animus vincique laborat* (39). This is close to a Stoic definition of freedom, as comparison with 106-14 shows. While he "labors to be conquered" by reason, others are conquered by such passions as avarice (54-55), gluttony (56), athletics, gambling (57), and lust (58). They realize too late that they have wasted their lives. This is the sequence of thought which leads to the dramatic, but not unprepared for, *libertate opus est* (73). Persius has legal freedom; true freedom is subjection to a life in accordance with reason.

In the discussion from 73-188, humor is intermixed. It is most sustained in the description of the slave Dama, made free by a turn. The scene, 76-82, must be visualized, but the humor lies in the speed with which the images change. A Stoic corrects the logic of Dama's protest; through him, *aurem mordaci lotus aceto* (86), Persius laughs at himself.

The satire ends with illustrations of the kinds of masters within, the passions mentioned only briefly before. One slave to passion is torn between Avarice and Luxury, both of whom address him. There is humor in the urgency of Avarice's appeal against the sensuousness of Luxury's. A scene from comedy shows a slave to love. Ambition leads an aedile to sponsor an extravagant Floralia while Superstition provokes adherence to foreign cults. Persius chooses the most conspicuous aspects of each cult and makes fun of them, although the references themselves are not funny. *Caput gustaveris ali* (188) comes *para prosdokian*.

The laughter of the centurion puts an abrupt end to this philosophy. By the repetition of *cent-* in *centuriones* (189), *centum* (191), and *centusse* (191), Persius links the end with the beginning.

Satire 6 is the least humorous and perhaps the least successful of the poems.[31] The deflation of elevated or pompous language is employed at the beginning when Persius makes the transition from addressing Bassus to describing his own way of living at Luna. 6.9-11:

'Lunai portum, est operae, cognoscite, cives.'
cor iubet hoc Enni, postquam destertuit esse
Maeonides Quintus pavone ex Pythagoreo.

Seeming overstatement makes line 24 humorous: *nec tenuis sollers turdarum nosse salivas.* The sustained humor, however, comes from visualizing the scene with the heir, 37-74. We can see the heir's dismay when Persius announces he is going to exhibit two hundred gladiators and give away food because of the imperial victory over the Germans. The humor builds as Persius lists all of the possible heirs he does not have. The climax comes in the description of some future heir for whom Persius is to live frugally, 69-74:

ungue, puer, caules. mihi festa luce coquatur
urtica et fissa fumosum sinciput aure,
ut tuus iste nepos olim satur anseris extis,
cum morosa vago singultiet inguine vena,
patriciae inmeiat volvae? mihi trama figurae
sit reliqua, ast illi tremat omento popa venter?

The poem ends *para prosdokian*, 75-77: *vende animam lucro . . ./ . . . ne sit praestantior alter/ Cappadocas rigida pinguis plausisse catasta*; and in irony, 78-80:

> rem duplica. 'feci; iam triplex, iam mihi quarto,
> iam decies redit in rugam. depunge ubi sistam.'
> inventus, Chrysippe, tui finitor acervi.[32]

By reference to the *De Officiis, Orator*, and *De Oratore*, I have endeavored to explore ancient concepts of humor and to show how well the satires of Persius conform to Ciceronian precepts. Cicero divided *iocus* or *ludus* into *ingenuus* and *illiberalis*; Persius claims *ingenuus ludus*. Cicero divided that which arouses laughter into *dicacitas* "wit" and *facetiae* "humor," with humor best shown in narration and wit, in ambiguity. The humor in Persius' satires draws most on scene painting in narration combined with ambiguity.

J. P. Sullivan has suggested that Persius qualifies as an exponent of what Pound calls *logopoeia*, that is, "the dance of the intellect among words."[33] In Sullivan's terms this is a "refined sensitivity to how language is used in other contexts." Perhaps Pound's *phanopoeia*, "which is a casting of images upon the visual imagination," can be used also to indicate the best way to enjoy Persius' poetry. First one must accept that it is not altogether serious; then one must be willing to see the word pictures which Persius paints. If these things are done, the satires will be viewed in a new, more sympathetic light.[34]

NOTES

1. R. A. Harvey, *A Commentary on Persius* (Leiden 1981) 2.

2. Cynthia S. Dessen, *Iunctura Callidus Acri: A Study of Persius' Satires*, Illinois Studies in Language and Literature (Urbana 1968) vii-viii.

3. Harvey, 5.14 n., 129-31.

4. For a discussion of these passages of Cicero, see Mary A. Grant, "The Ancient Rhetorical Theories of the Laughable: The Greek Rhetoricians and Cicero," *University of Wisconsin Studies in Language and Literature* (Madison 1924) 71-158. See also J. C. Bramble, *Persius and the Programmatic Satire: A Study in Form and Imagery* (Cambridge 1974) 190-91.

5. J. E. Sandys, *Marcus Tullius Cicero: Ad Marcum Brutum Orator* (Cambridge 1885; repr. Hildesheim 1973) 98-99, ad loc.

6. I must join him in this disclaimer.

7. Grant, 107-12.

8. This interpretation is also required by the context where, however, the emphasis is on *ingenuo*. Satire 5 asks the question, What is freedom? Thinly veiled but commonly unnoticed references in the first 51 lines lead to the open discussion which follows. See below, pp. 53-55.

9. G. C. Fiske, "Lucilius, The *Ars Poetica* of Horace, and Persius," *HSCP* 24 (1913) 31, reaches this same conclusion by reference to Aristotle.

10. Cf. Fiske, 17.

11. See above, p. 45.

12. See above, pp. 43-44.

13. See, e.g., Niall Rudd, "Imitation: Association of Ideas in Persius," *Lines of Enquiry: Studies in Latin Poetry* (Cambridge 1976) 62; and W. S. Anderson, "Persius and the Rejection of Society," *Essays on Roman Satire* (Princeton 1982) 188.

14. Respodents appear and disappear, sometimes disconcertingly, in Persius' satires. He himself calls attention to this feature of his style in 1.44: *quisquis es, o modo quem ex adverso dicere feci*.

15. See Kenneth J. Reckford, "Studies in Persius," *Hermes* 90 (1962) 476-83, for a discussion of ears as the controlling metaphor of Satire 1. Clausen in his *OCT* reads *articulis* for *auriculis* in 23, but if *articulis* is read, the poem and jokes are immeasurably damaged. See Reckford, 477.

16. Because of the difficulties of 22-23, a translation is in order:
    Are you, you dirty old man, collecting for others' ears tidbits
    to which you, ruined in ears and skin, would say, 'enough'?

17. The sexual overtones in the scene are discussed at length by Bramble, 71-99. He suggests, p. 79, that *lumbum* (20) means *culus* and that "instead of *aures* ..., *lumbum* and *intima*." These suggestions are repeated on p. 95; he allows the possibility of the "punning division of *auriculis*" (22) to support his claim for a pun on *innata* (25). But he seems not to connect these suggestions with the structure of the entire poem nor to see punning as a regular device for humorous effect in Persius. He translates *cute perditus* (23) "with *ruined prepuce*" but discusses other interpretations, 79-89.

18. See n. 17.

19. See J. N. Adams, *The Latin Sexual Vocabulary* (Baltimore 1982) 136-38, 194.

20. In my opinion, both *ceves?/ men moveat?* and *de Iove quid sentis?* can compete with anything (I've seen) in Latin which is supposed to be funny. Certainly both are funnier than any of the illustrations of kinds of humor in *De Oratore* 2.216-90.

21. Basically, I agree with the structure suggested by Niall Rudd, "Persiana," *CR* 20 (1970) 286-88, apart from assigning the first line. Up to line 14, Persius is establishing the scene. The friend speaks 5-6. Persius speaks half of 7-8, *verumne . . . nemon*. From 15 to the end belongs to the friend except for 19 *an tali studeam calamo*, 108 *nil calet hic*, and 109 *non frigent*. These words are spoken by Persius.

22. From *Persi Vita*, 33

23. See above, p. 46.

24. Dessen, 66-67; see also Reckford, 486.

25. See Adams on such words as *res, tracto, pilus, cauda*, and *nervus*.

26. There is controversy over attribution of voices in Satire 4. 1-2 asks the reader to pretend Socrates is speaking. There is no indication that he does not continue speaking through the end. Therefore, other than lines 20, 25, 26, 46-47, which belong to Alcibiades, *cuius* line 25 and 27-32, which belong to someone with whom Alcibiades is conversing, and 35-41, which belongs to the stranger, the rest of the poem is spoken by Socrates.

27. Reckford, 485-87, concurs in the opinion that the tail belongs to a peacock but does connect 15 closely with 35-41.

28. The commentators, perversely it seems to me, believe that Alcibiades is depilating himself in public and so deservers the stranger's disgust. He was probably only idly pulling at an odd hair or two as he sunned himself. The condition is less vivid.

29. Cf. a similar treatment of a miser in Plautus, *Aulularia* 296-310.

30. Persius is so subtle that commentators usually divide the poem into three parts, 1-51, 52-72, 73-191. But see Anderson, op. cit., "Part versus Whole in Persius' Fifth Satire," 153-68.

31. Dessen, 84, suggests that Satire 6 was composed first.

32. I depart from Clausen's punctuation of the last two lines.

33. J. P. Sullivan, "In Defense of Persius," *Ramus* 1 (1972) 59-60.

34. I wish to thank Professors Kenneth J. Reckford and David L. Thompson for their helpful comments.

MYTHOPOEIC FORTUNE IN APULEIUS, BOETHIUS, DANTE, AND CHAUCER

Gertrude C. Drake

Of the ancients' many deities, only Fortune and Nature survived in Christian literature. The archaic philosophical underpinning of the two goddesses' essence was that Fortune is in eternity God's handmaiden, Prima Providentia. As Secunda Providentia, Dame Luck is fateful Nature (Physis) in time.

The subject is enormously ramified. Thus, for this short study of the goddesses, I have chosen Apuleius, Boethius, Dante, and Chaucer who not only understood the dual aspects of Lady Fortune in and above time, but also reclothed her so dazzlingly as to assure her sway among poets through the eighteenth century. Apuleius, living in the second century A.D., in his philosophical works summarizes ancient thought on Fortune and Physis. Isis in his *Metamorphoses* is clearly the goddess of Eternity and of Fate. Boethius, the first Christian author to recap pagan interpretations of Fortune and Nature, is the essential link to Bernardus Sylvestris, who clearly fuses Fortune and Nature, and hands them on to Dante who provides a highly original concept of them, yet also adhering to Fortune's dual aspects, passing them on to Chaucer who memorialized her two functions specially in his masterpiece, *Troilus*.

"Time," says Apuleius in *De Platone et eius dogmate*, in part a compendium of Plato's *Timaeus*, "is the shadow of eternity, but whereas time is constantly being moved, the nature of the everlasting is fixed and immobile. Time can enter into eternity and flow into its vastness but can be dissolved whenever God, the maker of the world, so decrees."[1] In *De mundo*, a reworking of the Aristotelian Περὶ κόσμου, Apuleius explains that the moon, the eighth and lowest sphere of the heavens, is the border between the celestial regions and changeable mortality.[2] His *De deo Socratis* records Chaldaean and other beliefs that the moon is illuminated on one side but dark on the reverse, and that it receives its light from the sun.[3]

Franz Cumont has shown in his great study of Roman funerary symbolism that this notion of the dual aspect of the moon as the horizon between time and timelessness, widespread in archaic eras, was rooted in a naive conception of rudimentary cosmology which avowed that the spirits of the dead went to inhabit the moon.[4] That she is the way-station to solar or astral immortality becomes emblematically stylized in mortuary art where the crescent moon is shown beneath the sun or the stars.[5]

Plutarch's *De facie quae in orbe lunae apparet* traces the multi-colored strands of this lunar *mythos* woven into the rich symbological tapestry of late antiquity which reconciles time and timelessness. He puts his myth of the moon into the mouth of Sulla who is from Carthage, the great crossroads during the empire where mystical faiths from Asia Minor, Egypt, North Africa, Greece, and Rome met. Midway between sun and earth, the moon supervises life and death (945).[6] She herself is soul, the *anima mundi*, who receives mind from the sun and body from the earth, and from these aspects of being she reforms for new life on earth those terrestrials who have been pure enough to rise through the elements to reach her sphere, or sends them on their way to astral divinity (945C, 943A, 942F).

Mythopoeically Apuleius expresses the same eschatology in the *Metamorphoses*. The moon is the epiphany of Isis, the cosmic mother, mistress of all the elements, the highest of divine powers (11.5). She is Fortuna Videns (11.15), Seeing Fortune, in timelessness. Her aspect in time is Fate that decrees the eternal dichotomy of womb and tomb, good and evil, bad fortune and good. The irreligious worship her as Blind Fortune (11.15), for they are disciples of the destructive principle in time, the ass-god Set. The religious worship her as Seeing Fortune, for they are disciples of Horus, the structuring temporal principle, who ever battles Set in the world. Above time, her lunar orb resolves all conflict.[7] As Sallustius says, "Fortune (as Luck) has no sway above the moon."[8]

This symbological shorthand for temporal Fortune as the efficient cause of Fate pious men of late antiquity could instantly apprehend. Pindar tells us that Tyche (Fortune) is more powerful than her sisters, the Fates.[9] On the back of a round Etruscan mirror, c. 320 B.C., itself symbolic of time as but a reflection of the great lunar orb of the eternal Mother, one sees winged Fortune, hammer in hand, about to drive the Year Nail, the inevitability of temporal Fate.[10] Now the temple of Nortia, the Etruscan Tyche, was situated in the sacred grove of Voltumna, the androgynous *numen* of Fortune beyond the pair of opposites in time.[11]

The same symbology of Fortune controlling Fate is carved on a sarcophagus at Rome. Centrally there is a mother who has just given birth to a child. On the left, turned away from her, are the three Fates, but a fourth goddess, Fortune as Nemesis, who holds a sceptre, faces us, linking the Parcae who control destiny with the mortal mother and child.[12] At the right, the child, having been instructed in the lore of the Muses who save men from temporal illusion by teaching them to fly upward to hear the music of the spheres, ascends in a winged chariot above the earth to immortality.[13]

In late antiquity Fortune also becomes ever more assimilated to winged Victory. Temporally Fortune may be the Victory of a city, hence the shrine of Fortuna Redux in the Campus Martius. Supratemporally she is the victorious winged soul rising to bliss on the moon which Macrobius identified with Tyche.[14]

But to rise to the moon requires moral purity; and so we find that the winged griffin of Nemesis is one of the aspective icons of Fortuna Victrix.[15] That Fortune is Divine Justice we also know from inscriptions to *Deae Nemesi sive Fortunae*.[16] In Apuleius's *Metamorphoses*, once Lucius has doffed his ass's hide after the dark night of temporal asininity, he is united with lunar Isis, the *numen invictum* (11.7). From her orb as the dead Osiris he sees the sun at midnight. The next day, beatified as the risen Horus, he is crowned with the masculine solar rays of spiritual victory and wears a *chlamys* embroidered with Hyperborean winged griffins, the symbols of feminine lunar Tyche-Nemesis, which are engendered in the otherworld (*generat mundus alter*, 11.24), probably on the moon, one of the Isles of the Blessed.[17]

That Fortune is also fertile Mother Nature is symbolized by her carrying the cornucopia or a sheaf of wheat as both statues of her in the Vatican Museum show. In the *Orphic Hymns*, Physis is extolled as mother of all, she who steers, Rhea first-born, ruler of the gods, justice, eternal life, and immortal providence.[18] Apuleius's Isis is crowned with garlands, blades of wheat, and the moon, and her garment is bordered with flowers and fruits (11.34). She proclaims to Lucius that she is the mother of nature, mistress of all the elements, the first begetter of time, the highest power, queen of the shades of the dead, first of heavenly spirits, a single manifestation of all gods and goddesses.[19] Clearly here is Agatha Tyche, Fortuna Providens—she who oversees and provides, she who is God's thought expressed in nature.

But Apuleius's *Metamorphoses*, which so clearly records mythopoeically the late pagan theological complex of lunar Providence, Nature, Victory, Fate, Nemesis, and Blind Fortune, did not survive Christian onslaughts against Isiacism.[20]

It is therefore in Apuleius' *De Platone*, *De mundo*, and *De deo Socratis*, all of which were extant in the Middle Ages, that we find one of the paths over which Providence or Seeing Fortune, with all her temporal multiplicity but unity above time, walked from ancient to Christian glory.

In Apuleius's *De Platone* 1.12, a difficult chapter because it is so huddled, we find that Prima Providentia is God's thought (*Sententia*) expressed as the cosmos which she rules. Since no evil issues from God, all is right with the world. Fate, or Secunda Providentia, is divine law in time which fulfills God's intellection and undertakings. In the *Metamorphoses*, 11.6, Providential Isis, or Seeing Fortune, controls Fate. The highest of celestial and terrestrial powers, Providence ranks and assigns all *deos*, intermediary spirits, to keep God's order terrestrially according to established laws. Thus Fate in the world is the means whereby both Providences fulfill God's will celestially and terrestrially. Chance or Luck (Blind Fortune of the *Metamorphoses*), which seems to erupt irrationally into life, is men's burdensome misconception of Providence and her handmaiden Fate.[21]

(There is another principle in time, and that is free will which men can exercise to some extent.)

The Boethian chain of command in his *Consolation of Philosophy* is exactly as in Apuleius, also with rejection of indeterminate luck, as so postulated by Aristotle and supported by Albertus Magnus and Aquinas.[22] God is ineffable. Providence is the effable cosmic expression of God. Fate, her handmaiden in temporality, is the enforcer of God's laws. Fortune, either good or bad, is an illusion constructed by men's limited perception (*Cons.* 5.p.1.). Lady Philosophy patiently explains to Boethius, a somewhat backward pupil on occasion: "I say emphatically that chance is entirely non-existent, and I maintain that, beyond its signifying something in bondage to it, it is an empty word."

Plaintively Boethius then asks: "Do you mean to tell me that there is nothing that can rightly be called either bad luck or good?"

Philsophy answers by quoting the famous topos in Aristotle (*Met.*1025a14,f.) of the man who digs his garden to plant seed, but finds a pot of gold. Philosophy concludes her lesson by saying that chance is a final cause, unexpected from man's point of view, of two inevitable efficient causes which merge (*concurrere* and *confluere*). All things are in fact disposed by the material cause of Providence in time and place. The metric ends:

> So Luck, who seems to course with loosened reins,
> Yet endures the bit and maunders under law. (5.m.1.11-12)

In *Consolatio* 4.p.6. Boethius uses Cicero's serial notion of fate as an unbraiding of a rope (*quasi rudentis explicatio*): "Fate directs all things which have motion and are assigned to places and times so that this unfolding of the temporal order is a unified whole providentially; and this same unity above time is called in temporality Fate, which is multifarious and unfolds."[23] The simplicity of Providence becomes the temporal multiplicity of Fate. Providence, the handmaiden of God, is the unmoving and simple form of what is. Fate is the moving nexus of temporal orderings. This is essentially a restatement of Apuleius's *De Platone*.

Boethius's great treatise ends: "There is great necessity imposed upon you ... that you be upright since you live in the sight of your judge who sees all" (5.6.). Apuleius also closes his tract *De mundo* with moral necessity, conceived mythopoeically: "God is the beginning and the end of all. He penetrates all things and illumines them.... The avenger Necessity follows his every step, always prompt to punish those who have departed from holy laws; but as prompt, when God decrees, to become gentle towards him who has understood God from his tender youth, has feared him, and given himself wholly to him."[24] In both treatises Necessity or Nemesis is the moral principle of fateful temporality.

Thus far I have briefly tried to show that in imperial times, and later, to religio-philosophical minds like that of Apuleius or Boethius, Fortune was more than merely Lady Luck, the fickle goddess of purposeless change. It goes without saying that many of the superstitious must have knocked on wood, so to speak, by glorifying temporal Fortune in order to appease her savagery towards them. According to Nilsson her widespread worship in Hellenistic times indicated "the last stage in the secularizing of religion."[25] And Dodds remarks that when the Inherited Conglomerate of belief disintegrates "almost any perishable bag of bones may be hoisted into 'the vacant seat' of divinity."[26]

But Lady Luck, if perishable, reached a ripe old age. She lasted in religious and artistic representations for more than 1500 years. Her popularity in both pagan and Christian art and literature attests, I think, to a *tremendum* experienced by the pious as they gazed on her icons, the meaning of which escaped cynics or rationalists.

It is Fortune's symbols that best reveal to the student of religion what the fervid believer experienced mystically. As Bachofen has so profoundly observed: "Myth is the exegesis of the symbol. It unfolds in a series of outwardly connected actions what the symbol embodies in a unity. It resembles a discursive philosophical treatise in so far as it splits the idea into a number of connected images. ..."[27] Philosophically, for instance, Aristotle argues that Tyche is deprivation of mind, and luck (*automaton*) a deprivation of nature.[28] But symbolically, for the religious at least, all the facets of Tyche formed a transcendental oneness reconciling time and eternity. Just so the Father, Son, and Holy Ghost, although portrayed separately in art, yet project a triune entity for the pious Christian.

In Boethius Dame Fortune's most perdurable symbol was derived from her orb of the moon representing supratemporal divine simplicity and eternal peace. Temporally, it becomes a ball thrown at random up or down, or the sphere of the world signifying her absolute dominion, or more commonly a wheel to the spokes of which men desperately cling as Fortune ever turns it. Here is Chaucer's charming translation of Philosophy's famous speeches to Boethius on the constant mutability of Fortune's wheel (2.p.1.): "What eyleth the man? What is it that hath cast the into moorning and into wepynge? Thou wenest that Fortune be chaunged ayes the: but thou wenest wrong.... Sche hath rather kept ... hir propre stableness in the chaungynge of hirself.... Thou hast bytaken thiself to the governaunce of Fortune.... Enforcestow the to aresten or withholden the swyftnesse and the sweigh of her turnynge wheel? O thow fool of all mortel foolis! Yif Fortune began to duelle stable, she cessade thanne to ben Fortune."[29]

Fortune then lectures Boethius on his ungrateful acceptance of her bounties and refusal to play the game by her rules when he loses: "Worth up yif thow wolt, so be it by this lawe, that thow ne holden at that I do the wroong though thow descende adown whan the resoun of my pley axeth it." That Fortune is the cause of god's providential salvation is clear when she asks: "What eek if my mutabilite yeveth the ryghtful cause of hope to han yet bettere thinges?" This is the testing and chastising function of Fortune as Seneca portrays her in *De Providentia* (5.4) and as Apuleius conceives Blind Fortune whose seeming malice drives Lucius to Providential Isis (*Meta.* 11.15).

H. R. Patch in *The Goddess Fortuna in Mediaeval Literature* says that it remained for Dante to show that Fortune is a ministering angel of the Christian God.[30] It should be emphasized, however, that her theological essence in the *Commedia* is unchanged from that of paganism. Of the worshippers of temporal Fortune who run for ever in Hell (*Inf.* 7.64f.) Virgil says: "All the gold beneath the moon, or ever was, could not give rest to a single one of those weary souls (che tutto l'oro ch'è sotto la luna/ e che già fu, di quest' anime stanche/ non poterebbe farne posare una).''[31] Virgil then reveals to the poet that Fortune is one of God's governing spirits: "With the other Primal Creatures joyful, she wheels her sphere and tastes her blessedness (con l'altre prime creature lieta/ volve sua spera e beata si gode)." She does not hear men reviling her and her permutations, which Necessity makes swift.

Just as in the seventh canto the moon is the orb under which the worshippers of Fortune for ever run, so also there is a lunar image in the fifteenth canto where sinners against nature, the sodomites, are for ever on the move: "and each looked at us, as in the evening men are wont to look at one another under a new moon (e ciascuna/ ci riguardava come suol da sera/ guardare uno altro sotto nuova luna)." This simile adumbrates the theme of the canto, that perverted men scarcely see one another in waxing and waning time because they live only for the shadowy present, glorifying what illusory temporal Fortune and Nature bring. Fortune is mentioned four times in the canto, destiny once, and treasure once. Hence sodomy is set in the larger context of aberration that perversely worships Fortune's naturalistic world of time rather than her eternal Providence.

While Fortune and Nature often became two separate goddesses in the Middle Ages, the tradition of Fors Fortuna as the ancient fertility goddess who gives the fruits of the earth, symbolized by Fortuna's cornucopia, also persisted.[32] As Curtius shows, Bernardus Silvestris, fl. 1150, in his *De mundi universitate* still subordinates Nature to the feminine emanation from God called *Nous* who is the Intellect of the highest God, or Providence. *Nous* is none other than Apuleius's Fortuna Providens above time whose servant is Nature. Bernardus also depicts Mercury forming hermaphrodites, and thus provides the link between temporal Fortune, Nature, and sodomy as Dante constellates them in canto 15.[33]

It is in this canto that Dante meets the scholar Brunetto Latino, one of the sodomites who run endlessly in eternity like Blind Fortune herself in time.[34] Latino therefore appropriately speaks to Dante in terms of Fortune's temporal aspects in the natural world: "What chance or destiny brings thee, ere thy last day, down here (Qual fortuna o destino/ anzi l'ultimo dì qua giù ti mena)?" He then tells Dante that, if he but follow his star, Fortune will bring him much honor; Fortune, he says, will also honor Dante politically.

But Dante wisely replies that he is prepared for temporal Fortune: "Therefore let Fortune turn her wheel as pleases her, and the boor his mattock (però giri Fortuna la sua rota / come le place, e 'l villan la sua marra)." With fearful irony Dante says that he has learned from Latino "come l'uom s'etterna": Latino is running eternally in Hell because of his surrender to eternally moving time but Dante will see God in unmoving timelessness.

Again with fearful irony Latino asks Dante to think well of his *Tesoro* (*Li Livres dou Trésor* and the *Tesoretto*) which glorifies temporal Nature and "nel qual," says Latino, "io vivo ancora." Latino's "treasure," his fortune as it were, is his love of the natural world rather than his love of God. That Dante intended the reader to connect this perverse idolatry of Nature with temporal Fortune is made clearer in the next canto where three sodomites form a wheel, looking back as they run forward (*Inf*.16.21-27). They create their own miserable wheel of perverse Fortune.

After Dante has emerged from Hell and climbed to the top of the Mount of Purgatory, he is wafted to the moon, the first celestial orb beyond time (*Par*.2). As he ascends from there to the Empyrean, the order of the planets is reversed from Cicero' *Somnium Scipionis* (*De Re*. 6.17).[35] Thus Dante's paradisal progress is through 1. the Moon; 2. Mercury; 3. Venus; 4. the Sun; 5. Mars; 6. Jupiter; 7. Saturn; 8. the Fixed Stars; 9. the Primum Mobile; 10. the Empyrean where abide God, his angels, and his saints.

Chaucer unfortunately is inconsistent. In some places he reckons from the moon up, and in others according to Cicero's downward enumeration.[36] Thus there arises a problem of exegesis in an important passage in *Troilus*. Troilus, who has lost his beloved Criseyde to the Greek Diomede because of the foul envy of Fortune, despairingly seeks death in battle and is ultimately accommodated by Achilles.

> And when that he was slayn in this manere,
> His lighte goost ful blisfully is went
> Up to the holughnesse of the eighthe (seventhe, *var*.) spere.
>
> (5.1807-10)

Troilus's ghost is light enough to ascend through the elements, to the moon.

So Lucius in Apuleius's *Meta.*, 11.24, passes through the elements when he is resurrected on the moon and sees the sun at midnight. Dante, rising with Beatrice from Purgatory, goes through purifying fire just before reaching the moon. Thus he is transmuted from mortality to beatified spirit (*Par.* 1.49-69).

Troilus goes "up to the holughnesse of the eighthe spere," a translation, as mentioned above, of Boccaccio's "la concavità." This hollowness of the eighth sphere is possibly an imitation of Dante's beatiful metaphor for the moon: "Within itself the eternal pearl received us (Per entro sé l'etterna margarita/ ne recevette)" *Par.* 2.34-35.

Chaucer does not tell us in what sphere Mercury finally "sorted" Troilus to dwell after having been first wafted to the eighth orb, probably the moon.

Folco the troubadour tells Dante: "This heaven (Venus) is stamped by me as I was stamped by it (questo cielo/ di me s'imprenta, com'io fe'di lui)" *Par.*9.95-96. To the end that he may lead the reader to think of Venus as Troilus's permanent abode in eternity, Chaucer has framed the third central panel, which invokes Venus with mythic aspects of time. The invocations of books 1 and 2 respectively to Thesiphone, the "cruwel Furie," and to Cleo, Muse of History, counterpoise book 4 to Fortune, the "traitour comune," and the opening emphasis of book 5 on Destiny and the "angry Parcas." These four aspects of time framing Venus point up Chaucer's concern that the reader understand that Troilus's great love on earth within time will in timelessness bring him "in hevene to solas" (1.31) where his earthly love will be transformed to the power of beatified love, Venus.

In like manner Chaucer has given the reader sufficient clues for identifying the moon as the eighth sphere to which Troilus's ghost is first wafted. Troilus says in his piteous address to Fortune that he has always honored her "above the goddes alle" (4.268). It is hardly coincidental that her symbol of inconstancy in time, Criseyde's waning and waxing moon, is alluded to some seventeen times in *Troilus*. Chaucer, the master of proleptic innuendoes that later become constellated in enlarged contexts, puts the first lunar allusion in Troilus's mouth:

> Thi lady is, as frost in wynter moone
> And thou fordon, as snow in fire is soone.

> God wold I were aryved in the port
> Of death.

Here Chaucer is already adumbrating the final reversal from a litel tradgedye to a *commedia* on the moon, paradoxically the port of death and of joy. Throughout the rest of the poem the temporal aspects of the moon as the symbol of changing Fortune are kept before the reader.[38]

When the great reversal from temporal tragedy to heavenly joy occurs, Troilus, from the hollowness of the eighth sphere,

> gan despise
> This wrecched world, and al vanite
> To respect of the pleyn felicite
> That is in heavene above.
>
> (5.1816-19)

Chaucer closes his poem by recommending to "yonge, fresshe folks, he or she," that they should return from worldly vanity to God. "What nedeth," asks the poet, "feynede loves for to seke?" Here the word "feigned" implies that romantic love is but an imitation, a shadow in time of the soul's ever-lasting love of God. "Time," as Apuleius said, "is the moving shadow of eternity."

NOTES

1. *De Platone*, 1.10 (P. Thomas, *Apulei Platonici Madaurensis de philosophia libri* [Leipzig, 1921]), p. 92-93: "Tempus vero aevi esse imaginem, si quidem tempus movetur, perennitatis fixa et inmota natura est; et ire in eam tempus et in eius magnitudinem fluere ac dissolvi posse, si quando hoc decreverit fabricator mundi deus." Cf. *Timaeus*, 37D f.

2. *De mundo* 2 (P. Thomas, p. 139): "et ultima omnium Luna altitudinis aetheriae principia disterminans . . . ." Cf. pseudo-Aristotle, *De mundo*, 2.392a27—b11; also Cicero, *De re pub*. 6.17.17 (Loeb): "in infimoque orbe luna radiis solis accensa convertitur. infra autem iam nihil est nisi mortale et caducem praeter animos munere deorum hominum generi datos, supra lunam sunt aeterna omnia."

3. 1 (P. Thomas, p. 7): "ut Chaldaei arbitrantur, parte luminis compos, parte altera cassa fulgoris . . . seu tota proprii candoris expers, alienae lucis indiga, denso corpore, sed laevi, ceu quodam speculo radios solis obstipi vel adversi usurpat . . . ." Cf. Plutarch, *De facie quae in orbe lunae apparet,* 929A, B; Anaxagoras, frag. B 18 (Diels-Kranz); Empedocles, frag. B 43 (Diels-Kranz).

4. *Recherches sur le Symbolisme Funéraire des Romains* (Paris, 1966), p. 177.

5. Ibid., plate facing p. 208, and figs. 48, 49, 51, 52, 54-6, 62.

6. See also Plutarch's *De genio Socratis,* 591B.

7. A.de Buck, *The Egyptian Coffin Texts* (Chicago), 1935-61, 4.22c, translates: "The great Isis, who renders the two men, Horus and Set, contented. She brings Horus the whole eye, the moon, to purge his body of evil." The hallmark of the Egyptian faith was the reconciliation of duality; see P. Derchain, *Mythes et dieux lunaires en Égypte* (Paris, 1962), p. 23; also my "Lucius's 'Business' in the *Metamorphoses*" *Papers on Language and Literature,* 4 (1968), p. 346, n. 21, and 347, n. 23.

8. Sallustius, *De dis et mundo* 9. Cf. Cicero, n. 2 above: "supra lunam sunt aeterna omnia."

9. Quoted by Pausanias, 7.26.8. Also see A. Turyn, *Pindari carmina cum fragmentis* (Cambridge, Mass., 1956), Frag. 164.41. Pindar, *Olympian Odes* 12.1, calls Tyche the Savior-Goddess and Daughter of Zeus the Deliverer.

10. Joseph Campbell, *The Masks of God: Occidental Mythology,* p. 310, fig. 29. That Fortune is winged probably indicates that she is above time or winging to timelessness.

11. *PW* s. v. Voltumna, vol. 33, pt. 1, p. 851, col. 2, line 40 f.; cf. Propertius 4.2.43.

12. Cumont, plate 1 facing p. 336.

13. Pierre Boyancé, *Le Culte des Muses chez les Philosophes Grecs* (Paris, 1937), p. 290. Cf. Plato's *Phaedo* 69D.

14. *Sat.* 1.19.17.

15. John Ferguson, *The Religions of the Roman Empire* (Ithaca, N.Y., 1970), p. 86.

16. *CIL* 3.1125: from Dacia, mid-third century A.D.

17. For the sun and the moon as Isles of the Blessed see Iamblichus, *Vit. Pyth.* 18.12; cf. also Plutarch, *De genio Socratis* 590B-C. The Hyperboreans lived in the vicinity of the moon, according to Hecataeus, frag. 2 (*PW* vol. 9, p. 271, col. 1, line 63). In Egyptian mythology the griffin is Nemesis, a Set-animal, a winged aspect of Set (also sometimes winged). Set is the

principle of disorder and fated death so that man battles him to rise to immortality. Hence, although the griffin is a beast of ill omen, the religious *tremendum* is that the griffin is also a guardian angel (te Velde, p. 18-21). For the connection of the griffin with Nemesis and Adrasteia, yet also with the sun and Apollo, see *PW*, vol. 7, p. 1922, col. 2, line 60 f.

18. Wilhelm Quandt, ed., *Orphei Hymni* (Berlin, 1955), p. 10, number 10.

19. 11.5 (R. Helm): "En adsum tui ⟨ s⟩ commota precibus, rerum naturae parens, elementorum domina, saeculorum progenies initialis, summa numinum, regina manium, prima caelitum, deorum dearumque facies uniformis. ..."

20. The *Metamorphoses* by Apuleius would have been a scandal in mediaeval times, but it may have been known by the intelligentsia to some extent. The source for all later texts is an eleventh-century MS (Laurentian Cod. 68.2). In 1427 it was found by Poggio Bracciolini in the possession of a Florentine citizen who may have obtained it from Monte Cassino; see E. Haight, *Apuleius and his Influence* (New York, 1963), p. 91-92; 106-107. M. Kawczynski, "Ist Apuleius im Mittelalter bekannt gewesen?" *Bausteine zur romanischen Philologie* 47 (1905), p. 193-210, argues that the *Meta.* was known in the Middle Ages. Q. Cataudella, "Dante e le Metamorfosi di Apuleio," *Studi Santangelo* 8(1955), 183-87, after examining three passages in the *Commedia* that seem analogous to parts of the Psyche tale, (*Inf.* 30.139 and *Meta.* 6.19; *Inf.* 20.25 and *Meta.* 6.18; *Purg.*, *inter alia* 17.46 f. especially, and *Meta.* 5.3) concludes that there was "un rapporto di conoscenza, se non dipendenza, tra i due scrittori."

21. (P. Thomas, p. 95-96). Cf. Plato, *Timaeus* 29D-30A, 41D-42E; *Sym.* 202E; *De leg.* 4.709A-B; also Plutarch, *Moralia*, *De fato* 568E: the Cosmic Soul consists of three parts—the *moirai*, 572F: there are three Providences. See also Chalcidius (J. Wrobel, *Platonis Timaeus interprete Chalcidio cum eiusdem commentario* (Leipzig, 1876), 1963[2], *Com.* 143-52.

22. Aristotle, *Met.* 1025a225; *Anal. Pr.* 32b10; Albertus Magnus, *Ethics* 1.7.6-9; Aquinas, *Phys.* 2, *lectio* 8. See V. Cioffari, *Fortuna and Fate from Democritus to St. Thomas Aquinas* (New York, 1935), p. 16-32; 92-118.

23. Cicero, *De divinatione* 1.56.127; Boethius (Loeb) p. 34, lines 37-42.

24. *De mundo* 38 (P. Thomas, p. 175): eundem deum ultrix Necessitas semper et ubique comitatur eorum, qui a sacra lege discesserint, vindex futura, quam faciet ille mitificam, qui statim a tenere et ipsis incunabulis intellexit extimuit eique se totum dedit atque permisit. Cf. Plato's *De legibus* 4.715E; *Phaedrus* 246E.

25. M. P. Nilsson, *Greek Piety*, trans. H. J. Rose (Oxford, 1948), p. 86.

26. E. R. Dodds, *The Greeks and the Irrational* (Berkeley and Los Angeles, 1966), p. 242.

27. J. J. Bachofen, *Myth, Religion, and Mother Right* (Princeton, 1967), trans. R. Manheim, p. 48.

28. *Met.* 1070a6; *Phys.* 201b26.

29. F. N. Robinson, *The Works of Geoffrey Chaucer* (Boston, 1957), p. 329-30. This text is also used for all subsequent quotations from Chaucer.

30. Cambridge, Mass., 1927, p. 19.

31. Italian quotations from Dante throughout are from Natalino Sapegno, ed., *Dante Alighieri La Divina Commedia* (Milan and Naples, 1967). All English translations are from Isaac Gollancz, ed., *The Inferno* (London, 1966), transl. Carlyle-Wicksteed.

32. Patch, p. 65, 75.

33. E. R. Curtius, *European Literature and the Latin Middle Ages* (New York and Evanston, 1963), trans. W. R. Trask, p. 106. Bernardus Silvestris's neo-Platonic pantheism can be summed up as *Deus omnia, omnia Deus; creator et creatura idem.* See C. Barach and J. Wrobel, *Bernardi Silvestris De mundi universitate libri duo* (Frankfurt, 1964²), p. vii-xxi, for a summary of Bernard's pervasive influence; esp. p. xii for his sources, Apuleius, Chalcidius, Boethius. Bernard's cosmic trinity is Hyle (ΰλη, i.e., *materia*), Noys (i.e., Providence), and God. Cf. *Breviarum*, lines 18-20 (Barach-Wrobel): "Natura ad Noym, id est Dei providentiam, de primae materiae, id est hyles, confusione querimoniam ... agit"; also "Ea igitur Noys summi et exsuperantissimi Dei est intellectus et ex eius divinitate nata natura" (1.2.152). Cf. Chalcidius (Wrobel), p. 176: "Deinde prouidentia, quae est post illum summum deum secundae eminentiae, quem νουν Graeci vocant." In the second book Noys orders her handmaidens Natura and Urania to seek Physis who will fashion Man. Noys decrees that his mind will probe the supralunar heavens (*tractus aethereos*), the laws of Fate, and mutable Fortune (2.4.31-5). The moon is the "limes aeris aetherisque" (2.5.191-3). Noys Providentia gives to Urania her mirror (speculum igitur Providentiae est mens aeturna, 2.11.25-26), to Nature the table of Fate, to Physis the book of Memory (2.11.16-18). Each sphere in the heavens has its ruling *numen.* Mercury whose nature is bisexual (communis ambiguusque) fashions homosexuals and hermaphrodites (Epicoenum sexusque promiscui in communi signoque bicorpore hermaphroditos facere consuevit); bisexuality is not evil, for society may either justify it or debase it (2.5.160f.). The final glorification of sexual naturalism (its overtones are heard in *The Wife of Bath's Tale*) occurs towards the end of the last metric (2.14.153-56):

> Corporis extremum lascivum terminat inguen
> Pressa sub occidua parte pudenda latent.
> Iocundusque tamen et eorum commodus usus
> Si quando, qualis, quantus, oportet, erit.

Bernardus's heretical " 'freiweltlich' Richtung" (Barach-Wrobel, p. xix) influenced Alamarich's and David of Dinanto's works, which were condemned in 1209 and 1215. And Dante likewise condemns Bruno Latino's pagan deification of matter and nature. In his *Tresor*, Latino loses himself in the woods of matter where he meets towering Nature.

Having confessed his sins, he nevertheless returns to pagan Nature and is ultimately beatified on Olympus.

34. Regarding Latino's sodomy Sapegna notes (p. 175): "Che avesse fama di sodomita, lo sappiamo soltanto da Dante (oltre, si capisce, i commentatori antichi del poema, che s'appoggiano alla sua testimonianza); ma la notizia trova conferma nell' espressione testé citata del Giovanni Villani, che lo definiva 'mondano uomo' [*Cron.* 8.10]." Paget Toynbee, *Concise Dictionary of Proper Names and Notable Matters in the Works of Dante* (Oxford, 1898), p. 100, points out that Latino's *Tresor* indicts especially the vice of sodomy.

35. Apuleius, *De dogmate Platonis* 1.11 (P. Thomas, p. 94), lists the Fixed Stars first, then Saturn, etc., in descending order. *De Mundo* 3 starts with Saturn.

36. Chaucer counts upwards in *The Franklin's Tale*, 1280, and *The Astrolabe*, 1.21.56. See R. K. Root, *The Book of "Troilus and Criseyde"* (Princeton, 1954), p. 562. Chaucer counts downwards in "Lenvoy de Chaucer a Scogan," 8-12, where Venus is the fifth sphere, and in "The Complaint of Mars," 29-31, where he is the third.

37. For a summary of the scholarship on this problem, see my article, "The Moon and Venus: Troilus's Havens in Eternity," *Papers on Language and Literature*, vol. 11, no. 1, p. 3-17.

38. R. K. Root, *The Textual Tradition of Chaucer's Troilus*, (London, 1916), p. 245 f. says that 5.1807-27 was added in a revision. If so, like Troilus, Chaucer must have laughed when he realized how neatly he could clinch the doctrine of Time as but a copy of Eternity by having the hero on the duality of the Moon—ever-changing in Time, but perduring in Eternity.

FOOD AND THE COMIC SPIRIT IN THE PLAYS OF PLAUTUS

Brent Froberg

Food, while rarely eaten on stage and infrequently seen, does much to promote Plautine humor. Plautus often has his characters speak either directly about things to eat or has them mention food indirectly in figures of speech. I shall survey both uses—direct and figurative—and adduce where possible parallels or precedents from Greek comic poets to help establish the extent of Plautus's originality or dependence.

Lists of foods and seasonings lie scattered in Plautus's plays. There are tantalizing shopping lists: *Menaechmi* 210-11, *Casina* 492 ff., *Aulularia* 373-75; tasty menus: *Captivi* 849-51, *Stichus* 359-60; a fantastic list of spices: *Pseudolus* 814-15 and 831-36; and a list of sweets: *Pseudolus* 740-42. Protracted itemization is one standard feature of the comic tradition, and the fragments of Middle Comedy reveal that comic playwrights before Plautus regularly had their characters recite immense lists of viands.[1] Webster says that, "The audience of Greek comedy had always enjoyed hearing about food and drink," and suggests that this interest can be traced to a time "back beyond Aristophanes."[2]

The great bulk of quotations predominately on gastronomy which Athenaeus took from the comic poets may tend to exaggerate the significance of food in Middle Comedy and may have unduly influenced Webster's criticism, but there is general agreement on dating the emergence of the cook, the parasite, and the *hetaira* to the period of 400-370 B.C.[3] The development of these characters probably reflects a change in Greek society—

at least at its upper levels where sophisticated dining was a possibility. Rankin concludes that the popularity of the art of the cook grew to great proportions in Greece, particularly after the oriental influences began to assert themselves in the fifth century.[4]

Thus a heightened regard for fine eating is a plausible explanation for the introduction into the plays of cooks and parasites. In explaining the presence of the long lists of food, Webster makes the proposal that lyric poetry, parodied in comedy, is the prime inspiration. Webster cites the *Deipnon* from Athenaeus (iv.416) as a source for Aristophanes's parody in the *Ecclesiazousai* where there appears the name of an immense dish—a melange composed of some twenty-five words strung together.[5]

Besides gaining the comic impact of parody, there were likely other reasons why comic poets chose to include long lists of food in the texts of their plays. Three other possibilities come to mind: audiences enjoyed exhibitions of stunning elocution (and memory); lists of "unaffordables" fascinated—even amused—audiences of modest means; the length and the absurdity of these lists could strengthen the characterization of a comic role.

To audiences accustomed to the chokers in Aristophanes's plays, there would be nothing unusual in "patter" songs in New Comedy. Perhaps actors especially skilled in elocution were selected for virtuoso roles as cooks. Though the lyrics might be frivolous, great talent was required of the actor for effective recitation of tongue-twisting lists.

Also, audiences loved to indulge in the fantasy that was part of comic performances. Since meat was rarely eaten by Athenians and vegetables were scarce, the menus of comedy must have had irresistible attraction. Where bread and fish were dietary staples, a description of sumptuous meals and redolent seasonings could cause spectators momentarily to share, if only vicariously, in a great feast.

The lists of food and spices in Plautus's plays are all considerably shorter than the virtuoso pieces in the fragments of Middle Comedy. The longest recital is given by the proud cook of the *Pseudolus*, but even in shorter helpings, these recitations must have tickled the audience's palate and ears. Plautus achieved much more than amusement, though, with these lists. He used them successfully to characterize (or to caricature) comic roles. The cook, for example, in *Pseudolus*, Act III, has the same loquacious, boastful nature familiar in Middle and New Comedy.[6] But this cook's role has a dimension that extends further than self-parody. His style and character reflect on the character of Ballio, the man who hired him. The buffoonery is contagious: the man who would engage for his own birthday celebration the services of so extravagant and foolish a cook becomes himself a buffoon. The cook's elaborate plans are a reflection of Ballio's selfish character, and so the cook makes Ballio's already egregious nature seem even worse. Ballio is all the more deserving a target for the efforts of the huckster, Pseudolus. The transferred characterization, from cook to master, is extremely effective. Those who suppose that the cook has been inserted here merely to amuse and to give comic relief have limited the dramatic possibilities of this passage.[7]

Parasites, for the most part, play insignificant parts in the comedies, but sometimes, like the cooks, they may serve to develop the characters of their associates. Menaechmus, who tantalizes Peniculus with the prospect of a lavish lunch, carefully and thoroughly itemized (*Menaechmi*, 208-13), shows that he can tease pesky parasites; likewise, Hegio keeps Ergasilus at bay in the *Captivi* by constantly hinting at the skimpiness of the meals at his home.

Masters, too, and other men of means characterize themselves by the food that they order and by the way that they order it. Ballio, for example, is willing to entrust the purchase of everything to his slaves except for the fish which he prefers to go to buy for himself (*Pseudolus*, 169). The sharp practices of fishmongers were a frequent *topos* in comedy, and shrewd Ballio feels that he alone is a match for them. Another shopping list (*Aulularia*, 373-76) reflects Euclio's penury as the adjective *carus* intrudes itself repeatedly into his itemization. Lysidamus is made to look delightfully ridiculous in his decadence when he gives Olympio instructions for purchasing food for the wedding night (*Casina*, 490 ff.). He wishes to spare no expense and gives him orders to buy diminutive fish. For Ballio, Euclio, and Lysidamus, their basic character flaws are given added dimension by the food that they order and the way that they order it.

Compared to Plautus, Menander does not achieve so much characterization with lists of food. The bill of fare for the wedding in the *Samia* is scanty, perhaps demonstrating Athenian rigor (*Samia*, 190). Cnemon characterizes himself by telling what he does not have in the *Dyscolus* (505-508). In another passage (425-55), Cnemon considers his spare diet and imputes motives of gluttony to those who sacrifice sheep. Kallippides, arriving late in the play, reinforces this notion of gluttony by expressing fears that the sacrificers may have left him nothing to eat (*Dyscolus*, 775 ff.).

Too little is left of Menander to make a complete, comparative judgment between Plautus and Menander in their use of food to characterize roles. The food passages in Plautus amuse and characterize by their variety and their length. For both Plautus and Menander we shall know their characters better by observing everything that they eat or do not eat.

Much briefer and much more explicit than these long lists of food are Plautus's characterizations of whole nationalities by their eating habits. Plautus was using an old variety of humor found even in the writing of St. Paul who quoted a Cretan prophet characterizing his countrymen as "slow bellies (Titus 1:12)." In this vein Plautus jokes about the title of the *Poenulus*, calling it *Pultiphagonides*, or the "Porridge Eater." Collins says that Plautus is here caricaturing the Carthaginian, "just as we used to affect to believe that Frenchmen lived upon frogs."[8]

In the *Mostellaria*, the verb, *pergraecamini* (22 & 64) is closely linked with riotous living—eating and drinking in high fashion in particular. That the criticism implied by this verb should be placed in the mouth of an actor playing the role of a Greek is peculiar: apparently Plautus temporarily "forgot" his setting just to include a popular, Roman prejudice. In *Rudens* (588) Plautus makes Charmides say that Neptune had poured sea water into them as if they were Greek wines, thereby poking fun at the Greek practice of "cutting" wine.

Compared to the Athenian playwrights, Plautus had at hand a more limited number of targets for this kind of humor; otherwise, he probably would have used it more often. Greeks and Carthaginians were obvious butts who would appeal to the Romans, but the diversity of the Greek people offered greater opportunities for their playwrights. Thus, ethnic humor is more popular in Middle and in New Comedy. As Legrand observed,

> The fragments of the Middle period are full of allusions to the gluttony and dullness of the Boeotians, to excesses of every kind committed by Sicilians, Thessalians, and Corinthians, and to the exaggerated frugality of the Spartans. The same themes continued, from time to time, to inspire the authors of the subsequent period. Menander himself was not above sneering at the Boeotian "asses' jawbones."[9]

In the *Samia* (98ff.) Menander lets Niceratus speak of the fat men of Byzantium who have vast quantities of fish and everything flavored with wormwood. Their habits in dining must have been notorious, because a fragment of Diphilus (17K) also mentions this same excess.

"In addition to their dress and speech, what comedy appears most frequently to have noticed in foreigners was their ignorance of good manners and in particular of good manners at table, of the refinements of cooking and of the usages of polite society."[10] Plautus and his Greek predecessors may well have taken to heart the sentiment of the proverbial pun, *"Man ist was man isst."* On a small scale, for Plautus at least, food was a means of developing international caricature.

Plautus's figurative use of expressions concerning food finds little comparison with that of other ancient playwrights; the colorful metaphors, similes, and puns that concern food are almost an exclusive feature of the plays of Plautus. Rarely are Plautus's tropes subtle; they are earthy and concrete, and by their incongruity, they are sometimes outrageous and usually funny.

The frequency with which food appears metaphorically as a term of endearment evinces a close, figurative relationship between food and sex. In a way that seems particularly natural to speakers of English, Plautus often uses the word *mel* and its diminutives for endearment. A variety of forms throughout the plays includes the feminine *mellila* and the masculine *melliculus*. Other examples can be cited, too. A catalogue begun with standard terms of endearment in the *Poenulus* (365-67) ends cleverly with two items of food suggestive of a Roman dessert—*mea colustra* and *meus molliculus caseus*. Olympio, in the *Casina* (135-38), recites some endearments which include, "*meus pullus passer, mea columba, mi lepus.*" This allusion is doubly appealing, because these little animals might be household pets or entrees.

Endearment expressed by metaphors which name food is typical of vulgar speech and was surely part of the *sermo plebeius* of Plautus's day. MacCary in the introduction to his edition of the *Casina* states that: "Erotic language is always full of implied comparisons with food."[11] Plautus's language is laced with such comparisons; Menander and Terence, whose language is perceptibly more elevated than that of Plautus, offer nothing similar to this usage.

So, too, the American anthropologist, Marston Bates observes that: "In human behavior the parallels are shown by a whole list of words that can pass back and forth between the contexts of food and sex: appetite, hunger, satiated, starved."[12] There are metaphorical expressions which relate love to satiety: *Casina* (795), where, "*qui amat, tamen hercle, si esuriet, nullum esuriet,*" makes the equation clear; *Asinaria* (169) uses *expleri* in a way that equates sex with eating; and Alcmena emerges from her house after her night with Zeus looking, *saturam* (*Amphitryon*, 667).

Some metaphors are indirect, and a word that connotes food implies the comparison. For example, Mercury says in the *Amphitryon* (309) that anyone who gets in his way will eat fists (*pugnos edet*). (The verb *edo* turns the fists into food.) When Palaestrio (*Miles Gloriosus*, 316) says that he would not exchange a rotten nut for Sceledrus's life, he implies that Sceledrus is worth a little less than a rotten nut. Finally, money may be vomited—"coughed up" as we say—(*Curculio*, 687 and *Epidicus*, 582), and plans, like food, may be "cooked up" (*Persa*, 51) or "baked" (*Miles Gloriosus*, 208).

The food similes are short and the points of comparison are few. With startling frequency, violence is the quality that Plautus most often compares in these one-line similes. In the *Amphitryon* (319), for example, Sosia fears Mercury who threatens to bone him like a lamprey. Not only does Mercury assume the character of a cook in this simile, but also Sosia assumes the inconsequential identity of a limp, slimy eel. The same simile occurs in *Pseudolus* (382), perhaps because Plautus had discovered that this simile was certain to raise a laugh. The *Rudens*, also, has two violent similes taken from the art of cookery: Trachalio (659) orders Demeas's slaves to beat out the eyes of Labrax just as cooks beat cuttlefish, and Demeas adds the instructions that Labrax be thrown out by the heels like a dead pig.

The few longer, more extended similes, frequently liken women to fish. "We're considered to be like pickled fish—too salty and unappetizing; we must properly adorn ourselves," says Anterastilis to her sister (*Poenulus*, 240-47), to which Milphio replies, "The girl is a cook." The connection between women, cooks, and cosmetics is made again in an extended simile in the *Mostellaria* (273 ff.) where Scapha complains that when a woman's perspiration and her perfume come together, the effect is as unpleasant as when a cook combines his sauces.

Sometimes women become anglers. Twice the *meretrix* appears as a fisher. The courtesan, Cleostrata, (*Asinaria*, 177ff.) proclaims that she considers lovers as one would regard fish: No good unless they are fresh. Her enumeration of the virtues of a fresh fish (=lover), that he is juicy, stewable, cookable, and always willing to give, are qualities that pertain both to his ability to pay expenses and to his ability to play the lover. In the *Truculentus*, Diniarchus complains that Phronesium is like an expert fisher and he is like a fish in her nets (35ff.). Cleostrata, (*Asinaria*, 200ff.) also compares herself to bakers and vintners who, just as she, must have cash for their commodities.

One simile which occurs three times in Plautus's plays has a proverbial ring. Sosia (*Amphitryon*, 601) says, "*neque lac lactis magis est simile quam ille ego similest mei.*" Likewise in *Menaechmi* (1089), "*neque aqua aquae nec lacte est lactis, crede mi, usquam similius.*" Also in the *Miles Gloriosus* (551-52) "*nam ex uno puteo similior numquam potis aqua aquai sumi quam haec est atque ista hospita,*" as well as the expression, "*tam similem, quam lacte lactist,*" occur to describe identical twins. Grace Beede has convincingly demonstrated Plautus's fondness for including proverbs in his plays, and so it is not surprising to find Plautus using an expression that reminds us of the English idiom, "Alike as two peas in a pod."[13] The sentiment is the same, and coincidentally both languages use nutritive imagery to express it.

Puns are inescapable in Plautine comedy. Only a few of them have to do with food—several short puns and one virtuoso piece that plays on the names of cities appear. In the *Amphitryon* (732) there is the obvious malum (apple), malum (evil). Two clever puns on the names of fish occur in the *Casina*: *soleas* (495) is taken as a fish and as a pair of sandals; *lingulaca* (497) may be a dogfish or a virago. There is a play on the verb *pulto* (knock) and the noun *puls* (pottage) in *Poenulus* (728-29) where the inflected forms appear to be identical. Nixon, in his translation for the Loeb series, has rendered the pun effectively into English with the words, "batter" and "dough."[14]

Ergasilus, the hungry parasite of the *Captivi*, turns punster when he threatens a larder with a spectacular *tour de force* reminiscent of the long lists of food found elsewhere in Plautus's plays. These lines (160ff.) pun upon the names of food and the names of towns:

> . . . primumdum opus est Pistorensibus:
> eorum sunt aliquot genera Pistorensium:
> opus Paniceis est, opus Placentinis quoque;
> opus Turdetanis, opus Ficedulensibus;
> iam maritumi omnes milites opus sunt tibi.

Morris in his edited text of the *Captivi* explains the significance of these names:

> The names of troops pun upon names of articles of food and names of towns: *Pistorensibus* from *pistor* (miller, baker) and *Pistoria* in Etruria, *Placentinis* from *placenta* and *Placentia* on the Po, *Turdetanis* from *turdens* and perhaps a Spanish tribe whose name might have become known through the military operations during the Second Punic War. The geographical reference of *Paniceis* (*panis*) and *Ficedulensibus* (*ficedula*, a small bird) can only be guessed at. The last vs., of course, refers to fish.[15]

Finally, there is a small group of selections which use food and cooking and are mythological or legendary in their imagery. In the *Captivi* (877), Ergasilus swears an oath by the goddess Saturitas, and so satirizes the Greek and Roman tendency to deify any number of abstractions. Charmides, in the *Rudens* (508-09), conjures up the worst of fare by telling Labrax that he fed him food inferior to the offerings of Thyestes or Tereus. Plautus has two of his cooks achieve ridiculous bombast through food and myth: In the *Pseudolus*, Ballio's cook calls fish, *pecudes Neptuni* ("the cattle of Neptune," a metaphor as mixed as "Chicken of the Sea") and claims for his cooking (as he faultily remembers his mythology) rejuvenative powers similar to those of Medea for Pelias. Cylindrus, Erotium's private cook in the *Menaechmi* (330), has a similar, characteristic flair for alliterative hyperbole and calls the fire over which he will cook dinner, *Volcani violentiam*. The tone here is mock heroic, and the notion is ludicrous.

The metaphors, similes, and puns on food assign people the qualities of fish, elevate everyday events to an absurdly heroic level, and reduce sublime emotions, such as love, to the level of a condiment. The verbal style which imparts such an absurdly comical flavor to the plays is characteristically Plautine.

The comically long passages descriptive of foods and banquets may be found in Plautus and in other comic playwrights. The word play, i.e. the figurative expressions that involve food, is typical of Plautus. Food is an old theme in classical drama; in *The Origin of Attic Comedy* Cornford argues that the cooking and eating of a feast in ancient Greek plays is a practice as old as the primitive, fertility ritual of archaic folk-drama.[16] Plautus, when he adapted so freely from Greek originals, may have placed himself in this ancient tradition. But Plautus's immediate Greek predecessors mention food far less frequently than he. By increased allusions to food, Plautus was likely giving realism to his plays with language that imitated the common speech of his time. In so doing, Plautus was deliberately appealing to the basic, human needs of an audience of common people. Plautus wrote successful comedies by using themes that he knew to be universal, and in part, through the imagery of food, he secured an enduring popularity for his plays.

NOTES

1. *e.g.* Alexis (110K); Philemon (60, 79K); Archedicus (2K). All fragments notated with K are from Theodorus Kock, *Comicorum Atticorum Fragmenta* (Leipzig 1880).

2. T.B.L. Webster, *Studies in Later Greek Comedy* (Manchester 1953) 64.

3. *Ibid.*

4. E.M. Rankin, *The Role of the Mageroi in the Life of the Ancient Greeks* (Chicago 1907) 92; P.A. Legrand, *The New Greek Comedy* tr. J. Loeb (New York 1917) 222, ". . . luxury in eating increased and became more common in the course of the fourth century." Legrand states that Plato reflects this change of habit and cites several passages from the *Gorgias* as evidence.

5. Webster, *Ibid.* 22.

6. A.W. Gomme and F.H. Sandbach, *Menander, A Commentary* (Oxford 1973) 25.

7. J.N. Hough, *The Composition of the Pseudolus of Plautus* (Lancaster, Pa. 1931) 85; Webster, *Ibid.* 194, cites the scene as a "showpiece."

8. W.L. Collins, *Plautus and Terence* (Edinburgh 1873) 87.

9. Legrand, *Ibid.*, 56-57, cites Philemon (76K); Diphilus (22, 96, 119K); Menander (462K); and Eudoxus (2K). Also Menander (211K).

10. Legrand, *Ibid.*

11. W.T. MacCary and W.M. Willcock, *The Casina of Plautus* (Cambridge 1976) 32.

12. M. Bates, *Gluttons and Libertines: Human Problems of Being Natural* (New York 1967) 18.

13. G.L. Beede, "Proverbial Expressions in Plautus," *CJ* 44 (1949) 357-362.

14. P. Nixon, *Plautus IV* (Cambridge 1959) 72.

15. E.P. Morris, *The Captivi and Trinummus of Plautus* (Boston 1898) 15.

16. F.M. Cornford, *The Origin of Attic Comedy* (Cambridge 1914).

CARL ORFF AND THE *CARMINA BURANA*: *CANTIONES PROFANAE*

Judith Lynn Sebesta

The scion of a traditionally military Bavarian family, Carl Orff (1895-1982) died a musician as well-known for his many stage compositions as for his influence on children's musical education. As a young boy he learned to play the piano, cello, and organ, and also began composing at a very early age. At the time of his birth, Munich was a center for music in all forms— theatre, dance, orchestra—and influenced as well by the music of other countries, especially of Italy. One of Orff's earliest recollections was singing the Italian duets from *Figaro* and *Cosi fan Tutte* to his mother's piano accompaniment. The first opera, however, which he saw was Wagner's *Flying Dutchman* in 1909 which affected himn as much musically as symbolically, for as a young boy, Orff had a particular attachment to that sea-wanderer of Homer, Odysseus. The music of the opera performance and the cross-cultural mythical archetype resounded in him so deeply that in the days following the performance, he fell silent for hours on end, and, to the consternation of his mother, lost his appetite.

In view of his early response to music, it is not surprising that Orff in beginning his musical career became deeply interested in children's musical education. After holding the position of Kapellmeister at the Munich Kammerspiele (1905-1917), the National theater, Mannheim (1918-1919), and the Landestheatre, Darmstadt (1918-1919), he founded, in 1924, together with Dorothee Günther, the Güntherschule for the musical education of children. The curriculum of this school, emphasizing music and gymnastics, reflected Orff's basic assumption that the completely unmusical child is non-existent, or, at most, an extremely *rara avis*. He wrote many musical compositions for children to teach them, or to educate them (in the Latin sense of the word, *educere*) in perceptions of pitch, rhythm, and musical form. He encouraged them to interpret his music with improvisation. By the early 1930's the Günther-Orff experiments in music with children were so successful that the Ministry of Culture recommended their expansion to Berlin, but the rise of the Nazi Party brought these plans to a halt. In 1948, however, German broadcasting authorities gave Orff another forum to present his theory and methods to German children, their parents, and teachers. Though now well into his composing career (he was working on *Antigonae* at the time), he responded enthusiastically to the challenge of this new medium. He produced five basic collections known as *Musik für Kinder* (1950-1954), which he later developed into the *Orff-Schulwerk*. These collections and their songs have been translated into many languages, including Greek, English, Portuguese, and even Welsh and Japanese. The multi-national response to Orff's *Schulwerk* comes from his going back to what he found cross-culturally common in children's early musical expression—inarticulate calls, rhymes, singing of melodic phrases, and simple pentatonic scales. Orff's search in children for the cross-cultural musical response is parallel to his similar search in stage composition.

His radio success led Orff to begin training pupils in his improvisational and aural techniques at the Salzburg Mozarteum and, in 1961, he was able to begin the Orff Institute which soon drew teachers from all over the world for courses on musical pedagogy and which guided research into various applications of his method, including music therapy.

The basic pedagogical theory of Orff—that music must not be an isolated experience for a child, but should be integrated with movement, dance, and theatre—is reflected, as is his musical compositional style for children, in his work for the stage. His pedagogical and stage works are not two isolated areas in his career, but two mutually reflective expressions of his basic intellectual comprehension of music.

CARL ORFF AND THE *CARMINA BURANA*

For his children's music Orff went back to the musical expression common to all children; in his stage works he likewise reverts from the rich polyphony, extended melodic writing, and thematic development of modern composers, to what he saw as the basic musical forms common to all cultures, that is, to the primordial musical expression of humankind. In essence his musical style is heavily rhythmic, relies on much percussion and block harmony and uses, *inter alia*, the devices of pedal point and *ostinato*. The simple harmony and driving rhythm of his works can evoke positive response to his music in the Chinese audiences as well as in the German. A man from China present at the Salzburg premier of *Antigonae* commented, "Antigone—wonderful—just like Peking 5000 years ago."

Likewise, for his subject matter, Orff returns to what he regards as primordial themes, which cross centuries and cultures. Orff has used the plays of Sophocles and Aeschylus (*Antigonae, Oedipus der Tyrann, Prometheus*); the erotic Greek and Latin poetry of Sappho and Catullus (*Trionfo di Afrodite, Catulli Carmina*); Bavarian folktales (*Die Bernauerin, Astutuli*); fairy tales and legends (*Der Mond, Der Kluge*); medieval and renaissance sources (*Carmina Burana, Ein Sommernachtsraum, Ariadne, Orpheus, Tanz der Spröden*; and Christian mystery plays and beliefs (*Comoedia de Christi resurrectione, Ludus de nato infante mirificus, De temporum fine comoedia*). In doing so he drew on the humanistic validity such sources had for him, which he had experienced as early as 1909 at the performance of the Flyin Dutchman. Orff himself once said, "I am often asked why I nearly always select old material, fairy tales and legends for my stage works. I do not look upon them as old, but rather as valid material. The time element disappears, and only the spiritual power remains. My entire interest is in the expression of spiritual realities. I write for the theatre in order to convey a spiritual attitude."[1]

One of his works which illustrates his musical style, use of old material, and humanistic response is the *Carmina Catulli*, which, due to the explicit eroticism of the prologue and poems selected from the Catullan corpus, is not as well-known to students of Latin as the title would suggest. The driving rhythm of the prologue sung by a chorus of young men and women reflects the driving sexual instinct which rises in youth; they are carried along with the instinct just as the audience is carried along by the relentless tempo of this prologue. For the main part of the work, arranged in three acts and twelve scenes, Orff has selected eleven poems (one is repeated) which he arranges to tell the story of Catullus' unfortunate love affair with Lesbia (in order: *Odi et amo*; *Vivamus, mea Lesbia, atque amemus*; *Ille mi par esse deo videtur*; *Caeli, Lesbia nostra, Lesbia illa*; *Nulli se dicat mulier*; *Iucundum, mea vita*; *Desine de quoquam*; *Odi et amo*; *Amabo, mea dulcis Ipsithilla*; *Ameana puella defutata*; *Miser Catulle*; *Nulla potest mulier tantum se dicere*). These scenes comprise a play within a play, for the prologue and brief epilogue is a confrontation between the chorus of young men and women and a chorus of old men. Bored and irritated by the love words so constantly and repeatedly exchanged by the young lovers, the old men crossly try to show them the folly of their love by telling of Catullus' fate which is then enacted on the stage before them. Only love can distract the young lovers from each other, and though they listen to and observe the "moral tale," it no sooner finishes than they return to their avowals of passion, *"Eis aiona, tui sum!"* Orff points the message of the whole of this play within a play by quoting on the title page of the score this line from Catullus: *rumoresque senum severiorum omnes unius aestimemus assis*.

Likewise Orff's other works which followed his *Carmina Burana* are dramatic; in them he explores human experience through what has been called a "tragedy of archetypes and a visionary embodiment of metaphysical ideas." However, his *Carmina Burana* is his seminal work in that, though not his earliest work, it is the one in which he believed he had first truly expressed his conception of musical style and philosophy. Thus, with whimsical truth he wrote this palinode to his editor following the overwhelmingly successful first staging of his *Carmina Burana* in 1937 at Frankfurt am Main: "With the *Carmina Burana* my whole work begins." He even went so far as to revise three of his earlier works in his new vein of composition: *Ariadne* (1925; rev. 1940), *Orpheus* (1925; rev. 1940), and *Tanz der Spröden* (1925; rev. 1940).

Of all his works, nonetheless, his *Carmina Burana* remains the best-known and liked and the most frequently performed. What, then, is his *Carmina Burana* in terms of his musical expression and his intellectual comprehension of music and human experience?

The type of musical expression ranges from a metricized plainchant (*Fortune plango vulnera*) to a slow waltz (*Floret silva nobilis*), from a lilting round dance (*Reie*) to fanfares of trumpets and trombones (*Were diu Welt alle min*). Orff interprets aurally the wavering of a mind (*In trutina mentis dubia*), an epiphany (*Ave formosissima*), the breaking of winter's icy bonds (*Veris leta facies*) and drunken revelry (*In taberna quando sumus*). The mood of the work changes from awesome solemnity (*O Fortuna*) to flirtation (*Chramer, gip die varwe mir*), from bacchic exultation (*Tempus est iocundum*) to cynicism (*Estuans interius*) and includes even punning fantasy (*Cignus ustus cantat*). In short it is a *tour de force* of human emotion, experience, and situation. Though Orff would further develop his musical techniques, all elements of his style are present already: rhythm, evocative and obsessive at times; simple melody; plainchant, *ostinato*; muted harmonics, especially thirds; changes in rhythm and tempo within a piece; striking use of percussion and percussive playing of various instruments.

The source which Orff drew upon for this work, too, has a range of subject, tone, and mood. Browsing through a secondhand book store in Wurzberg, he came upon, by good fortune, a copy of "*Carmina Burana Lateinische und Gedichte einer Handschrift des XIII Jahrhunderts aus Benediktbeurn/ herausgegeben von J. A. Schmeller*. Fortune also played a major role in the discovery of the manuscript itself. The Benedictine monastery of Beuron was being secularized in 1803 when Baron von Aretin discovered this collection of more than 250 medieval Goliardic poems. Eventually the manuscript was transferred to the Munich Staatsbibliothek where Johann Andreas Schmeller first edited it in 1847.

Fortune was looking after herself it seems, for the opening poem, a hymn to her (*O Fortuna*) is preceded by the now widely known portrait of her symbolically enthroned on her wheel controlling the lives of men. The opening lines of this poem Orff made into his opening, and closing, songs. Following a sleepless night, the next day saw him sketch out *Fortuna plango vulnera*, the second song, and the third day, appropriately Easter morning, a hymn to the epiphany of spring, *Ecce gratum*. With his imagination captivated and excited by the pictorial quality of the other poems and suggestive, concise language of the Latin words, he was able to finish by June of that same year the preliminary libretto comprising 24 poems or *carmina*, written mainly in Latin, but also in old German and Old French.

While later Orff incorporated his *Carmina Burana* into a musical triptych, of which the other elements are *Catulli Carmina* and *Trionfo di Afrodite*, it originally stood alone, just as today it is usually performed apart from the other two members. It was conceived from the first as a dramatic work; Ludvig Seivert's design for the the first performance shows a stage in the center of which is Fortuna and her wheel, exactly as in the manuscript, flanked by choruses and soloists dressed in medieval costume who enact in movement, gesture, and dance the story of each poem or *carmen*. Today's performances, where budget permits, also provide, by costume, dance troupe, and scenery, a visual feast for the eye.

Aristotle defined a play's essential parts as a beginning, a middle, and an end, and surely, as a dramatic piece, Orff's *Carmina Burana* must have such a structure as well. Generally though, his *Carmina Burana* is described as a musical patchwork of brilliantly individual dance rhythms, tunes, and harmonics, and as a thematic patchwork of poems grouped loosely into three sections on spring (*Primo Vere*), drinking (*In Taberna*), and love (*Cour d'Amour*), framed by the opening and closing apostrophe to Fortuna. His subsequent works embody, however, primordial themes, and obviously, since Orff later incorporated his *Carmina Burana* into the triptych, it too must have a theme giving it structure. His other works express their themes through archetypes and enact before our eyes metaphysical ideas. It would be strange were the *Carmina Burana*—which Orff at age 42, with more than 20 years of musical creativity behind him regarded as his first, true work—only a crazy quilt of musical pieces and medieval poems, however enjoyable *per se* to an audience.

To comprehend fully the theme and the archetypal exposition of metaphysical ideas that are Orff's *Carmina Burana*, we must turn first to the persona of Fortuna whose vitality as a concept immediately acted upon Orff when he first opened Schmeller's edition in 1937.

(In the following paragraphs, "*carmen* 1," "*carmen* 2," etc., refer to those poems which Orff selected and numbered in his libretto.)

Of all the ancient divinities, only Fortuna survived through the change in religion that occurred when Christianity became the dominant religion of the Roman Empire. Why she was able to do so is a complicated question to answer. Part of the answer lies in the fact that she was not a deity with a specialized function or sphere of influence. She was an omnipotent deity, like Jupiter, whom she supplanted as supreme pagan god. Her survival after the advent of Christianity also lies in the collapse of the Roman Empire, which seemed to portend for Christians the increasing disorder and conflict which was to herald the Second Coming of the Lord. The breakdown of Roman society and government, together with the sudden, unpredictable invasions and calamities of the fifth and sixth centuries A.D., showed Fortuna to be an entity increasingly active in the world, and the unpredicability of her character became more and more pronounced.

No one could influence her, let alone control her. She respected not rank, not wealth, not merit. She favored the good and bad equally and abandoned them with equal disregard to their deserts. The despair expressed by *carmen* 1 was an emotion readily understood by medieval men and women, who surely, in weeping for the speaker, wept for themselves. That Orff chose to have a chorus sing this *carmen* shows his recognition of the universality of this theme to the medieval mind.

Fortuna's character is mysterious; not only do men's fortunes wax and wane, but even her power over the world seems to wax and wane, viewed from man's standpoint. Thus she is like the moon, which waxes and wanes. *Carmen* 1 abounds with contrasts which describe her power: *crescis aut decrescis, obdurat et curat, egestatem potestatem, immanis et inanis, est affectus et defectus.* Truly she is *obumbrata et velata,* obscure and cloaked as to her presence, intent, and effect. Controlling all, a natural force as immanent in the universe as heat and cold, she is rightly called by Orff *Imperatrix Mundi.*

Surely then, she is the major character of Orff's *Carmina Burana.* Yet in the selections *"Primo Vere"* and in *"Cour d'Amour,"* Venus appears as the ruling deity. Upon those who follow her commands to love, Venus, not Fortuna, bestows honor and happiness. This apparent contradiction as to the relative importance and influence of the two divinities in the world become more puzzling when one looks at the *carmina* of "*In Taberna*," which intervene between the two sections just mentioned. In the *Taberna carmina*, Venus is mentioned only once, and as for Fortuna, she is not mentioned at all by name, though a synonym of hers, *sors*, occurs in *carmen* 13.

Who then is truly the *Imperatrix Mundi*? And is there a thematic structure which links these three sections together, and to the prologue formed by *carmen* 1 and 2 and the epilogue formed by a repeat of *carmen* 1?

Since Orff calls her *Imperatrix Mundi*, Fortuna must be the main character. That she does not appear to be so in the main sections of the opus is due to her character: the ambiguity inherent in her character effects the ambiguity of the thematic structure of the whole work.

Her character is clearly described in *carmen* 1: she is *variabilis*, *obumbrata*, *velata* in intent and purpose. Her apparent blessings may be in reality losses and vice versa. She is the *sors salutis et virtutis*, two words which are ambiguous, having pagan and Christian meanings. *Salus* can mean mundane prosperity, i.e. riches and power, but also, in the Christian sense, spiritual prosperity: from the latter notion develops the word "salvation." *Virtus* can mean, in pagan terms, worth, power, excellence, strength; to a Christian it means virtue, moral excellence. Which meanings, pagan or Christian, do the words have here? Or are both meanings implied? Already Fortuna's ambiguity is clear!

Carmen 2, however, clarifies the meanings of *salus* and *virtus*. Fortuna bestows *munera*, *prosperitas*, *gloria*. The one favored by her is *felix et beatus*, and like a king is crowned with flowers; the floral imagery is important since it is a link between *carmina* 2 and 3, and 2 and 22.

Let us turn now to the *carmina* of "*Primo Vere*." The imagery of the fortunate one flourishing (*florui*), crowned with flowers (*flore coronatus*) is reiterated in these *carmina*. In *carmen* 3 Phoebus is covered with flowers as he reclines in Flora's lap; even though it is Venus (through Flora) who crowns the devoted lover, Phoebus, the floral motif still carries with it the associations of *felicitas* and *beatitas* given to it in *carmen* 2. Though the subsequent *carmina* do not employ so expressly the floral motif as this picture in *carmen* 3, yet the equation has been established: flowers = love = divine happiness. The floral motif is used in other ways as well. Flowers set the scene for spring and describe the physical charms of the loved one, e.g. *suzer rosenvarwer munt* (*carmen* 9). This latter use of the floral motif reappears in *carmina* 17, 20, and 24, and so links the section *"Primo Vere"* with *"Cour D'Amour."* Other linking motifs between these two sections are Cupid (*carmina* 4, 5, and 15) and the antithesis winter: frozen emotion:: spring: awakened emotion. This antithesis occurs in *carmina* 3, 4, 5, 7, and 16 and 22.

Yet if there is a single major theme of the *carmina* of *"Primo Vere,"* it is that of Venus' supremacy. We are ordered in *carmen* 5 to obey Venus' commands to love, to praise her for the happiness she bestows through this love and for the glory and honor this love gives the beloved. The culminating picture of *"Primo Vere"* is that of the supreme glorification love can bring. As the singer of *carmen* 8 states, love is ennobling, and the poet of *carmen* 10 would indeed lose the whole world for love and count it gain.

From this zenith of human happiness we fall to the nadir, or so it seems as we begin the section *"In Taberna."* The mood and tone of the *carmina* of this section contrast diametrically with the blithe and merry mood of *"Primo Vere."* In fact, in tone and arrangement these *carmina* are more akin to *carmina* 1 and 2. Orff has, however, scored *carmina* 11-14 as three solos (for the most part) and a chorus, and this scoring contrasts them to the two opening *carmina*. *Carmina* 1 and 2 are solo statements of Fortuna's power sung by a chorus to emphasize the universality of Fortuna's power over men. *Carmina* 11-13 are solos scored as solos to personalize the helplessness of man in life: he is like a boat without a pilot, a leaf buffeted by the wind. When Orff changes the score from solo to chorus as he does for part of *carmen* 13, his scoring emphasizes the universality of man's helpless condition.

But before whom is man so helpless? In overt imagery and language there appears only one mention of Venus, in *carmen* 11. Again she appears as a pleasure-giving goddess, but the singer seems to lack the joy expressed by the *carmina* of *"Primo Vere."* Her connection with the despair and hopelessness of the poet of *carmen* 11 is unclear. For surely, if he has obeyed Venus, he should be feeling as exalted as the lovers in *"Primo Vere."*

Hidden among the words of *carmen* 11 are clues as to the direction the whole opus is taking. Here appear the key words of *carmen* 1, *salus* and *virtus*. Which meaning, pagan or Christian, do they have in *carmen* 11?

As a further complexity, there is in this section no overt, clear mention of Fortuna, by name, though she seems to be addressed by a synonym, *sors*, in *carmen* 13. The choral scoring of this part is significant, for it reminds us of the omnipotent Fortuna, bestowing pain and loss, as described in *carmina* 1 and 2.

Carmina 12-14 further mystify the direction and total meaning of the opus at this point. All they appear to have in common is that they are drinking songs, but in topic and theme they seem unrelated to each other and to all the other *carmina*.

Although it appears initially obscure in thematic function, the *"Taberna"* section is central to the drama of the *Carmina Burana*, which is the cosmological battle between Fortuna and Venus for the *Imperium Mundi*, that is, for the domination of the human soul; for though Fortuna is initially hailed as *Imperatrix*, Venus, in *"Primo Vere,"* is the apparent ruler of the world who, usurping Fortuna's role, bestows *munera, gloria, prosperitas*. To understand the dramatic action in the *"Taberna"* section, the second "act" so to speak, we must understand in what way Fortuna is *Imperatrix Mundi* and what her relationship is to God, the supreme governor of the universe. For if she is independent of Him, He is not omnipotent. If she is subservient to Him, in what way is she *Imperatrix*?

Boethius tried to resolve this theological impasse which was not a mere logical problem for him, but a personal one. Imprisoned at Pavia and ultimately condemned to death, he wrote the *De Consolatione Philosophiae* to explain why good, and bad, men do not receive their just deserts in this life. He concluded that all fortune, whether harsh or kind, comes to reward and employ the good or to punish and correct the bad; in the case of the latter, even bad fortune is "good," since it chastises the erring soul and directs it towards its ultimate redemption. In his own case, he has lost ephemeral, worldly pleasures, but has retained the good fortune of redemption through Christ. Everything that is good proceeds ultimately from God, and Boethius sees Fortuna, whether she is kind or harsh, as working to bring forth good in every situation, through God's providence (*Cons. Phil.* 4 *pr.* 6 and 7, 5 *pr.* 1).

Medieval theologians developed Boethius' solution of making Fortuna one of God's chief servants. Dante was, after Boethius, most responsible for the Christianization of Fortuna. In the seventh canto of *The Inferno*, Vergil explains to Dante Fortuna's true role in God's scheme, a role, the Roman *vates* states, which is commonly misunderstood by men: just as He created the angels to guide the celestial phenomena, so God created Fortuna to guide the Earth's splendors. To the extent that she is above men, as the angels are, men cannot totally comprehend her or her actions so that she appears *obumbrata et velata* to them. Other medieval authors, such as Chaucer and Chrestien de Troyes, followed Dante in making Fortuna one of God's servants. Orff, also, follows Dante: he calls Fortuna *Imperatrix Mundi*, Ruler of the Earth.

Created by God to be his minister on earth, to reward the good, and particularly to punish and chastise the bad in this life, so that they might serve as a warning to the rest of mankind, Fortuna emphasizes her lessons by heaping honor upon honor, wealth upon wealth, on anyone deserving punishment and then by suddenly bereaving him of all. Thus the sinner would learn not to seek or value any transient honor or prize of beauty, sexual love, or glory, but turn his mind to seek God, virtue, and salvation. Of all the seven deadly sins—Lust, Pride, Gluttony, Envy, Anger, Sloth, Covetousness—the deadliest is Pride, because it is the mental attitude of consciously or unconsciously comparing oneself to God. For the sin of Pride Lucifer was banished from Heaven to reign in Hell.

Let us now return to Orff's *Carmina Burana* and examine the dramatic action so far. In the prologue, *"Fortuna Imperatrix Mundi,"* Fortuna's role as God's agent on earth is asserted. In "Act I" (*"Primo Vere"*), Venus, however, reigns supreme, arrogating to herself Fortuna's sphere of action. "Act II" (*"In Taberna"*) brings out the latent conflict between Fortuna and Venus through allegory and recondite allusion, devices much used by medieval poets; all the *carmina* of this section have strong Christian overtones.

Carmen 11 has the clearest Christian overtones of all the *carmina* in this section; they can hardly be missed. It makes three references to the Gospels and ends by parodying the *Dies Irae*. Lines 9-11 refer to the parable of the House on the Rock and

House on the Sand told by Jesus in *Matthew* 7.24-27 and *Luke* 6.46-49. In lines 12-13 the skipperless ship out of control recalls the incident recounted in *Matthew* 14.23-33 where the disciples, sailing across the lake without Jesus, were storm-tossed; when Jesus appeared walking on the water, the storm was calmed and the disciples saved. The *via lata* of line 33 is from *Matthew* 7.13, "Wide as the gate and broad is the way that leadeth to destruction and many there be that go in thereat." The last line of the poem is a parody of the concluding line of the *Dies Irae*, the famous plea of a sinner on Judgement Day who begs his Lord, "*Gere curam mei finis.*" Such Christian overtones lead to our understanding *virtus* in line 36 and *salus* in line 39 as Christian vocabulary, the virtue and salvation of the soul. Significantly Fortuna is called in *carmen* 1 and 25 *sors salutis et virtutis*.

Such strong Christian overtones lead to a search for other Christian overtones in the remaining poems of this section. If there are several, then, taken all together, they would suggest that this section is an assertion, in a velate and obumbrate way as befits her, of Fortuna's real presence and dominion in the world.

Carmen 11 has a roasted swan, a medieval table delicacy, sing his swan song to the diners awaiting him. The white swan was sacred to Venus, primarily because of its beauty; according to some poets, a pair of white swans drew her chariot. Bachelard states the swan, in myth, legend, and literature, represents a naked woman, of chaste nudity and immaculate whiteness. Cirlot mentions that the swan is a symbol of complete satisfaction of desire; the swan-song, the song of death, is an even more potent symbol of such satisfaction.[2] In this *carmen*, Venus' white bird is roasted black, the color of death and sin. I suggest that this roasted swan symbolizes the devotee of Venus who followed Venus' commands to the utmost and has surrendered her chastity to her lover; in the section, *"Cour d'Amour,"* the key word *pulcher* also is used to describe the beloved in *carmina* 16, 18, 20, and, by implication, 24. In obeying Venus to the utmost, the woman has "died to Christ" and become black with sin.

What awaited such a damned soul? Medieval imaginations often pictured one of the punishments of Hell as an eternal roasting of the soul in its fires. The chorus of diners in *carmen* 12 represents the devils who chomp their teeth as they dine on the agony of the damned soul; on of the witty touches of this poem is the chewing motion jaws make in saying *"dentes frendentes!"*

Carmen 13 contains a reference to Fortuna veiled under the epithet *sors turpissima*. Its theme is gambling, *ludus*, which is also mentioned in *carmen* 14. The word *ludus* appears elsewhere in Orff's *Carmina Burana*. In the *"Cour d'Amour"* *ludus* is the *ludus ineffabilis amoris* (carmen 19). In *carmen* 11 the poet likens himself to a leaf *de quo ludunt venti*. In short *ludus* has three meanings, the game of dice, the game of love, and the game of life. Gambling, then, is a metaphysical metaphor.

Carmen 14 contains obvious and irreverent references to the Pope, Christians, sisters and brothers of the church. As a poem it is a parody of the Litany, the penitential office for Lent. Only here, the carousers drink to, rather than pray for, "All manner and conditions of men." It concludes with an irreverent comment that again refers to the Day of Judgement, the *Dies Irae*. Scorned by the virtuous, the drunkards pray, *"Qui nos rodunt confundantur et cum iustis non scribantur."* This concluding reference recalls the parody in *carmen* 11 of the poem *Die Irae*; occurring in the beginning and end of the section *"In Taberna,"* this apocalyptical theme—like the hymn to Fortuna which forms *carmen* 1 and *carmen* 25, the beginning and end of the *Carmina Burana*—makes a circle, the pattern representative of Fortuna's wheel, and thus a final link to her.

Thus language, symbolism, and theme connect the section *"In Taberna"* to the other two sections of Orff's *Carmina Burana* and also to his prologue and epilogue. Its strong Christian overtones and veiled references to Fortuna make it serve as an appropriately veiled statement of her dominion. The next section, *"Cour d'Amour,"* or "Act III," tells the story of a pair of lovers from initial meeting to final consummation.

With the opening of "Cour d'Amour," we seem to return to the mood of *"Primo Vere,"* where there exists love, and loving youth and maidens, and happiness. The only sadness occurs when Venus has not yet provided a lover; here *carmen* 7 parallels *carmen* 15. As the *carmina* unfold, we find that they tell the story of a love affair. The floral imagery, especially that of the rose, and the metaphor of the icy heart not yet warmed by love harken back to that earlier section. Slowly the image of the beloved one is painted before our eyes in *carmina* 17, 18, and 20, culminating in the first utterance of the beloved woman who has finally been touched with love. In her soliloquy she vacillates between *pudicitia* and *lascivus amor*, two concepts with definitely moral, Christian overtones. Having made her decision to follow Venus' commands, she calls her service *suave*, the same word the poet of *carmen* 11 used to describe his service to Venus. This word makes an ironic link between the two *carmina*. The poet of *carmen* 11 seems to have gotten little pleasure and certainly not permanent pleasure from his service to Venus. What will be the final reward for this young woman, who decides to serve Venus?

Finally of all the *carmen* in "*Cour d'Amour*" the language of *carmen* 22 is the most reminiscent of "*Primo Vere*" as the following lists shows:

Primo Vere	*carmen* 22
Flore, floret, flore	*floreo*
gaudia, gaudere	*gaudeo, congaudete*
iocundus	*iocundum*
ver	*tempus iocundum*
hyemis	*tempus brumale*
lascivit	*lasciviens*

Clearly then the *carmina* of "*Primo Vere*" and "*Cour d'Amour*" are linked in tone, subject, imagery, and language. If they may be reduced to one theme, it is the glorification of love, that service to Venus which brings supreme joy, felicity, and honor. One question, however, still remains: how do these two sections, and the "*In Taberna*" section, function as Acts I, II, and III in the cosmological drama that is the *Carmina Burana*?

A key to answering this question is to note that the *carmina* in "*Cour d'Amour*" actually themselves form a drama; as he would later do in the *Catulli Carmina*, Orff uses the structure of a play within a play to express the "spiritual reality" of this particular work. *Carmen* 24 is significantly set apart from the other *carmina* of "*Cour d'Amour*" with its own title, "*Blanziflor et Helena*" and serves as the culmination of "Act III."

The imagery and message of *carmen* 24 are complex. Both Helena and Blanziflor were, for the poets of courtly love, models of the feminine lover. Both women devoted themselves to love and their lovers; Helena left her husband and country to follow Paris, while Blanziflor remained faithful to her love, even though she was sold to a slave merchant and ultimately to an emir.

Hailed as another Helena and another Blanziflor for her devotion to love, the woman who has yielded herself in loyal obedience to Venus becomes yet another exemplar. Nor is this the only height of honor she attains. For she is hailed with the epithets used to praise the Virgin (*decus virginum, virgo gloriosa, mundi luminar, mundi rosa*). Lastly she is identified as *Venus generosa* because she had bestowed happiness, glory, and honor on her lover through her submission. Bestowing the rewards which Venus bestows, the woman essentially becomes Venus, becomes her avatar on earth.

The context of *carmen* 24 in the Beuron manuscript provides a further dimension for this poem in terms of understanding its function as the culmination of the play that is Act III, i.e. "*Cour d'Amour.*" *Carmen* 24 is not an entire poem in itself, but is taken from a longer poem in the manuscript, *Si linguis angelicis loquar et humanis*, in which it forms the eighth stanza. *Si linquis* is a later, poetic version of the treatise *Rota Veneris* written by Boncompagno (1240). The Beuron poem, like Boncompagno's treatise, has the author encounter the Rose who is both Venus and his beloved. *Ave formosissima* is the praise he utters upon seeing this vision. The poet describes a transcendant experience contemporaneous with an earthly experience, and, in so doing, makes recourse to liturgical language and metaphors, not in order to blaspheme, but to express in more familiar language a new concept of love.[3]

Orff, however, does not end his *Carmina Burana* at this point with Venus transcendant and obeyed by all. The last *carmen*, 25, is the final comment on the action of this play within a play and on the larger play that is the *Carmina Burana*. The epilogue, titled "*Fortuna Imperatrix Mundi*," is a reprise of the prologue. As epilogue, it asserts Fortuna's true dominion and at the same time makes the whole *Carmina Burana* end as it began—or rather the *Carmina Burana*, like a circle, has no beginning and end. With prologue and epilogue identical, this work is as circular as Fortuna's wheel. The work has come full circle and asserts structurally as well as thematically Fortuna's domination as *Imperatrix Mundi*, God's agent on earth.

"Pride goeth before destruction, and a haughty spirit before a fall." (*Proverbs* 16.18) Fortuna is especially the agent of punishment for Pride. Appropriately then Orff concludes his opus with *carmina* 24 and 25. The former is the apotheosis of the woman who has chosen Lust (Venus), not *Pudicitia* and prides herself on the glory she thereby wins. Rolling upwards on Fortuna's wheel, compared to Venus and Mary, Queen of Heaven, she, in her splendor, epitomizes Pride before its fall. The latter *carmen* asserts Fortuna's role of *Imperatrix Mundi*, punisher of the sinner and servant of God. Through imaginative use of music, chorus, and solo singers Orff has shaped his *Carmina Burana* into his version of a medieval morality play.

With his *Carmina Burana*, Orff not only began, as he saw himself doing, his career in terms of musical style and expression, but also his exposition of what he regarded as the spiritual and humanistic truths of all mankind's experience, unbounded by time, culture, and place. He would henceforth continue to develop his humanistic conception of music through synthesis of literary and folkloric themes, mythical and religious archetypes, music and theatre.

BIBLIOGRAPHY

W. Beare, *Latin Verse and European Song*. Methuen (London) 1957.

F. Brittain, *Medieval Latin and Romance Lyric to A.D. 1300*. Cambridge University Press (Cambridge) 1951.

P Dronke, *Medieval Latin and the Rise of European Love Lyric*. 2 vols. (Oxford University Press) 1968.

E. Helm, "Carl Orff," *The Music Quarterly* XLI.3 (July, 1955), pp. 285-304.

H. R. Patch, *The Goddess Fortuna*. Harvard University Press (Cambridge, MA) 1927.

J. Sebesta, *Carl Orff Carmina Burana Cantiones Profane: Original Text with Introduction, Facing Vocabularies, and Study Materials*. Bolchzy-Carducci Publ. (Chicago), 1984.

J. Stevens, *Medieval Romance: Themes and Approaches*. Norton (New York) 1973.

G. F. Whicher, *The Goliard Poets*. Harvard University Press (Cambridge, MA) 1949.

J. J. Wilhelm, *The Cruelest Month: Spring, Nature and Love in Classical and Medieval Lyrics*. Yale University Press (New Haven) 1965.

NOTES

1. "Carl Orff," Everett Helm, *The Music Quarterly* 41 (1955) p. 286.

2. J. E. Cirlot, *A Dictionary of Symbols* (transl. J. Sage), (Philosophical Library, New York, 1962), pp. 306-307. Cirlot cites G. Bachelard's comments in his book (i.e. Bachelard's) *L'Eau et les Rêves. Paris, 1942.*

3. *For a more detailed discussion of Si linguis,* see Dronke, *Medieval Latin Love-Lyric,* (Oxford, 1968, 2nd ed.), pp. 318-331.

TACITUS AND SUETONIUS PAULLINUS

Herbert W. Benario

Our ancient sources for the revolt of Boudicca in 60 A.D.[1] are Tacitus and Dio.[2] Not only are there important differences between the two but there are some variations in what Tacitus says in the two places where he discusses the terrible event, in the *Agricola*, briefly, and in the *Annals*, at considerable length. Dio's narrative, which we know only in the epitome of Xiphilinus, is imprecise and overwhelmingly rhetorical, almost totally lacking in detail. We cannot be certain of Dio's source, but I do not think that it could have been Tacitus, nor do I think that we should contemplate a common source.[3] Two significant points need to be kept in mind: that Tacitus had access to sources which Dio either did not know or chose to ignore and that Tacitus, writing in the next generation of an event which had occurred within his lifetime, had a point of view which was inevitably very different from that of Dio, who wrote about a century and a half after the uprising in a principate totally unlike that which, with all its changes, Tacitus had known.

I wish in this paper to focus attention especially upon the variations in his comments about Suetonius Paullinus, the governor and general. Why should these have appeared? Several explanations follow.

"Clearly Tacitus is mistaken somewhere, and the only likely conclusion is that the careful and explicit denial in the latter work is a correction of his earlier, probably less well researched, statement."[4]

"The *Agricola* narrative, it appears, is rather more impartial and judicious, while that in the *Annals* betrays Paulinus' personal prejudice."[5]

"Tacitus is far more accurate and detailed in his account in *Annals* XIV than he is in the *Agricola*, which is highly rhetorical."[6]

"Yet there remains the further problem of the discrepancy between Tacitus' two accounts. The usual explanation is to say that he used for the account in the *Annals* a source that he had not yet read when he wrote the *Agricola*, namely, the memoirs of Suetonius Paullinus himself."[7]

"La vera ragione della differenza è dunque da ricercare nel fatto che ora Tacito è ancora fiducioso nella bontà e nella validità del dominio romano, mentre negli *Annales*, come vedremo, il suo pessimismo incrina anche la fiducia nella legittimità e nella capacità dell'amministrazione di Roma sui barbari."[8]

Where such disagreement rages, conviction seems impossible. A reason different from those given may, perhaps, offer itself. Since the text of the two passages is so crucial, I offer them herewith in full; I shall then consider the at least apparent contradictions and attempt an explanation, and finally suggest what may have been in Tacitus' mind, and what may have been his intent, when he wrote the two works.

AGRICOLA—14. Suetonius hinc Paulinus biennio 3 prosperas res habuit, subactis nationibus firmatisque praesidiis; quorum fiducia Monam insulam ut vires rebellibus ministrantem adgressus terga occasioni patefecit.

15. Namque absentia legati remoto metu Britanni 1 agitare inter se mala servitutis, conferre iniurias et interpretando accendere: nihil profici patientia nisi ut graviora tamquam ex facili tolerantibus imperentur. singulos sibi olim reges fuisse, nunc binos imponi, ex 2 quibus legatus in sanguinem, procurator in bona saeviret, aeque discordiam praepositorum, aeque concordiam subiectis exitiosam. alterius manus centuriones, alterius servos vim et contumelias miscere. nihil iam cupiditati, nihil libidini exceptum. in proelio 3 fortiorem esse qui spoliet: nunc ab ignavis plerumque et

imbellibus eripi domos, abstrahi liberos, iniungi dilectus tamquam mori tantum pro patria nescientibus. quantulum enim transisse militum, si sese Britanni numerent? sic Germanias excussisse iugum; et flumine, non Oceano defendi. sibi patriam coniuges parentes, 4 illis avaritiam et luxuriam causas belli esse. recessuros, ut divus Iulius recessisset, modo virtutem maiorum suorum aemularentur. neve proelii unius aut alterius eventu pavescerent: plus impetus felicibus, maiorem constantiam penes miseros esse. iam Britannorum etiam 5 deos misereri, qui Romanum ducem absentem, qui relegatum in alia insula exercitum detinerent; iam ipsos, quod difficillimum fuerit, deliberare. porro in eius modi consiliis periculosius esse deprehendi quam audere.

16. His atque talibus in vicem instincti Boudicca 1 generis regii femina duce (neque enim sexum in imperiis discernunt) sumpsere universi bellum; ac sparsos per castella milites consectati, expugnatis praesidiis ipsam coloniam invasere ut sedem servitutis, nec ullum in barbaris saevitiae genus omisit ira et victoria. quod nisi Paulinus cognito provinciae motu propere 2 subvenisset, amissa Britannia foret; quam unius proelii fortuna veteri patientiae restituit, tenentibus arma plerisque, quos conscientia defectionis et proprius ex legato timor agitabat, ne quamquam egregius cetera adroganter in deditos et ut suae cuiusque iniuriae ultor durius consuleret. missus igitur Petronius Turpilianus 3 tamquam exorabilior et delictis hostium novus eoque paenitentiae mitior, compositis prioribus nihil ultra ausus Trebellio Maximo provinciam tradidit.

ANNALES XIV—29. Caesennio Paeto et Petronio 1 Turpiliano consulibus gravis clades in Britannia accepta; in qua neque A. Didius legatus, ut memoravi, nisi parta retinuerat, et successor Veranius. modicis excursibus Siluras populatus, quin ultra bellum proferret, morte prohibitus est, magna, dum vixit, severitatis fama, supremis testamenti verbis ambitonis manifestus: quippe multa in Neronem adulatione addidit subiecturum ei provinciam fuisse, si biennio proximo vixisset. sed tum Paulinus Suetonius obtinebat 2 Britannos, scientia militiae et rumore populi, qui neminem sine aemulo sinit, Corbulonis concertator, receptaeque Armeniae decus aequare domitis perduellibus cupiens. igitur Monam insulam, incolis validam et receptaculum perfugarum, adgredi parat, navesque fabricatur plano alveo adversus breve et incertum. sic pedes; equites vado secuti aut altiores inter undas adnantes equis tramisere.

30. Stabat pro litore diversa acies, densa armis virisque, intercursantibus feminis, quae in modum Furiarum veste ferali, crinibus deiectis faces praeferebant; Druidaeque circum, preces diras sublatis ad caelum manibus fundentes, novitate adspectus perculere militem, ut quasi haerentibus membris immobile corpus vulneribus praeberent. dein cohortationibus ducis et se ipsi stimulantes, ne muliebre et fanaticum agmen pavescerent, inferunt signa sternuntque obvios et igni suo involvunt. praesidium posthac impositum victis excisique luci saevis superstitionibus sacri: nam cruore captivo adolere aras et hominum fibris consulere deos fas habebant. haec agenti Suetonio repentina defectio provinciae nuntiatur.

31. Rex Icenorum Prasutagus, longa opulentia clarus, Caesarem heredem duasque filias scripserat, tali obsequio ratus regnumque et domum suam procul iniuria fore. quod contra vertit, adeo ut regnum per centuriones, domus per servos velut capta vastarentur. iam primum uxor eius Boudicca verberibus adfecta et filiae stupro violatae sunt; praecipui quique Icenorum, quasi cunctam regionem muneri accepissent, avitis bonis exuuntur, et propinqui regis inter mancipia habebantur. qua contumelia et metu graviorum, quando in formam provinciae cesserant, rapiunt arma, commotis ad rebellationem Trinovantibus et qui alii nondum servitio fracti resumere libertatem occultis coniurationibus pepigerant, acerrimo in veteranos odio. quippe in coloniam Camulodunum recens deducti pellebant domibus, exturbabant agris, captivos, servos appellando, foventibus impotentiam veteranorum militibus similitudine vitae et spe eiusdem licentiae. ad hoc templum divo Claudio constitutum quasi arx aeternae dominationis adspiciebatur, delectique sacerdotes specie reli-

gionis omnis fortunas effundebant. nec arduum videbatur exscindere coloniam nullis munimentis saeptam; quod ducibus nostris parum provisum erat, dum amoenitati prius quam usui consulitur.

32. Inter quae nulla palam causa delapsum Camuloduni simulacrum Victoriae ac retro conversum, quasi cederet hostibus. et feminae in furorem turbatae adesse exitium canebant, externosque fremitus in curia eorum auditos, consonuisse ululatibus theatrum visamque speciem in aestuario Tamesae subversae coloniae; iam Oceanus cruento adspectu, et labente aestu humanorum corporum effigies relictae, ut Britannis ad spem, ita veteranis ad metum trahebantur. sed quia procul Suetonius aberat, petivere a Cato Deciano procuratore auxilium. ille haud amplius quam ducentos sine iustis armis misit; et inerat modica militum manus. tutela templi freti, et impedientibus qui occulti rebellionis conscii consilia turbabant, neque fossam aut vallum praeduxerant, neque motis senibus et feminis iuventus sola restitit: quasi media pace incauti multitudine barbarorum circumveniuntur. et cetera quidem impetu direpta aut incensa sunt: templum, in quo se miles conglobaverat, biduo obsessum expugnatumque. et victor Britannus, Petilio Ceriali, legato legionis nonae, in subsidium adventanti obvius, fudit legionem, et quod peditum interfecit: Cerialis cum equitibus evasit in castra et munimentis defensus est. qua clade et odiis provinciae, quam avaritia in bellum egerat, trepidus procurator Catus in Galliam transiit.

33. At Suetonius mira constantia medios inter hostes Londinium perrexit, cognomento quidem coloniae non insigne, sed copia negotiatorum et commeatuum maxime celebre. ibi ambiguus, an illam sedem bello deligeret, circumspecta infrequentia militis, satisque magnis documentis temeritatem Petilii coercitam, unius oppidi damno servare universa statuit. neque fletu et lacrimis auxilium eius orantium flexus est, quin daret profectionis signum et comitantes in partem agminis acciperet: si quos imbellis sexus aut fessa aetas vel loci dulcedo attinuerat, ab hoste oppressi sunt. eadem clades municipio Verulamio fuit, quia barbari omissis castellis praesidiisque militare

horreum, quod uberrimum spolianti et defendentibus intutum, laeti praeda et laborum segnes petebant. ad septuaginta milia civium et sociorum iis, quae memoravi, locis cecidisse constitit. neque enim capere aut venundare aliudve quod belli commercium, sed caedes patibula, ignes cruces, tamquam reddituri supplicium, at praerepta interim ultione, festinabant.

34. Iam Suetonio quarta decuma legio cum vex- 1 illariis vicesimanis et e proximis auxiliares, decem ferme milia armatorum, erant, cum omittere cunctationem et congredi acie parat. deligitque locum artis faucibus et a tergo silva clausam, satis cognito nihil hostium nisi in fronte et apertam planitiem esse, sine metu insidiarum. igitur legionarius frequens ordinibus, levis circum 2 armatura, conglobatus pro cornibus eques astitit. at Britannorum copiae passim per catervas et turmas exultabant, quanta non alias multitudo, et animo adeo feroci, ut coniuges quoque testes victoriae secum traherent plaustrisque imponerent, quae super extremum ambitum campi posuerant.

35. Boudicca curru filias prae se vehens, ut quamque 1 nationem accesserat, solitum quidem Britannis feminarum ductu bellare testabatur, sed tunc non ut tantis maioribus ortam regnum et opes, verum ut unam e vulgo libertatem amissam, confectum verberibus corpus, contrectatam filiarum pudicitiam ulcisci. eo provectas Romanorum cupidines, ut non corpora, ne senectam quidem aut virginitatem impollutam relinquant. adesse tamen deos iustae vindictae; cecidisse legionem, quae proelium ausa 2 sit; ceteros castris occultari aut fugam circumspicere. ne strepitum quidem et clamorem tot milium, nedum impetus et manus perlaturos. si copias armatorum, si causas belli secum expenderent, vincendum illa acie vel cadendum esse. id mulieri destinatum: viverent viri et servirent.

36. Ne Suetonius quidem in tanto discrimine 1 silebat. quamquam confideret viruti, tamen exhortationes et preces miscebat, ut spernerent sonores barbarorum et inanes minas: plus illic feminarum quam iuventutis adspici. imbelles inermes cessuros statim, ubi ferrum

virtutemque vincentium totiens fusi agnovissent. etiam 2
in multis legionibus paucos, qui proelia profligarent;
gloriaeque eorum accessurum, quod modica manus
universi exercitus famam adipiscerentur. conferti tantum et pilis emissis post umbonibus et gladiis stragem
caedemque continuarent, praedae immemores: parta
victoria cuncta ipsis cessura. is ardor verba ducis seque- 3
batur, ita se ad intorquenda pila expedierat vetus miles
et multa proeliorum experientia, ut certus eventus Suetonius daret pugnae signum.

37. Ac primum legio gradu immota et angustias loci 1
pro munimento retinens, postquam in proprius suggressos hostis certo iactu tela exhauserat, velut cuneo
erupit. idem auxiliarium impetus; et eques protentis
hastis perfringit quod obvium et validum erat. ceteri
terga praebuere, difficili effugio, quia circumiecta
vehicula saepserant abitus. et miles ne mulierum
quidem neci temperabat, confixaque telis etiam iumenta
corporum cumulum auxerant. clara et antiquis victoriis par ea die laus parta: quippe sunt qui paulo minus
quam octoginta milia Britannorum cecidisse tradant,
militum quadringentis ferme interfectis nec multo
amplius vulneratis. Boudicca vitam veneno finivit. et 3
Poenius Postumus, praefectus castrorum secundae
legionis, cognitis quartadecimanorum vicesimanorumque prosperis rebus, quia pari gloria legionem
suam fraudaverat abnueratque contra ritum militiae
iussa ducis, se ipse gladio transegit.

38. Contractus deinde omnis exercitus sub pellibus 1
habitus est ad reliqua belli perpetranda. auxitque copias
Caesar missis ex Germania duobus legionariorum
milibus, octo auxiliarium cohortibus ac mille equitibus,
quorum adventu nonani legionario milite suppleti
sunt. cohortes alaeque novis hibernaculis locatae, quod- 2
que nationum ambiguum aut adversum fuerat, igni
atque ferro vastatum. sed nihil aeque quam fames
adfligebat serendis frugibus incuriosos, et omni aetate
ad bellum versa, dum nostros commeatus sibi destinant.
gentesque praeferoces tardius ad pacem inclinabant,
quia Iulius Classicianus, successor Cato missus et Suetonio discors, bonum publicum privatis simultatibus

impediebat disperseratque novum legatum opperiendum esse, sine hostili ira et superbia victoris clementer deditis consulturum. simul in urbem mandabat, nullum proeliorum finem exspectarent, nisi succederetur Suetonio, cuius adversa pravitati ipsius, prospera ad fortunam referebat.

39. Igitur ad spectandum Britanniae statum missus 1 est e libertis Polyclitus, magna Neronis spe posse auctoritate eius non modo inter legatum procuratoremque concordiam gigni, sed et rebelles barbarorum animos pace componi. nec defuit Polyclitus, quo minus 2 ingenti agmine Italiae Galliaeque gravis, postquam Oceanum transmiserat, militibus quoque nostris terribilis incederet. sed hostibus inrisui fuit, apud quos flagrante etiam tum libertate nondum cognita libertinorum potentia erat; mirabanturque, quod dux et exercitus tanti belli confector servitiis oboedirent. cuncta 3 tamen ad imperatorem in mollius relata; detentusque rebus gerendis Suetonius, quod paucas naves in litore remigiumque in iis amiserat, tamquam durante bello tradere exercitum Petronio Turpiliano, qui iam consulatu abierat, iubetur. is non irritato hoste neque lacessitus honestum pacis nomen segni otio imposuit.

Careful reading of the two passages will reveal only two instances where Tacitus appears to contradict himself or offer substantially more information in one place than in the other. Both involve the military activities and desolation of the Britons.

Agr. 16.1 *ac sparsos per castella milites consectati, expugnatis praesidiis*

Ann. 33.2 *barbari omissis castellis praesidiisque militare horreum . . . petebant*

The two statements need not be taken as contradictory. The first report may refer to actions before the sack of Camulodunum, the latter after. So Tacitus suggests in the order of the narratives. We do not know how much time passed between the beginnings of the revolt and the first rampage and the later wanderings after Camulodunum had been destroyed. Food for such a mass of people became increasingly important as time passed, since no crops had been sown. The assaults early on of the *castella* and *praesidia* likely yielded them little, since we know that one of Agricola's innovations was to furnish each *castellum* with a year's provisions to enable it to withstand siege.[9] On this interpretation, the two statements are supplementary, and both present the kind of intimate detail which must have come from a first-hand source.

Agr. 16.1 (this continues the sentence begun above) *ipsam coloniam invasere ut sedem servitutis*

Ann. 31.4 *templum divo Claudio constitutum quasi arx aeternae dominationis adspiciebatur*

32.3 *templum, in quo se miles conglobaverat, biduo obsessum expugnatumque.*

33.1 *Suetonius ... Londinium perrexit . . . unius oppidi damno servare universa statuit.*

33.2 *eadem clades municipio Verulamio fuit*

Much is made of the seeming discrepancy between the two works on this point. Some scholars are unhappy that Tacitus mentions only one city in the *Agricola* but three in the *Annals*. Compounding the difficulty is the fact that both Suetonius[10] and Dio mention only two. But Tacitus' narrative in the biography is very brief and compact; he takes us with him up to the destruction and torment of the capital of the province, which is variously yet similarly described as *sedes servitutis* and *arx aeternae dominationis*, and then ignores all the remainder of the campaign until brief mention, almost parenthetically, of the climactic battle. In the *Annals* the narrative is fuller, and there is space for the accumulation of disaster. Indeed, Tacitus seems to be alluding to a powerful phrase in the earlier work by an equally stunning one in the later; *unius proelii fortuna* appears to lurk behind *unius oppidi damno*, which will be redeemed by the almost boastful assertion, *clara et antiquis victoriis par ea die laus parta* (37.2).

If there is no meaningful inconsistency between what Tacitus reports on the revolt of Boudicca in his two narratives, how important are the seeming differences in mood and the final judgment on Suetonius Paullinus.[11] Can they be explained by differing sources, or by a change in Tacitus' own viewpoint?

Need they be so explained? I think not; the answer, I suggest, lies rather in the difference in the character of the two works than in the character of their author.

But before we arrive at our conclusions, we must put and then attempt to answer several further questions. These are:

1. Did Suetonius Paullinus write *Memoirs*?

2. If he did, did Tacitus use them?

3. If that seems to be the case, did he know them directly or indirectly?

4. Was he familiar with them when he wrote the *Agricola*?

5. If not, when did he become acquainted with them, in order to affect the *Annals*?

6. If the answer to 4 is positive, why are there differences between the two accounts?

We know from Tacitus that Domitius Corbulo wrote *Commentarii*;[12] the historian not only mentions them but questions their veracity in the report of another's disaster and disgrace. These *Commentarii* served as an *apologia pro vita sua* and included much valuable material on astronomy and geography, which Pliny exploited for his *Natural History*. Pliny similarly reports that Suetonius was the first Roman commander to cross Mount Atlas in Mauretania and march far to the south; his source was most likely Suetonius himself.[13] Another interesting detail in Pliny is the distance between Mona (Anglesey) and Camulodunum (Colchester),[14] which is precisely the kind of first-hand information that a reader would expect in a general's memoirs.

We are nowhere told that Suetonius did write *Commentarii* to rival those of Corbulo, his great military rival. It nonetheless is a reasonable conjecture; they would have been composed after the death of Nero, when at last he could freely give his version of the events which had led to his recall after the great disaster and great triumph.[15] The man whom Tacitus depicts as *scientia militiae et rumore populi, qui neminem sine aemulo sinit, Corbulonis concertator, receptaeque Armeniae decus aequare domitis perduellibus cupiens*[16] would hardly have let the opportunity pass to have the final word in the popular matching of him and Corbulo; the latter had had his say before his enforced suicide in 65. Suetonius was luckier; he survived both rival and emperor, and with some honor. He *may* have been consul in 66, an iteration which is unfortunately nowhere recorded; if not he himself, it was likely his son.[17]

Our answer to the first question is affirmative; so too is our answer to the second. Tacitus had an unparalleled source of information for the details of the Boudiccan revolt in his father-in-law. When would the conversations between the two have occurred? Agricola was governor from 77-83 and Tacitus away from Rome from 90-93.[18] The years 84 to 89, when Agricola was in retirement and Tacitus in Rome for at least part of the time (he was praetor in 88)[19] would have furnished much opportunity. Agricola could hardly have had any feelings toward Suetonius other than the friendliest, although he might have taken exception, with the advantage of hindsight and his own experience of government in the island, to details of the general's strategy. He had, after all, been especially favored by Suetonius: *Prima castrorum rudimenta in Britannia Suetonio Paulino, diligenti ac moderato duci, adprobavit, electus quem contubernio aestimaret.*[20] Agricola would certainly have been interested in his old commander's *Memoirs*, and Tacitus would not have been unfamiliar with them. If that seems the case, the conclusion must follow that Tacitus knew them directly, and he must surely have read them before he began composition of the biography of Agricola in 97.

Since our answer to question 4 is likewise positive, question 5 becomes unnecessary. We can at last return to our chief inquiry, why there should be differences in Tacitus' treatment of the revolt in the two works.

The reason is to be found in Tacitus' intent and character delineation. The scale and scope of the *Agricola* and the *Annals* are very different. In the earlier work he merely sketches in outline the events which he will later describe in detail. The design of the biography has no place for a lengthy narrative which does not have Agricola for its protagonist. Tacitus recounts practically nothing of strategic or tactical interest. He sweeps immediately from report of the disaster at Camulodunum to statement of a great triumph: *nec ullum in barbaris saevitiae genus omisit ira et victoria. quod nisi Paulinus . . . propere subvenisset, amissa Britannia foret.* We learn what happened, we do not discover how it happened. Since Agricola's role, whatever it was and whatever his own achievements, was subordinate to Suetonius', he could not be given credit. That was a given in the relationship of senior and junior officer: *cuncta etsi consiliis ductuque alterius agebantur, ac summa rerum et recuperatae provinciae gloria in ducem cessit, artem et usum et stimulos addidere iuveni.*[21]

In the *Annals*, needless to say, the canvas is broader, many people "strut and fret their hour upon the stage," and Tacitus can be more critical. Extensive narrative dealing with foreign affairs and with military campaigns relieves the tedium and frequent disgust with affairs of the capital and the doings of the emperors, particularly when one who could be considered *capax imperii* is involved. Further, twenty years or more had passed since Tacitus wrote the *Agricola*; that passage of time guaranteed that practically none was alive who had participated in those events. *Quotus quisque reliquus, qui haec eventa vidisset?*[22]

This interval is, I submit, crucial. Tacitus had never been an uncritical admirer of Suetonius Paullinus. Even in the *Agricola* he had recognized his excessive harshness and bitterness after the revolt: the Britons were driven by *proprius ex legato timor, ne quamquam egregius cetera adroganter in deditos et ut suae cuiusque iniuriae ultor durius consuleret.* We do not know whether Tacitus ever had any personal relationship with Suetonius; through Agricola, however, he certainly had a vicarious one. There may well have been some details which could have embarrassed the old man, and the ever-present tension between *ira* and *studium* would have had impact. Tacitus did, after all, give Suetonius generally consistent praise. During the civil war, his influence was great, although not overriding. Some even thought that, if the soldiers on both sides could come to their senses, he might be chosen as emperor, *quod vetustissimus consularium et militia clarus gloriam nomenque Britannicis expeditionibus meruisset*[23] (no hint of criticism here). He was a man of *prudentia*[24] and with no military rival, *nemo illa tempestate militaris rei callidior.*[25] He was by nature cautious, *cunctator natura et cui cauta potius consilia cum ratione quam prospera ex casu placerent.*[26] But caution was preferable to rashness, which marked the career of Petillius Cerialis, who had served under Suetonius in Britain and had lost a substantial body of the ninth legion and barely escaped with his own life.[27]

One of the unanswerable problems of Tacitean studies is the gap between the end of the *Annals*, which must have concluded with the death of Nero and the consequent end of the Julio-Claudian dynasty in mid 68, and the beginning of the *Histories*, which commenced with January 1, 69. Why the gap of some six months in what was obviously intended to be a continuous narrative? It may well be, as has been often suggested, that Tacitus chose not to detail the events in which Verginius Rufus played a major role. There may have been some discreditable circumstances which Tacitus chose to spare the memory of the now legendary figure.[28] If another author could challenge Verginius with the statement that the latter would not approve what he was going to write,[29] so Tacitus might have had some information which could have done harm to the reputation of Suetonius Paullinus. The historian has chosen to give us hints of failings in the latter, with little detail.

I conclude with a brief recapitulation of my main points:

1. Whatever Tacitus knew of the Boudiccan revolt, he knew when he wrote the *Agricola*.

2. Seeming contradictions in the two narratives are easily explained.

3. Tacitus' opinion of Suetonius did not change over a span of some twenty years.

4. He considered Suetonius Paullinus one of the great men of his age, like Agricola a victim of bureaucracy and jealousy and, like Agricola, a potential emperor.[30]

NOTES

1. Tacitus dates the revolt to the year 61. See R. Syme, *Tacitus* (Oxford 1958), App. 69, for arguments on the historian's "inadvertence in dating." Accepted by G. Webster, *Boudica: the British Revolt against Rome AD 60* (Totowa, N.J., 1978), the most recent discussion, particularly valuable for its marshaling of archaeological evidence.

2. 62.1-12.

3. See, for differing argumentation, C. Questa, *Studi sulle fonti degli Annales di Tacito* (Rome 1963²) 219-24; G. B. Townend, "Some Rhetorical Battle-Pictures in Dio," *Hermes* 92 (1964) 467-81; J. C. Overbeck, "Tacitus and Dio on Boudicca's Rebellion," *AJP* 90 (1969) 129-45; D. P. Orsi, "Sulla rivolta di Boudicca," *AFLB* 16 (1973) 529-35; and N. Reed, "The Sources of Tacitus and Dio for the Boudiccan Revolt," *Latomus* 33 (1974) 926-33. The best discussion of Dio is F. Millar, *A Study of Cassius Dio* (Oxford 1964).

4. Overbeck, *op. cit.*, 138.

5. Reed, *op. cit.*, 928.

6. L. A. du Toit, "Tacitus and the Rebellion of Boudicca," *A Class* 20 (1977) 153.

7. M. T. Griffin, "Nero's Recall of Suetonius Paullinus," *SCI* 3 (1976/77) 149.

8. E. Paratore, *Tacito* (Rome 1962²) 183-84.

9. *Agr.* 22.2.

10. *Nero* 39.1.

11. See *PIR* S 694; A. R. Birley, *The Fasti of Roman Britain* (Oxford 1981) 54-57.

12. *Ann.* 15.16.1.

13. *NH* 5.14.

14. *NH* 2.187.

15. See H. Bardon, *La Littérature Latine Inconnue* II (Paris 1956) 172-73.

16. *Ann.* 14.29.2.

17. Griffin, *op. cit.*, 147.

18. *Agr.* 45.5.

19. *Ann.* 11.11.1.

20. *Agr.* 5.1.

21. *Agr.* 5.3.

22. This is a paraphrase of Tacitus' comment in *Ann.* 1.3.7, *quotus quisque reliquus, qui rem publicam vidisset?*

23. *Hist.* 2.37.1.

24. *Hist.* 2.37.2.

25. *Hist.* 2.32.1.

26. *Hist.* 2.25.2.

27. See A. R. Birley, "Petillius Cerialis and the Conquest of Brigantia," *Britannia* 4 (1973) 179-90.

28. See, inter alios, J. B. Hainsworth, "The Starting-Point of Tacitus' *Historiae*: Fear or Favour by Omission?," *G&R* 11 (1964) 128-36; D. C. A. Shotter, "The Starting-Dates of Tacitus' Historical Works," *CQ* 17 (1967) 158-63; idem, "Tacitus and Verginius Rufus," *CQ* 17 (1967) 370-81.

29. Pliny *Ep.* 9.19.5.

30. H. W. Benario, " *Imperium* and *Capaces Imperii* in Tacitus," *AJP* 93 (1972) 14-26.

PROFILES AND POLICIES
OF ATHENIAN CONSERVATIVES
IN THE EARLY FOURTH CENTURY B.C. (403-378)

Dionysios A. Kounas

With the declaration of the anmesty, Archinus' *paragraphê* in 403/2, and the reunion of Athens and Eleusis in 401/0 an artificial reconciliation was effected between the dissident factions in Athens,[1] and generally speaking, the civil discord between oligarchs and democrats ceased. But, despite the amnesty and *paragraphê*, the Athenian body politic remained divided into two distinct camps designated as *hoi ex asteos*, those who apparently supported the Thirty's régime and oligarchy in general, and *hoi ek Peiraios*, those who favored the democratic constitution. From the latter came the nucleus of the faction traditionally known as "imperialists" or "radical democrats."

The radicals thoroughly disapproved of the conciliatory temperment among the moderate elements of *hoi ek Peiraios* towards the oligarchic men of the city. It was one thing to forgive and quite another to forget the excesses of the Thirty, the humiliation of a Spartan victory over Athens, and the menial position relegated to Athens resultant with its defeat. They were especially loathe to accept the terms of reconciliation, for with the oligarchs, radicals associated the evils that had befallen Athens since 404.[2] It is not surprising, therefore, that the imperialists tingled with hatred for oligarchs and Sparta. Nor is it improbably that they entertained thoughts of *timoria* against Sparta and its supporters in Athens. In order to satisfy their lust for revenge the radicals undertook to convince the Athenians that their only hope of redemption from subservience to Sparta and of allaying their fears lest another oligarchic revolution occur lay in reascending the imperial escalator.[3]. The implication here, of course, is that imperialism had necessitated, prompted, and underscored control of Athens by the *demos*.

Of course *hoi es asteos* were by nature diametrically opposed to such liberalism, for their conservatism to a great extent was commensurate with their previous and present political, economic, and social background. One's clues are derived from the political catch-phrases with which Athenians designated oligarchs. Through the fifth and fourth centuries oligarchs were frequently called *plousioi, dynatoi, kaloi kagathoi, beltistoi, chrestoi, aristoi, gnorimoi kai charientes*,[4] and of course, after the democratic restoration in 403, *hoi ex asteos* was in vogue. At the outset, however, it must be firmly established that *hoi ex asteos* does not simply mean that all the urbanites living in the city proper were oligarchs. And in reverse, neither does *hoi ek Peiraios* imply that those Athenians residing in the Piraeus and in other *demes* apart from the *asty* were naturally democrats.[5]

In the mid-fifth century this might have been the case, but certainly not in the late fifth or early fourth centuries. During and after the Peloponessian war numerous Athenians who previously resided in the Piraeus and countryside of Attica now took up residency in the city proper. And one's residence in a particular *deme* both within the *asty* and without ceased to be of tantamount significance, if in truth it ever did, in determining one's party affiliation.[6] Moreover, for Lysias, Xenophon, Isocrates, and Aristotle *hoi ex asteos* and *hoi ek Peiraios* are convenient epithets with which to denote the Athenian civil war of 403 and temporary strongholds of the parties involved. On the subsequent pages it will become clearly evident that many oligarchs fled the city during the civil strife and fought alongside the democrats. By the same token, there is sufficient evidence to suggest that several of the democrats did not participate with Thrasybulus and other Athenians but remained in the city during the oligarchic administration. Henceforth for purposes of clarity and simplicity the epithetic use of *hoi ex asteos* and *hoi ek Peiraios* to denote oligarchs and imperialists will be abandoned in favor of those synonyms commonly employed by most modern authors.

In light of the above observations and the complexity of the primary sources, one's first inclination might be to shy away from any attempt to describe the nature of Athenian oligarchs from 403 to 378, and in truth, careful analysis of the sources does prescribe the exercise of restraint on many points. Nevertheless, after sifting through the storehouse of information available, it is possible to find molds within which to cast the basic character and temperament of the oligarchs.

After the democratic restoration the conservative faction in Athens was by no means small in number. By virtue of the political amnesty of 403/2 and the reunion of Athens with Eleusis its membership swelled considerably, and understandably so. It will be recalled that the amnesty was extended not only to those who participated in the conspiracy of 404/3, but even to those exiled earlier during the Peloponessian War because of oligarchic conspiracies, like Andocides.[7] Moreover, prior to the reconciliation with Eleusis, Archinus, observing the large number of oligarchs who wished to avail themselves of the opportunity to migrate to Eleusis and join their former colleagues, compelled many conversatives to stay by arbitrarily eliminating the last days allowed for taking up residence in Eleusis.[8] Once the reconciliation with Eleusis was effected, naturally more oligarchs returned to the city proper.

Consequently one segment of the oligarchic faction drew its clientele mainly from the élite Three Thousand, the rich element in Athens whose wealth was derived by serving the Thirty and from their own crimes, Eratosthenes being a case in point. Added to these were several citizens who had not suffered any malice under the Thirty, or Ten, and who remained in Athens during the Thirty's reign to protect their property or serve as henchmen like Melêtus or Epichares.[9] Generally speaking, they represented the old landed gentry of Athens which comprised the aristocracy. But wealth alone was not the sole prerequisite for enlisting in the oligarchic ranks, nor was the possession of land. The burdens of trierarchies during the Peloponessian War and liturgies to the state had impoverished many nobles, and this in part explains the occurrence of the oligarchic revolutions of 411 and 404. Undoubtedly several nobles recouped their losses through participation in the property confiscations under Critias' and Eratosthenes' direction. But for many notables their entire patrimony was lost forever, and under the guise of polemic with the *demos* they contrived in vain to steal another's. To them democracy was despicable. These, then, were the hard core reactionaries who were not a few in number and who constituted the extreme, conservative element in the oligarchic camp which came to the fore when Eratosthenes was on trial for his life.[10]

The left wing of the oligarchic camp was occupied by "moderate conservatives" such as Callimachus, Nicomachus, Thrasybulus of Collytus,[11] Mantitheus, Evandros, Phormisius, Anytus, and Archinus. The latter three had gravitated around the leadership of Thereamenes in opposition to both democrats who hoped to extend the franchise and oligarchs who felt Athens must be ruled absolutely by a select few. They were more inclined to favor the ancestral constitution of Solon in which men of hoplite and *hippeis* status administered the affairs of state. But, as Theramenes woefully discovered, moderate oligarchy was not what Critias and Eratosthenes had in mind, and conversely that "a moderate democracy is only possible as a step in development, but cannot be artificially created from an extreme democracy."[12] Lest the "moderate conservatives" experience a fate similar to Theramenes, they departed Athens and made common cause with the democrats against the extreme oligarchs.[13] Upon their return to the city several moderates, in the manner of Archinus and Anytus, recanted oligarchy and cast their lot with the moderate democrats. Others it seems, in the fashion of Phormisius, Nicomachus, Thrasybulus of Collytus, and Evandros, kept one foot in both camps. It was they especially whom the imperialists feared and viewed with circumspect because of their continued affiliation, or so the imperialists contended, with the extreme oligarchs.[14] Nevertheless, both groups shared some common bondage with the right wing by virtue of their basically conservative temperament which, for all intents and purposes, they did not abandon after the reconciliation. Furthermore, they experienced equally the suspicion and invectives of the *demos*' mistrust for anyone bearing the faintest resemblance of an oligarch, and this animosity perhaps welded them closer together than any single political issue.

In addition to the liberal oligarchs, one can justifiably assume oligarchs garnered a few members from the small farmers and businessmen in Attica of recently attained *hippeis* status, or who at least appeared to be of that class. Provided Mantitheus' defense and the writ against Alcibiades the younger are reliable,[15] it would seem that the security of serving in the cavalry, tendentiously oligarchic as always, was offered to many who by lineage or tradition did not belong to that class. Obviously from the comments made in the trials such security was not proffered at random, but to select individuals of oligarchic disposition who could justify, or appear to warrant classification of *hippeis* status. In a manner befitting oligarchs they lamented democracy and imperialism and subscribed to conservatism. Understandably their patience may have worn thin with the peculations of certain radicals and the duration of the previous war. Hence they welcomed the opportunity to ally with the *aristoi* in the hope of preserving and increasing their income by thwarting the radicals. Of equal importance in their minds, no doubt, was also the factor of social prestige which came with their identification and association with the conservative aristocracy.[16]

Summarily speaking, after 403 the conservative, oligarchic party had crystalized into three distinct smaller cliques. First and foremost was the vanguard of extreme conservatives comprised of traditional reactionaries. Its central figures were Eratosthenes, Melêtus, and Epichares. They staunchly adhered to the precept of rule by a select few on the basis of wealth and lineage, and customarily speaking, dedicated themselves to undermining democracy by subversive tactics. Second in line were the *hetaireiai* of Phormisius, Nicomachus and Evandros. These "buckskins," as Critias would call them, tolerated democracy with severe limitations and thus were supple enough to move freely from the democratic to the oligarchic camp as the need arose. Finally, there crept out of the political woodwork the smaller group of *parvenus* of moderate wealth. They shuddered at the thought that the new winds of imperialism and radical democracy might sweep away their newly acquired wealth. Therefore they shared some affinity with the oligarchs. Despite the shades of differences on constitutional issues, however, all three cliques were firmly untied in opposition to liberal democracy and the revival of Athenian imperialism and gave ground grudgingly whenever these issues came to the fore.

But the conservatives and their confreres as oligarchs dared not oppose publicly the radical democrats. The ostracism of Thucydides, the son of Melesias, in 443 instructed oligarchs to remain inconspicuous in their efforts to subvert democracy. As a result oligarchs became the handmaidens of deceit to further their schemes which successfully came to fruition in 411 and 404/3. After 403, however, the position of conservatives in the mask of oligarchy was extremely precarious because the *demos* equated oligarchy with treason.

Oligarchs, and oligarchy in general, suffered the malaise of complicity in the revolution of 411, the trial and condemnation of the generals after Arginusae, the Athenian defeat at Aegospotami, Spartan occupation, the loss of the fleet and fortifications, the rapine of Thirty, and more recently, of attempting anew to subvert the democracy.[17] Indeed the rancid odor of oligarchic treason and conspiricay had so thoroughly fouled the political atmosphere of Athens it became expedient for the notables to renounce superficially extreme conservatism and profess conversion to the moderate or imperialist democratic faith. As ardent defenders of the democratic constitution, oligarchs subversively hoped to foil imperialism and democracy, guarantee their property rights, retain their political influence and simultaneously avoid persecution for previous evils which befell the Athenian state.[18] Succinctly put, oligarchs wisely returned to the caverns of deception to remove the stain of treason. That not a few successfully exonerated themselves is partially attested by the prominent political roles played by Archinus, Anytus, Mantitheus, Andocides, Phormisus, and Evandros. The exact number of others who participated in the administration is lacking, but that other oligarchs served in the government is evident.

In order to fortify the amnesty of 403 with some semblance of authenticity the Athenians Thrasybulus, Archinus, and Anytus, no doubt under the pressure of Sparta, selected ten representatives each from the democrats and the oligarchs as a provisional government to re-draw the laws. To further assist in the re-establishment of democracy five hundred *monothetai* were selected from the entire population. There is no reason whatsoever for not concluding that among the *nomothetai* were several members of the oligarchic faction.[19] The likelihood of this belief becomes even more plausible upon reflection that the provisional government and *nomothetai*'s first inclinations were to imitate as nearly as possibel Solon's constitution, all of which suggests a strong oligarchical influence. The circumstances had changed radically since the days of Solon and democracy of the late fifth century prevailed. At any rate, several oligarchs were active politically as administrators. Others, however, like Eratosthenes were not to be entrusted with the affairs of state.[20] To escape any further detection the notables and their *hetaireiai*, as was their custom, deliberated secretly in the evenings the conservative policies to be pursued in domestic and foreign affairs.[21]

With respect to internal politics, at best it can be said the *gnorimoi*, as always, violently opposed Athenian rule by the *demos* and the imperialists with whom they identified radical democracy. Indicative of their antipathy are the vitriolic oath sworn by oligarchs against democracy and Critias' severe censure of democracy. In both inflamed hatred for the *demos* and avowed calculations for its ruin run at fever pitch.[22] But the excesses of the Thirty were so vividly recent in Athenian memories that oligarchs perforce compromised their extremism somewhat to reap support from the moderate democrats. Naturally to expect the moderates to endorse another overthrow of the democracy was more than oligarchs could ever have hoped for in view of the political temperament of Athens generally. What they did expect and did receive from the moderates, although half-heartedly at times, was support in stunting the growth of the *demos*' power and discrediting the imperialists. And this the conservatives achieved principally by disavowing any further extension of the Athenian franchise and by opposing the increase of state expenditures.

Shortly after 403 two proposals were laid before the *Ecclesia* which reflect oligarchic refusal to grant more power to the *demos*. Phormisius moved to limit citizenship to property owners, an act which if passed would have reduced the body-politic by at least five thousand. Theoretically the proposal served a two-fold purpose: to cement a reconciliation between the conservatives and moderates by reverting to a pre-Cleisthenean constitution and to provide at the same time effective administration by responsible conservative citizens. In reality, however, Phormisius intended to weaken as much as possible the radical democrats because a major portion of democratic support was drawn from the non-propertied segment of the populace in Attica. But Archinus quickly recognized Phormisius' proposal had serious limitations that might prove detrimental not only to the moderates, but to the entire city-state as well and prevented its passage into law.

In the first place, many moderate democrats would be disenfranchised, for like Anytus they lost their property under the Thirty and had not retrieved it. In the second place the clamour of another civil war was imminent, for the democrats, through the eloquence of Lysias, seized upon the motion as being another attempt to undermine the democracy in favor of oligarchic élitism. Inasmuch as the proposal failed enactment, one can safely conclude moderate support was not forthcoming. Nevertheless, the conservatives received ample moderate support when they reject Thrasybuls' motion.

Thrasybulus, either out of commitment for aid provided or devout sympathy with radical democracy, proposed to confer citizen ship on everyone including slaves and metics who had returned with the democrats from Piraeus. Again the astute Achinus, as spokesman for both moderates and oligarchs, perceived inherent dangers in the measure and declared it unconstitutional, more to the relief of the oligarchs than the moderates. Were in enacted, the democratic ranks would have swelled considerably and accordingly state expenditures because of pay for state services. Conversely conservative and moderate influence in political administration would decrease while their taxes soared to provide *misthos* for the rabble.

In Phormisius' proposal and the failure of Thrasybulus' motion to receive the support of the people and in the ease with which Archinus annulled the latter, one definitely observes a temporary prevalence of oligarchic and moderate conservatism over the Athenian *demos*.[23] Be that as it may, the rejection of Thrasybulus' measure was for the oligarchs merely a token victory in internal politics, for the antecedent democracy of post-Periclean Athens was restored, state expenditures increased continually, and likewise their share of the liturgies. By 394/3 Agyrrhius had raised the *misthos ekklesiastikos* to three obols and the oligarchs regretfully observed the Pnyx overflowing with the lower elements of Athenian society.[24] Perhaps in concession to the *aristoi*'s opposition to the *misthos*, which they undoubtedly put forward, Archinus and Agyrrhius hoped to mitigate the economic burden of liturgies for the notables when they reduced the amount of state subsidies comic poets received to produce plays.[25] But to a *bona fide* oligarch the concession presumably appeared small compared to the large number of *mochtheroi* who ran pell mell to the *Ecclesia* to obtain their meal tickets.

Even more revolting was the sight of imperialist leeches that infested the coffers of Athena, sucking the economic blood of the *polis* while it was in the grips of another war for survival. In union with moderate democrats the malevolent conservatives immediately assailed the radicals in the courts, 392 to 387, and deprived them fo the leadership of Agyrrhius, Aristophanes, Ergocles, Philocrates, and Epicrates. Fate too seemed to favor the oligarchs when it removed Conon and Thrasybulus from the political scene. Unfortunately in the process, however, the oligarchs had to sacrifice one of their own, Phormisius.[26]

In retrospect, then, the oligarchs acheived only minor successes in internal affairs. Politically the *beltistoi* for the most part restricted temporarily Athenian extension of the franchise but did not halter the influence of the *demos*. They continued to serve as magistrates in the government but always under the close scrutiny of the imperialist democrats, for the notables only partially erased the stigma of their previous crimes. Their one major acheivement *via* the courts was to deprive the radicals of their leaders, although here the *gnorimoi* were not solely responsible because the imperialist chauvinists removed themselves through their inaptitude, peculations, and chicanery.

As for economics, here the conservatives did not enjoy one major victory to speak of, save perhaps the reduction of aid to comic poets. The liturgies and the *misthos* increased accordingly, and failure in this sphere of activity must be attributed to two factors. By 378/7 the tradition of receiving *misthos* for magisterial service and attendence in the Assembly was firmly entrenched as an integral part of Athenian political life. An economic platform which called for the reduction, much less for the abolishment, of the *misthos* courted staunch resistance and certain failure. Along those same lines, the exigencies, complexity, and expansion of governmental activity in the early fourth century necessitated some sort of inducement to enlist the aid of the populace in the reconstruction and maintenance of the Athenian state. The intensified individualism resultant with the Peloponessian War in terms of the demands made upon the citizenry for thirty years had to be offset somehow. This the oligarchs failed to perceive and appreciate. Their immediate and only concern was the sacrifices demanded of them, and this is quite understandable, considering the heavier burdens of liturgies oligarchs bore than the individual members of the *demos*.

Yet, in spite of their setbacks at home politically and economically, and perhaps in spite of themselves, the oligarchs unknowingly benefited Athenian democracy. Their niggardliness generally and their watchful eye for malfeasance of office were instrumental for the eventual introduction of professionalized financial adminstrators. Moreover, they unwittingly forced the *demos* to weigh carefully, but not always, the virtues of imperialist administrators and policies, particularly in foreign affairs. And in that realm of political activity the oligarchic party again enjoyed minor successes.

In foreign politics, as in domestic politics, the temperament of the oligarchs was predicated on the principles of conservatism and subterfuge. The apple of discord among democrats and oligarchs was whether or not Athens should throw off the yoke of docility to Sparta and pursue an aggressive, independent course of action. To the radical democrats self-determination in international politics meant political and economic imperialism, which in turn denoted the revival of Athenian hegemony. To the *beltistoi*, however, imperialism was anathema. Renewed hegemony conveyed an unrestrained *demos* and onerous trierarchies, two results which conservatives could ill-afford. The *beltistoi*, therefore, were content to remain *la chose de Sparte* because it suited their purposes of checkmating Athenian democracy. The radicals, as devout Athenian chauvinists, interpreted oligarchic submissiveness as "laconization."[27]

Considering the previous history of Athenian oligarchs, laconization, or appearance thereof, was only natural. Laconia in several instances had been the friend and benefactor to oligarchy. This was especially true after the Peloponessian War. From 404 to 395 Athenian oligarchs were heavily indebted politically and economically to Sparta. Upon the wings of Spartan victory oligarchy prevailed in Athens; a Spartan government and garrison sustained the Thirty's rule in its initial stages; subordination to Sparta was the cardinal rule of Critias and his colleagues; Spartan subsidies assisted the oligarchs in their war with the democrats; Spartan troops were enlisted in their war with the democrats; Spartas troops were enlisted by the Thirty, Ten and exiles in Eleusis when Thrasybulus' forces appeared to gain the upper hand; the Spartan Pausanias arbitrated the civil war and imposed the peace and amnesty; the presence of Milon, a Spartan harmost, nearby on Aegina probably intimidated the Athenians to observe the amnesty; and finally, Sparta favored and observed with keen interest the progress of Phormisius' proposal.[28]

In connection with the latter, it is quite apparent from the stylus of Lysias that the threat of Spartan intervention was imminent should the Athenians reject the motion, and that same fear of oligarchic appeal to Spartan intervention may, to some extent, have prompted Archinus to persuade the *Boule* to execute without trial an Athenian citizen who refused to abide by the anmesty's covenants.[29] Therefore, let it be established at the outset that guarantees were lacking the radical and moderate democrats that Sparta would not, or could not intervene in behalf of the oligarchs should their position in Athens worsen.

In testimony of that one must consider carefully that Sparta had a profound dislike for Athenian democracy, which accounts for Sparta's concurrence to Lysander's requests that the democracy be supplanted with oligarchy and later that the oligarchy must be supported in the civil war. Moreover, even Pausanias in 395/4 experienced Sparta's hatred towards the democracy when he was censured and condemned for his setback at Haliartus. Among the charges brought against him was that of allowing the Athenian democrats to escape in 402 though he had them in his power.[30] That the Athenians in general were aware of Sparta's enmity for the *demos* can justifiably be presumed to be a foregone conclusion.

On the reverse side of the coin, one should further consider the irrefutable fact that nowhere in the primary sources does one find assurances from the oligarchs to the *demos* that they would not betray the city again to Sparta in any given situation. In Athens oligarchs were especially notorious for betraying the city to other powers. Under the dominion of a foreigner the *gnorimoi* chafed less than under the subjugation of compatriots.[31] And this too both the oligarchs and the *demos* were cognizant of, which helps to explain in one sense why so many Athenians in Lysias' orations are constrained to prove their fidelity in deed and thought to the democracy, especially during the Corinthian War against Sparta. Hence Spartan intervention and oligarchic treachery complemented one another. Yet, in all fairness to the *beltistoi*, one must define their interpretation of laconization in foreign policy in the years preceeding the establishment of the Second Athenian Confederacy.

Intuitively speaking, an oligarch's definition of laconization never at any time implied the reduction of Athens to *helot* status. Simply put, it evolved from the basic premise that the Athenians should recognize without dispute the superiority of Sparta's military and political leadership on both sides of the Aegean. More benefits of a political and economic nature would accrue to Athens as a satellite member of the Peloponessian League than as a contender for Greek hegemony, despite Corinthian and Theban withdrawal from the confederation. The underlying rationale in the arguments which the conservatives offered in resistance to deviation from this norm was perhaps similar to the following.

Politically and militarily Athens would enjoy security from possible invasion by the Persian or a hostile Greek state and the elimination of *stasis* that arose over imperialism. Sparta, on the surface at least, had proven repeatedly the truth of this argument. After the Peloponessian War Sparta prevented Corinth and Thebes from ravaging Athens; Spartan mercenaries, for the most part, marched into the very heart of Artaxerxes' empire and returned virtually undefeated; and Lysander, Thibron, Dercylidas, and Agesilaus scored repeated victories in Asia Minor. Of no little import along these same lines was the facility with which Sparta chastized the Eleans without fear of reprisal from any Greek state. In other words, Sparta appeared more formidable in 395 than in 431, and oligarchs preferred to let sleeping dogs lie. And what could be said of Athens politically and economically from 403 to 395 in comparison, except in a negative sense?

To contest successfully Spartan supremacy and to re-enter the arena of imperialism required political stability, faithful allies, and naval rearmaments. Political stability was not in evidence in Athens, nor was there any hope of a unified, concerted effort at hegemony as long as the scrutiny trials against oligarchs held complete reconciliation between the parties in abeyance. Athenian allies in the previous conflict with Sparta proved totally unreliable, and Corinth and Thebes were not to be trusted because of their hegemonistic aspirations and all too recent conversion to the Athenian cause. Naval armaments were virtually non-existent, save for the twelve triremes Athens was permitted to keep at Sparta's pleasure. Even the walls were gone thus exposing Attica to invasion on land and the bays of Phalerum, Munychia, and Piraeus were menaced by the harmost on Aegina. In addition Athens lacked competent admirals who had proved their worth in naval encounters with Spartan corsairs. Apart from that, there was the economic situation to consider, and that more than the political or military aspect was of immediate concern to the wealthy who espoused the oligarchic cause, for in the absence of tribute their liturgies must underwrite the new venture of imperialism.

According to the *gnorimoi*, economic conditions in Athens were such that laconism was preferable to imperialism. The internal peace assured with membership in Sparta's league afforded Athenians an opportunity to recover fully from the distress of inflation and decline in agriculture, commerce, and industry, if in truth the decline after the Peloponessian War was as extensive as many authors traditionally report. With the necessity of naval rearmament, refortification, and maintaining anew garrisons abroad removed, state expeditures could be diverted elsewhere to enhance reconstruction generally and hasten the reinstitution of a sound coinage. This argument was fortified considerably when the oligarchs further pointed out the absence of allies and tribute meant the entire expense for imperialism must be borne by the Athenians, a factor which no doubt weighed heavily upon every mind and which more than any other confirmed the support of the moderate democrats. All things considered, the gamble for a new hegemony was not commensurate with the risks involved. That, to be sure, is precisely the meaning of the Oxyrhynchus historian's observation that the *gnorimoi* and moderates preferred to retain the *status quo*, laconism and impassiveness *in lieu* of imperialism and activism. Indeed, it would be superfluous to say anything other than oligarchic commitment to laconism was labored on the sincere belief that such a policy was in the best interests of the Athenianian state.

Inadvertently, however, oligarchs had overlooked the one major flaw in their laconization policy which the radicals seized upon to whip them into tacit agreement on imperialism. To be specific, laconization in foreign affairs was not a safeguard against Spartan rapacity in Attica. Inasmuch as this will be explored more fully later on, little need be said at this point beyond the statement that repeatedly imperialists hammered this argument home to the Athenians whenever the issue was debated. As for the oligarchs, the evidence clearly indicates that they remained unshaken from this view for the major part of the period under examination. Although expressions of laconization took a variety of forms, its prime outlets were through the media of philo-Spartanism and act calculated to enfeeble the war-spirit and the advent of imperialism.

In any discussion of a philolaconian faction in Athens during the early fourth century obstacles are encountered in the ancient sources and modern accounts. In the primary sources it is admittedly difficult to separate philolaconism from panhellenism because often times the latter served as a mask for the former, at least as far as the oligarchs are concerned. As the image of Sparta progressively tarnished from 403 to 378, thus did philolaconism meld ever more into panhellenism. For want of reliable sources which do indeed distinguish between the two, the discussion presented below will be confined solely to examples which are undeniably manifestations of affection for things laconian. The other obstacle was created by modern authors[32] who argue that Sparta had completely alienated everyone in Greece so that by 395 there was not in truth a laconophile faction in Athens. If there was, it had no connection with foreign policy. Needless to say, the validity of such an interpretaion of the primary sources warrants careful consideration, but as always the paramount factor must be what the Athenians thought, in particular the radicals. It is dubious to suppose that they viewed the actions of the oligarchs in any other light than the reflection of philolaconism. And there are other germane points worth considering which render neglibible resolute support of this hypothesis.

Inasmuch as the *demos* took a dim view of philolaconism, one could not expect the oligarchs to have flaunted carelessly admiration for Sparta. In the countenance of overt philolaconism Athenians were constantly reminded of their menial position in Greece, the rapine of the Thirty, and the loss of autonomy at home and abroad. Going further, public display of true oligarchic sentiments in politics was inconstant with the subsersive nature of the *gnorimoi* unless they were in complete control of the political machinery. To be precise, until the time was opportune, oligarchs usually avoided the hazard of risking everything by means of flagrant professions of laconism. To draw attention to themselves was to invite more scrutiny trials and rebuke from the *demos*, something which periled the effectiveness of oligarchy.

Yet their inhibitions concerning philolaconism can not be construed to imply that the fear of their fellow Athenians rescinding the amnesty provoked oligarchs into make a complete about-face in foreign policy in just eight short years after decades of acknowledging Spartan hegemony and undermining the constitution to please Sparta. Earlier above it has been shown that the threat of another Spartan intervention primarily validated observance of the amnesty which *Sparta itself dictated*, not the Athenians! Furthermore, one must reiterate two salient facts which bear directly on this discussion.

After 403 oligarchs had found refuge in the camp of the moderate democrats with whom they shared common ground on the question of absolute democracy and rampant imperialism. Hence it follows that some tempering of philolaconism was necessitated, but not complete negation. And in reverse, it is quite conceivable that oligarchs produced a tempering effect upon certain moderates, i.e., they became more tolerant and amiable towards Sparta.[33] In conjunction with this, it would be well to remember that oligarchs could not jeopardize the much needed support of the moderates by continuous display of philolaconism and *vice versa*. Undoubtedly this partially explains why the primary sources do not abound with examples of philolaconism during this period. Should the opportunity offer itself whereby oligarchs did not fear public reproach and reprisal and feel the need for continued moderate support, of one thing there can be no doubt. The *aristoi* definitely would be the first to sing paeans openly to Sparta as they did before in 403, and it is certain their number would not be small.[34] But to continue this line of argument is senseless, especially when the sources provide obtrusive examples of philolaconism.

At Thereamenes' trial in 403 Critias, oligarchy's leading protagonist prior to his death, pronounced emphatically the disposition of oligarchs towards Sparta. "The Spartan constitution is the superlative of covenants, whereas democracy is a harsh system for Athenians. The *demos* would never befriend Sparta, while the *beltistoi* would remain faithful to Sparta until the bitter end. It is for that reason Sparta condoned and helped us establish the present oligarchy. Therefore, in imitation of that *politeia* Theremenes must die."[35] Not a few oligarchs present on that occasion were still in Athens years later. While it is impossible to speculate on the number of those continued to adhere to these beliefs, nevertheless, it can be assumed that at least several remained faithful to Sparta.

Although the heated pen of Lysias does not state explicitly such was the case, in 403/2 philolaconism is clearly the inference in his vituperation of Athenians who advocated Phormisius' proposal because it would please Sparta.[36] In 396/5, however, he does not mince words in derisive censure of Athenians who bend over backwards to remain loyal to Sparta, who value oaths to Sparta more than pledges to their own citizens, and who are incensed if other Greeks surpass them in philolaconism.[37] Conceivably so Lysias' sharp words were directed primarily at the *gnorimoi* and those particular moderates who for the moment expediently "assumed the yoke of submissiveness to Sparta with unfaltering acquiescence," not the body politic in general.

Illustrative examples of tempered philolaconism are even found in Athenian pottery made in this period. Afraid that they might kindle the *timoria* wrath of the *demos*, artists of the early fourth century meticulously selected innocuous Spartan figures to be represented on cups and bell-craters. Apparently it was their belief that the figures of *Sparte* and Leonidas would excite Athenian rancor less than Spartans of more recent notoriety. Of course there is no way to prove that the potters or artists were oligarchs; but, bearing in mind the market appeal of pottery with philolaconian motifs, surely some of this ware found its way into the homes of several Athenian oligarchs.[38]

Before returning to the discussion of the anti-imperial demeanor of the *beltistoi*, another relevant fact must be pointed out which further attests to the existence of a philolaconian group in Athens during the first half of the fourth century. It is in this particular period of Athenian history that Critias, Xenophon, Plato, *et al.*, studied and extolled the virtues of the Spartan *rhetra* and venerated Spartan generals like Agesilaus. To say that their literary works influenced Athenians extensively would be fallacious. Yet the fact remains their words were read with avid interest by many *aristoi* who came into contact with them, and again the conjecture is self-evident that some impact was made.

To return to the original issue at hand, the conservatives' anti-imperial and laconizing manifesto called for retention of the *status quo* as faithful allies of Sparta and resistance to attempts that might alter the situation. To prevent the radicals from swaying the *demos* in favor of imperialism, the *gnorimoi* again drew upon the support of the moderates. Three incidents occurred before the outbreak of the Corinthian War which attest to the collusion of oligarchs and moderates and even reflect more leavens of philo-Spartanism.

Once the democracy was restored the Athenians were faced with the repayment of foreign loans contracted at Sparta and Thebes respectively by the oligarchs and democrats for pursuing the civil war. At first the Athenians decreed that each party assume responsibility for its own debts, then later made it incumbent upon both parties to share equally the burden of each other's debts, which in fact they did. The reasoning for the reversal according to the majority of authors[39] was the efficacious hope of total reconciliation and a question of material resources. That is to say, the oligarchs had impoverished the democrats with their rapacity and the civil war that ensued. Legally they were directly responsible for the foreign loans and since they retained the profits from what they stole, they should pay. Sentiment was not then the sole determining factor. Yet the very simplicity of such an explanation renders it circumspect in that it fails to relate in detail why oligarchs felt obliged to assume the debts of their enemy the *demos*. That answer is to be found in the advantages for the oligarchs.

In the first place, the oligarchs would not bear the expense alone. The change of mind made the *polis* responsible for the indebtedness and should the *polis* default on its payments to Sparta and Thebes, democracy would reap the blame, not oligarchy.

Secondly, repayment meant Athenian oligarchs *via* democracy honored their economic endebtedness to Sparta and simultaneously remained faithful allies. Finally, here was proffered an opportunity to efface more of the stigma of treason which hamstrung their effectiveness. Basically the same train of thought ran through their minds when they sent mercenary contingents to serve with Sparta and when they disavowed the expedition of Demaenetus.

Xenophon, anti-Athenian throughout, would have his readers believe that the contingents Athens sent to Elis and Persia *ca.* 399 were mainly cavalrymen who supported the Thirty because it would be a gain for democracy.[40] Accepting his interpretation at face value, one may further assume among these knights were ready volunteers from the oligarchs and moderates who welcomed the opportunity to prove Athens did not intend to contest Sparta's leadership in Greece and to escape the spiteful scrutiny trials of the radicals.[41] Four years later, 396/5, the Oxyrhynchus historian points out the *gnorimoi* and the moderates amassed their forces and prevailed upon Athens to repudiate Demaenetus' expedition to aid Conon in a state warship. According to the author, moderates and oligarchs were indignant because the imprudence of Demaenetus proclaimed an open breach in the peace with Sparta, a peace which contented both oligarchs and moderates.[42] Economic considerations enter into the picture to help explain why the oligarchs did not wish to undertake an open war with Sparta at this time, but compounded with that must go the reluctance of oligarchs to relinquish their attachment to Sparta.[43]

If the latter be true, to what does one attribute the willingness of the *gnorimoi* to forsake readily one year later their commitment to anti-imperialism and ally with Thebes against Sparta? Those who argue against the presence of a philolaconian faction quickly bring into contention Xenophon's assertive statements that the Athenians considered it their right to rule and as a result they voted unanimously for the Boeotian alliance.[44] Since it was common knowledge that Sparta threatened Thebes with imminent invasion, the only logical explanation for the unanimity of minds is the absence of pro-Spartan Athenians. Yet Xenophon himself provides evidence to the contrary, and in so doing invalidates his own report of the unanimous vote.

Precisely how many Athenians participated in the *Ecclesia*'s deliberations on that day is unknown; however, oligarchs were in attendance and were expected to demur when the motion was put to a vote. At one point in particular the Theban envoys appealed to the oligarchs to forsake their Lacedaemonian allies and regard them as enemies because of their duplicity.[45] Although the authenticity of the speech is questionable, it remains to be seen that Xenophon was aware that several oligarchs remained pro-Spartan in sentiment and opposition might arise from that quarter. Hence the speech and the appeal to the oligarchs serves the purpose of substantiating his earlier statement concerning Athenian claims to Greek hegemony. Of a similar nature is Xenophon's abortive attempt, as a prime exponent of philolaconism *himself,* to absolve Sparta as the aggressor and violator of the peace. For Xenophon the convenient scapegoats were Thebes and Athens. What better way to convince his readers than to report Thebes convinced everyone and the Athenians unanimously clamored for war.[46] But one must examine both sides of the coin to account for the abrupt change in foreign policy.

If, in fact, there was a unanimous vote, unanimity on this one occasion is insufficient proof for complete disbelief in the existence of an oligarchic, pro-Spartan party in Athens in 395. Nor does it necessarily imply a complete reversal in the temperament of the *gnorimoi,* especially in light of their reluctance later to sustain the war effort. A facile way of accounting for oligarchic caprice would be to suppose that the Theban envoys and the Athenian orator, whoever proposed the alliance,[47] were so convincing the heat of the moment all caution was thrown to the wind. But the plausibility of this view does not harmonize with Athenian attempts antecedent to the Theban embassy to forestall war, with the deliberations subsequent to the speech of the emissaries, nor with the overtones of reservation in Thrasybulus' reply to the envoys.

Somehow Athens had received information beforehand of Sparta's intent to mobilize against Boetia and fruitlessly pleaded with Sparta to submit to arbitration. After the Theban envoys arrived in Athens and made their plea, the deliberations in the *Ecclesia* saw the need for "many other orators" to speak in behalf of the alliance. Thrasybulus, in conveying the Assembly's reply to the Thebans, took care to add that Athens, failing walls, nevertheless would "risk the danger" of war with Sparta.[48] In comparison with oligarchic and moderate concern with the disavowal of Demaenetus' enterprise the year before, all of the above would further suggest that moderates and oligarchs hesitated on the issue of war in 395. A more credible explanation, however, for their acquiescence is to be found in the vicissitudes and developments in foreign affairs from 403 to 395. Each was of equal importance and is mutually related in inducement for oligarchs and moderates to consent to war.

By 395 Sparta's aggressiveness and predation in Greece and the eastern Aegean militated against its Athenian partisans from acting favorably to maintain the peace. Repeatedly complaints must have reached Athenian ears concerning Lacedaemon's corruption of Greek independence. Even Athens had felt the oppressive hand of Sparta. The subtle restraints Lacedaemon exercised in Athenian domestic policies nurtured the undying hatred of the *demos* for Sparta. Although Athens and other city-states had faithfully made good their debts and promises of aid for Spartan enterprises, Sparta sacrilegiously transgressed the limits of international law when it imposed upon the states noxious garrisons, violated the sanctity of their ambassadors, and refused to submit its grievances against Thebes to arbitration. Corinth, Thebes, Argos, and Persia were all dissatisfied with Sparta. Hand in hand with these considerations went the defensive nature of the alliance, the presence of powerful Theban hoplites, Persian finances and ships, and the checkmates of Thebes and Persia against renascent Athenian imperialism. All of the above served to cool philolaconism and to sway the *gnorimoi* over to the war effort, but not for long.[49]

Once the war was underway, oligarchs soon discovered that hostilities with Sparta had confirmed their premonitions that renascent imperialism would inevitably ensue. Fortifications, allies, and triremes reappeared in rapid succession along with rising taxes and increased power of the *demos*. In consequence the oligarchs restored to every device at their command to stop the war and stay imperialism. At Haliartus and Nemea in 394 a martial spirit was absent among the hoplites and cavalry whose members usually came from the inzealous, well-to-do oligarchs and moderates. The *demos* inveighed against them for their heartlessness as testified by the invectives heaped upon Alcibiades and Mantitheus' constrained defense in behalf of his participation in the campaigns. Yet, in a manner befitting the *beltistoi*, Mantitheus could not refrain from casting reproach upon the moderate imperialist Thrasybulus who favored continuing the hostilities.[50] A year or two later this ploy was used when the conservatives shirked their responsibilities as trierarchs and protested a possible tax increase to meet the rising costs of the war. Others, likely as not, numbered among those Athenians who falsely professed to be merchants, and thus take advantage of the law exempting men of commerce from liability to military service.[51] In spite of their efforts the war continued; nevertheless, their lack of martial spirit had a corrosive effect on the war-effort. At this point, providence took a turn in favor of the oligarchs.

The allies were unable to bring about a decisive victory over Sparta who seemed to gaining ground as the war progressed. Consequently the struggle degenerated into a war of attrition and deprived Athens of some of its allies who were totally unprepared for a prolonged effort to unseat Sparta. The real blow to Athens, however, came through a diplomatic maneuver on the part of Antalcidas. In 393/2 Antalcidas dexteriously convinced the Persian Satrap, Tiribazus, the machinations of Conon had effected a new Athenian imperialism detrimental to the interests of both Sparta and Persia. Tiribazus thereupon imprisoned Conon as a traitor to the King, thus depriving the imperialists of their leading protagonist and Athens of a competant admiral.[52] Nothing further need be said than the oligarchs were likely as not overcome with joy.

At the same time the oligarchs and their moderate comrades, it is not too much to say, prevailed upon the Athenians to listen, along with the Thebans, to the peace overtures of Sparta. Andocides and other envoys were dispatched to Lacedaemon to negotiate the terms of settlement. Based on the eloquent testimony of Andocides, it behoved Athens to come to terms because of the advantages Sparta offered. Corinth and Thebes, it seems, had negotiated not in the interests of the allies, but in their own behalf. Athens would do well to follow their example. Athens could retain Lemnos, Imbros, Scyros, its fleet, fortifications, and share Greek hegemony with Sparta.

Try as he may, however, to convince the radicals that the peace he negotiated was equitable and sincere, Andocides could not hide the diffuse strains of oligarchy in his words. His overlying theme stressed the munificence and amity of Sparta towards Athens, words which to the radicals and *demos* were treasonous and devoid of truth. Moreover, the peace offer was an empty one and negligible. Sparta's concessions, as far as the war hawks were concerned, were simply nothing more than belated *de jure* recognition, if that, of *de facto* Athenian accomplishments. Moreover, Sparta, in return for Persian aid, again was willing to bargain away the Ionians into Persian bondage. True enough it was that Athenian imperialism had previously abridged the autonomy of several Aegean states, but Athenian imperialism undeniably had always defended successfully the Ionians against Persia. To accede to Sparta's terms was to accept a dishonorable peace and whatever vestiges of new found hegemony Athens enjoyed in Greece might be lost. These and other arguements the radicals offered proved unassailable to the *demos* which rejected the hybrid peace of the moderates and oligarchs and sent Andocides into exile.[53]

Failing to stop the radicals in 392, the moderates and oligarchs found recourse through the media of the courts in an effort to discredit the imperialists. Here they repaid in kind the imperialists by indicting them for peculation and malfeasance of office. Playing upon the hatred of the *demos* for anyone who dipped into the public trough, the coalition with malediction by 387 stripped the imperialists of their leaders by employing basically the same arguments they used before in 399. They complained that radicals under the aegis of democracy were more tyrannical than the Thirty before them. Being poor they became wealthy rapidly. They held offices without rendering account; they pushed for war vehemently; and they caused the Athenians to be distrusted among the other Greeks. Such caustic indictments made a profound impression upon the citizens and robbed the imperialists of Agyrrhius, Ergocles, Aristophanes, Nicophemus, Philocrates, Dionysius, and Epicrates. Were it not for the inhabitants of Aspendus, the eminent Thrasybulus would have experienced a similar fate as well.[54] To retain the faith of the populace the *gnorimoi* sacrificed Phormisius for accepting bribes while on service abroad, but of late he may have proven expendable.[55]

The success achieved here convinced the oligarchs that the time was ripe to make another plea for peace. They keenly observed that the international situation had changed radically since 392. Persia had upset the balance of power in favor of Sparta by shifting its support from the allies to Lacedaemon. Dionysius of Syracuse foresook neutrality and offered Sparta the services of his war fleets to offset somewhat Sparta's naval loss at Cnidus. Corinth, Thebes, Argos, and other allies subsequently had either rejoined the Spartans or displayed discontent with the duration of the war. Teleutias under the cover of night had boldly sailed into Piraeus destroying triremes and hauling of much needed merchant vessels with grain. Thrasybulus of Collytus added a final touch to the situation by surrendering without resistance his command of triremes in the north. But the gravity of the situation spoke for itself and the oligarchs had only to remind the Athenians of the comparable situation they faced at the end of the Peloponessian War when Athens was helpless. The tide of opinion turned in their favor and Athens accepted the barbarians's peace. For the time being conservatism had won out.

Unfortunately for the years 387/6 to 378 the paucity of references to the oligarchic faction grieviously restrict any thoroughgoing analysis of their domestic and foreign policies. That which follows, therefore, must of necessity remain conjectural. At first glance it would appear that the oligarchs either vanished from the political scene or stood by innocuously in the wings of the Athenian stage. That such was not the case can be inferred from the scrutiny trial of Evandros, Sparta's capture of the Cadmea, and Sphodrias' invasion of Attica resulting in the ravaging of Thria in 397.

The trial of Evandros implies that oligarchs, like Thrasybulus of Collytus and the defendent himself, continued to serve in Athenian administration. The case against Evandros was a weak one, and Lysias himself was not convinced. The gist of the rhetor's complaint against Evandros does, however, suggest that oligarchs still masked as democrats to undermine democracy and continued to utilize the courts to remove their political adversaries like Leodamas. Simultaneously they expunged a little more the stigma of insidious oligarchy, for Evandros apparently survived the ordeal of *dokimasia* and became archon in 381/1.[56] But Athenian democracy persisted in spite of the oligarchs, and the subsequent years of Athenian history saw the *demos* increase its power. At any rate, the *chrestoi* probably became aware democracy was ringing its own death knell and it would not be long before pure individualism in Athens would force the *polis* to give up the ghost.

In foreign affairs it is equally possible that oligarchs enjoyed some inkling of success. Athenians made a concerted effort to adhere to the peace and rampant imperialism is not in evidence. A few, like Thrasybulus of Collytus, tenaciously preferred to practice laconism and 382 estranged Boetia from Athens for Sparta.[57] After the Cadmea was recovered and Sparta threatened Athens with reprisals, the possibility exists that oligarchs had a hand in punishing the impetuous Athenians who aided the Thebans. The circumstances in this incident compare favorably with oligarchic reaction to Demaenetus' expedition seventeen years earlier.

Nevertheless, Sparta, in the form of Sphodrias' invasion and its inexcusable failure to chastize him, did not stay its aggression. As a result whatever vestiges of oligarchic philolaconism remained in Athens perforce dwindles more and more into panhellenism. But the imperialists were not to be denied and oligarchs painfully observed the genesis of a new thalassocracy swaddled with the old burdens of trierarchies. True the new empire was a mere shadow of its former self, and in this too there may be kernels of oligarchic influence, for the character of the Second Athenian Confederacy explicitly forbade cleruchies. Until more evidence is brought to light, however, one must content oneself with the generalization that the conservative faction failed to prevent renascent imperialism, extension of the *demos'* power, and increased taxation. As a preventive agent, then, the oligarchic party was a failure, but as a restraining force it succeeded. And, without the support of the moderates, it is highly unlikely that the conservatives would have enjoyed these minor victories.

That, however, does not explain fully why oligarchic policies die not prevail in internal and foreign politics. A multiplicity of factors are worth comment, to be sure. Superficially speaking the failure of the oligarchs can be ascribed to their complicity in the defeat of Athens in 404, the recentness of the Thirty, and their association with Sparta. For the *demos* these factors were of prime consideration, but the underlying reasons must be sought in the nature of oligarchy itself and its tenêts in the declinng years of the fifth century and early decades of the fourth.

Oligarchs and oligarchy were ingrained with intellectual and political élitism and extreme conservatism. Intellectual élitism had fostered the maleficence and malignity of Pisander, Antiphon, Theramenes, Critias, Eratosthenes, Thrasybulus of Collytus, and others. Political élitism, be it in the pre-Solonian or pre-Cleisthenean mode, was totally incomprehensible and unpalatable to an Athenian *demos* which had thriven upon more than a century of increased rule. By 378 Athenians generally were inclined to believe most assuredly that, as one modern author so aptly phrased it, "democracy, then, as the rule of the whole people meant the perfection of the *polis*.[58] In face of that oligarchs and oligarchy waxed most pale and their succes was attainable only through deceit, subversion, terror, and treason. As an Athenian fifth column which wetnursed *stasis* and treachery, oligarchs could not hope to curry for any sustained period the favor of the commoners, whom they inherently despised anyway.

Moreover, their professions of extreme conservatism imbued them with a negative hindsight which did not allow for positive foresight. To attempt to revive the halcyon ancestral constitution was to alienate a citizenry which prided itself on progressivism in all levels of Athenian culture. By the end of the fifth century liberal democracy and thalassocracy had become synonymous, or, at the very least, implied one another in the minds of most Athenians. Any thought of deviation from this norm they regarded as anathema and the deviators as radical reactionaries. They synthetic quality of democracy's appeal politically, economically, and socially hence had captured the imagination of the Athenians. Briefly put, Athenian hegemony and democracy, then, constituted the ultimate expressions of pride in the city-state of Attica, and every citizen was afforded opportunity to participate and to share in the rewards. This the oligarchic reactionaries failed to perceive or refused to comprehend.

Oligarchy, in contrast, could not cope with these benefits. Politically the conservatives savored the exclusion of the lower elements of the body-politic from the citizenry. Socially they would have rendered the lower classes inferior. Economically they did not grasp the significance that trade and prosperity followed the flag of thalassocracy. Actually they were not atuned to the times in which they lived and were grieviously unaware that *eunomia, isonomia*, and *isegoria* depended upon the majority's will and not an élite, select few.

NOTES

1. On the amnesty and *paragraphê* see Aristotle, *Athenian Politeia*, XXXIX-LX; Xenophon, *Hellenica*, II. iv. 37-43; Lysias, XXV, 28-35; Isocrates, XVIII, 1-4; Aristophanes, *Plutus*, 11. 1146-4148; Ancocides, I, 90-91; Cornelius Nepos, *Thrasybulus*, III. ii.-iii.; Paul Cloché, *La restauration démocratique à Athénes en 403 avant J.-C.* (Paris, 1915), pp. 251-404, a thorough but belabored treatment; G. Busolt, *Griechesche Statskunde*, Zweite Hälfte, ed. Dr. Heinrich Sowboda, in *Handbuch der Altertumwissenschaft*, ed. Walter Otto, Vol. IV.1.1. (Munich, 1926), pp. 916-922; & C. Hignett, *A History of the Athenian Constitution to the End of the Fifth Century B.C.* (Oxford, 1952), pp. 293-298.

2. "εἰ μὲν οὖν οἴονται, ὅσα ὑπὸ τῶν τριάκοντα γεγένηται τῇ πόλει, ἐμοῦ κατηγορηκέναι, ἀδυνάτους αὐτοὺς ἡγοῦμαι λέγειν ... μέγα μὲν οὖν ἡγοῦμαί (μοι) τεκμήριον εἶναι, ὅτι, εἴπερ ἐδύναντο οἱ κατήγοροι ἰδίᾳ με ἀδικοῦντα ἐξελέγξαι, οὐκ ἄν τὰ τῶν τριάκοντα ἁμαρτήματα ἐμοῦ κατηγόρουν, οὐδ ἄν ᾤοντο χρῆναι ὑπὲρ τῶν ἐκείνοις πεπραγμένων ἑτέρους διαβάλλειν, ἀλλ αὐτοὺς τοὺς ἀδικοῦντας τιμωρεῖσθα» κ.τ.λ." Lysias, XXV, 2, 5-7.

3. Cf. K.J. Beloch, *Die attische Politik seit Perikles* (Leipzig, 1884), pp. 113-114, who keenly observes that Athenian fears of another oligarchic revolution were groundless because the Thirty and its predatory deeds did more to ensconce democracy in Athens than anything the democrats had done for a century.

4. Leonard Whibley, *Political Parties in Athens During the Peloponessian War* (Cambridge, 1889), pp. 48-49; & idem, *Greek Oligarchies Their Character and Organization* (London, 1896), pp. 22-31. Cf. Robin Seager, "Thrasybulus, Conon, and Athenian Imperialism 396-386 B.C.," *Journal of Hellenic Studies*, LXXXVII (1967), 95, who reports γνώριμοι καὶ χαρίεντες is a phrase equivalent with "such meaningless modern collectives as *tous les honnêtes gens*." Hence it does not refer to a party or permanent political group in *Hellenica Oxyrhynchia*, I. ii. Meyer, however, *Theopomps Hellenika*, (Halle a./S., 1909), p. 49; I. A. F. Bruce, "Athenian Foreign Policy in 396-395 B.C.," *The Classical Journal*, LVIII (April, 1963), 290; idem, *An Historical Commentary on the 'Hellenica Oxyrhynchia'* (Cambridge, 1967), p. 53; Georges Mathieu, "La réorganisation du corps civique athénien à la fin du Ve siècle," *Revue des Études Grecques*, XL (1927), 67, demonstrate the reverse is true.

5. Beloch, *A.P.P.*, p. 119, is especially guilty of this line of reasoning when he cites Aristophanes, *Ecclesiazusae*, 1. 300, as conclusive proof that oligarchs were excluded from political administration until Conon's return. The improbability of his view is explored more fully below n. 19.

6. A. W. Gomme, *The Population of Athens in the Fifth and Fourth Centuries B.C.* (Oxford, 1933), pp. 37-39. In any discussion of Athenian political parties one must always bear in mind the caprice of the rank and file with respect to particular issues of the day. Lysias, XXV, 8-11, is most explicit on this point. "πρῶτον μὲν οὖν ἐνθυμηθῆναι χρὴ ὅτι οὐδείς ἐστιν ἀνθρώπων φύσει οὔτε ὀλιγαρχικὸς οὔτε δημοκρατικὸς, ἀλλ' ἥτις ἂν ἑκάστῳ πολιτεία συμφέρῃ, ταύτην προθυμεῖται καθεστάναι! ... σκέψασθε γάρ, ὦ ἄνδρες δικασταί, τοὺς προστάντας ἀμφοτέρων (τῶν) πολιτειῶν, ὁσάκις δὴ μετεβάλοντο.... οὔκουν χαλεπὸν γνῶναι, ὦ ἄνδρες δικασταί, ὅτι οὐ περὶ πολιτείας εἰσὶν αἱ πρὸς ἀλλήλους διαφοραί, ἀλλὰ περὶ τῶν ἰδίᾳ συμφερόντων ἑκάστῳ." Basically this same view is expresed by M. I. Finley, "Athenian Demagogues," *Past and Present*, XXI (April, 1962), 3-24.

7. Modern authors have not satisfactorily resolved the question whether Andocides was an oligarch, moderate, or democrat after his return to Athens. Nor for that matter do his orations provide conclusive evidence one way or another. The significant factor is that the Athenians thought he carried the "odour of oligarchy" with him no matter what he professed to be. So R. C. Jebb, *The Attic Orators*, I (London, 1893), pp. 83-85.

8. Aristotle, *Ath. Pol.*, XL. 1-2.

9. Andocides, I, 12, 35, 63 94-101; Xenophon, *Hell.*, II. iv. 36; & Jebb, *Att. Orat.*, I, pp. 114-115, n. 1 p. 115.

10 "..: ἐπίστασθε γάρ ἐν ταῖς ἐφ' ἡμῶν ὀλιγαρχίαις γεγενημέναις οὐ τοὺς γῆν κεκτημένους ἔχοντας τὴν πόλιν, ἀλλὰ πολλοὺς μὲν αὐτῶν ἀποθανόντας, πολλοὺς δ' ἐκ τῆς πόλεως ἐκπεσόντας, ..., ἄλλως τε καὶ μεμνημένοι τῶν περὶ τῆς ὀλιγαρχίας μαχομένων, οἳ τῷ λόγῳ τῷ δήμῳ πολεμοῦσι, τῷ δὲ ἔργῳ τῶν ὑμετέρων ἐπιθυμοῦσιν.... Καὶ εἰ μὲν ἑωρᾶτε, ὦ ἄνδρες δικασταί, σῳζόμενα τῇ πόλει τὰ ὑπὸ τούτων δημευόμενα, συγγνώμην ἂν εἴχομεν νῦν δ' ἐπίστασθε ὅτι τὰ μὲν αὐτῶν ὑπὸ τούτων ἀφανίζεται, τὰ δὲ πολλοῦ ἄξια ὄντα ὀλίγου πιπράσκεται." Lysias, XXXIV, 4-6; XVIII, 19-20; XII, 81, 85-92; XXVI, 22-23; XIX, 45 f.; XVI, 5-6, *et passim*; XXV, 2-3, 9-12, 18; XXX, 9-10, 15-17; Isocrates, VII, 66-67; & George Grote, *History of Greece*, vol. VIII (New York, 1897), pp. 292-293.

11. There is ample evidence to prove Thrasybulus of Collytus was an oligarch, espec. in Lysias, XXVI, 21-24; Xenophon, *Hell*, V. i. 26-28; Aeschines, *Against Ctesiphon*, 138; Jebb, *Att. Orat.* I, pp. 237-240; Walter Schwahn, "Thrasybulos aus Kollytos," *Pauly-Wissowa Realencyclopädie der Classischen Altertums-wissenschaft*, Zweite Reihe, Elfter Halband, ed. W. Kroll and K. Mittelhaus (Stuttgart, 1936), p. 575; & *Prosopographia Attica*, ed. Johannes Kirchner, rev. Siegfried Lauffer (Berling, 1966), 7305, where it is shown he surrendered ships without a fight in the Hellespont to Sparta in 387, was a member of an oligarchic clique, extracted bribes from Athenians to secure their release as Spartan

prisoners of war, and aided the Spartans in their capture of the Cadmea thus depriving Athens of an ally.

12. Whibley, *Polit. Parties*, p. 15.

13. It is odd to note that many sources, both primary and secondary, state clearly that these moderate oligarchs did indeed fight alongside the democrats to win back the city from the Thirty. What they fail to mention is whether they left the city before or after Theramenes' death. I am inclined to believe they left after because their association with Theramenes, or other members of the régime, afforded them some measure of security.

14. "καὶ τούων μὲν οὐ θαυμάζω, ὑμῶν δὲ τῶν ἀκροωμένων, ὅτι πάντων ἐστὲ ἐπιλησμονέστατοι ἢ πάσχειν ἑτοιμότατοι κακῶς ὑπὸ τοιούτων ἀνδρῶν, οἳ τῇ μὲν τύχῃ τῶν Πειραιοῖ πραγμάτων μετέσχον, τῇ δὲ γνώμῃ τῶν ἐξ, ἄστεως." Lysías, XXXIV, 2-3; XVI; XXVI; XXX; Aristotle, *Ath. Pol.*, XXVII. 5, XXXIV, 3, XXXVI. 1-2; Xenophon, *Hell.*, II. iii. 47-50; & *Hell. Oxy.*, I. ii.-iii. Cf. Bruce, *C.J.*, 290-291, who, based solely on Platon, *Presbeis*, frag. 119-122, takes exception to Phormisius because he was on an embassy with an imperialist to the King shortly after 394 and received bribes. Associations with imperialists and acceptance of bribes do not make a radical. Besides the majority of primary and secondary sources definitely agree Phormisius' sympathies lay more with the moderate oligarchs.

15. Lysias, XIV, 8 f.; XV; XVI, 13, 15, 18,; Xenophon, *Memorabilia*, III. v. 19.

16. In addition to those ancient sources cited above, the brief description of the conservative party's membership is further based on those comments in the following modern accounts. Cloché, *R.D.A.*, pp. 11-12, 42, 69-71, 86-87, 366-385, 405-412, 420-446, 474-475; idem, *La politique ètrangère d'Athènes de 404 à 338 avant Jésus-Christ* (Paris, 1934), pp. 6-8;, idem, "Les conflicts politiques et sociaux à Athènes pendant la guerre corinthienne (395-387 avant J.-C.), "*Revue des Études Anciennes*, XXI (1919), 157-159; Mathieu, *R.E.G.*, 67-72, 104-111; Beloch, *A.P.P.*, pp. 111, 113-114; Busolt, *G.S.*, II, pp. 917-920; Meyer, *Theo. Hell.*, pp. 48-50; Donald Kagen, "The Economic Origins of the Corinthian War," *La Parola del Passato*, LXXX (1961), 325-326; Bruce, C.J., 290-292; Whibley, *Polit. Parties*, pp. 37, 79-91; & idem, *Gk. Olig.*, pp. 1-45, 105-139.

17. Thucydides, VIII. lxiv.-lxxviii., xc.-xcii.; Xenophon, *Hell.*, I. vii. 8-12, 28-29, II. ii. 16-24, iii. 27-29, 30, 32, 45-47; & Lysias, XII, 36, 38-41, 43-46, 51,68, 70-72, XIV, 34-35, XXX, 10-14.

18. Lysias vividly intones the *demos*' hatred for the oligarchs in XII, XVI, XVIII, XXV, XXVI, & XXXIV. On the superficial conversion of the oligarchs see in particular Lysias, XII, 81, 86-87, XVIII, 19-20, XXV, 12-14, XXVIII, 10-17, XXX, 7-17, XXXIV, 1-3; Isocrates, VIII, 108; Busolt, *G.S.*, II, pp. 923-924; Beloch, *A.P.P.*, pp. 114-115; & Cloché, *P.E.A.*, pp. 6-8. I seriously question, however, the number and success with which oligarchs infiltrated imperialist ranks. Doubtless the number would be small considering imperialist distaste for anything or anyone oligarchic.

19. Beloch, *A.P.P.*, p. 111, concedes this point as far as Archinus and Anytus are concerned. But later, p. 119, he maintains, relying completely on Aristophanes, *Eccles.*, 1. 300, that oligarchs were excluded from political administration until Conon's return to Athens in 394/3. In this, it seems to me, he is grossly mistaken for three reasons. First, *hoi ex asteos* in this instance does not refer to the oligarchic party in any way whatsoever. Within the context, 11. 300-310, *hoi ex asteos* is in reference to the apathetic lower element of urban Athens which Aristophanes berates for its refusal to attend the *Ecclesia* until the introduction and increase of the *ecclesiastikos*. Since oligarchs traditionally opposed any measure which swelled the *Ecclesia* with the *demos'* influence, they least of all would have absented themselves from the Pnyx until pay for attendence was provided. Their presence is especially noted in 396/5 opposing the venture of Demaenetus and again in 395 when Thebes proposed the Attic-Boeotian alliance—*Hell. Oxy.*, I. ii.; & Xenophon, *Hell.*, III. v. 9-10. Second, even with the *ecclesiastikos* only the wealthier citizens could afford to serve as magistrates and not everyone who attended the *Ecclesia* was compensated—so A. H. M. Jones, *Athenian Democracy* (Oxford, 1964), pp. 17-18, 51-50. Finally, the amnesty would have been meaningless if oligarchs were totally excluded from the administration—see n. 20 *infra*. Moderates especially would not have tolerated their exclusion because a major portion of their support came from the oligarchic faction.

20. Aristotle, *Ath. Pol.*, XXXIX-XLI; Xenophon, *Apology*, XXIX-XXX; *idem, Hell.*, II. iv. 43; Andocides, I, 82, 84, 85, 150; Lysias, XVI, XXII, 8 f., XXVI; Hignett, *H.A.C.*, pp. 294-296; Eduard Meyer, *Geschichte des Altertums*, 3rd ed., Vol. V (Berlin, 1921), 216, 231; Mathieu, *R.E.G.*, 82-98; Cloché, *R.D.A.*, pp. 251 *et passim*; *idem, P.E.A.*, pp. 9, 12; Busolt, *G.S.*, II, pp. 916-919, 922-924; Jebb, *Att. Orat.*, I, pp. 237-243, 256-264; & n. 14 *supra*, all concur oligarchs actively participated in the administration except Eratosthenes.

21. These nocturnal conclaves are discussed in George M. Calhoun, *Athenian Clubs in Politics and Litigation*, in *Humanistic Series, No. 14, Bulletin of the University of Texas*, CCLXII (Austin, Jan. 8, 1913), pp. 10-39.

22. "καὶ τῷ δήμῳ κακόνους ἔσομαι καὶ βουλεύσω ὅ τι ἂν ἔχω κακόν, ... ἡμεῖς δὲ γνόντες μὲν τοῖς ὅοις ἡμῖν τε καὶ ὑμῖν χαλεπὴν πολιτείαν εἶναι δημοκρατίαν, ... καὶ ἐάν τινα αἰσθανώμεθα ἐναντίον τῇ ὀλιγαρχίᾳ, ὅσον δυνάμεθα ἐκποδὼν ποιούμεθα κ.τ.λ." Aristotle, *Politica*, 1310 a; & Xenophon, *Hell.*, II. iii. 25-27.

23. Aristotle, *Ath. Pol.*, XL; Lysias, XXXIV; Aeschines, III, 195; Hignett, *H.A.C.*, pp. 295-298; Meyer, *G.D.A.*, V, pp. 216, 220-222; Mathieu, *R.E.G.*, 82-98; Ulrich von Wilamowitz-Moellendorff, *Aristoteles und Athen*, II, 2nd ed. (Berlin, 1966), pp. 223-230; Beloch, *G.G.*, III.1, pp. 13-15; Cloché, *R.D.A.*, pp. 420-469; & Grote, *H.G.*, VIII, pp. 294-295.

24. Aristophanes, *Eccles.*, 11. 176-188, 289-310, 375-393; Aristotle, *Ath. Pol.*, XL. 3; & Benjamin B. Rogers, *The Comedies of Aristophanes*, V (London, 1919), p. 18, n. 102. Not a few authors, based on Aristophanes' strictures of Agyrrhius and the *misthos*, believe irresponsible government ensued as a

result of the masses attending the Assembly merely to obtain their daily bread. Busolt, *G.S.*, II, pp. 921-922, is particularly adamant on this point, for "Nun füllte sich die Versammlung mit der Masse des anwachsenden Stattvolkes, das fortan mit seinem zahlenmässigen Übergewicht die Enscheidung.... Die Menge gewöhnte mehr und mehr daran, Tagegelder für mühelose, unveranwortliche Staatsdienste zu empfangen." Jones, n. 20 *supra*, justifiably calls for moderation of this view. In addition, far too many authors forget that Aristophanes had a particular bone to pick with the *misthos* because it was introduced and later raised by the same men who was partly responsible for reducing the state gratuity doled to comic poets to defray production expenses. See Rogers *supra*, also pp. 56-57, n. 367; & *Scholia Aristophanica*, II, ed. Wm. G. Rutherford (London, 1896), pp. 517-518, n. 102.

25. See n. 24 *supra*; & W. Judeich, "Archinos," *Pauly-Wissowa*, II.1, pp. 540-541.

26. Lysias, XXVII, XXVIII, XXIX; Demosthenes, XXIV, 134, *De Falsa Legatione*, 315; Platon, *Presbeis*, frag. 119-121; Andocides, I, 133-135; Cloché, *R.E.A.*, 160, 186-192; *idem*, *P.E.A.*, pp. 29-30, 45 f.; & Beloch, *A.P.P.*, pp. 122-123, 130-131.

27. "τὸ δ' οὖν κεφάλαιον τῆς ἑκατέρον διανοίας τοιοῦτον ἦν· οἱ μὲν (ὀλιγάρχαι) γὰρ ἠξίουν τῶν μὲν πολιτῶν ἄρχειν, τοῖς δὲ πολίταις δουλεύειν, οἱ δὲ (δῆμοι) τῶν μὲν ἄλλων ἄρχειν, τοῖς δὲ πολίταις ἴσον ἔχειν." Isocrates, VII, 69-70, IV, 110-115.

28. Lysias, XII, 58-61, 94-95, XVIII, 22, XXVI, 19-21, XXXIV, 6-11; Isocrates, IV, 110-113, VII, 65-70; Plutarch, *Lysander*, XV. 5, XXI; Aristotole, *Ath. Pol.*, LXXXIV. 2, XXXVII. 2, XXXVIII. 2-XXXIX, XL. 3; Xenophon, *Hell.*, II. iii. 13-15, 41, iv. 4, 10-12, 28-43; Cloché, *R.D.A.*, pp. 186-250; & nn. 17, 23, *supra*.

29. Aristotle, *Ath. Pol.*, XL. 2; Isocrates, XVIII, 2-5, 20; Lysias, XXV, 7 f. Cf. Mathieu, *R.E.G.*, 110-111; Meyer, *G.D.A.*, V, p. 216; & espec. Cloché, *R.D.A.*, pp. 441-443, who believe that the Spartan threat was not immediately imminent should Phormisius' measure fail enactment because the rivalry between Pausanias and Lysander rendered intervention improbable and Sparta was too preoccupied with Elis. All things considered, I doubt if the Athenians were as certain of that as Cloché *et. al.*, and that is the essential factor which must not be overlooked, i.e., what the Athenians thought might happen and what actually did occur are quite different.

30. Besides those references cited in n. 28 above, see further the statements of Xenophon, Hell., III. v. 25; & Plutarch, *Lysander*, XXI.3-XXII. Along these same lines, cf. Pausanias, *Description of Greece*, III. v. 1-3, who dates the censure of Pausanias in 403/2.

31. "To the Greek, (especially to the Athenian), to be ruled by his political opponents was an intolerable humiliation, to be averted at any cost, even if it became necessary to deliver his state into the hands of its foeman.... Athens was no exception to this rule." Calhoun, *Athenian Clubs*, p. 141.

32. Especially Bruce, *C.J.*, 291-294; & S. Perlman, "The Causes and the Outbreak of the Corinthian War," *Classical Quarterly*, XIII-XIV (1963-64), 70, neither of whom seems to be aware of the other's theories although both are identical. To dismiss completely their arguments would be unfair to the conservative faction. The crux of their view is based on primary sources which refute rather than substantiate *in toto* the non-existance of a philolaconian faction. Perlman in particular strains hard to apply a Thucydidean formula to explain the outbreak of the Corinthian war, i.e., fear of Spartan imperialism. Relatively speaking the blame perhaps lies more on the Oxyrhynchus historian, Perlman's main source, for he tries even harder to follow the path of Thucydides. At any rate, the improbability of thier view will be discussed more thoroughly on the subsequent pages above.

33. That is exactly what Cloché, "Notes sur la politique athénienne au début du IVe siècle et pendant la guerre du péloponèse," *R.E.A.*, XLIII (1941), 18; & *idem*, *P.E.A.*, pp. 7-8, 11-12, means when he states "... ; mais cette attitude 'philolaconienne' m'est pas précisément la même que celle de Cimon: fervent admirateur de Sparte, assurément, le fils de Miltiade n'avait jamais subordonné—comme le feront jusqu'en 395 les dirigeants de la démocratie restaurée—l'activité athénienne aux exigences de la puissante cité du Péloponèse; son idéal, c'était l'hégémonie commune d'Athènes et de Lacédemone, et non la soumission de l'une aux volontés de l'autre." Cf. Kagan, *P.d.P.*, 329, who also adheres to this interpretation.

34. Thucydides, VIII. lxvi.-lxvii., basically imparts this line of reasoning in discussing the success of the oligarchic revolution and the astonishment of the Athenians at those of their neighbors whom no one would have thought capable of joining oligarchy. In sum, to be an oligarchic in this period was to be philolaconian because it suited their purposes of stopping democracy. See also Whibley, *Polit. Parties*, pp. 79-81; & Calhoun, *Athenian Clubs*, p. 142 f., whose statements are ignored by both Perlman and Bruce.

35. "ἡμεῖς δὲ γνόντες μέν τοῖς ὅοις ἡμῖν τε καί ὑμῖν χαλεπὴν πολιτείαν εἶναι δημοκρατίαν, γνόντεδ δὲ ὅτι Λακεδαιμονίοις τοῖς περισώσασιν ἡμᾶς ὁ μὲν δῆμος οὔποτ', ἂν φίλος γένοιτο, οἱ δὲ βέλτιστοι ἀεὶ ἂν πιστοὶ διατελοῖεν, διὰ ταῦτα οὖν τῇ Λακεδαιμονίων γνώμῃ τήνδε τὴν πολιτείαν καθίσταμεν.... καλλίστη μὲν γὰρ δήπου δοκεῖ πολιτεία εἶναι ἡ Λακεδαιμονίων κ.τ.λ." Xenophon, *Hell.*, II. iii. 25, 34; & G. E. Underhill, *A Commentary on the Hellenica of Xenophon* (Oxford, 1899), p. 59. Along these same lines, see also Isocrates, IV, 110, VII, 61.

36. XXXIV, 6-7.

37. "οὐκ οὖν αἰσχρόν, εἰ ἅ μὲν Λακεδαιμονίοις συνέθεσθε βεβαιώσετε, ἅ δὲ αὑτοῖς ἐψηφίσασβε οὕτω ῥαδίως διαλύσετε, καὶ τὰς μέν πρὸς ἐκείνους συνθήκας κυρίας ποιήσετε, τὰς δὲ πρὸς αὑτοὺς ἀκύρους· καὶ τοῖς μὲν ἄλλοις Ἕλλησιν ὀργίζεσθε, εἴ τις Λακεδαιμονίους ὑμῶν περὶ πλείονος ποιεῖται, ὑμεῖς δ' αὐτοὶ φανήσεσθε πιστότερον πρὸς ἐκείνους ἢ πρὸς ὑμᾶς διακείμενοι;" XVIII, 15-16. Neither Bruce nor Perlman grasp the full significance of this passage. Nor, for that matter, do many authors cited in n. 16 above.

According to them, here is *carte blanche* evidence to prove *all* Athenians were loyally submissive to Sparta. But again, taking into account the basic nature of the oration, I call for moderation to the extent that submissiveness was expedient and that only the oligarchs and certain moderates were philolaconian.

38. J. D. Beazley, Vol. III of L. D. Caskey, and J. D. Beazley, *Attic Vase Paintings in the Museum of Fine Arts, Boston* (Boston, 1963), p. 91-92; & Peter E. Corbett, "ΛΕΩΝ ΕΠΙ ΛΕΩΝΙΔΗΙ," *Eesperia*, XVIII (1949), 104-107.

39. Aristotle, *Ath. Pol.*, XXXIX. 6, XLI. 3-4; Isocrates, VII, 68-69; & those references in n. 16 *supra*.

40. *Hell.*, III. i. 4-5.

41. Cf. Meyer, *G.d.A.*, V, pp. 218-219, who pays lip service to this line of reasoning.

42. *Hell. Oxy.*, I.-II.; B. P. Grenfell, and A. S. Hunt, *The Oxyrhynchus Papyri*, Part V (London, 1908), pp. 202-203, nn. i.3 & i.16; Bruce, *Comm. Hell. Oxy.*, pp. 50-57; & *Idem*, *C.J.*, 292-294.

43. Bruce, n. 42 above, objects because the Oxyrhynchus historian neglects to mention that a pro-Spartan group existed at Athens in 396; that the democrats and oligarchs were not divided on domestic issues; and that thus they were not divided on foreign politics. In refutation of the latter I refer the reader to the discussions within the text where it has been shown there was division on domestic issues. Moreover, taken *prima facie*, Bruce thereupon presumes the reconciliation was genuine and complete harmony existed between the various factions in Athens, despite primary source evidence to the contrary in Lysias, Isocrates, *et. al*. Needless to say, Bruce would do well to examine these sources more closely. In response to his first objection, not a few ancient sources fail to mention that which is assumed to be common knowledge, e.g., Herodotus and Thucydides. Xenophon himself is most aggravating on this score for this period, for his *Hellinica*, among other things, ignores Demaenetus' expedition and details concerning the reconciliation. See Underhill, *Comm. Hell. Xen.*, ix-xxxi. In sum, the silence of one particular biased source is inconclusive and insufficient evidence for discounting the presence of a philolaconian group in Athens.

44. *Hell.*, III. v. 2, 16. Andocides, III, 25 f., does explain the reasoning for concluding the alliance. His comments, however, reveal in the main those arguments with which the imperialists persuaded the populace to join the war effort. Bruce, n. 42 *supra*, lays too much stress on the unanimity of the vote. Yet his principal source, Grote, *H.G.*, IX, pp. 292-294, after praising the Athenians for thie unanimity of mind, gives full consideration to the other factors involved, which also will be discussed within the text.

45. "πολὺ δ' ἔτι μᾶλλον ἀξιοῦμεν, ὅσοι τῶν ἐν ἄστει ἐγένεσθε, προθύμως ἐπὶ τοὺς Λακεδαιμονίους ἰέναι. ἐκεῖνοι γὰρ καταστήσαντες ὑμᾶς εἰς ὀλιγαρχίαν καὶ εἰς ἔχθραν τῷ δήμῳ, ἀφικόμενοι πολλῇ δυνάμει ὡς ὑμῖν σύμμαχοι παρέδοσαν ὑ-

μᾶς τῷ πλήθει· ὥστε τὸ μὲν ἐπ᾽ ἐκείνους εἶναι ἀπολώλατε, ὁ δὲ δῆμος οὑτοσὶ ὑμᾶς ἔσωσε." *Hell.*, III. v. 9-10; & Underhill, *Comm. Hell. Xen.*, p. 114. Bruce dismisses in a cavalier fashion the import of this speech, but Grote does not. Cf. further how this passage echoes Thrasybulus' admonitions to the oligarchs after the civil war ended—II. iv. 41-42.

46. Along these same lines see Grote, *H.G.*, X, pp. 287-288; & Seager, *J.H.S.*, 96-97. Although Grote is cognizant of the laconian bias which permeates Xenophon's discussion of the war's causes, he directs his attention more to Timocrates' bribery of the various states. Underhill, *Comm. Hell. Xen.*, p. 112, vindicates Xenophon somewhat by showing that Xenophon's report of the Attic-Boeotian alliance is an attempt to prove that Thebes was conducting a more energetic foreign policy than previously assumed. Cf. Cloché, *R.E.G.*, 315-343; & *Idem, Thèbes de Béotie*, pp. 95-116, who agrees with Underhill.

47. A veritable host of modern authors on the basis of pure inference only maintain that Thrasybulus of Steiria advocated and proposed the conclusion of the Attic-Theban alliance of 396/5. Inasmuch as I intend to disprove this fallacy in a future essay, suffice it to say that the actual inscription itself does not warrant such a conclusion. See Tod, *G.H.I.*, II, "101."

48. *Hell.* III. V. 16; and Pausanias, III. ix. II.

49. *Hell. Oxy.*, I. iii.-II. iv.; Pausanias, III. ix. 11; Xenophon, *Hell.*, III. v. 14; Andocides, III, 25 f.; T. T. B. Ryder, *Koene Eirene, General Peace and Local Independence in Ancient Greece* (London, 1965), pp. 22-25; Coleman Phillipson, *The International Law and Custom of Ancient Greece and Rome*, I (London, 1911), pp. 309, 328-330, II, pp. 182-189; Kagan, *P.d.P.*, 325-326, 328-329; Cloché, *P.E.A.*, pp. 13-16; *idem, R.E.A.*, 164-165; & Grenfell-Hunt, *Oxy. Papyri*, pp. 203-205, nn. i.30-36. Bruce, *C.J.*, 94, is incredulous with respect to the defensive nature of the alliance. For him it is too simple and no other philolaconians were so morally inclined *par example* Leontiades of Thebes. But Cloché, *R.E.G.*, 333 f., & Perlman, *C.Q.*, 66, show that Leontiades did in fact compromise his sentiments for expediency, as, I might add, the Athenian oligarchs wisely did. Apart from Bruce's unawareness of Cloché and Perlman's views, he does not appear to comprehend the underlying rationale behind the formation of defensive alliances as opposed to offensive convenants.

50. Lysias, XIV, 8 f., XV, XVI, 13, 15, 18; Xenophon, *Memorabilia*, III. v. 19; Cloché, *P.E.A.*, pp. 16-17; & *idem, R.-E.A.*, 166-167. Upon reflection of present day events, the unwillingness to serve in the ranks is not so unique. One might muse upon the number of bonfires lit with oligarchic draftcards in Athens.

51. Aristophanes, *Eccles.*, 11. 195-198, 825-829, 1027; *Plutus*, 11. 904-906; Rogers, *Com. of Arist.*, V, pp. 32-33, n. 197, 128-129, n. 825, 156, n. 1027; Beloch, *A.P.P.*, pp. 124-125; & Cloché, *R.E.A.*, 170-174.

52. Xenophon, *Hell.*, IV. viii. 12-17; Lysias, XIX, 41-42, 44; Nepos, *Conon*, V; Isocrates, IV, 180; & Grote, *H.G.*, IX, pp. 358-361.

53. Andocides, III, 3-7, 10-20, 21-24, 32-33, 39; W. Judeich, "Die Zeit der Friedensrede des Andokides," *Philogus*, LXXXI (1926), 141-154; Cloché, *P.E.A.*, pp. 16-17, 22-30; *idem, R.E.A.*, 177-183; Meyer, *G.d.A.*, V, pp. 252-253; Beloch, *A.P.P.*, pp. 122-123; & Jebb, *Att. Orat.*, I, pp. 83-85.

54. Lysias, XXV, 30-35, XXVII, XXVIII, 10-17, XXIX; Demosthenes, *De Falsa Legatione*, 134; *idem*, XXIV, 135; Meyer, *Theo. Hell.*, pp. 52-54; Cloché, *R.E.A.*, 160, 186-192; *idem, P.E.A..*, pp. 29-30, 41-45; & Beloch, *A.P.P.*, 130. On the use of the courts as common media for the dissemination of slanderous propaganda and political attack see Calhoun, *Athenian Clubs*, pp. 98-104.

55. *loc. cit.*

56. Lysias, XXVI; Jebb, *Att. Orat.*, I, pp. 237-240; & n. 11 *supra*.

57. *loc. cit.* I find it difficult not to believe that Thrasybulus the Collytean did enlist the aid of other oligarchs when he alientated the Boeotians from Athens. The sources are silent, nevertheless, it is a point worth considering.

58. Victor Ehrenberg, *The Greek State* (Norton, 1964), p. 43.

IN THE FULNESS OF TIMES
Richard Luman

"But when the fulness of the time was come, God sent forth His Son, made of a woman, made under the law, to redeem them that were under the law, that we might receive the adoption of sons."

Galatians 4:-45

St. Paul echoes the words of Jesus Himself (Mark 1:15): "The time is fulfilled, and the kingdom of God is at hand...." From the earliest Christian times, it occurred to the followers of the Christ that it was—at the very least—a curious coincidence that this "fulness of times" should have come at the very moment in which Caesar Augustus had established Roman hegemony over the whole of the civilized world: a settlement which allowed free access to the whole Mediterranean and the three continents to apostolic missionaries; which affirmed peace throughout that great area; and which proposed, in place of regimes of caprice and tyranny, one of law and justice. Could the contemporary appearance of the Messiah and of the social order necessary for the dissemination of His Gospel to all men with unprecedented facility be anything less than providential?

Indeed, when coupled with the New Pentecost of Constantine, could there be any doubt that God's hand was in history guiding events, Roman emperors, and men's hearts to His saving purpose, and therefore that the reigns of Augustus, Constantine, and Theodosius I were moments in salvation history, bearing, as did the Exodus and the Incarnation, the burden of ultimate meaning? The Emperor Constantine—the first, to our knowledge, to interpret Virgil's *Ecloga* IV as Messianic prophecy[1]—perhaps thought so, as his house historian, Eusebius of Caesarea, certainly did.

Christian and post-Christian historians, the latter often in reaction against the views of the former, have had to reflect on the contemporaneity of the work of Caesar and Christ. But there is no unanimity of view in either camp, for there are Christian sacralizers and Christian de-sacralizers of the Roman order, while there are critical historians who grant a kind of secular sacrality to the Empire (perhaps Gibbon's famous encomium of the Antonines "If a man were called to fix the period of history of the world during which the condition of the human race was most happy and prosperous . . ." would fulfill the role of exemplary text). There are others who regard it as interesting but in principle no different from any other even of the same sort. The range from eudaimonic evaluations to kakodaimonic appears on both sides of the fence. The purpose of this article is to examine four influential readings of Roman Imperial history, those of Eusebius of Caesarea, Augustine of Hippo, Otto of Freising, and Montesquieu, seeking to discover any consistent evaluative thread or strategy in 1400 years of historical reflection, and at least asking whether such a review can tell us something about (a) whatever "really happened"; (b) what, why, how these thinkers placed the establishment of the Empire in their larger conceptions of human history; and (c) the process of thinking about and writing history.

In fact, plural evaluations of Augustus and his work are known to us from pagans writing before the coming of Christians to power. Tacitus' dark conception of both Augustus and his Principate in the *Annals* is too well known to require repetition. On the other hand, not least in the reign of Augustus himself, others saw his work as transcending the boundaries of merely human artifice. The founding of temples to Rome and Augustus (beginning in 9 B.C.) as well as that very Virgilian *Ecloga* (without Christian glosses) testify to that.[2] Charles Norris Cochrane, seeking to summarize the more general pagan attitude, describes the Empire as "the last act of creative politics."

The inherent contradictions of classical political theory and practice, analyzed from Plato to Cicero, were seen to be transcended and hence resolved by the establishment of a government built on men a little more than human. The philosopher kings of Plato, the romantic Alexander, the ancient despots of the Orient, the Latin *paterfamilias*, and the civil magistrate of Rome combine to yield the god by decree of the Senate. The classical commonwealth was at last to be given a chance to achieve its peculiar genius: men could pursue the virtues, live honest lives, work out their corporate fate with the tools of philosophy and politics. The Empire had given humanity a new chance, for it was a rededication of the City to the great goal of civilized government under law for all men, establishing decency and order in political life, standing as patroness to arts and civil virtues, giving peace and justice to all, an "effort to erect a stable and enduring civilization upon the ruins of the discredited and discarded systems of the past. As thus envisaged, it constituted not merely a decisive stage in the life of the Roman people, but a significant point of departure in the evolution of mankind."[3] Thus Cochrane summarizes his understanding of Vergil's vision of the new chance for humankind—and for Rome—given by Augustus: the "religion of culture."[4] Mob-rule and the irresponsibly powerful would be curbed; endemic στάσις would be transmogrified into universal harmony; violent Rome the conqueror and exploiter would become Rome the bringer of peace and plenty, and the patron of the quiet joys of culture, all through political action, "through . . . the instruments which organized society affords ..... especially through submission to the 'virtue and fortune' of a political leader ..... a hero-saviour."[5] It should hardly be surprising therefore that—as Quispel points out—there was an apocalyptic tradition of *Nero redivivus* among pagans as there was among Christians.[6] The role of Emperor as human but transcendant culture-hero, a kind of secular Messiah, was already there, for "the *Pax Augusta*" stood as the "final and definitive expression of the spirit of classsical antiquity;[7] "unique associations were to cling to the reign of Augustus as the dawn of a new and better epoch for humanity."[8]

Eusebius of Caesarea[9]

Eusebius, disciple of Origen, bishop of Caesarea, intimate of the Emperor Constantine, and "Father of Church History," speaks for that generation which saw the transformation of the *Pax Romana* into the *Pax Christiana*, and the *Imperium romanum* into the *Imperium romanum christianum*. From the terrible scenes of martyrs dying for the Cross before the implacable soldiers of Caesar to the Constantinian Pentecost of Nicea in which the Emperor surpassed the earlier efforts of the unaided Holy Ghost,[10] was but a moment in time yet a Copernican revolution in understanding. Constantine dominated the imagination of the generation rescued from the prison-house. Eusebius compares him frequently with Moses;[11] both led their people out of oppression and suffering into a promised land. He compares his reign to the Messianic Age;[12] Constantine too, brings about universal peace, prosperity and the worship of the true God. Eusebius' conception of the office and person of the Savior is such that he is able to use language concerning Constantine which recognizes a distance between the Emperor and the Son of God, but which also sees the Emperor and his work as "decisive evidence" of God's hand in history.[13] Constantine, like St. Paul, is called upon the road to Rome to be God's champion.[14] Constantine, unlike all other men, is elevated to the purple by God alone, without human contribution.[15] Constantine seems to have shared such an exalted conception of his role. He lectured his court on theology.[16] He constructed the great Church of the Holy Apostles in Constantinople, with twelve cenotaphs for those who walked with Jesus, and a thirteenth for himself.[17] Constantine had instituted a new age, an age in which God's will would rule, and things could never return to the old ways: Eusebius and his friends knew of the terrors of persecutors; they were as yet unaware—or shut their eyes to—the dangers of Greeks bearing gifts.[18] Cochrane suggests that Eusebius saw Constantine's work as fulfilling the Roman imperial promise (never yet realized because of the violence and injustice visited on Christians and the worship of false gods) of universal peace and harmony by undergirding it with the Gospel, the new alliance of the victorious Emperor with God the Father of Jesus Christ and giver of victories.[19] The Gospel provides that real reconciliation among men without which the Roman Imperial program must always remain but a shadow, a straining forward to what it can not achieve by itself alone. But when enriched by the Gospel —and only then— Rome can fulfill its promise. For paganism is divisive and degrading; universal peace can truly exist only under the aegis of the universal and only true God.[20]

This optimism concerning the Constantinian settlement, this willingness to embrace the Roman world and its self-defined civilizing mission, along with the recognition of the inadequacy of Rome without Christ, meant the foundation of the Empire must be seen to be both providential and yet incomplete. In that sense, Constantine must transcend Augustus, for he has brought about Messianic banquets[21] in the real world of Roman politics.

The achievements of Augustus and his successors are recognized; but Romans have misapprehended the source of their power, Eusebius says, quoting with approval, Melito of Sardis and echoing Tertullian.[22] God brought about the Roman peace, used it (beginning in the reign of Tiberius) to spread the Gospel. As a consequence, the Gospel has become, since

> the great reign of thy ancestor Augustus , . . . to thine empire a blessing of auspicious omen. For from that time the power of the Romans has grown in greatness and splender . . . . And a most convincing proof that our doctrine flourished for the good of an empire happily begun, is this—that there has no evil happened since Augustus' reign, but that, on the contrary, all things have been splendid and glorious, in accordance with the prayers of all.[23]

"Our doctrine flourished for the good of an empire happily begun . . ." The greatness and mission of Rome have succeeded because it has been the cocoon for the Gospel.

The success of Rome in her self-chosen mission is thus seen as a proof of the Gospel. And the good Emperors have all recognized this relationship. Beginning with Tiberius[24] they have fostered and protected the Church. Only evil Emperors, men recognized by all rational men as monsters, tyrants such as Nero and Domitian (and even they were persuaded by "calumniators"), have abandoned this salutary course. For those recognized by all rational men as noble and honorable have in fact patronized the Church. Therefore God blessed them with long and useful reigns, while he brought down terrible destruction on the tyrants. Thus Eusebius and his sources appropriate the history of Rome for Christians, as they have appropriated the history of Israel as Christian. As the Patriarchs, from Adam to Abraham are Christians in all but name,[25] so are the good Emperors friends of the Church in all but name. The succession of bishops who descend from the Apostles, spread the Gospel, maintain the unity of the Church and the purity of the Faith, are thus to a small degree paralleled by the succession of sensible Emperors.[26] And as the shadow succession of heresiarchs, aping the bishops yet serving the devil, have brought trouble to the Church, so the evil Emperors, feigning good but serving devils, brought persecution on the Church and suffering to Rome. In Constantine and his councils these two virtuous successions meet: the succession of good Emperors from Augustus, and the succession of the bishops from the Apostles. It would seem a natural alliance, since, while the one stemmed only from the "natural understanding" while the other derived directly from "divine guidance," the first was not outside the general activity of God through his Logos, and the second, directly derived from Him. Heresiarchs and tyrants were both agents of Satan, seeking to disrupt God's activity both in the natural order of political association and the supernatural order of salvation. Now earthly peace and perfect unity have been brought about by Constantine under God; and the Gospel has added to his realm the blessings of eternal peace and the unity of true faith.

The foundation of the Empire and its transformation into a Christian Empire can thus be seen as moments in salvation history. The sacralization of the Empire, already a portion of the cultural package ("Romanitas") offered by the Antonines to their subjects, could be continued under Christian Emperors, just as Constantine remained Pontifex Maximus even while presiding over Christian councils. The foundation of the Empire was thus read through two key interpretative events: the Incarnation of Jesus Christ and the conversion of Constantine.

Augustine of Hippo

If the generation of Eusebius could be overwhelmed by the warmth of the sun of Imperial favor and receive Imperial beneficence uncritically as—at the very least—"a picture of Christ's kingdom ... shadowed forth, and a dream rather than a reality,"[27] two generations of Imperial meddling in Church life led to caution. Already *Athanasius contra mundum* had to include *contra imperatorem Constantium*.[28] Constantius seeking to overcome Nicaea by creating more Nicaeas, calling ever more councils to find acceptable Arian formulae enforceable by authority; Julian's apostacy and notorious School Laws; Imperial meddling in episcopal elections in Alexandria, Rome, and Milan—all must lead a prudent man of the late Fourth Century to ask whether a Christian Empire was either a dependable ally or even a blessing. Augustine, observing both the policies and perturbations of theologians in the purple and the wavering of Roman order symbolized by the fall of the City in 410, could not but reconsider such an absolutization of the social and political order. He was wary of all human structures, which he regarded as the consequence of the Fall—bulwarks against the excesses of depraved humanity—rather than as realizations of human created potential. He had suspicions even of the empirical Church. Not, of course of that Church which lives forever in fellowship with divine grace, but of the sociological institution in which fallen man, *incurvatus in se*, sought power over other men, restrained only by the Divine beneficence of institutional order and limits. Yet, engaged in a struggle for control of the African Church and the souls of his congregation with the Donatists, he was prepared to invoke the aid of that very political order, both Imperial and ecclesiastical, and needed to justify that appeal. And for all his devotion to the new order, Augustine was a loyal Roman, full of admiration (tempered but real) for republican virtue, Vergilian rhetoric, and the cultural burden of Roman order.[29] Like Jerome, his attitude toward the classical world from which he sprang was profoundly ambivalent: fearful, contemptuous, deeply loving, distrustful, yet grateful and respectful. His problem thus became, once he had placed the triumphalism of the generation of Eusebius under the powerful microscope of his mind, how to relativize the Roman world and its culture without consigning it to the rubbish heap; how, on the other hand, to conserve and value the abiding virtues of this great community without making it an integral part of salvation history.

Shortly after the sack of the City, which shocked at least the West,[30] Augustine was asked to undertake a defence of the Christian community against the charge of having caused—by contempt for the rites of the gods—this apocalyptic misadventure. In his reply, *De civitate Dei*, he sought to show that the attack of the Goths, though appalling to all decent men, was precisely *not* apocalyptic, but was a historical event fundamentally no different from many similar events in human history: Rome, preeminent for law and wisdom, was yet only a city, subject to all the vicissitudes of human fortune. A great City, a City to which mankind owed much, our City—but not the heavenly Jerusalem. As a consequence, its ravishing, though of terrible import for men of that time, required in principle no explanation more cosmic than that invoked for the fall of Troy or the fall of Carthage. But in order to show that this event in the history of the City was not qualitatively different from similar events in the history of other communities, he had to desacralize the Empire. Its founding, its development, even its conversion to Christianity, must be seen as similarly contigent events, produced by the same forces which led to the same results elsewhere. Desacralizing the Empire did require that cosmic explanation which he denied Rome itself. What state of affairs obtained in the world such that some of the events of human history may, on the one hand, bear the burden of showing forth God's true intentions for men, while others remain but the cumulative experience of mankind? How could the Crucifixion of Jesus—the execution, after all, of a trivial criminal by Rome—be absolutely truthful concerning God and man, while the destruction of Rome, which many had regarded as a carrier of divine meaning in history, saved or damned no one? Only if one could understand the whole of human history could one establish the values of these specific moments.[31] For that, one needed a plan encompassing the entirety of man's experience and God's action, from creation[32] to consummation.

Augustine examines Cicero's definition of a commonwealth as that community which establishes and delivers *justice*. But no human community, Augustine shows, does that. All human states are born in violence and destruction: the history of Rome, replete as it is with stories of extraordinary bravery, nobility and virtue (such as the life of Regulus), nevertheless demonstrates that fully. States are only violence, robbery and fear legitimized by time and size. In principle they differ not at all from a gang of thugs and bank robbers.[33] The Roman Empire is no exception; indeed, in some respects, it is the preeminent example. Justice can only be achieved in a community in which God rules perfectly. Cicero's definition therefore fits a divine commonwealth, but no association known empirically to mankind's history.[34]

The easiest move then would be to consign the state, its culture, and all its values, to the realm of Satan, as some early Christians had in fact done. It would have been thouroughly consistent with the Manichaeism of Augustine's college days. It would have drawn the metaphysical battle lines clearly, not only in heaven, but on earth; it would have pointed out friends and enemies unambiguously. But the mature Augustine recognized that no such simple transcription or "instant replay" on earth of the cosmic struggle would deal adequately with the complex data of human experience and divine intention.

Instead, Augustine proposes looking at the bond which characterizes all human associations, the common goal, passion, enthusiasm, purpose (his word is "love") which alone makes of diverse people a community. The goal might be noble or base; the purpose is neutral, and the association is itself neutral. Filled with what its members bring to it, it may serve God or be seized by demonic forces. Thus kingdoms and bandits are indeed examples of the same species. The two greatest associations in human history, the bearers of meaning, are similarly defined by their loves: the City of God by its love for God, the Earthly City by its love for self and its aggrandizement. The whole of human history is the story of the decisive interactions of these two communities from the Fall to the Consummation.[35] Within that scheme, of course, the Earthly City has only temporary existence: it is neither a part of Creation nor will it persist into eternity. The two Cities are characterized, in the Preface to Book I, by contrasting quotations, the one from *James* (4:6: "God resists the proud but He gives grace to the humble") and the other from the *Aeneid* (6:853: "To spare the conquered, and beat down the proud" is taken as the Earthly City's self-characterization). If to any degree, however tempered, Vergil is the "theoretician of Roman Imperial power," that choice of texts could easily lead to the view that the Earthly City and the Roman Empire are the same. Can these cosmic characters be found so easily in human affairs?

R.A. Markus, in a brilliant analysis of *Saeculum: History and Society in the Theology of St. Augustine*, argues that one cannot slip from transcendent associations to empirical institutions with such ease. Neither the Roman Empire nor the Roman Church may be identified with their principals simply.[36] All institutions exist in an area between and within the two Cities, for in this world the Parable of the Wheat and the Tares applies: the two cannot be separated by any method of inspection or judgment except God's alone. The wars of heaven are carried out not only *between* institutions but *within* them.

The Roman Empire is such an empirical association. Its origins are in greed, bloodshed, war, brutality, aggression, theft, murder, rape; but also in ambition for glory, hard work, peasant shrewdness, passion for honor. Its history is typical of that of all such associations.[37] Rome, therefore, like all human cities, must fall, and its fall, whatever its repercussions, is but one sound in the cacophony of human experience. Yet it did grow out of virtues: and its rise to temporal eminence is God's reward to the Romans for their temporal virtues: now they can have no complaint. Not that all Romans were virtuous: but a creative leadership set the tone. Though *sub specie aeternitatis* their virtues may be nought but splendid vices, in the realm of civil righteousness they are of relative value, and they have been rewarded relatively.[28] On the one hand, therefore, the rise of Rome has always been under God's hand; but, on the other, it is perfectly explainable by principles applicable to all such cases. It has a preeminent but not interpretatively a privileged position: remarkable but not redemptive.

This view clearly makes it possible for Augustine to make meaningful relative judgments. The values of associations can be estimated by comparing their goals, means, and structures. There is a spectrum along which institutions can be arranged. And all is in flux: institutions may improve or worsen. Thus, Rome has learned great things in its time, and in its last days has recognized the true God. It has therefore, despite its origins, moved in a positive direction: but it does not thereby transcend the limits of history; it is not a necessary term in the series of cosmic events which actually determine man's fate. No moment of history other than those narrated in Scripture is redemptive. And God's *use* of ambiguous human institutions does not sacralize or establish divine endorsement.[39] God gave power to Augustus, but also to Nero, to the Christian Constantine but also to the Apostate Julian. Men such as Julian rose through their ability, and they—without wishing to—served the divine purpose.[40] The foundation and history of Rome is therefore no more or less providential than is the history of any other kingdom. Rome rose through discernible virtues and comprehensible causes; and God found it useful in His own secret ways. Christian Rome is better than pagan Rome but in principle no different, no more redemptive, no more permanent.

Otto of Freising

Augustine's influence, as in so many areas, worked its way deeply into medieval thinking on the social and political order. One of his major disciples was Otto, Bishop of Freising (c.1110-1158), author of *Historia de duabus civitatibus*, a universal history from the Creation to 1146, and of the *Gesta Friderici I imperatoris* (left unfinished at his death). Otto was extraordinarily well-prepared for such work, for he was at the center both of the intellectual and the political movements of his day. On his mother's side, he was great-grandson of the Emperor Henry III, who deposed two popes and nominated a third at the Synod of Sutri in 1046; the grandson of Henry IV, who confronted Gregory VII; the nephew of Henry V; half-brother of Konrad III; and uncle of Frederick I Barbarossa. His father was Leopold III of Austria, his brother the great Henry Jasomirgott, his family the Babenbergs. He was a student at Paris from about 1127 to about 1133; there he knew and was much influenced by Abelard and other great teachers. In 1133, he joined St. Bernard's burgeoning Cistercian Order and became Abbot of Morimond. In 1137 he was made Bishop of Freising. He spent several years in the East on the Second Crusade. He thus could be said to have authentic access to both sides of most of the great controversies of his time. A reflective man of philosophical training, devoted to Empire and Church, monk, bishop, member of the imperial house, "he merits the encomiums bestowed upon him as the leading philosophical historian of the twelfth century, if not of the whole medieval period."[41]

The Two Cities (this seems to have been Otto's own title) proclaims its Augustinian lineage clearly. But Otto writes not in the immediate shadow of the fall of Rome, but that of the Investiture Contest.[42] The relations between society and the Christian faith are different for him from what they were for Augustine. Seven hundred years of Christian civilization, including the conversion of Europe and the conquest of the classical heritage, lie between him and the Bishop of Hippo. For him, society as *corpus Christianum* is a reality.

Yet there is another shadow: the impending end of the world. Eschatology is, in fact, the binding structural element in the *Two Cities* (but not in the *Gesta*).[43] All of history is moving toward the terrible persecution of the Antichrist which itself will be followed by the glorious triumph of Christ. All this seemed to Otto to be imminent. The reflections on the course of human history which the doctrine of sin and the conviction of the imminent *eschaton* together provoke are often dark and bitter.

Yet there is real change: man, must, for example, move from his primitive state of violence and brutality to a condition ready to receive the Savior. The events of human history are always under God's hand, and so there is an *order to experience*, and even evil makes its contribution to good. That order must be discovered and explained (e.g., why did God wait until the reign of Augustus to undertake incarnation? It did mean, after all, the apparent abandonment of many generations of people to the dominion of sin).[44] There must be strands of events which are significant, forms of behavior, classes of occurrences. Civilization and empire travel steadily toward the West; when they reach the limits of the West (which they seem to have done), the *eschaton* will be upon us. *Translatio imperii* (*translatio sapientiae*, *translatio sanctitatis*) is one of the mechanisms of change he explores. As one Empire fades, another is always born. History also gains meaning through noting a series of heroic and tragic correspondences: Scipio and the Maccabees, or Carthage and Corinth. History displays ironic repetition: the histories of Babylon and Rome, the fates of the first and last "queens" of Carthage.[45] Sometimes these strands of history (e.g., the four monarchies of Daniel) are illuminated by prophecy. More often, and especially since the Incarnation, authoritative prophetic interpretation is not available, and the historian must do the best he can with his human insight.[46] Yet even secular history can furnish us with useful *exampla*: the sudden death of Alexander the Great at the height of his worldly fortune, overthrown by a simple cup, can demonstrate dramatically the mutability of all things, the fragility of greatness, and hence the hollowness of all values built upon the sandy foundation of such fortune. Hence, history is a *useful* source of sad reflection for all serious persons even when not given an undoubtable meaning directly by God.

All of these ideas together suggest to Morrison that there is, alongside the Two Cities structure and the eschatological structure, a third structure[47] in the *Two Cities*, not always coherent with the first two. This is a view of human progress in social organization, in learning (especially philosophy), and even in sanctity. Thus, Otto can assert that Plato knew all of the Gospel except for the Incarnation.[48] Progress through suffering (of which Regulus is a secular example) leads to the present moment, when monastic piety in particular, and the Church in general, has come to dominate society. Mankind is thus on pilgrimage from the Fall to some indefinite consummation, and history is "the education of mankind."[49]

Roman history is the backbone of the early books, and the necessary background to the later. Otto recognizes both the tragedy and triumph of the growth of the Empire, the Romans' bravery and virtue and at the same time deceitfulness and treachery. Yet it could not have been sustained except through God's hidden plan. "The reason for this . . . we shall, by God's grace, set forth hereafter when we shall have come to the principate of Augustus Caesar."[50] So both the valor of the Romans and God's intent created the Empire. But the vices of the Romans produced not merely conquest and law, but also civil war, and the destruction of the Republican constitution: how ironic that Romans called out the whole conquered world to fight Romans! Similarly, the last days of the Jewish Commonwealth are characterized by *prophetic* silence. The conflicts in the Earthly City were resolved by Augustus, just as the silence of prophecy was ended by the utterance of the ultimate divine Word, Christ.

There are other correspondences between the lives of Augustus and Christ which Otto feels are significant. The reign of Augustus can even be seen as a kind of secular prophecy or at least shadow of the Incarnation. Augustus was received, for example, in Rome as ruler of the world on the sixth of January. Augustus is for Otto (and generally for the Middle Ages, for Tacitus' views were not known) the model of a moderate, sensible, wise ruler, the best example of a human ruler using human wisdom.[51]

Why, then, did God wait until Augustus' reign to be born? By then, progressive revelation, through which God had prepared men, was ready for fulfillment. God had given the City of the World ample time and warning; whether men attended to that, Christians at least could learn from the example provided by that history. Men had been taught by Rome to think in universal terms and were thus prepared for a universal Gospel and a universal Christian community. The Roman world provided, under Augustus, peace and unity, not only for the spread of the Gospel (although it did specifically do so), but also as a kind of preparatory experience. The *Pax augusta* therefore came about as a consequence neither of accidental causes, nor of the machinations of pagan gods. The reign of Augustus was intended by the true God. Why He chose Rome rather than, say, Alexandria, Otto does not know, unless it was because of the merits of Blessed Peter, which He foresaw. If so, it is more appropriate that that City which was head of the universal Empire should become the head of the universal Church. But, finally, in such matters, God's will is inscrutable.[52]

Clearly, Otto has a far more positive view of the pagan world than did his master Augustine. It was possible, using simple reason and virtue, to attain to the true faith in every respect except a knowledge of that particular historical manifestation of God's purpose, the Incarnation. It should not surprise the reader that Otto envisaged a kind of penultimate conflation of the City of Man with the City of God. When the Apostles were martyred in Rome, the secular prestige of the City began to decrease. The Roman Empire, identified by Otto with the City of Man, faded as the City of God, the Church, grew, until eventually the latter replaced or absorbed the former. The first instrument of that transformation,[53] chosen by God Himself, was the Emperor of the Romans, Constantine. Now the royal and kingly powers are both within the Church, though not exercized by the same person (here Otto seems to be echoing St. Bernard's teaching on the Two Swords). Hence, Constantine rightly donated the Empire to the Church and the Church rightly accepted it (but Otto rightly rejects the story of the Emperor's leprosy as apocryphal).[54] In Otto's own time, that mastery, represented by Gregory VII, a series of monastic popes, and the Investiture Contest, is becoming evident and effective.

However Otto understands the content of the eschatological Two Cities, he does not continue Augustine's subtle ambiguities, reservations, and fears concerning the making of history "a theological prop for a sacral society, a Christian political establishment in which the divine purpose in history lay enshrined."[55] The Roman Empire was providential. It acted almost as a type for the Imperial Church. In Otto's time the City of God seemed to have triumphed over and replaced the Earthly City.

Montesquieu

Charles Louis de Secondat, Baron de la Brède et de Montesquieu (1689-1755), is, through *L'Éspirit des Lois* (1748) one of the theorists most influential in establishing the eighteenth century's understanding of social order and change. The *Considérations*[56], first published in 1734, was less significant historically, but was much read, especially by Gibbon. Along with Machiavelli's *Discorsi*, it is one of the few early modern attempts to think through the philosophical and historical issues raised by Roman history, and it is partly from that study that ideas such as "separation of powers" arose.

Perhaps the most striking difference between Otto's philosophical history and that of Montesquieu is the absence from the latter of the magisterial hand of God. The "causes" of human greatness and decline are social and this-worldly. Whether ordered or not, the events of human history owe little to a divine plan (although Montesquieu never denies such divine supervision, his few references are ironic).[57] God is principally notable for His inactivity. The great events of Christian history pass almost without notice. This, then, is a history recognizably modern in its devotion to causation within the process of history itself, its assertion of history's autonomy, and hence its relegation of divine action to a decent obscurity.[58] It is a study of the ways in which power is acquired and lost; it is a history of war and conquest.

Early Roman society was uniquely suited to become a machine of conquest. The Romans were very adaptable and willingly learned from their foes. Many shrewd leaders guided Roman policy. Roman history was a series of warlike challenges triumphantly overcome. Hence, Rome became great in part simply because she won: success begat success. War produced spoils and the hunger for further spoils. Government was well-suited to expansion in Italy. Romans had the virtues and vices of a small community: canniness, hard-headedness, tight-fistedness, willingness to work, prudence, liberty, perseverance, passion for glory, tough leadership.[59] It is thus the virtues of the pagan, republican city-state that made Rome great (=powerful), and it was the corruption of those virtues which destroyed the Republic, established the Empire, and eventually destroyed Roman power. The Empire is thus the consequence of the decay of the body politic. True, there were great Emperors—Augustus and Trajan—and there were still military successes for a time, but the heart had gone out of the Roman enterprise. It failed for discernible social reasons: lust for wealth and power among the generals, the decay of property-holding citizen armies, the vast scale of Roman conquests, which went beyond the regulatory capacities of a city-state constitution. Designed for expansion, the Republic succeeded too well and too quickly: the Roman Republic died of immoderate greatness—indeed, she committed suicide by betraying her own peculiar genius. Success brought out those dissensions always present in communities, but on too grand a stage and without adequate controls. Epicureanism became popular among the ruling class, helping to destroy the state religion (and hence patriotism and morals). Those who had had excessive luxury or power and lost them sought to regain them through demagoguery. The electorate was corrupted. The army became greedy and devoted to its generals rather than to the state. The generals destroyed the balances and checks of the republican constitution, making the concentration of power in the hand of one man both necessary and inevitable. The Republic therefore fell because of basic human characteristics (well exemplified by the Romans) formed in Rome's peculiar situation.[60] Neither the guidance of God nor the machinations of Satan caused the Empire to be: neither original sin nor heroic sanctity, but what men are. Only to a secondary degree *individual* men's talents and schemes: rather the way communities develop in response to conditions which provide such opportunities as great men may seize upon. Thus the Empire became inevitable: but its peculiar form was born in the failures of the Republic and in the cowardice and deviousness of Augustus. Tacitus' Augustus, the "artful" Augustus (as Gibbon will call him), replaces the noble, wise, moderate ruler who foresaw and in a sense modeled the coming of Christ.[61] Emperors evaluated by whether they persecuted Christians or (like Tiberius) secretly recognize Christ and foster the Church are replaced by men working out the implications of monarchy. So one sees that the blood and the sacrifice and the planning, statecraft, courage, prudence—all end in "satiating the happiness of five or six monsters .... This senate had brought about the extinction of so many kings only to fall into the meanest enslavement to some of its most contemptible citizens, and to exterminate itself by its own decrees!"[62] But as the greatness of the Republic was fatal to the Republic, so eventually the greatness of the Empire was fatal both to the lives and fortunes of the Emperors.[63] The "wisdom of Nerva, the glory of Trajan," the best prince of all, "the valor of Hadrian, and the virtue of the two Antonines" (for in thinking of Marcus Aurelius "we have a better opinion of ourselves because we have a better opinion of men") only delayed the certain collapse.[64] For,

> It is not chance that rules the world .... There are general causes, moral and physical, which act in every monarchy, elevating it, maintaining it, or hurling it to the ground. All accidents are controlled by these causes. And if the chance of one battle—that is, a particular cause—has brought a state to ruin, some general cause made it necessary for that state to perish from a single battle. In a word, the main trend draws with it all particular accidents.[65]

Here it is, perhaps, that Montesquieu most decisively departs from his predecessors and anticipates his successors, such as Gibbon.

Conclusion

Augustine was primarily a philosopher and theologian. He felt uncomfortable writing history, and indeed, disliked professional history as it was written in his day.[66] Otto and Montesquieu thought themselves "philosophical historians" (Gibbon also so conceived of himself), yet they came to very different conclusions about the meta-meaning of the history they wrote. Eusebius, Augustine, and Otto are all Christians seeking to understand the whole of history as God's plan, yet they, too, disagree about Rome's place in that plan. Did we arrive at Ranke's kind of historical truth ("wie es eigentlich gewesen") about Augustus from our review of these four writers? Was the Principate providential or simply the result of natural causes, empty of cosmic meaning? Or did we learn, by observing these four historians side by side, anything about the craft of history? Did there emerge a progression, a gradual conquest of the past with the establishment of permanent monuments of true understanding: did we discern a *tradition* in formation: a *direction*, a *building* of one upon another? Is it illegitimate, for example, for a historian to look to divine causation as an interpretative principle, and was Montesquieu's recognition of that fact a move of permanent value which—in spite of his defects as a historian, and they are many—placed the historical enterprise on a higher plane of discourse? How do we go about establishing *meaning* in history? Indeed, can we even find universally defensible and persuasive standards and methods for establishing it? No brief article can do more than point to such fundamental puzzles.

Four thinkers engaged in a common quest; and in the process, each created his own "Roman Empire" (as Gibbon later did for himself and us). All are bound together by a common set of events and persons in a common past, but each uses those to construct a picture protraying his own fundamental assumptions about man and God. Recognizing that, we can ask: can any one of them claim a privileged interpretative position, one from which to judge all the others, Montesquieu more than Augustine, Otto more than Eusebius? Each is telling the story consistent with his own understanding of the past and needing to be told to his time and his community. Could Augustine have told Montesquieu's story?

A tradition has been defined as "an extended conversation about the meaning of that tradition."[67] If one excludes a conception of *progress* and substitutes that of *response*, our conversation about the Roman Empire surely constitutes such a tradition. For it has not merely a common topic, but shares, passes on, negates, transmutes, revises, reinterprets that topic, thus building into our conception of ourselves, our basic identity as a historical community, this set of events: not only as fundation, but as continuing building stone. What "really" happened is, to a degree, less important than what has been thought, rethought, and argued about what happened. Thus the Roman Empire became—if not quite providential—an important "bearer of meaning" within our tradition, and a major element in the myth of Western identity. Rome and her fate dominated the Western historical imagination for centuries. That role was solidified and given precise content in Gibbon's masterpiece,

The Decline and Fall of the Roman Empire (surely one of the great mythopoeic programmatic titles in literature!).[68] We can now see some of the steps which led to his formulation of the issue (definitive, but not final, for the tradition goes on, with Gibbon now as subject as well as participant). So gradually crystallizes our understanding of ourselves in relation to our past. Augustus Caesar, whether as master builder or as one of those heroes "whose function (it) is to tear a society apart by applying to it the logic of its own corruption,"[69] must always remain with us as long as our tradition lives, as text for our commentary.

NOTES

1. In his *Oration to the Assembly of the Saints*, Chs. XIX-XXI; he has already invoked the authority of the Sibyl in previous chapters. Some of these citations Augustine echoes, *De civitate Dei*, X, 27, but in his own way.

2. The passages are thought to refer to the birth of an heir to Augustus. See Tacitus, *The Annals (Ab excessu divi Augusti)*, I, x, for that historian's summary of criticism of Augustus.

3. Charles Norris Cochrane: *Christianity and Classical Culture*, London, Oxford University Press, 1972, p. 27. The description of Augustus' work, with its claims to "eternity," as the culmination of the classical effort to "create a world that should be safe for civilization" and hence as "the last act of creative politics" can be found, for example, on p. v.

4. *Ibid.*, p. 29.

5. First section of quotation, *Ibid.*, p. 23; the second, p. vi; the third, pp. 86-87.

6. Gilles Quispel: *The Secret Book of Revelation*, New York, McGraw-Hill, 1979, e.g., pp. 120, 131-132.

7. Cochrane, *op. cit.*, p. 17.

8. *Ibid.* p. 27. Two recent reviews of the reign of Augustus and its interpretation are Donald Earl: *The Age of Augustus*, New York, Crown, 1968; and John M. Carter: "Augustus Down the Centuries," *History Today*, March 1983, Vol. 33, pp. 24-30. The writing on this period is of course very extensive, i.e., Sir Ronald Syme, *The Roman Revolution*, Oxford, 1939.

IN THE FULNESS OF TIMES 171

9. The best work of evaluation is Robert M. Grant: *Eusebius as Church Historian*, Oxford, the Clarendon Press, 1980. A convenient text of the *Historia ecclesiastica* is that of Kirsopp Lake in the Loeb Classical Library, 1953. But the translation with extraordinary notes (with the *Vita constantini*, etc.) in the *Select Library of Nicene and Post-Nicene Fathers*, Series II, Volume I, by A.C. McGiffert (1890) is not to be ignored because of its age. See also A. H. M. Jones, *The Later Roman Empire*, Norman, Oklahoma, 1964 and Johannes Quasten, *Patrology*, Westminster, Maryland, 1983, esp. III, 309-345.

10. *Vita constantini*, III, 8. Eusebius describes the formal banquets but says little about the theological issues of the Council, which is here compared with Pentecost, to the Council's enlargement.

11. *VC*, I, 12. The V. C. is less reliable than H. E. See Quasten, loc. cit.

12. *HE*, X, 1-4, 9; *VC*, III, 15.

13. See Eusebius' *Oration on the Thirtieth Anniversary of Constantine's Reign*.

14. *VC*, I, 28-32. In the liturgy for the Feast of St. Constantine, the Emperor is described as "like Paul, he received a call not from men." See Alexander Schmemann: *The Historical Road of Eastern Orthodoxy*, New York: Holt, Rinehart and Winston, 1963, p. 63.

15. *VC*, I, 24.

16. See the address mentioned in fn. 1. See also *VC*, III, 24, 17-20, etc.

17. *VC*, IV, 58-60.

18. Cochrane, *op. cit.*, p. 186.

19. *Ibid.*, p. 185.

20. *VC*, II, 19.

21. *VC*, III, 15.

22. *HE*, IV, 26, 5-11.

23. *HE*, IV, 26, 8.

24. *HE*, II, 2.

25. *HE*, I, 3-4, esp. 4,6.

26. On successions of orthodox bishops as the frame, see *HE*, I, 1, 1.

27. *HE*, III, 15.

28. See Athanasius: *Apologia de Fuga*; *Apologia ad Constantium*; *Narratio ad Ammonium* (account of his flight from Julian).

29. Regrettably, any brief account of Augustine's view of any great subject is so compressed and telegraphic that of necessity important distinctions and qualifications, and—as he himself recognized—developments and even contradictions in his thought must be smoothed over. I am much indebted here to what I regard as the most splendid investigation of Augustine's thought on institutions and history, R. A. Markus' *Saeculum: History and Society in the Theology of St. Augustine*, Cambridge University Press, 1970. The principal source will be St. Augustine, *De Civitate Dei* (DCD). On Augustine's view of the empirical church, see Markus, p. 178 ff. But see also *DCD*, XX, 9. where the tension between the eschatological church and the church militant is discussed. On Augustine's historical experience, see Peter Brown, *Augustine of Hippo*, University of California Press, 1969, and Markus, pp. 22-44. On Augustine's experience in Africa, see F. van der Meer: *Augustine the Bishop*, Harper, 1965 and W. H. C. Frend, *The Donatist Church*, Oxford, 1952, as well as Markus, pp. 105-153. Lidia Storoni Mazzolani: *The Idea of the City in Roman Thought, From Walled City to Commonwealth*, Indiana University Press, 1970, and Jeremy duQuesnay Adams: *The POPULUS of Augustine and Jerome*, Yale, 1971, are also relevant. An easily available dependable text of *DCD* is that of the Loeb series, ed. G.E. McCracken, seven volumes, Harvard, 1957.

30. On the attitude of the East, see Walter Emil Kaegi, Jr.: *Byzantium and the Decline of Rome*, Princeton University Press, 1968.

31. See Arthur C. Danto: *Analytical Philosophy of History*, Cambridge University Press, 1965 on this issue. The whole interest in *narrative*, its meaning, and its relation to history and literature which has grown up recently, illustrates the continuing force of this problem.

32. As Augustine points out in the last three books of the *Confessions*, attempts to get behind creation are fruitless. Even creation will not tell the whole story, since the Earthly City does not come onstage until the Fall.

33. *DCD*, II, 21. The citation is from Cicero's *De republica*, 2, 42f. Scipio argues, Augustine says, that a commonwealth which does not deliver justice is not merely corrupt, it in fact ceases to exist. Hence, Sallust already demonstrates that Rome was not such a functional commonwealth. The discussion continues in *DCD*, XIX, 21; the definition of association is in XIX, 24. Robber bands and kingdoms: *DCD*, IV, 4.

34. *DCD* II, 21.

35. The *locus classicus* for the Two Cities and their Two Loves is *DCD* XIV, 28. Augustine, like Luther, tended to think in polar opposites. On common love, see Markus, p. 66 and elsewhere.

36. Because in their pure form they are of necessity mutually exclusive; yet in real life people may belong to both Church and Empire. For this whole discussion, see Markus, Chapters 3 and 4.

37. On the origins of the Empire and its virtues and faults, see *DCD*, Books I-V. He writes virtually a history of the Republic there.

38. On Roman virtues rewarded by God, see *DCD*, IV, 33; V, 1; V. 12; V, 19. On the "creative leadership of the few," see *DCD*, V, 12. On the temporal reward for temporal virtue, *DCD*, V, 15.

39. Markus argues that a *central concern* of *DCD* is the rejection of the Eusebian imperial theology. He shows how Augustine avoids the use of prophetic categories when talking of the Empire; how he includes his own time (post-Constantine) in the condemnation of the wickedness of the world; and how he avoids or reinterprets passages from Scripture Eusebius had used in reference to Empire or Emperor. Markus, pp. 48-58.

40. *DCD*, V, 21.

41. Hofmeister, the principal editor of his works, says that there is "scarcely another individual in whom we see so clearly and so impressively revealed the riches and the variety of the movements that filled the 12th century—the complete fulness of the opposing tendencies that live in this time and its people—as in Otto of Freising." Qt. in C. C. Mierow's translation of *The Two Cities*, Columbia University Press, 1928, pp. 22-23. A thorough review of his family and life may be found in the Introduction to that volume (pp. 1-79). The quotation in the text is taken from the Introduction to Meirow's translation of the *Gesta Friderici* (*The Deeds of Frederick Barbarossa*), Columbia University Press, 1953, p. 5. Text: A. Hofmeister, ed.: *Ottonis Episcopi Frisingensis Chronica sive Historia de duabus Civitatibus*, Hanover, 1912.

42. Whether Otto in fact continued Augustine, or betrayed him (see Markus, *op. cit.*, pp. 162-165); whether Otto was in any way original; whether the manifest inconsistencies in and between the texts can be explained, are outside the scope of this article; a good review (with ample references to the literature) can be found in Karl F. Morrison, "Otto of Freising's Quest for the Hermeneutic Circle," *Speculum*, 55, #2, April 1980, pp. 207-236. In Markus's view, Otto's "vision of history owed almost everything to Orosius, almost nothing to Augustine," *op. cit.*, pp. 164-165. The relationship between the framework of Otto's history and the Investiture Contest is discussed in Morrison, p. 210 and elsewhere.

43. The difference between the two works—eschatology vanishes altogether in the *Gesta* and the tone is optimistic—are discussed in Morrison, *art. cit.*

44. Otto: *The Two Cities*, Prologue to Book III.

45. *Ibid.*, Prologue (Meirow translation, pp. 94-95). Scipio and Maccabees, II, 42 (p. 204); queens of Carthage, II, 41 (p. 202); Babylon and Rome parallel histories, VI, 22 (p. 383).

46. Silence of prophecy, II, 47 (p. 211); insight of historian, Book III, Prologue (pp. 218-219); Alexander, II, 25 (pp. 182-184).

47. Morrison, *art. cit.*, summarized well on p. 220. Actually Morrison sees this as the second, eschatology as the first, the two cities not counting.

48. *The Two Cities*, II, 8 (pp. 162-163).

49. Morrison, *art. cit.*, p. 216.

50. *The Two Cities*, II, 36 (pp. 196-197).

51. Irony of Civil Wars and terrible cost of Roman conquests, II, 50-51 (pp. 214-215); silence of prophets broken by Logos, II, 47 (p. 211); *Pax augusta*, Prologue, Book III (esp. p. 221); correspondences between Augustus and Christ, III, 6 (p. 230).

52. Prologue to Book III (pp. 217-222).

53. Persecution of Apostles, III, 16 (p. 243); Church=City of God, III, 22 (p. 251); the two Cities become one: "But from that time on, since not only all the people but also the emperors (except a few) were orthodox Catholics, I seem to myself to have composed a history not of two cities but virtually of one only, which I call the Church. For although the elect and the reprobate are in one household, yet I cannot call these two as I did above; I must call them properly but one—composite, however, as the grain is mixed with the chaff . . . . the City of Earth was laid to rest and destined to be utterly exterminated in the end; hence our history is a history of the City of Christ," Prologue to Book V (pp. 323-324); God's choice of Constantine, Prologue to Book IV (p. 271).

It is Morrison's contention that one of Otto's deeper concerns is to find a way of explaining change and transformation, one of the topics upon which he has recourse to philosophy.

54. The two swords, Prologue to Book IV (p. 272); the legitimacy of the Donation of Constantine, *Ibid.* (pp. 273-274).

55. Markus, *op. cit.*, p. 164.

56. Montesquieu: *Considérations sur les causes de la grandeur des Romains et de leur décadence*, in Vol. I, *Oevres complètes de Montesquieu*, ed. A. Masson, Paris, 1950-55 (vol. I facsimile of 1758 edition). Translated by David Lowenthal, Cornell University Press, 1968. A brilliant analysis of Montesquieu's thought and influence may be found in Isaiah Berlin: *Against the Current, Essays in the History of Ideas*, Viking, 1980, pp. 130-161.

57. In Ch. XXII, he discusses why God, for example, had permitted the replacement of Christianity by Islam throughout so much of the East.

58. He thought he had, "for the first time in human history, . . . uncovered the fundamental laws which govern the behaviour of human societies, much as natural scientists in the previous century had discovered the laws of the behaviour of inanimate matter." Berlin, *op. cit.*, p. 134. Montesquieu speaks of this experience as the dawning of great light "after a long and painful period of intellectual wandering." It will at last permit serious history to replace irrational stories built on unprovable theological or metaphysical explanations. *Ibid.*, p. 133. Once those fundamental laws were grasped, human societies should become intelligible, a science of

society should be possible, and rational communities can be developed. Berlin, *op. cit.*, pp. 134-136. But, although one can regard him as one of the founders of sociology, anthropology, and social psychology, one should note that he in fact never wrote on the basis of such universal laws, but attended carefully to the varying situations in which men in fact lived: "I have seen, in my life, Frenchmen, Italians, Russians . . . but as for *man*, I declare that I have never met him in my life" Berlin summarizes, quoting De Maistre (p. 139). He regarded societies as organic growths, each following its own particular ways.

59. Virtues of the Romans: *Considérations*, Chs. I and III.

60. Corruption of the Republic: *Ibid.*, Chs. VI, IX, X, XI. Constitutions arise from the interweaving of basic human characteristics with the particular conditions under which a community develops. See the famous passage from *De l'ésprit des lois*, qt. in Berlin, *op. cit.*, p. 135.

61. *Considérations*, Ch. XIII (Lowenthal, p. 122). "Augustus, a scheming tyrant, conducted them gently to servitude" (Lowenthal, p. 123).

62. *Ibid.*, Ch. XV (Lowenthal, p. 138).

63. *Ibid.* (Lowenthal, p. 139)

64. *Ibid.*, Ch. XVI (Lowenthal, pp. 145-146)

65. *Ibid.*, Ch. XVIII (Lowenthal, p. 149).

66. See, among other works, A. Momigliano: "Pagan and Christian Historiography in the Fourth Century A.D.," in A. Momigliano, ed.: *The Conflict Between Paganism and Christianity in the Fourth Century*, Oxford, 1963, pp. 79-99.

67. A rough summary of Alasdair MacIntyre's argument in Chapter 15 of his very stimulating book *After Virtue*, Notre Dame, 1981, esp. p. 207.

68. For the background of Gibbon's judgments, see Howard D. Weinbrot: *Augustus Caesar in "Augustan" England: The Decline of a Classical Ideal*, Princeton, 1978; David P. Jordan: *Gibbon and His Roman Empire*, University of Illinois Press, 1971; Lynn White, Jr., ed.: *The Transformation of the Roman World: Gibbon's Problem After Two Centuries*, University of California Press, 1966; the Summer 1976 issue of *Daedalus: Edward Gibbon and the Decline and Fall of the Roman Empire*; Leo Braudy: *Narrative Form in History and Fiction: Hume, Fielding, & Gibbon*, Princeton, 1970; Shelby T. McCloy: *Gibbon's Antagonism to Christianity*, London, 1933. The standard edition of the *Decline and Fall* is that of J. B. Bury, in seven volumes, London, 1909.

69. This felicitous phrase is taken from Charles Barr: *Ealing Studios*, Overlook Press, 1977, p. 130.

GERMANO-ROMAN NUMISMATIC ART

James E. Spaulding*

The Germanic invasions of the fourth and subsequent centuries transformed late classical civilization into the medieval world. In the course of this transformation, both the Roman and German cultures weakened before the forces of political decay and social dislocation. In their stead a new tradition arose, one shorn of both the decadence of aged Rome and the rudeness of the youthful barbarian, yet marked by the lingering elegance of *Romanitas* and the vigor of the new, Germanic blood. This synthesis permeated every aspect of contemporary life: the economy, the political structure, religion, the law, the arts. The development of a Germano-Roman society in western Europe is of special interest to the historian of numismatic art because it confronts him with a series of questions the likes of which had not been posed since the beginnings of coinage in the seventh and sixth centuries B.C.: (1) Did coin design still constitute an art and to what extent? (2) If the coinage remained a medium of artistic expression, in what way did it reflect that fact? (3) Did numismatic art share in the unity imposed on other artistic forms by a common tradition or mixture of traditions and, if so, to what extent? This study is limited to a consideration of the first two queries, which must be answered before approaching the broader and more significant problems inherent in the third.

In late antiquity Roman art came under the influence of a number of barbarian traditions: Celtic, Germanic, Sassanian, and others. The coinage of the period, although it may have obliquely felt these many influences, in continental Europe and North Africa directly reflected the clash of only two differing aesthetic traditions, the classical Roman and the German.

Roman coin art at the end of the fifth century represented, in its general features, a continuation of the naturalism of the earlier Empire, but it betrayed a greater degree of uniformity and a lack of vigor and inventiveness. Its was a naturalism greatly corrupted by the decadence of the age. The portraits of the obverses lost their three-dimensional nature and the modeling of successive planes of interest gave way to a layering of individual levels as the head or bust became a mass raised above the field. Contours were replaced by lines engraved into the elevated surface. The only attempt to impart a sense of unity to the design was a blending of the outlines of the back of the head, the neck, and the jaw. The planes of the facial details were merely intimated by a thickening of the lines sketching the more prominent features. The breasts and shoulders of the bust types were increasingly represented in a facing attitude, even when the portrait was in profile. The folds of the garments were suggested by simple lines and a balance was achieved through the depiction of sleeve and fibula. The result was not a barbarization, rather a simplification and stylization that often was very pleasing. Reverse figure types were likewise rendered naturalistically but in line and without modeling (figs. 1, 2). This, at the time of the first Germanic coin issues, was the Roman ideal in numismatic art, centered on the mints of northern Italy and Constantinople and characterized by the continued domination of portraiture and diluted naturalism.

Portraiture and naturalism were ideals alien to the Germanic artistic tradition. Germanic art was essentially decorative, and in this it reflected the habits and needs of a migratory society. The absence of permanent settlements had prevented the early Germans from developing painting and sculpture, those art forms that encourage the evolution of naturalistic representations. The craftsman expressed aesthetic impulses within the physical framework of the accoutrements of a people constantly on the move: weapons, horses' trappings, tents, and clothing; and the shape of such objects led in the direction of abstract design and geometric form. The Germans excelled in the embellishment of leather and metal and gloried in the use of semi-precious stones, glass, enamel, and gold. Theirs was an art of imaginative shapes and brilliant color, the use of which the Goths had learned from the Sarmatians and Scythians and passed on to the other Germanic tribes.

When the Germans first settled inside the Roman Empire, they had no metallic currency of their own. When their kings initiated regal coinages in Gaul, Spain, and Italy, they had to accept, *faute de mieux*, the artistic conventions represented on the coins already circulating there. But those were conventions of naturalism and figure depiction non-existent in and at odds with the usages of the German past. The inevitable outcome was a conflict of opposing traditions, the ultimate resolution of which must needs have followed one or more of four courses. First, the mint technicians might have failed to maintain the Roman tradition or to impose a Germanic alternative on the moneys. The result would then have been progressive stylistic deterioration to the point where the coinage would cease to be a medium of artistic expression. Second, the Roman concept of numismatic figure representation might have been maintained, but with the forms of the figures modified by the imposition of Germanic ideals until a new, Germano-Roman style evolved. Third, the Roman tradition could have given way completely to the Germanic, the figure types yielding to abstractions derived from the Imperial designs. Such a goal was never fully realized by the Germans, although the creation of a Germano-Roman style may have represented a transitional phase in a course of development that lacked the necessary time to mature. Fourth, the die engravers might have retained the late classical tradition, but here is a course of development that can be highly misleading. A continuation of the outward *form* of the late Roman coinage is only *prima facie* evidence of the perpetuation of the Roman *spirit*. A mere slavish copying of a Roman prototype may be a technological triumph, but for the art historian it is no more indicative of artistic accomplishment than the degeneration that marks the first alternative. To continue the Roman tradition in the coinage, the die-sinkers in the Germanic kingdoms would have had to demonstrate that they were the heirs to the spiritual essence of late Roman numismatic art.

Of course, the ultimate direction Germanic coin design took was influenced by a great number of factors, not all of which were grounded in aesthetic principles. Some strengthened the cause of Roman tradition. In antiquity and the Middle Ages the concept of art for art's sake no more pertained to numismatic art than to the major forms of artistic expression. The numismatic artist had to function within a framework delineated by economic exigency and political convention. In the Germanic kingdoms coinage was intended primarily to serve the needs of commerce. In the fourth and fifth centuries, when the German kings began to strike, the money markets of the Mediterranean world were dominated by Roman gold, the integrity of which had been maintained in the face of the economic decline of the West. Cosmas Indicopleustes, who had journeyed as far as India in the reign of Justinian, summed up the rôle of the Roman coinage:

> There is yet another sign of the power which God has accorded to the Romans. I refer to the fact that it is with their coinage that all the nations carry on trade from one extremity of the earth to the other. This money is regarded with admiration by all men to whatever kingdom they belong, since there is no other country in which the like of it exists.[1]

The Germanic kings, then, were well advised to begin their own coinages in imitation of the world-accepted medium of exchange. Otherwise traders would reject their coins in the marketplace.

Custom and technological considerations reenforced the dictates of trade. The German nations had, of course, used coined money long before they settled in the Empire, and that money was Roman. As far back as the Republic, the Germans had expressed a preference for Roman serrate denarii.[2] Over the centuries they had become accustomed to Roman currency just as had the peoples along the Mediterranean Sea. But when they themselves began to coin, the Germans lacked a tradition of their own and so were forced to turn to craftsmen who had learned their trade at the Imperial mints or who had been taught by those who had been schooled in the north Italian and Gaulish workshops. These artisans made copies of the Roman coins, at first so worthy as to be indistinguishable from the originals. Subsequent generations of workmen, however, were less faithful to the prototypes; and stylistic differences, at first minute but more noticeable with growing removal from the emperor's mints, betrayed the Germanic origin of many coins struck after the close of the fourth century and the beginning of the fifth.

Since the time of Augustus, the coinage in the precious metals had been reserved to the emperor in his capacity of paymaster of the armies.[3] As the coinage of the Empire, the Imperial gold proclaimed the emperor's mastery of the civilized world through his image and inscriptions. The German kings were federates of the Empire and owed at least nominal recognition of the emperor's suzerainty. The mintage of gold coins being an Imperial prerogative, to the extent that they coined in that metal, the German kings struck for and in the name of the emperor, that is, they copied as faithfully as possible the coins issued by the Imperial mints. To have done otherwise would have been regarded as a usurpation of a right belonging to and only to the emperor.[4]

Not all external influences pointed Germanic numismatic art along paths of the current Roman ideal. There were other forces that had a moderating effect, and if they did not exactly encourage, they made possible, experiments in other directions. The Imperial exclusiveness of the gold coinage did not extend to the silver and bronze, and the Germanic kings could exercise a regalian right of coinage in the lesser metals. The barbarian rulers soon debased their gold coins so that they ceased to find acceptance outside their own territories.[5] This, with the rejection of Imperial suzerainty in the sixth century, created new opportunities for artistic emancipation in those kingdoms that could overcome the forces of monetary conservatism at home.

The attraction of late Roman canons of art was further weakened by the force of pre-Roman and barbarian traditions that had lingered on in Gaul or those that more recently had been imported from beyond the frontiers, as well as by a decline in the quality of Gallo-Roman work. In popular art, Celtic forms has survived the Roman occupation. The first German invasions had driven Celtic workers into Gaul from the fringes of the Empire. There they came under the protection of the Roman governors and soon exerted a noticeable influence on Gallo-Roman ornamentation. Metalsmiths from the Pontus and Danubian basin are known to have been working in Gaulish workshops in the fifth century. "Thus," in the words of Raymond Lantier, "a climate of taste was created in advance, ready for the new productions of barbarian art."[6] By the late fifth and sixth centuries, sculpture in the round had all but disappeared from Gaul, and high relief had given way to lines engraved in stone and colored to make them stand out from the background.

Which forces actually came to dominate Germanic numismatic art and the degree and geographical extent of domination can be determined only by an examination of the coinages of the Germanic kings.[7]

The Suevians

In the first decade of the fifth century A.D., Asding Vandals, Siling Vandals, and Alans, an eastern Sarmatian people, began moving from Pannonia in the direction of the Rhine. En route they joined forces with two Suevian tribes—the Marcomanni and Quadi—who, since pre-Christian times, had occupied the area from the headwaters of the Elbe to the Danube. In 406, these three peoples—Vandals, Alans, and Suevians—crossed the Rhine in the vicinity of Mainz and advanced through Gaul, where they pillaged for some three years. In October 409, they passed into Spain, aided by military factions revolting against the emperor Honorius. In the Iberian peninsula the Asdings and Suevians occupied Galicia, the Silings seized Andalusia, while the Alans settled in the Central Plateau. The Hispano-Roman population, following a century of debilitating Imperial exactions, was helpless to resist the invaders and so appealed to the Visigoths who, having ravaged the Balkans and invested Rome itself, had followed the Vandals and Suevians across Gaul. In 412, the West Goths skirted the Pyrenees as Roman allies. In the ensuing years they forced the Suevians into the northwest, destroyed the Silings, and drove the Asdings and Alans across the straits into North Africa. They then withdrew into Aquitania Secunda after having restored Spain to what remained of the Roman administration.

Because of their small numbers—perhaps 15,000 to 20,000—the Suevians could hardly have established any semblance of centralized political control over the population of northern Lusitania and Galicia. The contemporary chronicler Hydatius tells of wandering bands terrorizing the countryside and exacting tribute,[8] but much of this must be dismissed as exaggeration and as more rhetoric than history.[9] The Suevian presence may even have given a new impetus to municipal life by forcing the Hispano-Romans from the countryside to the relative safely of the towns.[10] There the crude invaders did not interfere with the vestiges of Imperial governance.

In the occupied territories, the Suevians came under a double cultural impress, that of the established Hispano-Roman population and that of the neighboring Visigoths who had long since effected the transition from disparate bands of warriors to a people united into a nation.[11] This double influence is reflected in the Suevian coinage, typologically derived as it was from both Roman and Visigothic models. It is in this coinage that we find our best glimpse of Suevian artistic achievement. Other than the coins, the extant physical remains of the Suevians consist of a few buckles and sarcophagus lids; and it is only in the last four decades that numismatists have succeeded in separating the Suevian coinage from the mass of imitative Germanic issues, largely as a result of the investigations of Wilhelm Reinhart.[12]

There are no extant documents relating to the Suevian coinage, but the mention on the coins of several towns suggests that the *jus monetae* may not have been a monopoly of the Suevian kings. The location of many of the mint sites near oriferous streams has led Reinhart to propose that panned gold was sometimes coined *in situ* for the payment of taxes.[13] Although most gold-bearing lodes in Spain had declined by Strabo's time,[14] the Duero, Miño, and Tajo still yield to the pan.[15] Quantities must not have been great for Saint Isidore does not record an abundance of gold as he does of various minor metals,[16] nor are the passages in the *Lex Romana Wisigothorum* which pertain to the mines carried over into later legislation.[17] In any event, the volume of gold required for the coinage could not have been large if the paucity of surviving coins be any index.

The Suevian coinage, with a single exception, consisted of gold solidi and thirds (tremisses).[18] The first recognizable pieces are fair copies of coins of Honorius (393-423). Solidi bear, on the obverse, the emperor's bust in profile with diadem and *paludamentum* and the legend D(*ominus*) N(*oster*) HONORIVS P(*ius*) F(*ilius*) AVG(*ustus*). The reverse, inscribed VICTORIA AVGGG (= *Augustorum*), shows the emperor standing facing right with his foot on a prostrate captive. In the right hand he holds a globe surmounted by a figure of Victory. In the field is the emperor's mintmark M/D (=*Mediolanum*), in the exergue CONOB (= *Constantinopolitam obryzum*, "pure gold of Constantinople"). There is a corresponding issue of tremisses, likewise Roman in style and executed with considerable care. The obverses are similar to those of the solidi; the reverses show a small cross within a crown and the inscription CONOB (fig. 3.) One might well wonder where the Suevians found craftsmen capable of so faithfully echoing in their coin dies Roman artistic traditions. The Suevians, as they crossed Gaul, had not had sufficient time to absorb the techniques of the Roman workshops, and there was no longer a tradition of coin manufacture in Spain, where the last Roman mint had closed soon after the middle of the first century. Hispano-Roman gem engravers or metalsmiths may have turned their skills to the demands of the mint, or possibly the newcomers brought with them experienced die-sinkers from Gaul. Whatever the origin of these artisans, their appearance was ephemeral.

Even greater mystery surrounds the issue of rare silver siliquae of elevated Italianate style which dates to the reign of king Rechiar (448-456). The obverse portrays a skillfully executed bust of Honorius, who had died a quarter century before the accession of Rechiar; the reverse depicts a Latin cross between the mint letters B R (= *Bracara*), all within a laurel wreath and surrounded by the Suevian king's inscription IVSSI RICHIARI REGES (fig. 4). Eckhel mentions the coin, then known from a single example[19] A second specimen from the same dies came to light subsequently. In 1943, Wilhelm Reinhart, with solid arguments, condemned the coin as a modern forgery,[20] in spite of the fact that the inscriptions reflect orthographical variants peculiar to Spain.[21] This coin's authenticity was placed beyond doubt when a third piece was unearthed during excavations at Castro de Lanhoso, twelve kilometers north of Braga. The fine style contrasts sharply with even the relatively careful earlier issues of solidi and tremisses. The output of the Roman mints at Milan and Rome had fallen off substantially by mid-fourth century, and perhaps an unemployed engraver had found his way from northern Italy to Galicia.

Whatever the explanation, for the art historian Rechiar's siliqua is an abberation and in no way a commentary of Suevian numismatic art; for in the gold coinage a degredation of style, fabric, and lettering set in almost immediately, testifying to a lack of appreciation of Roman culture and the absence of a viable artistic tradition of Germanic origin. Solidi, still with Honorius' types and inscriptions, assume an angularity of outline found also on tremisses struck in the name of Valentinian III (424-455) and probably issued during that emperor's reign. This barbarization of style was accompanied by a change of lettering in the reverse field from M/D to H NR, possibly an allusion to Honorius, more likely the mint signature of *Norba Caesarina* (*Colonia Norbense*, today's Cáceres), the H being a blundered representation of M(*oneta*).[22] The artistic deterioration of the thirds continued in concert. The inscriptions remain those of Valentinian III, even after that emperor's death, as is verified by the mint letters in the reverse field as was customary on coins of the eastern Empire only at the end of the fifth century. A fourth type of tremissis followed, with an even more careless representation of Valentinian III, whose inscriptions were now replaced by legends of a distinct national character and often negligently engraved: MVNITA GALLICA PAX, OCODIACCAREIGESONAI (fig. 5),[23] LATINA TVDE MVNITA, etc.

In the final years of the Suevian kingdom, a new form of tremissis appeared with fully Visigothic types: obverse, indecipherable legend around an angular profile bust of Justin II (566-578)[24] with the trapezoidal torso characteristic of early Visigothic tremisses; reverse, an insect-like figure derived from the Victory of the Byzantine coinage. Stylistically the new coins belong more to the Visigoths than the Suevians. The Suevian coinage, art-historically considered, no longer existed; and when the Visigoths marched into Galicia in 585, the Suevian kingdom followed its moneys into the dustbins of history.

The Visigoths

The Visigoths of southern France and Spain[25] were the sole Germanic people to reconcile Roman and Germanic ideals in their monetary art. All the conditions were ripe for the Visigoths to create a new artistic mode. They and their kindred Ostrogoths had, more than any other barbarian nations, come under the intense influence of both oriental and Roman traditions, which produced an ambivalence reflected in Visigothic coin design.

The West Goths established a kingdom in the most

thoroughly Romanized part of Europe outside Italy; yet in Spain, which became the heartland of their realm during the sixth and seventh centuries, there had been a hiatus in regular mint activity going back some 400 years. In Iberia they broached an independence of the Imperial coinage, metrologically by debasement as early as the time of Alaric II (484-507) and, politically, in the reign of Leovigild, who renounced his subjection to Constantinople at some time between 575 and 578; and, unlike the Frankish kings in Gaul, the Visigothic rulers maintained a close control over their coinage and the selection of coin types.

The Visigoths had enjoyed a longer and closer association with Rome and its culture than had those Germans who preceded them into Spain. Settled since the second century A.D. between the Empire's Danubian frontier and the Ostrogoths to the east, they could not help but absorb many Roman ways, but without compromising their own Germanic traditions and their Arian Christian faith. Bishop Ulfilas' Gothic translation of the Bible demonstrates, by its vocabulary, both the inroads of and the resistance to the institutions and products of the West.[26] When, after the middle of the fourth century, the Huns moved westward from Central Asia, absorbed the Ostrogoths, and threatened Visigothic independence, Alaric I (ca. 376-410) requested and received the emperor Valens' permission to settle his people in the Balkan peninsula. Smarting under the exactions of Roman provincial administrators, he again set his nation on the march in 387, inaugurating a progression of peregrinations that, in 412, brought the Visigoths to the Pyrenees. King Ataulphus (410-415) had a predilection for Roman institutions and culture and aspired to be the restorer of Roman civilization.[27] He and his successors campaigned in Spain on behalf of the Hispano-Romans, reducing the other Germans and carving out a kingdom for themselves in Spain and Gaul. At its widest extent the Visigothic domain stretched from the Atlantic to the Seine; but after a crushing defeat at the hands of the Franks in 507, the Gaulish territories shrank to a mere foothold in the Narbonese.

Ulfilas' use of Latinized vocabulary in reference to household utensils points to the presence, at an early date, of Roman traders among the Goths, so there can be little doubt that the Ostrogoths and Visigoths were more than casually acquainted with the use of coined money. The latter would certainly have been anxious to coin for themselves once they had constituted their own kingdom in Spain and Gaul. By the beginning of the fifth century they were striking slavish copies of Roman gold. However, the Visigoths, before and after their settlement in the Roman world, were a warrior folk; and it would be wrong to imagine that they possessed the requisite skills to cut dies and strike coins with any degree of sophistication. Nevertheless, in the course of their wanderings they did pass through or near several centers of monetary production: Thessalonica, Aquileia, Rome, Milan, and Ravenna, from any one of which they may have attracted or impressed employees of the Roman mint. Arles and Aquileia, as well as Lyons farther north in Gaul, ceased striking in the 420's, and Trier closed its mint about 450. The workshops at Rome, Milan, and Ravenna had declined by mid-fifth century. There must have been a large number of unemployed mint workers ready to serve a new master.

The earliest discernible Visigothic coinage dates to the reign of Theodoric I (419-451), who struck excellent copies of the issues of rulers at Constantinople. By choice, or more probably because of the lack of technical skills, subsequent generations failed to maintain this fidelity to the Imperial prototypes.

The first radical artistic change came with Alaric II, who, in 491, adopted as his sole types: obverse, D(*ominus*) N(*oster*) ANASTASIVS P(*ater*) P(*atriae*) AVG(*ustus*) around the profile bust of the emperor Anastasius (491-518), and reverse: a standing figure of Victory holding a palm branch and crown. In the reverse field are initials of the Visigothic mint and, in the exergue, CONOB (fig. 6). Succeeding kings down to Leovigild maintained Alaric's types with appropriate changes of the emperor's name, but almost immediately the designs underwent a stylistic transformation. While the engravers strove to retain a realistic image of the emperor, the facing chest quickly became a two-dimensioned geometrical simplification of the imperial original, assuming a square or trapezoidal shape of obvious barbarian inspiration. The winged figure of Victory took the abstract aspect of an insect (fig. 7). There can be no doubt that this metamorphosis represents the implementation of an aesthetic standard exhibiting elements of Germanic and Roman taste, for, once it had assumed its consummate form, it remained unchanged for the better part of a century; and when Leovigild replaced this Victory type in 579, it was to make way for another "national" design.[28]

The real blossoming of the Germano-Roman style occurred under Leovigild (573-586), who not only remade the image of the Visigothic monarchy, but initiated a revolution in monetary art. Leovigild's first coins, struck prior to 575, represent a continuation of his predecessors' types: obverse, Imperial bust and inscriptions and reverse, stylized walking Victory. At some point during the ensuing three years, the Visigothic king, following the example of Theodobert of Austrasia, rejected even nominal subservience to Constantinople and replaced the emperor's now pseudo-portrait and inscriptions with his own. The obverse bust retains its trapezoidal form, but the legend now reads LIVVIGILDVS or LIVVIGILDVS REX: and on the reverse, the qualificative INCLITV(s) displaces the *Victoria Augustorum* in use since Alaric II (fig. 8).

No other barbarian king, with the possible exception of the Ostrogoth Theodric I, had a greater appreciation of *Romanitas* than did Leovigild. He assumed the costume, titles, and regalia of the Romans; and, more important for the future, he sought to replace the traditional elective monarchy of the Germans by the heritable rule of the Leovigildine family. He or his ministers also understood the rôle the moneys might play in advertising the prince and his policies. No other medieval ruler would exploit the propaganda potential of the coinage as thoroughly as did Leovigild and his immediate successors. In 579, the king discontinued the profile and Victory types in favor of a new, autochthonous style. The obverse now presented a stylized portrait faintly reminiscent of the Byzantine facing busts, with an arc of hair worn long in the German fashion. At first the bust is cloaked with a *paludamentum* fastened by a fibula, which, in later years, is simplified in the direction of the geometric chest of the earlier Visigothic profile coins. His obverse inscriptions are D(*ominus*) N(*oster*) LIVVIGILDVS (or LEOVIGILDVS) REX. The reverse bears the facing bust of the heir to the throne and the name of the mint,[29] usually with a a qualifying adjective or substantive. Leovigild obviously intended the reverse type to broadcast his selection of a son as successor to the throne. At first this was his elder son, Hermenigild, who embraced Roman Catholicism and revolted against his father in 579, then Hermenigild's younger brother, Reccared.[30]

Leovigild gives us further proof of his grasp of Roman monetary conventions with various legends celebrating victories against Hermenigild during their civil war: CORDOBA BIS OPTINVIT, CVM D(eo) OPTIN(u)IT (I)SP(a)LI(m), CVM DI(e obtinuit) RODA(m), EMERITA VICTORI(a). Leovigild rebuilt and renamed the city of Reccopolis and, in good Roman fashion, glorified the act with a reverse inscription RECCOPOLI FECIT. Similar commemorative legends appear on coins of Reccared and, exceptionally, later kings.

During Hermenigild's revolt and after Reccared's conversion to Athanasian Christianity, the coins, again following Roman precedent, invoke the patronage of God with occasional religious formulae: CVM D(eo) (Leovigild), ERMENEGILDI REGI A DEO VITA (perhaps on the occasion of Hermenigild's conversion to Catholicism), IN D(ei) N(omine) (Chindasvinth, Wamba, etc.). The Visigoth moneyers also adopted the Roman practice of representing personifications and deities by religious symbols. The most notable is the cross as the emblem of the Christian faith. Ervig (680-687) transmuted the reverse portrait into a nimbate figure of Christ.[31]

Leovigild's facing-bust type found favor with all subsequent Visigothic kings through Chindasvinth (642-653) and lingered on as a facing head into the reign of Reccesvinth (653-672). Chintila (636-640) replaced the reverse busts on some of his coins with a cross-on-steps motif copied from the Byzantine coinage. This new combination of types continued almost to the end of the kingdom (fig. 9).

Sixteen kings struck facing-bust tremisses at some fifty mints, and so we should not be surprised to discover a great number of deviations in both the manner and quality of representation of the head and drapery; but throughout we are conscious of a single and vigorous artistic medium which joins, in no uncertain terms, the classical concept of portraiture with the Germanic love of geometric abstraction.[32]

Chindasvinth introduced yet one more combination of types: obverse, royal inscriptions surrounding a profile bust and reverse, mint signature and a cross on three steps in imitation of the East Roman type introduced by Tiberius II Constantine (578-582), but without the exergual CONOB of the Byzantine coins. The king's bust varies greatly: some examples display a well delineated geometric representation of the *paludamentum* and fibula, on others the costume is reduced to a wizened series of concentric or nearly concentric squares. Some are bareheaded, others portray the strapped helmet (*Spangenhelm*) or, in a single instance, domed helmet (*Haubenhelm*) of the Visigothic man at arms (fig. 10).[33] The presence of patently German armor points up once again the deliberate attempt of the Visigothic coin designer to fuse Germanic and Roman elements in his work.

Towards the end of the Visigothic period new types appeared. During the joint reign of Egica and Wittiza (698-702) the moneyers compressed, with evident lack of success, the facing heads of the two kings separated by a scepter onto an obverse die bearing Egica's inscription. The reverse, with the co-ruler's name and title, contains either a monogram or full name of the mint (fig. 11). A similar obverse marks coins of the shared rule of Chindasvinth and Reccesvinth (649-653) with, as reverse, cross on steps. The latter kings also struck tremisses with a profile-bust obverse and monogram reverse. Most of these pieces are too crowded to allow the engravers to display their talents, and the level of design and manufacture falls well below that of the more conventional issues. Even the standardized facing-bust type from Wamba (672-680) until the end of Visigothic rule in 711, assumes a coarseness of treatment which is not to be attributed to artistic degeneration as much as to the turbulence of an era marked by internal unrest and foreign invasion.

For 250 years the Visigothic moneyers developed and maintained a genre of numismatic art unique in that age when the ancient world was giving way to a new Europe, unique in that it represented the successful fusion of traditions. On the one hand were the pictorial types, iconography, and inscriptive formulae of classical monetary usage; on the other the tendencies to abstraction and linear decoration that the Visigoths had transplanted from the steppe lands of Central Asia and southeastern Europe.

Writers on numismatic art are prone to denigrate the achievements of Visigothic design, pointing to a technological deterioration[34] and failure to "find artists who could represent [the Gothic idiom] with much more skill than that possessed by a normally ingenious metal-smith."[35] This misses the very essence of Visigothic art, which is precisely an art of the metalsmith. Once the age of servile imitation had passed, there was in Spain no need to imitate the mechanical accomplishments of the Roman mint. The Visigothic die-sinker's talent—it would be an exaggeration to say genius—lay in his ability to respond to economic and political realities in terms intelligible to his compatriots, i.e., to respond with the primitive simplicity with which his ancestors had decorated their instruments of war. And this was a positive accomplishment, not the chance result of irresistible artistic retrogression.

Only in Visigothic Spain, among the Germanic kingdoms, do the coins reflect the persistent jousting of *Romanitas* and *Germanentum* found in other areas of public life. In religion there was constant tension between the Roman Christianity of Hermenigild, Reccared, and many of their successors and the Arianism of the earlier kings and a large segment of the Gothic aristocracy down to the Moorish conquest. In political life we witness a continuing struggle between the Constantinian and post-Constantinian system of familial rule and the elective processes of customary Germanic law. The numismatic artist realized what the nobility of Church and state could not: he resolved the dichotomy of Visigothic life.

The Franks

The Franks were a heterogeneous group of tribes who settled along the lower Rhine and North Sea in the course of the first three Christian centuries. The largest were the Ripuarian Franks of the Rhine basin and the Salians of what are now parts of Belgium and the Dutch Netherlands. Each of these was divided, in turn, into subgroups ruled over by petty chiefs. In the late third and fourth centuries many Frankish tribes served as *foederati* in the Roman armies, but relations between Franks and Romans were, more often than not, strained. So when the Salians began moving south of the Rhine, following the other German intrusions into the Empire in 406, they not only occupied Roman centers in Belgium and the Rhineland, but quite often leveled the Roman adminstrative ediface. King Clovis (481-511), first great representative of the Merovingians, and his sons united the Franks into one great kingdom and, in the process, put an end to Roman political ascendancy in Gaul. Unlike the Visigoths, the Merovingians were unable to maintain the unity of the kingdom because of repeated divisions of the patrimony and, finally, surrender of power to the regional aristocracy. Dagobert I (ca. 629-639) was the last Merovingian king whose power was more than nominal. After his death mayors of the palace exercised the *dominium* in the various domains until the eighth century, when the Merovingian world was reunited under the authority of the Pepinid family, which, in 751, usurped the crown to establish a second race of French kings.

The Merovingian Franks[36] had no coinage typologically and metrologically distinct from that of the Empire prior to the reign of Clovis.[37] Clovis struck solidi and tremisses in the name of Anastasius (491-518), which already exhibited carelessness in the rendition of the emperor's portrait and the transcription of the legends, as well as tremisses of Visigothic inspiration.[38] When Clovis died, each of his four sons, following the Germanic customary law which treated the Frankish patrimony as personal property to be divided among surviving males, ruled over a kingdom of his own. Thus began a process of separation and reconsolidation that would condemn the Franks to 375 years of internecine warfare and sap the ruling house of the vigor required to sustain any semblance of order in Frankish monetary art. Clovis' sons continued their father's types with the substitution of the effigies and inscriptions of their contemporaries at Constantinople. The emperor's bust would remain the preferred obverse type down to the end of the Merovingian coinage (fig. 12).

Clovis' grandson, Theodobert I of Austrasia (534-538), was the first barbarian ruler to renounce the nominal suzerainty of the emperor by striking solidi in his own name, an act which Procopius condemned as an arrogation from which even the Persian kings forebore.[39] This, coupled with serious debasements of the coinage, offered opportunities for an independent development of Frankish monetary art, which Theodobert and his successors failed to exploit, in part owing to the strength of Imperial monetary conventions in Gaul and, in part, because of Frankish indifference to the physical aspects of the coinage. Theodobert's coins from Gaulish and Rhenish mints are more carefully engraved than those of his immediate predecessors, but they are not up to the quality of those struck at Imperial mints.

In a class apart are Theodobert's gold coins struck during his Italian campaign of 539. Some are on a par with the finest Imperial pieces of the age and must have been struck in the north Italian mints or by craftsmen carried from Italy to Gaul (fig. 13). In either case, they are representative of the artistic conventions of Italy rather than those of the Merovingians.

Not only did Theodobert's coiners fail to create a national numismatic art, he and his heirs lost their control over the monetary affairs of their kingdoms. The early Frankish kings, if they exhibited a disdain for things Roman, at first recognized the value of continuing the existing fiscal system in Gaul. In the late Empire, it had been the custom to reduce tax receipts in the precious metals to ingots, which were conveniant for transfer to the treasury.[40] The Merovingian kings aped this procedure, striking into coins the gold received as tax payments.[41] For this purpose, they turned the production of the moneys over to *monetarii*, individuals and associations of individuals who, for a share of the proceeds, managed the mints and signed the coins as a token of their responsibility. Also, the king shared the *jus monetae* with all manner of local authorities, lay and ecclesiastical; and these dignitaries farmed out their mints to *monetarii* of their own. The consequence was a proliferation of mints and fiscal accountability, which was aggravated by a weakening of the monarch's central authority. By the reign of Dagobert III (711-715), the political and military power had come to rest in the hands of the mayors of the palace and other great nobles. Dagobert III was the last of his race to sign the coinage. Where the Romans had maintained but three mints in Gaul, the Franks counted theirs in the thousands;[42] and this could only exacerbate the decline of royal supervision of the design and quality of the moneys and lead to artistic decay. The spiritual degeneration of the coinage was a *fait accompli* by the reigns of Clothair II (651-670) and Childeric II (660-673). By then, the barbarousness of engraving was at times so pronounced that it is impossible to attribute coins on the basis of style to homonymic kings who ruled as much as forty years apart.

In spite of the looseness of fiscal controls and the great number of mints, the profile bust of Roman inspiration remained, as we have seen, the foremost Frankish obverse type, and it is the form and quality of its execution that most clearly illustrate the vagaries of Merovingian numismatic art down to Pepin III's monetary reform of 755.[43]

Four principal schools of engraving dominated the Merovingian coinage.[44] Centering on the great cities of Marseilles, Trier, Chalon-sur-Saône, and Limoges, their influence often extended over a considerable area; and from each there developed a profusion of local styles.

At Marseilles, classical influences governed coin design throughout the Merovingian era, and there the stylistic deterioration that characterized the coinage of the age never reached the extremes that it did elsewhere. On the Roman profile bust a diadem divides the hair into three areas. The figure is well modeled with a clearly delineated chin and a long, properly proportioned neck. The *paludamentum*, at first not too far removed from that of the prototypes, becomes simplified in time but always remains recognizable. A peculiar feature of the bust is the peaked shoulders which may be a simplification of the fibula of the Imperial gold (fig. 14). The conservatism of the Massiliote types testifies to close commercial relations with Byzantine traders. The Marseilles school would exert a noticeable influence on the work representative of Chalon-sur-Saône.

The leading Austrasian mints were located at Trier in *Belgica Prima*, where the last Roman mint in Gaul had closed in the 450's, and at Cologne, Toul, Metz, and Rheims. On early tremisses the hair stands on end, with the exception of three locks, which fall downward over the cheek. The bow which ought terminate the diadem stands isolated behind the head, producing the class French numismatists term *boucle perdue*. The *epitogium* takes the form of fringed epaulettes (fig. 15). The details of engraving disappear rather early, but the overall impression that distinguishes the work of Trier remains until the style comes to an end in the reign of Guntram (561-593).

The artistic school that had Chalon-sur-Saône as its focal point developed out of the school of Trier, but with a strong influence from the direction of Marseilles. Later it would inspire a new center of engraving at Limoges. In Burgundy at Chalon, Lyon, Lausanne, and elsewhere the engravers no longer distinguished the *epitogium* from the remainder of the cloak. They dispensed with the locks that, at Trier, covered the cheek, but they retained the *boucle perdue*. Pure work of Chalon dates to the reign of Guntram, which king it does not survive. Later issues—those of the seventh century—came under the impress of Marseilles (fig. 16).

The numismatic art of Austrasia and Burgundy underwent a rapid localization of style. Three distinct forms developed before the end of the sixth century, each marked by a peculiar artistic degeneration. To the north of Burgundy, most notably at Besançon, the engravers distorted the head. The neck and cheeks run together; the lips and nostrils are merely intimated by dots entered into the die with puncheons. A crescent-shaped punch outlines the ear. The hair still stands on end, as at Trier and the mints under its influence; it is now bound by a ribbon. The modeling of the tunic deteriorates as the chest assumes the aspect of adjacent ladders (fig. 17).

In the regions of Metz and Toul, Burgundian engravers put an end to Trier's influence with a complete artistic metamorphosis culminating in a new mode peculiar to Austrasia. The chest is reduced to a square or oblong. An over-sized neck, not engraved but entered into the die by means of a rectangular punch, stands suspended between head and body. Patterns of dashes and dots form the hair, which is bound by a dotted ribbon, or the hair is completely missing. Facial details are similarly intimated by dots or pearls (fig. 18). At Rheims the engravers, taking scant inspiration from their prototypes of the Trier school, lessen facial features and reduce the body to the peculiar shape of a bearded almond (fig. 19). This barbarism found wide currency in those localities with which Rheims traded.

Along the Rhine from Strasbourg northward to the middle course of the Meuse, the stylistic and mechanical deterioration, while evident, is not as pronounced as at Lyons. The neck thickens, assuming a goitrous appearance; the ear cuts the fillet; and horizontal dotted lines barely hint at the remains of a bust (fig. 20).

In the early seventh century, Burgundian engravers fell under the artistic domination of Marseilles, although the Burgundian profile bust is stiffer. At Chalon a commercial revolution was at its height, and several mints worked to supply the currency demands of the increased volume of trade. The engravers met the challenge with dies cut in the Massiliote style and which reflect a high degree of sophistication (fig. 21). Engel and Serrure conjecture that the die-sinkers competed to produce the best coins.[45] Unfortunately, this artistic revival was short-lived.

Chalon lost her commercial prëminence after Clothair II's death in 628, and the coin inscriptions show that the *monetarii* abandoned the city for greener pastures.

Limoges was the fourth great center of coin design in Merovingian Europe. Early in the seventh century, she was developing in economic importance, which helped attract goldsmiths and *monetarii* from Chalon. Limoges quickly became the most important seat of artistic activity in Aquitaine. The distinguishing features of her coins are the hair line, which falls in bangs over the forehead, and the restraining diadem, which extends beyond the front and rear of the head. The facial outline is well sketched, the eye is almond-shaped as if seen in a frontal pose, and there is a profusion of pearls throughout the various components of the design. The finest extant representative of this idiom is a unique gold presentation piece of Dagobert I found in England (fig. 22).

Saint Eligius, the most capable goldsmith of the Merovingian age, was born in 588 near Limoges at the villa of Chaptelat. He was apprenticed to Abbo, a renowned goldsmith and *monetarius* of the principal mint at Limoges. He then became goldsmith and counselor to the king; and, in a career that spanned the reigns of four sovereigns, he reformed the coinage and signed the dies as *monetarius* at Paris, Marseilles, and Arles.[46] It was Eligius who carried the Limousin style to the Palatine mint where, during his tenure, the coins, while far from being great works of art, do exhibit a new realism and homogeneity of presentation at odds with the aesthetically debased tremisses of his predecessors. Eligius' coins fall into two inscriptional groups, those signed by Eligius alone and those bearing the names of both the king and the moneyer-saint. Two, possibly three, engravers prepared the dies for the latter. Eligius himself may have engraved the most respectable of these (fig. 23).[47] The dies where Eligius' name figures alone are stylistically less consistent and presage the rapid decline of the Limoges school, which was obvious by Clovis II's death in 656 (fig. 24). That Eligius was a competent craftsman is beyond question, but the existence of cruder specimens alongside those of superior execution implies that he was not endowed with an independence of spirit or true understanding of the classical past. No renaissance was afoot. Eligius' better pieces are no more than mirages in an artistic desert. So, ironically, the finest examples of seventh-century Merovingian numismatic art only serve to point up its degradation, while Eligius' pieces of poor appearance anticipate the end of Limousin primacy in coin design, a collapse that was already noticeable at the end of Clovis II's reign and consummate fact soon after. A tremissis of PAVLIACO (Pouillé or Poillé?), based on Eligius' palatine tremissis for Clovis II, demonstrates how far the descent (fig. 25).

The tendency to barbarization was broken here and there by ephemeral local types. Some were isolated attempts to reach back to classical models. An engraver at Maastricht imitated a bronze of Constantine the Great. Farther removed from Imperial prototypes are, from the Auvergne, an episcopal bust with hand raised in benediction (fig. 26); from Autun, a fair helmeted head (fig. 27); and, from the same mint, such less successful jugate busts (fig. 28).[48] Frankish *monetarii* chose Visigothic designs in the time of Childebert II, possibly to commemorate their king's marriage, in 580, to a daughter of Leovigild. In the late seventh century, bizarre copies of tremisses of the joint reigns of Chindasvinth and Reccesvinth or Egica and Wittiza were copied as far from Spain as Normandy and Maine. Of strictly local inspiration were a few religious and animal figures. Many of the latter are *types parlants* of the mint, such as a wolf's head on a tremissis inscribed LOCI VELACORVM (fig. 29). *Velacos* is Gaulish for "wolf." Devoid of any degree of sophistication, these moneys afford a glimpse at folk art of the basest sort and of attitudes of mind that are not represented in the literature of the day.

The Merovingian reverse types, from the art-historical point of view, parallel those of the obverses. The earliest Frankish coins have a Victory, generally facing in Burgundy, in profile in the northeast. Quickly degenerating, Victory fell from favor in the 570's, giving way to rough imitations of the Byzantine cross-on-steps or *globus cruciger*. In central, western, and northern France, the Victory type persisted longer and ultimately was transmuted into a Christian figure, becoming an angel in an attitude of prayer or the image of a local saint. Parochial varieties strayed from the Byzantine originals until little or no Roman element remained. The Victory reverse never appeared in Provence. Marseilles adopted current Byzantine cross motifs, no doubt influenced, as in her choice of obverses, by her trade relations with the East. As did the obverse types, the reverse designs occasionally reverted to classical models, aped foreign conventions, or comprised purely local inventions. Epigraphical types, common on the silver issues from the late seventh century, are of little interest to the art historian.

The Merovingian inscriptions receded from classical influence as quickly as did the coin types. They demonstrate none of that consciousness of Roman monetary practices that marked the coin legends of Visigothic Spain and which was a requisite to the perpetuation of the late classical tradition or creation of a new, mixed artistic convention. The inscriptions are almost entirely onomastic. The kings assume the title *rex* or *rix*, but only once do we find the Roman *dominus*: DOMNVS DAGOBERTVS REX FRANCORVM on Dagobert's medallion (fig. 22) and once the Visigothic formula HINCLITVS ET PIVS (on a tremissis of Clothair II). The modifiers of place names are descriptive, never honorific as is usual on Visigothic coins, where the mint city is *pius*. Historical references are rare: TRIECTO FIT PAX on a coin of Maastricht, PAX alone on several tremisses of the Gévaudan, CHLOTARI VICTORIA on pieces of Clothair II. Occasionally the religious inscription AΩ figures in the reverse field.[49] The inscriptions are further evidence of the regressive nature of Merovingian monetary art; they offer no indication of an appreciation of the Roman notion of sovereignity and the use of the coinage in the service of that ideal.

In Merovingian coin design, the classical element was quickly lost from view. Nowhere was there a transformation in the direction of purely decorative motifs such as had marked the numismatic art of pre-Roman Gaul, nor could there have been a stabilization at some point in its development marked by a fusion of styles and attitudes. Where schools of engraving evolved, they were no more than representatives of different forms of artistic retrogression. The course was negative and regressive. The rare appearance of local issues of good style attests to the possibility of an artistically worthwhile coinage and suggests that one of the reasons for the failure to develop a distinctive Merovingian coin art was the division of responsibility for monetary affairs. The Frankish *monetarii* were businessmen who coined for profit, and this criterion they imposed upon their engravers. This, joined to a dim or nonexistent classical tradition among the Franks and the political and social turbulence of the times, exacerbated the situation from the aesthetic point of view. These factors, taken conjointly, explain the general insouciance, in regard to the die-sinker's art and the moneyer's craft, that allowed no development of a Frankish national style.

The Burgundians[50]

The Burgundians, an East German people, appeared on the Rhine in the fifth century A.D. After wars against the Roman general Aetius and the Huns, they moved to the vicinity of Lake Geneva after 436, then to the Rhône valley. They fought as Roman federates against the Huns in 451, and for this the Burgundian kings received the Imperial title Master of the Soldiers. Gondebaud joined Clovis in his war against the Visigoths; then his son turned against the Franks, who destroyed the Burgundian kingdom in 534.

The first coins attributable to the Burgundians appeared ca. 500, when Kind Gondebaud (473-516) deposed his brother, Godegisel, and extended his authority over the entire Burgundian patrimony. Gondebaud's imitations of solidi and tremisses of Anastasius are of good style and distinguished by a royal monogram in the reverse field (fig. 30). His silver comprises two issues, one with obverse, Anastasius' bust and inscriptions; the other with reverse, standing winged Victory. The opposite faces bear the king's monogram. Both series are of high style. Mint abbreviations RM (*Roma*), RV (*Ravenna*), and MD (*Mediolanum*) are, as on contemporary Ostrogothic coins, in a form both older and more correct than those on Merovingian moneys. A small bronze piece has obverse, laureate profile head without legend and reverse, royal monogram and mint signature. Gondebaud's sons, Sigismund (516-524) and Gondomar II (524-534), struck copies of the gold and silver of Anastasius and Justin with an initial or monogram as a personal mark. The Burgundian coinage came to an end when the Franks and Ostrogoths divided the kingdom between them in 534 and before it could develop a character of its own.

The Herules

The Herules had emigrated from the Baltic to create, in the second half of the fifth century, an independent kingdom stretching from the Carpathian Mountains to the Danube. After having supplied soldiers to the Roman army, they moved westward from the Thracian frontier, marched on Rome in 476, and deposed Romulus Augustulus, the last Roman emperor in the West. Although an undisciplined people, they made few changes in the existing administrative system. Pretending to govern Italy as the agent of the emperor at Constantinople, the Herule king, Odoacer, struck, at Rome and Ravenna, small coins in silver and bronze with his own bust and inscriptions (fig. 31).[51] The Ostrogothic invasion of 489 and Odoacer's assassination five years later put an end to the Herule kingdom in Italy before it could develop more than a semblance of monetary autonomy.

The Ostrogoths

The Goths had moved southward to the shores of the Black Sea in the third century A.D. Occupying lands from the Danube mouths to the Dnieper, they raided into Dacia and Moesia, then separated into two nations divided by the Dniester River: the Visigoths to the west and the Ostrogoths to the east. Hunnish expansion checked Ostrogothic independence until the defeat of the Huns at Châlons in 451, after which the East Goths moved into the Balkans as Roman allies. At Zeno's request, Theodoric led his people against Odoacer, whom he defeated and murdered in 494, and Anastasius recognized him as ruler of Italy.

Theodoric the Great (493-526) had been a hostage at Constantinople in his youth, and he came to northern Italy with great respect for Roman institutions. Like Ataulphus eighty years before, he saw himself as the restorer of *Romanitas* rather than its enemy. He and his successors would carry over to the coinage this esteem for things Roman.

Until 497, Theodoric struck solidi and tremisses in imitation of those of Anastasius, who had succeeded Zeno in 491, differencing his own coins by the sole mention of the mint, using the highly proper abbreviations that we have already seen adopted by the Burgundians. In 498, Anastasius returned the West-Roman regalia to the Eternal City, and Theodoric accepted this gesture as constituting recognition of his own position in the West. From that moment we see the Ostrogothic king's monogram in the reverse field of coins in all metals, although he continued to strike in the Byzantine mode.

The only exception to this rule is a handsomely executed facing bust of the Ostrogothic king, which we find on a unique three-solidus piece struck not as currency but as a medallion or presentation piece. Theodoric is shown with long hair; he wears an elegantly decorated cuirass and cape; and he holds a *globus cruciger* in his hand. Both the obverse and Victory-type reverse carry the king's name and titulature.[52] Although outside the normal run of the coinage, this magnificent artifact verifies, at the beginning of Ostrogothic monetary history, an ability to depict German traits within the compass of Roman idiom and anticipates Theodahad's portrait bronzes of two reigns hence.

Athalaric (526-534) struck no gold, but his silver and most of his bronzes continued the Imperial types, now with the inscriptions and conventionalized portraits of Justin I and Justinian. Bronze issues from Rome break the stylistic monotony, all the while remaining true to Imperial artistic ideals. His most common coins from that mint are ten-nummus pieces with **INVICTA ROMA** and the goddess Roma on the obverse and reverse, D(*ominus*) N(*oster*) **ATHALARICVS REX** written out in four lines or contracted into a monogram. Another base-metal series represents, on the reverse, Athalaric leaning on a spear and shield and that king's inscriptions.

Theodahad (534-536) continued the issue of imitative silver. His small bronzes copy Justinian's types and inscriptions on the obverses, while the reverses are epigraphic: D(*ominus*) N(*oster*) **THEODAHATHVS REX** in four lines or monogram. Middle bronzes repeat the Invicta Roma types. Theodahad's numismatic *pièce de résistance* is a large 40-nummus piece in bronze: obverse, the king's name and titles around a crowned profile bust clothed in a sumptuous dalmatic and with a cross on the breast. A walking-Victory reverse is flanked by S(*enatus*) C(*onsulto*) and surrounded by either **VICTORIA PRINCIPVM** or **VICTORIA AVGUST**(*i*) (fig. 32). Wroth[53] and Babelon[54] interpret the bust as authentic portraiture; and the long hair, falling almost to the shoulders at the rear, intimates that this is more than a conventionalism. As with Theodoric's triple-solidus, we are in the presence of a Roman portrait of a German king.

Theodahad's successors were preoccupied by Justinian's war for the reconquest of Italy, which had begun in 536. Witiges (536-540), who was taken prisoner by Justinian's commander,

Belisarius, issued but two coins, a silver piece with Justinian's head on the obverse and his own inscription on the reverse: D(*ominus*) N(*oster*) WITEGES REX (fig. 33) and a bronze Invicta Roma type, also with an inscriptive reverse. Matasunda followed her husband to the throne for a short while in 540, and continued his silver issues with her own monogram on the reverse. Theodebald (540-541) appears not to have had time to initiate a coinage in his own name. After issues of silver in the name of Justinian, Totila (541-552) and Theia (552-553) showed their resentment of Justinian by reverting to models of Anastasius. On silver and bronze, Totila gives us his own conventionalized facing portrait and the incription D(*ominus*) N(*oster*) BADVELA REX on the obverse and as the reverse type (fig. 34). Bronze coins struck at Pavia borrow a theme from earlier Roman colonial coinages: obverse, turreted *tyche* of the city, which is described as FELIX TICINVS, and reverse, the king's inscriptions. Theia's imitative silver carries the reverse legend D(*ominus*) N(*oster*) THEIA REX. He struck no gold or bronze.

A number of anonymous bronze coins, perhaps struck at Rome early in the sixth century, feature patently Roman types: helmeted Roma (fig. 35), she-wolf and twins, Victory on prow, or a Roman eagle. An unnamed 10-nummus piece from Ravenna has obverse, a turreted head and FELIX RAVENNA and reverse, either *Ravenna* in monogram or an eagle and mark of value.

In 553, Narses, at the head of the Byzantine armies, defeated and killed Theia, and Ostrogothic dominion in Italy came to an end. For sixty years Theodoric and his successors had maintained the artistic integrity of their coinage, adapting Imperial monetary usages to their particular needs. Their coins show great originality, yet are thoroughly within the Roman tradition. Except for Theodoric's medallion, which is *sui generis* in every way, and a lone issue of Totila, the gold and silver portraiture is reserved to the emperors. The *Roma Invicta* and civic personifications echo the Roman past but touch the Italian present. The same is true of those inscriptions that announce the *dominium* of an Ostrogothic king who can lead his subjects back to the good life anticipated by *Felix Ticinus* and *Felix Ravenna*. This could eventuate only within a properly functioning Germano-Roman state growing on the bedrock of the traditions and institutions manifest in Roman coin types and legends. It is difficult to believe it might have been otherwise. Theodoric was the most Romanized of all the German kings, relations with Constantinople remained close until the Ostrogothic wars, the newcomers saw the advantages of maintaining the preexisting administrative structure, and there was no discontinuity in the operation of the mints at Rome and Ravenna and only a brief hiatus at Milan.

The Vandals[55]

By the second century A.D. the Vandals had migrated from northern Germany into the upper Danube valley. From there they raided Imperial territory. Aurelian warred against them in 271, then enrolled them as auxiliaries in the Roman armies. In the third century, following raids by the Goths, they received permission to settle in Pannonia. At the beginning of the fifth century they began a new migration, crossing the Rhine in 406 to ravage Italy and Gaul for three years before the Franks drove them beyond the Pyrenees. From Baetica, they crossed to North Africa in 428, leaving behind no artistic trace of their passage through Gaul and Spain. Establishing a capital at Carthage, they soon extended their rule over Roman Africa. Arian Christians, they persecuted the Athanasian population until they, in turn, fell victim first to the enervating influences of Roman life and then to Belisarius' army of liberation.

The Vandals had not coined in Spain, nor did they have moneys of their own during their first fifty years in Africa. They never struck in gold.[56] The earliest Vandalic issues date to Huneric (477-484), who struck imitations of the silver siliquae of Honorius with obverse, diademed profile bust and inscription HONORIVS not preceded by D(*ominus*) N(*oster*),[57] but with a regional reverse: standing and facing figure of Carthage holding a grain spike and, in the field, Huneric's regnal year (fig. 36).

Gunthamund's silver of certain attribution presents obverse, a conventionalized laureate bust with *paludamentum* and the king's legends D(*ominus*) N(*oster*) GVNDTHAMVND REX and reverse, wreath enclosing DN, which may abbreviate *denarii* (fig. 37). Thrasamund (496-523), Hilderic (523-530), and Gelamir (530-534) continued Gunthamund's types with appropriate inscriptional changes. Hilderic also struck siliquae with an additional inscription: KART(*ha*)G(*o*) FELIX (fig. 38).

The Vandalic bronze coinage may have begun as early as the reign of Gunthamund.[58] It consisted of copious issues of fourth bronzes and less numerous folles with their fractions. Besides bust obverses and Victory or monogram reverses, we have for Hilderic large bronzes of a cruder but more emancipated aspect: obverse, the standing, uniformed figure of king or warrior holding a spear and reverse, a horse's head, reproducing a type employed at Carthage since the fourth century B.C. The obverse is inscribed **KARTHAGO**, the reverse with a figure of value.

The Vandalic coinage confronts the art historian with an enigma. The style remains good but lacks the spontaneity of Ostrogothic monetary art. The Vandals came to North Africa lacking a discernible history in the arts and crafts. The artifacts that have come down to us from the African occupation have an affinity with Visigothic and Frankish rather than Roman work. By the end of the fifth century, the sloth and debilitation of character that was the price of acculturation and that would make the Vandals easy prey for the Byzantines were already well advanced, and the dependence on the Roman population for the conduct of public affairs must have been great. One is tempted to see behind the diademed and armored busts of the Vandal kings the hand of the Roman artist and even of a Roman mint administration.[59] Yet the Imperial mint at Carthage had closed in 308, more than a century before Germanic settlement there. This and the fact that the Vandals did not coin until a half century after they had moved from Spain suggests that some influence came from an external source. But from where? Engravers from Spain or Gaul would have brought a different artistic tradition. Captive or émigré artisans may have been capable of creating isolated dies of elevated style, as had been the case with Rechiar's silver in Spain, but would they or their successors have been able to maintain and pass on those standards for more than fifty years? In any event, the last raids into Italy had come to an end at least twenty years before the beginnings of Vandal coinage, and experienced mint workers from Rome or northern Italy would have found more congenial employment with the Ostrogothic kings, unless Vandalic fiscal affairs had come into the hands of Roman administrators once the religious persecution had eased. The motivating spirit of Vandal numismatic art was Roman; the source of that spirit remains in the realm of conjecture.

1 2 3

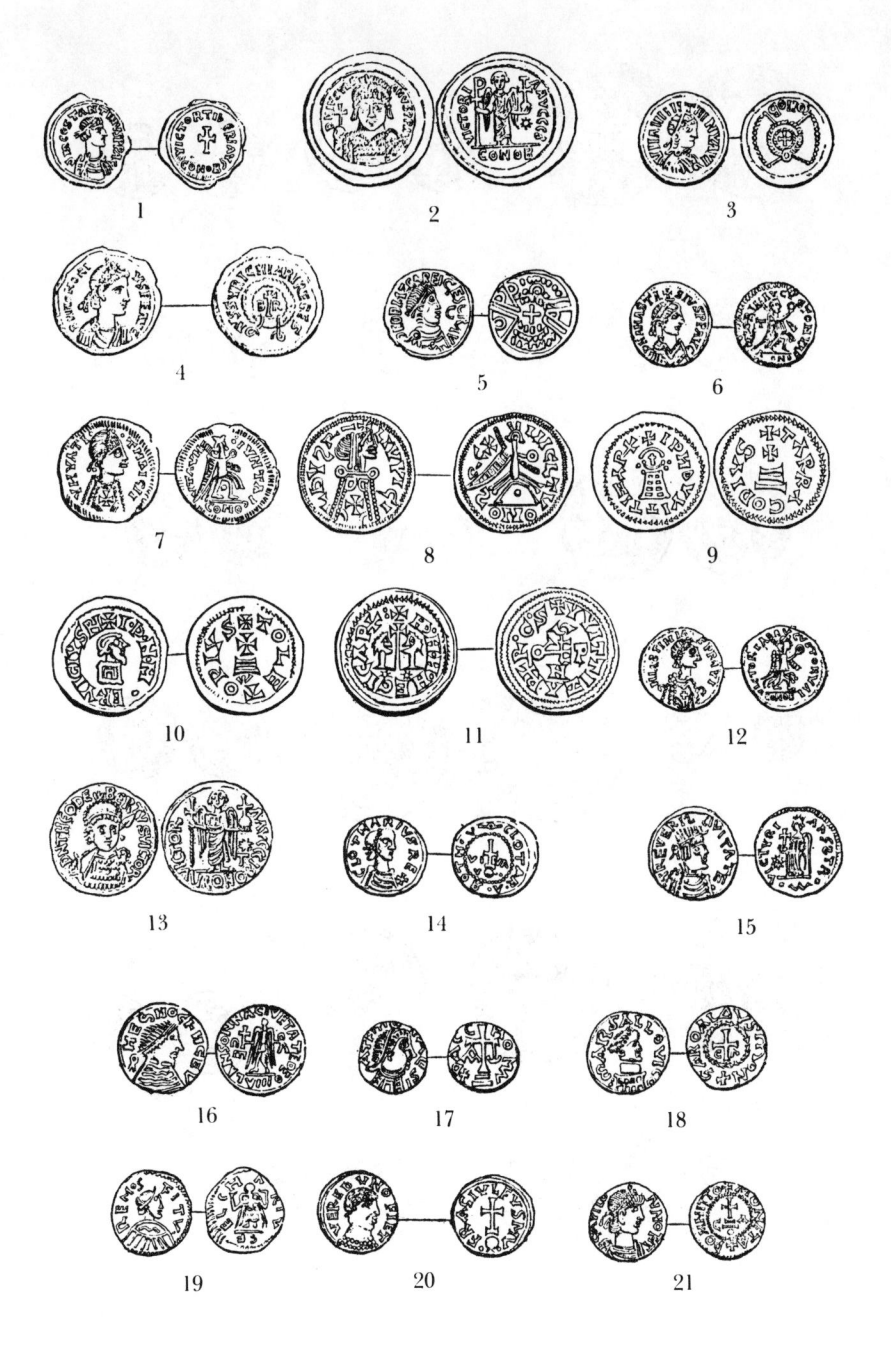

4 5 6

7 8 9

10 11 12

13 14 15

16 17 18

19 20 21

22

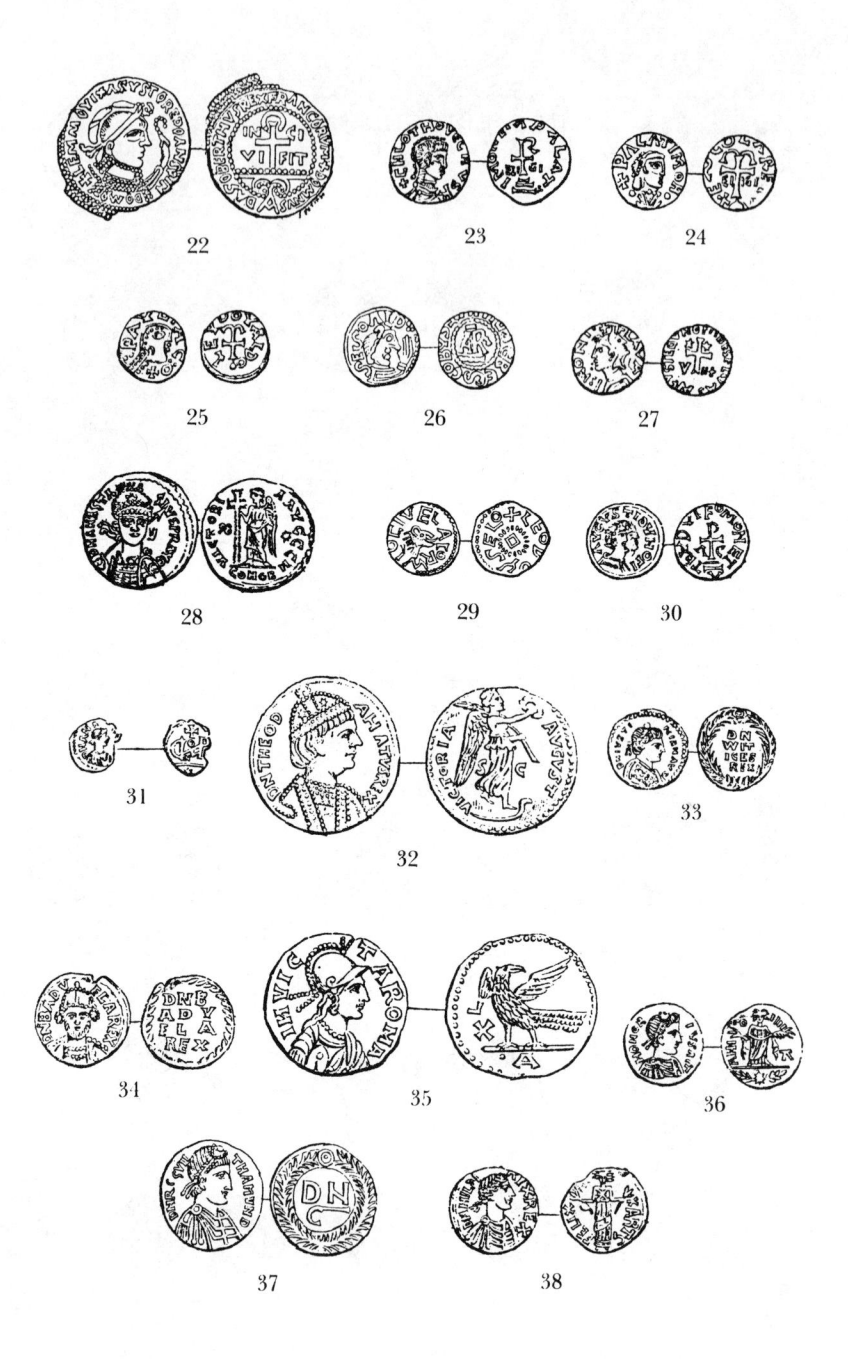

23

24

25

26

27

28

29

30

31

32

33

34

35

36

37

38

The coinage of each Germanic kingdom was the product of a process of development and change. In part this was the result of forces beyond the control of the numismatic artist; but in part, too, it mirrored his ability or failure to reply to those forces and, through his medium, to express the spirit of an age. Many factors determined whether or not a particular coinage would constitute an agency of conscious artistic assertion. Coin art is the offspring of a specific political and social milieu. The same factors that produce that setting influence the evolution of aesthetic standards and art forms. Some of these factors are political, others economic, sprititual, or technological, and they exert their influence to a dissimilar degree.

Coinage is, in the first instance, an economic institution, and it must be consistent with economic realities. As long as barbarian coins pretended to compete with those of the emperor's mints, their form was dictated by the features of the Imperial gold. This precluded any freedom of artistic expression. It was otherwise when debasement and political emancipation had changed barbarian gold into a strictly local currency. This and the creation of a coinage in silver or bronze for domestic use opened up avenues for experimentation in numismatic art.

Familiarity with Roman life and an appreciation of Roman institutions contributed to the creation of a workable administrative structure and a will to preserve or adapt Imperial coin art, but they did not necessarily dictate a course of growth; nor did the absence of an understanding of Roman tradition or even an abhorrence of *Romanitas* preclude the continuance of Roman monetary practices. The degree of temporal removal from Roman mints was a similar factor in the equation. Highly Romanized Germans may have been more apt to perpetuate late-Roman coin design if they enjoyed, in their midst, Roman mints with a history of uninterrupted operation, but long gaps in mint activity did not prevent the Vandals and Visigoths from copying or adapting Imperial conventions. The import of barbarian artistic fashions seems to have been closely related to the existence of working mints and the strength of Roman attitudes and institutions in the determination of the nature of Germanic coinages, but the relationship is too variable to allow the formulation of a general rule. The mixture of these factors might explain the Imperial styles of Germano-Italian mints and

West Gothic "national" numismatic art. Yet the Vandals, by religion and culture antipathetical to Roman ways, cultivated a Roman coinage where no coins had been made for more than a century and a half. This apparent inconsistency gives credence to the supposition that Vandalic fiscal affairs and mint administration were in the hands of elements of the Roman population.

Aesthetic principles, cultural affinities, and technological achievement are variables in our understanding of Germano-Roman monetary art. The degree of influence each exerted differed in the individual Germanic kingdoms. One factor, however, was not variable. Coinage can be a vehicle of aesthetic expression only when there is uniformity in the design and manufacture of metallic currency. The continuing exercise of centralized administrative authority is an ineluctable a priori to the maintenance of that uniformity, and an effective government must reserve for itself the exercise of the *jus monetae* or, at the very least, a large degree of control over those to whom fiscal responsibilities may have been delegated. Roman and Germano-Roman numismatic art was, then, a product of governments that were durable, unified, and at least reasonably effective. The Burgundian and Herule kingdoms were not permanent and lacked the time necessary to develop their own numismatic styles or consciously to adopt as their own those of the Byzantine mints. The Suevian kings never consolidated their power in their backward corner of the Iberian peninsula, and they may well have delegated much of the responsibility for the coinage to tax farmers. This, coupled with a lack of a strong artistic heritage, Germanic or Roman, explains the Suevian failure in monetary design. The Franks failed, too, in spite of traditions very much alive in Gaul. The death of Clovis I was the signal for the dissolution of Merovingian political unity. Responsibility for the coinage passed to hundreds, if not thousands, of individuals. Frankish insolvency in numismatic art derived from inefficiency in government, and both were the consequence of lassitude, insouciance, and want of discipline.

In those kingdoms in which political unity was the rule, the artistic results reflected that fact. The Visigoths developed a double tradition into an art style uniquely theirs. Freed of Imperial political control and economic restrictions and sponsored by a strong ruling house that gave him direction and protection, the Visigothic numismatic artist created a new mode symbolizing the union of Germanic and Roman influences. The Ostrogoths, settled in the heartland of the old Roman world and heir to the same mixed traditions as the Visigoths, continued the coin art of the Empire and ultimately made it theirs. A similar continuation of Roman numismatic conventions among the Vandals demonstrated a respect for Imperial monetary institutions inconsistent with their disdain for other things Roman.

The die engravers of late antiquity and the early Middle Ages were motivated by the same impulses and limited by the same restraints as were workers in other arts and crafts. Their legacy, however, is broader in geographical scope and chronological extent. This, joined to their greater chances of survival, endows the coins with an unrivaled significance for the recreation of the art of the Germanic invasions. The most important lesson to be learned from the coinage of the times is that numismatic art, like all forms of aesthetic expression, was both an integral part and a reflection of the society that gave it substance.

NOTES

*The author wishes to express his gratitude for support provided by the General Research Fund of the University of South Dakota.

1. Cosmas Indicopleustes, *Topographia Christiana*, in J. P. Migne, *Patrologiae cursus completus. Series Graeca*, (Paris: Lutitiae, 1857-1866), LXXXVIII, col. 115.

2. Tacitus, *De Germania*, V.

3. Harold Mattingly, *Roman Coins* (2d revised ed.; Chicago: Quadrangle, 1962), p. 102.

4. Procopius complained that it was not right for any sovereign "in the whole barbarian world to imprint his own likeness on a gold stater, and that, too, though he has gold in his own kingdom." *De bello Gothico*, VII.xxxiii.4-6 (trans. H. B. Dewing in *Loeb Classical Library*, IV; New York: The Macmillan Co., 1919), p. 439.

5. The Burgundians forbade in their territories the circulation of debased coins going back to the days of Alaric II (484-507). *Leges Burgundionum, Constitutiones extravagantes*, XXI, 7, in *Monumenta Germaniae historica, Legum, Sectio* I (ed. L. R. de Salis), *Tom.* II, *Pars* I (Hanover, 1892), p. 342.

6. "The Barbarian Invasions of the Early Middle Ages," *Larousse Encyclopedia of Byzantine and Medieval Art* (New York: Prometheus Press, 1963), p. 97.

7. The indirectly derived issues of the Lombards and Carolingian Franks have not been considered, nor have the Anglo-Saxon coinages, which are, in large measure, based on Celtic art forms. The Frisian coinage is not reviewed as it was the product of Merovingian and Burgundian engravers.

8. *Hydatti Lemici Continvatio chronicorvm hieronymianorvm ad a.* CCCCLXVIII, in *Monumenta Germaniae historica, Avctorvm antiqvissimorvm, Tom.* XI, CHRONICA MINORA SAEC. IV, V, VI, VII, *Pars* II (ed. Theodor Mommsen; Berolini, 1894), 47-49.

9. W. Reinhart, "El reino hispánico de los Suevos y sus monedas," *Archivo español de arqueológia*, XV (1942), 311.

10. A. Herculano, *Historia de Portugal* (2d ed.; Lisbon: Viuva Bertrand e Filhos, 1846 ff.), IV, 18-19; cf. Hydatius, 47-49; similar is Manuel Torres, "El estado visigótico: Algunos datos sobre su formación y principios fundamentales de su organización política," *Anuario de historia del derecho español*, III (1926), 381, 388.

11. Alfred von Halban, *Das römische Recht in den germanischen Volksstaaten* (Breslau: H. & M. Marcus, 1899-1907), I, 156; Torres, "El estado visigótico," 388.

12. W. Reinhart, "Die Münzen des Swebenreiches," *Mitteilungen der bayerischen numismatischen Gesellschaft*, LV (1937), 151-190; idem, "El reino hispánico," pp. 308-328.

13. "El reino hispánico," p. 317.

14. Strabo 3.2.8.

15. Sil. Ital. I, 234; A. Schulten in A. F. von Pauly and G. Wissova, *Real-Encyclopädie der classischen Alterstumwissenschaft* (Stuttgart: J. B. Metzler, 1894-1919), XIII, col. 2006.

16. *Isidori Hispalensis episcopi Etymologiarvm sive Originvm libre XX* (ed. W. M. Lindsay; Oxonii: e typographo Clarendoniano, 1911), XIV, 4, 28-29.

17. Manuel Torres, *Lecciones de historia del derecho español* (Salamanca: Libreria General "La Facultad de Germán Garcia," 1933-1934), II, 169.

18. In Spain there was no need to coin in silver and the base metals as Roman pieces would have been available in large quantities. Aloïss Heiss, the foremost French student of the Spanish coinage, found well worn Roman bronzes still being used in remote Spanish villages in the nineteenth century.

19. Joseph Eckhel, *Doctrina Numorum Veterum* (Vindobonae: Sumptibus Josephi Camesena et soc., 1798), VIII, 172-173, who refers to the catalogue of the Musée d'Ennery. The coin is now in the Bibliothèque Nationale.

20. "El reino hispánico," pp. 326-327.

21. *Reges* for *regis* (genitive). A. Engel and R. Serrure, *Traité de numismatique du moyen âge* (Paris: E. Leroux, 1891-1905), I, 32-33; F. Mateu y Llopis, Review of W. Reinhart, "El reino hispánico," in *Ampurias*, V (1943), 358-359.

22. H for N is found on certain issues where CONOB becomes COHOB.

23. Reinhart's transcription. Other authorities offer DEODIAZCAREIGESCRAV (Engel and Serrure) and OCODIACCAREIGESONAV. Reinhart, "El reino hispánico," p. 325.

24. At least one specimen bears a legible inscription of Justin II. The remainder are garbled beyond recognition. The weight corresponds to that of contemporary Visigothic coins.

25. A. Heïss, *Description générale des monnaies des rois wisigoths d'Espagne* (Paris: Imprimerie Nationale, 1872); F. Mateu y Llopis, *Catálogo de las monedas previsigodas y visigodas del gabinete munismático del museo arqueológico nacional* (Madrid: Cuerpo facultativo de archiveros, bibliotecarios y arqueológos, 1936); G. C. Miles, *The Coinage of the Visigoths in Spain: Leovigild to Achila II* (New York: The American Numismatic Society, 1952); W. H. Tomasini, *The Barbaric tremissis in Spain and Southern France* (New York: The American Numismatic Society, 1964); J. Lluis y Navas, "La repercusión de las artes en el estilo de las monetas visigodas," *Gaceta numismática*, No. 30 (Sept. 1973), pp. 8-17; W. Reinhart, "Die Münzen des westgotischen Reiches von Toledo," *Jahrbuch für Numismatik*, III-IV (1940-1941), 69-101.

26. F. Dahn, *Die Könige der Germanen* (2d ed.; Leipzig: Breitkopf & Härtel, 1855), pp. 12-22.

27. Orosius VII, 41, 43; Herculano IV, 10-16; Torres, "El estado visigótico," p. 381.

28. F. Mateu y Llopis, "El arte monetario visigodo," *Archivo español de arqueológia*, XVI (1943), 172-193; XVIII (1945), 34-58; Tomasini, pp. 173-182.

29. Miles recorded 78 mints. Others have been identified since.

30. Leovigild and Reccared issued, exceptionally, tremisses with obverse, profile bust and reverse, cross on steps. Except for the Visigothic kings' inscriptions, these imitated Frankish coins struck at Marseilles in the name of Maurice Tiberius. Issued in southern Gaul, the types belong more properly to Merovingian than Visgothic art history.

31. Mateu y Llopis, "El arte monetario," pp. 53-54.

32. There are many issues of inferior style. These may be copies made by rebels at war with the king rather than true regal issues.

33. W. Reinhart, "Germanische Helme in westgotischen Münzbildern," *Jahrbuch für Numismatik und Geldgeschichte*, II (1950/51), 43-46 and plate II.

34. Lluis y Navas, p. 10; C. H. V. Sutherland, *Art in Coinage* (New York: Philosophical Library, 1956), pp. 106-108.

35. Sutherland, p. 106.

36. A. de Belfort, *Description générale des monnaies mérovingiennes*, 5 vols. (Paris: Société Française de Numismatique, 1892-1895); M. Prou, *Les monnaies mérovingiennes* (Paris: C. Rollin et Feuardent, 1892); G. de Ponton d'Amécourt, "Description raisonée des monnaies mérovingiennes de Chalon-sur-Saône," *Annuaire de la Société Française de Numismatique et d'Archéologie* (1873-1876), pp. 37-152; M. Deloche, *Description des monnaies mérovingiennes du Limousin* (Paris: C. Rollin et Feuardent, 1863); idem, *Études de numismatique mérovingienne* (Paris: C. Rollin et Feuardent, 1890); J. Lafaurie, "Les monnaies de Marseille du VIe au VIIIe siècle," *Bulletin de la Société Française de Numismatique*, XXXVI (1981), 68-73; Alan M. Stahl, "The Merovingian CA Coinage of Austrasia," *American Numismatic Society Museum Notes*, No. 21 (1976), pp. 121-151 and plate XIII.

37. The tomb of Clovis' father, Childeric (458-481), contained some 300 gold and silver coins. All were Roman in origin or so carefully copied from Roman models as to be indistinguishable from Imperial issues.

38. The coins of Visigothic style are difficult to separate from Visigothic and Burgundian issues. They are discussed by W. Reinhart, "El elemento visigodo en el numerario merovingo," *Archivo español de arqueológia*, XIII (1950-51), 143-155, and W. Tomasini, *op. cit.*

39. *De bello Gothico*, VII. xxxii. 4-6.

40. *Codex Theod.* XII, Title 7, 1. 3, which is a law of Valentinian dating to 387 A.D.

41. Saint Ouen (*Vita sanctii Eligii episcopi Noviomensis* in J. P. Migne, *Patrologiae cursus completus. Scriptores Latini. Series secunda. Tomus* LXXXVII [Parisii, 1851], cols. 477-491) refers to the mint at Limoges as *publica fiscalis monetae officina*. Tremisses of Trier are inscribed CONSTIT(utio), "tax." M. Prou saw in the coin legends RACIO FISCI, RACIO

DOMINI an affinity with the *ratio fisci* of an inscription from the time of Marcus Aurelius and the later *res dominica*, which referred to the administration of the Roman treasury. *Revue numismatique*, 1889, p. 57, cited by Engel and Serrure, I, 88.

42. It is estimated that as many as 5,000 mints may have operated in Merovingian Gaul. Of these, some 800 are represented by extant coins. Engel and Serrure, I, 89.

43. Pepin III, the first Carolingian king, reformed not only the metallic content of his coinage but the types, which from 775 until 800, would be invariably epigraphic.

44. In this I follow Engel and Serrure, I, 151-171.

46. Saint Ouen, *Vita Eligii*.

47. Jean Lafaurie, "Eligius monetarius," *Revue numismatique*, VIe série, XIX (1977), 111-151 and plates XI-XIII; Jacques Dubois, "Numismatique mérovingienne et hagiographie," in P. Bastien, C. Morrisson, and F. Dumas (eds.), *Mélanges de numismatique, d'archéologie et d'histoire offerts à Jean Lafaurie* (Paris: Société Française de Numismatique, 1980), pp. 209-213.

48. M. Prou suggests the design used as a model may have been a double-struck coin. Quoted by Engel and Serrure, I, 163.

49. *Ego sum Alpha et Omega, principium et finis*. Rev. 1:8.

50. Charles Lenormant, "Lettres à M. de Saulcy sur les plus anciens monuments numismatiques de la série mérovingienne, VI et VII," *Revue numismatique*, 1853, pp. 19-39; Engel and Serrure, I, 37-39; Jean Lafaurie, "Les monnaies frappées à Lyon su VIe siècle," in *Mélanges de travaux offerts à Maître Jean Tricore* (édité sous les auspices de la ville de Lyon, III; Lyon: Audin, 1972), pp. 193-205.

51. W. Wroth, (*Catalogue of the Coins of the Vandals, Ostrogoths and Lombards . . . in the British Museum* [London: Printed by order of the Trustees of the British Museum, 1911], p. xliii) believes this to be an attempt at true portraiture.

52. Jean Babelon describes this piece as representing the ultimate in realism: "L'effigie est d'une laideur singulière, et c'est là une étrange apparition." *Le portrait dans l'antiquité d'après les monnaies* (Paris: Fayot, 1942). This medallion is the subject of Ernesto Bernareggi, "Il medaglione d'oro di Teoderico," *Revista italiana di numismatica*, LVII (1969), 89-106; Maria Alföldi, "Il medaglione d'oro di Theodorico," *Revista italiana di numismatica*, LXXX (1978), 133-141.

53. ". . . may be something of a likeness." Wroth, p. xliii.

54. ". . . portrait assurément authentique." Babelon, p. 186.

55. C. F. Keary, *The Coinage of Western Europe from the Fall of the Western Empire to its Reconstruction under Charles the Great* (London: Trübner & Co., 1879), pp. 25-42; Wroth, pp. xv-xxviii; J. Friedländer, *Die Münzen der Vandalen* (Berlin, 1849); C. Morrisson, "La monnaie d'argent d'Hilderic à Carthage," *Le Club Français de la Médaille: Bulletin*, No. 73 (1981), pp. 100-102.

56. Gold Coins previously attributed to the Vandals are now known to have been struck by other barbarian peoples, especially the Visigoths. Cf. W. Hahn, *Moneta Imperii Byzantini* (Vienna: Verlag der Österreichischen Akademie der Wissenschaften, 1973 ff.), I, 92.

57. The omission of D(*ominus*) N(*oster*) led Engel and Serrure (I, 19) to read into the legend a Latinized form of Huneric. . Morrisson reads the name as that of the Roman emperor in the West and dates the coin to early Gunthamund (487/488) or possibly, early Huneric (480/481). "Les origine du monnayage vandale," *Actes de 8ème Congrès international de numismatique* (ed. H. A. Kahn and Georges le Rider; Paris and Bâle: Association internationale des numismates professionales, Publication No. 4, 1976), pp. 468-470. The inscription may represent a purposeful confounding of names.

58. Hahn, I, 95.

59. Wroth, p. xxiv.

COTTON MATHER, *THE CHRISTIAN PHILOSOPHER*, AND THE CLASSICS

Winton U. Solberg

The ancient belief that God reveals himself in both nature and Scripture was reinvigorated by the scientific revolution of the early modern period, and the Puritan priest Cotton Mather (1663-1728) was a leader in disseminating this view in British North America. Like most New England clergymen of his age, Mather welcomed experimental philosophy as a handmaid of theology, a new instrument for discovering the Mind of God. Mather kept in close touch with intellectual currents and wrote prolifically in theology, history, medicine, and science. His interest in "natural philosophy" was far-reaching, and his scientific communications to the Royal Society led to his election as a fellow in 1713.[1]

Mather's most important writing on science is *The Christian Philosopher: A Collection of the Best Discoveries in Nature, with Religious Improvements*. He completed the manuscript in 1715, and the book was published in London in 1720, though it bears the date 1721. The author's purpose was to demonstrate "that *Philosophy* is no *Enemy*, but a mighty and wondrous *Incentive* to *Religion*" (p. 1).[2] Mather's order is approximately the conventional scheme for the study of natural philosophy in the Schools, which was based ultimately upon the order in which traditional Aristotelian texts were taken up. He treats the heavenly bodies first (astronomy), then earthly phenomena and the earth itself (physics in the largest sense), and finally living bodies, including man (the life sciences). Under each chapter heading Mather collects the "best discoveries" in nature encountered in his reading, to which he adds scientific observations of his own and reflections upon the religious significance of the facts and theories presented. Each section ordinarily closes with a "rhapsodical statement of how the new knowledge redounds to the glory of God."[3]

Scholars agree that this book is the best example of the way in which Newtonian science was first disseminated in British America, and that it is one of the major intellectual achievements of the colonial period.[4] In his effort to harmonize science with religion Mather emphasized the argument from design. This holds that one may reasonably infer the existence of a purposeful Creator responsible for the universe from evidences of intelligent planning found in physical nature. The design argument originated with the pre-Socratics, but Plato was the first philosopher to give it full expression. Christian writers later reaffirmed it, and the doctrine gained new vitality in England along with the birth of natural science in its distinctively modern form.

In his book, Mather cites some 415 authors. His greatest reliance is on men who lived during the early modern period, but he also draws on ancient, medieval, and Renaissance worthies. The present essay will emphasize his debt to classical and Christian antiquity. Mather had been educated in these traditions, for the revival of learning had made Greek and Latin authors more available, and the learned languages were still the mark of the educated man. Puritans insisted upon the need for an intellectual comprehension of the faith, and despite their commitment to classical learning, they always took care to insure that the pagan classics not undermine Christian truth.

Young Mather began his studies at the free public grammar school under Benjamin Thompson and later Ezekiel Cheever. The Boston Latin School prepared youngsters for college, and Cheever was one of the most respected schoolmasters in Massachusetts. At school Mather composed many themes and verses in Latin and learned to take Latin notes on sermons preached in English. He read several Latin authors, went through a great part of the New Testament in Greek, read considerably in Isocrates and Homer, and made "some entrance" in Hebrew grammar. Cheever brought the dead languages to life and taught Mather to love Christ above the classics.[5]

Harvard College in the seventeenth century was devoted to both Renaissance and Reformation ideals. Its purpose was to give Christian gentlemen a liberal arts education, not merely to train ministers. When Mather entered Harvard in 1674, he already knew more Latin and Greek than was required for admission. President Leonard Hoar himself tested the eleven-year old boy's fluency in Latin and his ability in the Greek tongue.[6] The Harvard curriculum was designed to give students a mastery of the learned languages and some knowledge of classical literature. Latin was the official language of college life; scholars were not to use English with each other unless called upon to do so in public exercises of oratory or the like. Mather's class spent most of their first two years studying Greek and Hebrew. Both were considered of general cultural value as well as of practical use in reading the Scriptures. Greek literature was available in a fat little anthology prepared by Jean Crespin. The emphasis on Hebrew and kindred languages, "the most distinctive feature of the Harvard curriculum," aimed primarily at improving Old Testament scholarship. The first two Harvard presidents had been excellent Hebraists, and Hebrew was their favorite subject. Though the study of Hebrew had fallen off before Mather entered, he composed Hebrew exercises as an undergraduate. In 1680 he started a revival of the language by arguing in his master's thesis that Hebrew vowel-points were of divine origin.[7]

In addition to classical languages and literature, Harvard emphasized most of the traditional studies—logic, ethics, metaphysics, mathematics, rhetoric, oratory, and divinity. Disputations and declamations were conducted two afternoons a week after students became proficient in logic. Mather ordinarily chose natural philosophy for his declamations, thus killing two birds with one stone. Harvard students also gained proficiency with the original languages in which the holy Scriptures were written by translations at prayer. At morning prayer every student took turn in reading some portion of the Old Testament out of Hebrew into Greek (Freshmen read it out of English into Greek), and at evening prayer everyone in turn translated a portion of the New Testament from English into Greek.[8]

Mather recieved a good grounding in the learned languages and was an omnivorous reader who bought many books and had access to an excellent family library.[9] He continued to learn about antiquity from the time of his graduation to the time he wrote his treatise on Newtonian science. Here our concern is with his knowledge of classical and Christian antiquity as demonstrated in *The Christian Philosopher*. He makes many references to the ancient world in his book. Most of these are to authors, several of whom are cited frequently. The Greek authors include Aelian, Aristotle, Democritus, Dio Cassius, Diodorus Siculus, Epictetus, Galen, Hippocrates, Homer, Plato, Plutarch, Strabo, and Theophrastus. Those named five times or more are Galen (20), Aristotle (16), Plato (7), Hippocrates (5), and Plutarch (5). The Latin writers include Ammianus Marcellinus, Ausonius, Cato, Cicero, Claudian, Columella, Curtius, Aulus Gellius, Horace, Juvenal, Livy, Lucretius, Ovid, Petronius Arbiter, Pliny, Seneca the Elder, Seneca the Younger, Suetonius, Tacitus, Valerius Maximus, Vergil, and Vitruvius. Those named five times or more are Pliny (32), Cicero (16), Vergil (7), Ovid (6), and Seneca the Younger (5). The Christian authors or writers on Scripture include Ambrose, Augustine, Basil, Chrysostom, Clement, Gregory of Nazianzus, Lactantius, Minucius Felix, Origen, Philo, John Philoponus, Theodoret, and Theophilus. Only Augustine (6) is named five times or more.

Mather's intention is to harmonize Newtonian science and religion, and at the outset he asserts the Platonic idea of the physical creation as an expression of the Mind of God. "The whole *World* is indeed a *Temple* of GOD, *built* and *fitted* by that Almighty *Architect*;" he writes, "and in this *Temple*, every such one ... will speak of *His Glory*" (p. 2).

Mather quotes many authors, and his Introduction states the hope that his constant quoting will not be censured for boasting his learning. In this connection he quotes in Latin St. Augustine's reproach of Julian and Jean La Bruyère's satire on Herillus of Carthage (fl. c. 260 B.C.) for always citing others whether he speaks or writes (pp. 2-3). The source of the former quotation is *Contra Julianum Pelagianum*, 4.15. (Migne, *PL*, 44: col. 776); of the latter, the 1699 English translation of La Bruyère's *Characters: Or, the Manners of the Age* (1688), p. 134.

Mather is grateful to those whom he quotes; Pliny has given him a rule: *"Ingenuum est profiteri per quos profeceris."*[10] He also believes it is just to name discoverers, especially "the Industrious Mr. Ray, and the Inquisitive Mr. Derham; *Fratrum dulce par*: upon whom, in divers Paragraphs of this *Rhapsody*, I have had very much of my Subsistence; (I hope without doing the part of a *Fidentinus* upon them) and I give thanks to Heaven for them" (p. 3). Marcus Valerius Martialis (c. A.D. 40-c. 104) had named Fidentinus as a plagiarist of his verses (*Epigrams*, 1. 29, 38, 53, 72). Mather may have been tender on this point, for he borrows extravagantly from the "delightful pair of brothers."

John Ray (1627-1705) was the leading English botanist and zoologist of his day. He published many scientific studies and became a fellow of the Royal Society. His most influential writing was *The Wisdom of God Manifested in the Works of the Creation* (1691). This popular work went through four editions during the author's lifetime and many reprintings after his death. "More than any other single book," Charles E. Raven writes, "it initiated the true adventure of modern science." Ray not only interpreted the significance of organic life rather than merely describing and classifying it, but his delight in the physical universe was a new and important attitude. "The direct insistence upon the essential unity of natural and revealed, as alike proceeding from and integrated by the divine purpose, had not found clear and well-informed expression until Ray's book was published."[11]

William Derham (1657-1735) was a theologian and scientist who "pursued both avocations with confidence in their essential harmony." He conducted research in many fields of science and became a fellow of the Royal Society. His Boyle Lectures were published as *Physico-Theology: Or, A Demonstration of the Being and Attributes of God, from His Works of Creation* (London, 1713). Ray's *Wisdom* forms the basis of this book, in which the footnotes, a relatively novel device which neither Ray nor Mather used, contain many valuable references.[12]

Mather acknowledges that he has consulted scores of philosophers besides Ray and Derham, and adds that those who value the essays of "the memorable Antients, *Theodoret*, and *Nazianzen*, and *Ambrose*, upon *the Works of the Six Days,* count it a Fault, if among lesser Men in our Days, there be found those who say, *Let me run after them*" (p. 4). Mather obviously knows the Hexaemeral literature, and here he names three Christian authors who wrote on the creation story as told in Genesis. Theodoret (c. 393-c. 466) was bishop of Cyrus in Syria and one of the greatest Greek interpreters of Scripture in Christian antiquity. An English translation of his *Orations on Providence* appeared as *The Mirror of Divine Providence* (London, 1602). St. Gregory of Nazianzus (329-389), a Cappadocian Father, wrote on the work of God in creation and on Divine Providence. St. Ambrose (339-397), bishop of Milan and one of the four traditional Doctors of the Latin church, treated the works of the six days in his *Hexaemeron*.[13]

After a long quotation from a "Mahometan Writer" which describes how man's reason leads to admiration of the works of Creation, Mather writes, "I was going to say *O Mentis aureae Verba bracteata*! But the Great *Alsted* instructs me, that we *Christians*, in our valuable Citations from them that are Strangers to *Christianity*, should seize upon the Sentences as containing *our Truths*, detained in the hands of *Unjust Possessors*; and he allows me to say, *Audite Ciceronem, quem Natura docuit*" (pp. 5-6). The "*O Mentis*" quotation is based on Ausonius (d. c. A.D. 395; *Gratiarum actio ad Gratianum*, 4).

Johann Heinrich Alsted (1588-1638), a German Reformed theologian, directed Mather to several classical references. He was professor of theology and philosophy at the gymnasium in Herborn and subsequently at the University of Weissenberg in Transylvania. A believer in the fundamental unity of divine and secular knowledge, Alsted wrote on nearly every branch of learning, but mostly theology. Mather relied heavily on Alsted's *Theologia naturalis exhibens augustissimam naturae scholam* (Hanover, 1623), but Alsted's fame rests ultimately upon his role in compiling the first encyclopedia of all human knowledge. Mather considered the *Scientiarum omnium encyclopaedia* of Alsted (4 vols., Leyden, 1630), "*a North-West Passage*" to "all the *Sciences*."[14]

Mather's Introduction concludes with a quotation from Minucius Felix (fl. A.D. 200-240), a Roman lawyer whose apology for Christianity in the form of a dialogue between a Christian and a pagan was modeled on Cicero's *De natura deorum*, draws on Stoic ideas, and was probably dependent on Tertullian's

Apology. "If so much Wisdom and Penetration be requisite to observe the wonderful Order and Design in the Structure of the World," Mather quotes from the dialogue *Octavius*, "how much more was necessary to form it" (p. 6)![15]

Astronomy enjoyed great prestige in the eighteenth century, and this section of *The Christian Philosopher* includes some twenty classical references. Acknowledging that he can treat only some of the works of God, Mather adds that "*Theophilus*, writing *of the Creation*, to his Friend *Autolycus*, might very justly say, That if he should have a *Thousand Tongues*, and live a *Thousand Years*, yet he were not able to describe the admirable Order of the Creation, διὰ τὸ ὑπερβᾶλλον μεγεθὸς καὶ τὸν πλοῦτον σοφίας τοῦ θεοῦ" (pp. 7-8). Theophilus, bishop of Antioch in the second century, wrote to show the pagan world the Christian idea of God and the superiority of the doctrine of creation over the immoral myths of the Olympian religion. His Apology addressed to Autolycus is the earliest Christian work in the Hexaemeral literary tradition.[16]

Chrysostom, Mather continues, mentions "a Twofold Book of GOD; the Book of the *Creatures*, and the Book of the *Scriptures*: GOD having taught first of all us διὰ πραγμάτων, by his *Works*, did it afterwards διὰ γραμμάτων, by his *Words*. We will now for a while read the *Former* of these *Books*, 'twill help us in reading the *Latter*" (p. 8). The source is Chrysostom's ninth Homily to the people of Antioch. Next Mather adds, "The Philosopher being asked, What his *Books* were; answered, *Totius Entis Naturalis Universitas*. All Men are accommodated with that Public Library" (p. 8). The ultimate source may have been either Socrates (c. 380-450) "Scholasticus," *Ecclesiastical History*, 4. 23 (Migne, *PG* 73: col. 518) or *Vitae Patrum: sive historiae eremeticae libri decem*, 6. 4, 16. Someone asked St. Anthony of Egypt (251?-356) how he managed to live without books, both sources relate, and the hermit replied that the whole world was his book. But Mather's source is Matthew Barker, *Natural Theology: Or, the Knowledge of God, from the Works of Creation* (London, 1674), p. 17.

The twelve essays on the heavenly bodies, about 15 percent of the book, discuss light, the stars, the fixed stars, the sun, the planets, comets, heat, and the moon. In the first essay, Mather writes that "Aristotle's Definition of Light; Φῶς εστιν ἡ ἐνέργεια τοῦ διαφανοῦς *Light is in the Inworking of a Diaphanous Body*; is worth an attentive Consideration" (p. 9). His source is Robert Hooke (1635-1702), the English scientist, but Hooke had written "Light is the in-working of the Transparent Body or Medium."[17] Aristotle, *On the Soul*, 2. 7, 418b 9-10, is the ultimate source; a modern translation of the definition by W. S. Hett reads, "Now light is the activity of this transparent substance *qua* transparent."[18]

In discussing light Mather, desiring to fetch lessons of piety from the whole creation, writes that "even a *Pagan Plutarch*" reminds one "That the World is no other than the *Temple* of GOD; and all the *Creatures* are the *Glasses*, in which we may see the *Skill* of Him that is the Maker of all. And his Brother Cicero has minded us, *Deum ex Operibus cognoscimus*." He then adds, "The famous Hermite's Book, of those three leaves the *Heaven*, the *Water*, and the *Earth*, well studied, how nobly would it fill the *Chambers* of the Soul with the most *precious and pleasant Riches*? *Clement of Alexandria* calls the World, *A Scripture of those three leaves*: and the Creatures therein speaking to us, have been justly called *Concionatores Reales*, by those who have best understood them" (pp. 13-14). The long passage of which these quotations are a part is based on Alsted, pp. 244-245. Plutarch reaffirms the Platonic idea which Mather had previously mentioned; it is found in Plutarch's treatise *De Iside et Osiride*. The quotation from Cicero is in *Tusculan Disputations*, 1. 28, 70. The "famous Hermite" is St. Anthony, earlier identified as "the Philosopher."

Mather returns to his beloved Platonic theme in his essay on the Stars. "It was a good Remark made by one of the Antients, *Quid est Coelum, et totius Naturae Decor, aliud, quam quoddam speculum, in quo summi Opificis relucet Magisterium*" (p. 18)? Alsted cites the passage, attributing it to Plutarch's *Of Isis and Osiris*, but identifying the concept as Platonic. Plato correctly said in the *Timaeus*, Alsted writes, "the world is an epistle of God the Father to the human race. And gentile philosophers and Christian savants rightly advise that the creatures are mirrors, in which we observe the singular art of him, who created the world" (Alsted, p. 265; *Encyclopaedia*, 3:327).

"The Pagan *Tully*," Mather continues, "contemplating *Coelestium admirabilem Ordinem, incredibilemque Constan-*

tiam, the admirable Order, and the incredible Constancy of the Heavenly Bodies and their Motions, adds upon it, *Qui vacare Mente putat, ne ipse Mentis expers habendus est*: Whosoever thinks this is not governed by *Mind* and *Understanding*, is himself to be accounted void of all *Mind* and *Understanding*" (p. 18). Here Mather borrows from Ray, pp. 76-77, who is quoting *De natura deorum*, 2. 56.

In treating the "Fixed Stars," Mather writes that Claudian mentions a new star in A.D. 388 (p. 21). Claudian, an Alexandrian who went to Italy, discusses the nova in his *Panegyric on the Third Consulship of the Emperor Honorius*, 7. 172, but Mather's information is from Joseph Walker, *Astronomy's Advancement: Or, News for the Curious; Being a Treatise of Telescopes* (London, 1684), p. 23.

Mather alternately displays and hides his knowledge. At the beginning of his essay on the Sun he writes, "There will be no *Athenians* now to arraign me for it, if I call it, *The Carbuncle of the Heavens*" (p. 25). Learned readers would have recognized the allusion to the philosopher Anaxagoras (c. 500-c. 428 B.C.), who was tried, fined, and exiled from Athens for saying that the sun was stone and the moon earth at a time when people regarded sun, moon, and stars as divinities. Mather may have been reminded of or directed to the story in a note (which does not recount the tale) in David Gregory, *Elements of Astronomy, Physical and Geometrical* (2 vols., London, 1715), Preface. Plato relates the episode (*Apology*, 26D), as does Diogenes Laertius (*Lives of Eminent Philosophers*, 2. 3,8).

"*Virgil* and *Ovid* intimate such a Darkness upon the *Sun* once for a whole Year together," Mather writes, "that the Fruits of the Earth could not be ripened" (p. 27). The author undoubtedly had read the classical sources in Vergil's *Georgics* (1. 463-468) and Ovid's *Metamorphoses* (15. 785-786), but in all probability he was reminded of these lines by Walker's *Astronomy's Advancement*, p. 9, which identified authors and locations. The darkness is said to have occurred in 44 B.C., the year of Caesar's assassination.

The essay on Saturn attributes the motions of the heavenly bodies to God alone and quotes two ancients to support this view. One is the early Christian apologist Lucius Caecilius

Lactantius Firmianus (A.D. 240-320), who had argued that *"There is indeed a Power in the Stars, of performing their Motions; but that is the Power of God who made and governs all things, not of the Stars themselves that are moved"* (p. 34). The source is Lactantius, *The Divine Institutes*, 2. 5, but Mather quotes it verbatim from Derham's *Astro-Theology: Or a Demonstration of the Being and Attributes of God, from a Survey of the Heavens* (London, 1715), p. 61. The other author is Plato, who, Mather says, had previously argued, *"Let us think, how it is possible for so prodigious a Mass to be carried round for so long a time by any natural Cause? For which reason I assert God to be the Cause, and that 'tis impossible it should be otherwise"* (p. 34). Plato's *Epinomis* (983A-B) is the source, but Mather takes it from Derham's *Astro-Theology*, p. 63.

In his essay on Mercury, Mather writes "The Philosopher, who gazing on the *Stars* with his attentive Observation, tumbled into a Pit that he observed not, was not so unhappy as he that has visited *Heaven* on the noble Intentions of *Astronomy*, but by an ungodly Life, procures to himself a Condemnation to that *Hell*, which is a State and Place of Utter Darkness. Wretched Astronomers" (p. 40)! "The Philosopher" is Thales, and the source is Diogenes Laertius, *Lives of Eminent Philosophers*, 1. 1,33-34.

In treating Comets, Mather refers to Seneca's prediction that a time should come when the mysteries of comets should be unfolded, though Seneca has not obliged us with the observation which encouraged this prediction. The forecast appears in Seneca the Younger's *Natural Questions*, 7. 25, 3-4, but one cannot be certain that Mather knew that work, since he probably took the reference from Edmond Halley, "A Synopsis of the Astronomy of Comets," in *Miscellanea Curiosa: Containing a Collection of Some of the Principal Phenomena in Nature, Accounted for by the Greatest Philosopher of this Age* (3 vols., London, 1708), 2: Appendix. Reaffirming the ancient superstition that comets demonstrate the wrath of God, Mather quotes "—*Si fractus illabatur Orbis,/ Impavidum ferient Ruinae*" (p. 45), which is from Horace, *Odes*, 3. 3, 7-8. To make this point more clear, he might also have quoted lines 1-2 as well as 7-8:

> The man tenacious of his purpose in a righteous cause
> is not shaken from his firm resolve ...

Were the vault of heaven to break and fall upon him, its ruins would smite him undismayed.

Mather combines the classics with superstition in discussing the Moon. Its influences upon sublunary bodies are wonderful, he writes, and lunatics are not the only instances. "Our *Husbandmen* will multiply the Instances upon us, till they make a Volume, which neither a *Columella*, nor a *Tom Tusser* have reached unto. The Georges of my Neighborhood just now furnished me with two Instances, which have in them something that is notable" (p. 51). Lucius Junius Moderatus Columella, a contemporary of Seneca the Elder, wrote *De re rustica*. "The Georges" is a pun on the Greek *georgos*, meaning "farmer." Mather goes on to relate some stories about how cutting wood in the waxing or waning of the moon affects its properties.

As we have seen, Mather demonstrates an affinity with Plato, and it comes as no surprise that he devotes little attention to the Antiplatonist doctrines of Epicurus. Later essays mention Epicureans (or Epicurism) four times (pp. 76, 134, 165, 289), but fleetingly and often deprecatingly. Lucretius, who taught Epicureanism, is mentioned once on the subject of ice (p. 73).

Mather turns from astronomy to physics in the broadest sense, devoting fourteen essays, about 23 percent of the book, to the subject. He treats rain, the rainbow, snow, hail, thunder and lightning, the air, wind, cold, the terraqueous globe, gravity, water and fluids, the earth, magnetism, and minerals. Over twenty classical authors appear in these pages, and some of them two or three times. Mather usually quotes Scripture in making the religious "improvement" on the report of scientific discoveries, but occasionally a classical quotation serves the purpose. "We are to expect," the essay on the Rainbow concludes, "*—Affore Tempus/ Quo Mare, quo Tellus, correptaque Regia Coeli,/ Ardeat, et Mundi Moles operosa laboret* (p. 58). He is citing Ovid, *Met.*, 1. 256-258.

Mather weaves the classics into his essay on Thunder and Lightning. The natural causes of thunder do not release one from considering the Providence of God in it. "It is he, who *Fulmina molitur dextra, quo maxima motu/ Terra tremit, fugere Ferae, et mortalia Corda/ Per Gentes humilis stravit Pavor*" (p. 63). Thus Vergil's *Georgics* (1. 329-331) reinforces a point. Thunder has the voice of God in it, as paganism itself owned, and the voice heard is that power belongs to God. "The very *Mountains* are torn to pieces, when—*Feriunt summos sua Fulmina Montes*" (p. 63). Horace (*Odes*, 2. 10, 11-12) does duty here. Yet God is merciful to a sinful world. "The Desolations of the World, how wonderfully would they be, *Si quoties peccant Homines sua Fulmina mittat*" (p. 64)! The source is Ovid, *Tristia* (2. 33), who writes of Jupiter hurling his thunderbolts. Men die as a result of such a calamity, and "their being asleep at the time has not preserved them, though there be a Fancy in Plutarch that it would" (p. 64). The statement shows familiarity with Plutarch, *Moralia*, 665B-666D. Guilt makes men "startle at a *Thunder-Clap; Hi sunt qui trepidant, et ad omnia Fulgura pallent,/ Cum tonat, exanimes primo quoque Murmure Coeli*" (p. 64). Mather may have remembered these lines from Juvenal, *Satire* 13, 223-224, but he probably takes them from Alsted, p. 198.

Insects have many orifices on their bodies to admit large quantities of air, Mather writes, and they die if these openings are stopped up with honey or oil. "Pliny knew not the reason of his own Observation; *Oleo illita Insecta omnia exanimantur*" (p. 68). Here Mather copies Ray, p. 82, who had simplified a phrase in Pliny, 11. 21.

The essay on Wind says that "*Plato* long since defin'd it, *The Motion* of the Air about the Earth" (p. 69). This is from Plato's *Definitions*, 411C, a work which scholars no longer attribute to Plato.

Philoponus tells us, Mather says in the essay on Cold, that Democritus assigned the cause of cold to "*Frigorifick Atoms*" (p. 73). John Philoponus (500-565), an eccentric Alexandrian philosopher and theologian, contributed to the Hexaemeral literary tradition which Mather knows well, and Democritus of Abdera (c. 460-357? B.C.) was a mathematician and physicist. Mather incorporates this information from Robert Boyle, *New Experiments and Observations Touching Cold: Or, An Experimental History of Cold, Begun* (London, 1665), Lucretius is named, and the author asks, was it not a mistake when Pliny defined ice as, "*Aquae Copia in Angusto*" (p. 73)? Mather quotes Livy as saying of the Alps, "*Aeternis damnati Nivibus*" (p. 74)! Mather is normally accurate in quoting, but I cannot locate the last two quotations in the authors named. Concluding the essay, Mather draws a moral lesson from nature by quoting a reflection of Petronius: "*Incultis asperisque Regionibus, diutius Nives haerent; ast ubi Aratro domefacta Tellus nitet, dum loqueris levis Pruina dilabitur. Similiter in Pectoribus Ira considit; Feras quidem Mentes obsidet, Eruditas praeterlabitur*" (p. 75). The source is the *Satyricon*, 99.

The Copernican hypothesis is now generally preferred, Mather states, and the earth's motions oblige us to acknowledge God as governor of the world. "Even a *Pagan Cleanthes*," as Cicero will tell us, would assign this as sufficient cause for belief in a deity. Cleanthes (331-232 B.C.) succeeded Zeno as head of the Stoic School. Mather then quotes Cicero on the uniform motion and revolution of the heavens and the ordered beauty of the sun, moon, and stars. Plutarch says this observation was the first that led men to acknowledge a God (p. 76). The ultimate sources are *De natura deorum*, 2. 5, 15, and Plutarch's *Moralia*, 880A-B, but Mather takes the material from Derham, p. 44 n. 3 (Plutarch is cited also in *Astro-Theology*, pp. 3-4).

Gravity is an effect "insolvable by *philosophical Hypothesis*," Mather thinks, and it must therefore be "religiously resolv'd into the immediate *Will*" of the Creator (p. 82). After discussing a particular aspect of the subject he quotes Cicero, "*Quod facit Natura per omnem Mundum, omnia Mente et Ratione conficiens*" (p. 84), taking the statement from Derham, p. 34 n. 4, who cites *De natura deorum*, 2. 44, 115. In a paragraph on various principles that animate the world, Mather says there is no such thing as "an *universal Soul*" as Plato taught; nor any "*substantial Forms*" as Aristotle held; nor any "omniscient *radical Heat*" as Hippocrates contended (p. 87). He bases this on George Cheyne, *Philosophical Principles of Natural Religion: Containing the Elements of Natural Philosophy, and the Proofs for Natural Religion Arising from Them* (London, 1705), p. 3.

In the essay on the Earth, following the assertion that earth and water nourish many vegetables and animals, Cicero is quoted: "*Quorum omnium incredibilis Multitudo, insatiabili Varietate distinguitur*" (p. 96). Mather borrows from Ray, p. 101, but Derham also (p. 37 n. 1) quotes this passage from *De natura deorum*, 2. 39, 98. The variety of soils declares the Wisdom of the Creator in providing for such diverse intentions, and yet, *"Nec vero Terrae ferre omnes omnia possunt"* (p. 96). Mather takes this from Derham, p. 62 n. 3; who attributes it to Vergil's *Georgics*, 2. [109]. Mountains have advantages for man; Hippocrates usually repaired to them for the plants by which he wrought the chief of his cures (p. 99). This detail about the famous Greek physican is from Arndt's *True Christianity*, 4. 3. The German theologian Johann Christian Arndt (1555-1621) first published that work in German (1606-1609); it was later translated into Latin and English. Though Arndt is a favorite author he provides few classical references. A discussion of mountains as a bulwark and defense prompts the statement that the *"Barbarians* in *Curtius"* were confident of the safety they provided (p. 99). The source is Quintus Curtius Rufus, a historian in the first century A.D. who wrote a ten-book history of Alexander the Great. Mather's information comes from Derham, p. 71 n. 1, who is quoting John Wilkins, *The Discovery of a World in the Moon: Or, a Discourse Tending to Prove, That 'tis Probable There May Be Another Habitable World in That Planet* (London, 1638). Mather calls upon the Greek physician Galen of Pergamon, an ardent believer in teleology, to chastise the pseudo-Christians who reproach the work of God in the conformation of the earth (p. 99), borrowing for the purpose a Latin quotation cited by Derham (p. 80 n. 12) from *De usu partium* (10. 9).

The subject of earthquakes leads to mention of the "old sinking of *Helice* and *Buris"* mentioned by Ovid, the twelve cities swallowed up in the days of Tiberius, and "huge *Atlantis,* mentioned by *Plato,* now at the bottom of the *Atlantick* Ocean" (p. 101). Ovid's reference is in *Met.* 15. 293-295, Pliny's on the twelve cities in 2. 86, 200, and Plato's in the *Timaeus* 24E-25D. But surely Mather draws this information from Ray, *Three Physico-Theological Discourses: Concerning I. The Primitive Chaos, and Creation of the World. II. The General Deluge, Its Causes and Effects. III. The Dissolution of the World, and Future Conflagration* (London, 1693), pp. 163-164, 183. Speaking of casualties induced by earthquakes, Mather observes that Ammianus Marcellinus tells us that in the year 365 *"Horrendi Tremores per omnem Orbis Ambitum grassati sunt"* (p. 102). Here too Ray's *Discourses* is followed (p. 13), though the ultimate source is the ancient author's *Rerum gestarum libri qui supersunt,* 26. 10, 15. "Chrysostom did well ... to call the Earth *our Table;* but it shall *teach* me as well as *feed* me: May

I be a *Deipnosophist* upon it" (p. 103). Here Mather draws on Chrysostom's seventh Homily to the people of Antioch and also alludes to a work by Athenaeus (fl. c. A.D. 200), which describes a "learned banquet" at which the guests discussed several weighty topics as well as the dishes before them.

In a chapter on Magnetism, Mather says that the ancients knew of the magnet, that Pliny writes on the subject, and that "*Aristotle* speaks of *Thales*, as having said, the Stone has a Soul, ὅτι τὸν σιδηρὸν κινεῖ *because it moves Iron*" (p. 104). He takes the first point from a German author, Johann Christoph Sturm (1635-1703). His other references are Pliny, 26. 25, 126-130, and Aristotle, *On the Soul*, 1.2, 405a21 but Mather must borrow them from an undiscovered intermediate source. In discussing the disposition of the *"magnetical Vertue"* throughout the globe, Mather writes: "The Medium itself may be always luminous; or the concave Arch may shine with such a Substance as does invest the Surface of the *Sun*; or they may have peculiar Luminaries, whereof we can have no Idea: As *Virgil* and *Claudian* enlighten their Elysian Fields; the latter, *Amissum ne crede Diem; sunt altera nobis/ Sydera; sunt Orbes alii; Lumenque videbis/ Purius, Elysiumque magis mirabere Solem*" (p. 110). Mather is probably alluding to the *Aeneid*, 6. 640-641; the quotation is from the *Rape of Proserpine*, 2. 282-284.

Mather makes sophisticated use of classical learning in his chapter on Minerals. In discussing various kinds of salt, he writes: "He deserves to be herded with the Creatures, which *Animam habent pro Sale*, who shall be so *insipid* an Animal, as to be insensible that the Benefits of *Salt* call for very great Acknowledgements. *My God, save me from what would render me unsavory Salt*" (p. 119)! The last sentence echoes Matt. 5:13 and Luke 14:34. The Latin phrase is found in various forms in Varro, Cicero, Pliny, Plutarch, Clement of Alexandria, and Porphyry. Mather's wording differs from that of the authors named, which suggests that he is rephrasing a familiar idea. The wordplay is clever. The Latin *sal* means both *salt* and *wit* or *intelligence*. The English *insipid* means *without savor or taste* or *lacking salt*, and more generally *dull* or *uninteresting*. In the classical writers the point of the Latin, to have a soul instead of salt, is that the pig, being good for nothing except banquets, has a soul for no other reason than to serve as a preservative (salt) for the flesh. Mather employs the classical tag not only to characterize the brute beast but also to suggest a vital function of the mineral under discussion.

In treating gold and silver, Mather speaks of the trade of *"effodiuntur Opes"* (p. 120), words which occur in Ovid's description of the bronze age in *Met.* 1. 140, though Mather probably saw the phrase in Alsted, p. 399. Castigating the love of gold, Mather notes that "The *Auri sacra Fames* is the worst of all Distempers" (p. 121). Perhaps he quotes the *Aeneid* (3. 57) from memory.

The essay's conclusion contains a baroque assortment of classical references. "The antient Pagans not only worshipped the *Host of Heaven* [justly called *Zabians*] but whatsoever they found *comfortable* to Nature, they also *deified*, even, *Quodcunque juvaret*. The River *Nilus* too must at length become a Deity; yea, *Nascuntur in hortis Numina*. And according to *Pliny, a Man that helps a Man becomes a God.*" Mather then quotes St. Paul and Philo to warn against admiring the creation more than the Creator (pp. 121-122). This material follows Barker, *Natural Theology*, pp. 62-63. The Sabeans were a religious sect mentioned in the Koran and by later Arabian writers, but Barker used the word erroneously to describe heathens who worshipped the sun, moon, stars, and planets as divine. Barker attributes *"Quodcunque juvaret"* to "the Poet," who is Ovid (*The Heroides*, 4. 133), and the *"Nascuntur"* line to Juvenal (the work is his satire on the Egyptians, *Sat.* 15. 10-11. Alsted also quotes Juvenal on the gods of the Egyptians, p. 66. Barker (p. 63) quotes Philo as saying Κόσμον μᾶγγον ἢ κοσλλ' ποῖον θαυμήσαντες, and he identifies the source of the quotation as *De mundi opificio*. Mather improves the Greek so as to make it read κοσμὸν μαλλὸν ἢ κοσμοποίον θαυμάσαντες.

Mather turns next to natural history, assigning seven essays, about 60 percent of his treatise, to what is known today as the biological sciences. He treats vegetables, insects, reptiles, fishes, birds, quadrupeds, and man. Classical references are frequent, but space compels generalization in treating this material.

According to the essay on Vegetables, the "Pagan *Pliny*" acknowledged the exceeding fertility of wheat as an instance of the divine bounty to man. One bushel in a fit soil, Pliny says, yields one hundred and fifty (p. 126). Here Mather follows Ray, p. 130, who relies upon Pliny, 18. 21. Mather cites Theophrastus on the uses of trees and on nature's ways for scattering and sowing seed. Some seeds are swallowed by birds, pass through their bodies, and are by them transferred to places where they fructify. Theophrastus affirms this of the mistletoe (pp. 129, 130-131). Both references are from Derham, pp. 444 n. 1, 454 n. 16. The Boston author also describes a plant which the ancients called "*Aeschynomenae*" (p. 130). Mather borrows the point from Derham, p. 452 n. 13. All the plants in the vegetable kingdom are useful; Plutarch reports that the Babylonians obtained over 300 kinds of commodities from the palm tree (p. 132). The source is Plutarch's *Moralia*, 724E.

Some ancient Romans confined their delight to a single vegetable; Cato doted on cabbage. In antiquity several plants bore the name of Hercules, probably to denote their extraordinary force. To the Romans, cabbage was their "grand *Physick*" as well as food for 600 years (pp. 134-135). As Mather probably knows, Marcus Porcius Cato spent several pages in *De agri cultura* explaining the medicinal values of cabbage (156-157). Pliny treats the plant called Hercules or similar names (25. 12, 15, 37), as did Dioscorides, *De materia medica* (4. 66), and Theophrastus, *Enquiry into Plants* (9. 12, 3).

"Everybody has heard," Mather writes, "*Cur moriatur homo cui Salvia crescit in hortis*" (p. 135)? Sage was in high repute in antiquity and the Middle Ages, and this Latin apothegm was probably well known in the early modern period. It has a corresponding English proverb: "He that would live for aye,/ Must eat Sage in May."[19] To Mather, the works of the Creator in the whole vegetable kingdom call for continual admiration. "It is a notable Stroke of Divinity methinks which Pliny falls upon, *Flores Odoresque indiem gignit Natura, magna (ut palam est) Admonitione hominum*" (p. 139). Here the author follows Derham, p. 448 n. 7, who is quoting Pliny, 21. 1. This essay concludes with a baroque efflorescence of Latin quotations from Alsted and Arndt which includes "a Saying of Austin's *Deum Creaturas singulas guttula Divinae suae Bonitatis aspersisse, ut per illas homini bene fit*" (p. 140). Mather's source is Arndt, *True Christianity*, 2. 37, but I have been unable to locate the passage in St. Augustine.

Aristotle and Pliny are the leading ancient authorities in the essay on Insects. Mather considers the "Divine Workmanship" of these animals astonishing. As Pliny tells us, *"In his tam parvis atque nullis, quae Ratio, quanta Vis, quam inextricabilis perfectio"* (pp. 141-142). The ultimate sources are Aristotle, *Historia animalium*, 1.1, 487a 32-33 and 4.1, 523b13-15, and Pliny, 11. 1, but Mather follows Ray, p. 196.

The capacity of spiders to move with speed and safety is admirable. They dart out and sail away by the help of their webs. Mather notes a hint of their darting in Aristotle and Pliny, "but the Antients knew nothing of their *sailing*" (p. 149). Here Mather follows Derham, pp. 403-404 n. 5; the original sources are Aristotle, *Hist. an.*, 9. 39, 623a and Pliny, 11. 24.

The sagacity of insects in providing for their necessities is also admirable. One of these providers is the bee, on whom Mather cites Aristotle in Greek and Pliny in Latin. Becoming lyrical, he quotes several lines of Latin verse on the king bee without identifying the source as Vergil, *Georgics* (4. 212-213, 216-218), and adds that "these *aculeated Preachers*" furnish moral instruction to man. As Pliny notices, *"Nullus Apibus, si per Coelum licuit, Otio perit Dies"* (pp. 152-155). This passage requires knowledge of Aristotle, *Hist. an.* (1. 1, 488a3,10), Pliny (11. 16, 51), Vergil, and Pliny (11. 4, 14), but Mather borrows it all from Moses Rusden, *A Further Discovery of Bees: Treating of the Nature, Government, Generation and Preservation of the Bee* (London, 1679), pp. 4-20 passim.

Some animals prefer to be housed in the bodies of other animals, Mather writes, and birds as well as some beasts have peculiar lice distinct from the two kinds with which men are infested. "It has been pretended that the *Ass* is free, and an odd reason assigned for it; but it has been rather supposed from a Passage in *Aristotle*, the *Chronology* whereof won't well suit with the *odd Reason* I refer to." This cryptic passage is made clear later. Some insects, Mather continues, work themselves into the very scales of the fishes. "There *Lumbricus innascitur, qui debilitat*; it was observed as long ago as the Days of the *Stagyrite*" (p. 157). Here the source is Derham, pp. 417-418 nn. 8-9. Derham, however, explains that the "odd reason" for the ass's freedom from lice is "because our Saviour rode upon one, as some think." Derham's authorities are Aristotle, *Hist. an.* (5.31, 557a 13-14; 8. 20, 602b

28), and Pliny (2. 33). But Aristotle had said that the ass has neither lice nor ticks.

Mather mentions Aristotle on the manner in which ichneumons carry spiders into their nests (he follows Derham, p. 228 n. 2, quoting *Hist. an.* 5. 20, 552b26), and Pliny on the nidification of the gnat, the story of whose proceedings "would give you a thousand Astonishments" (pp. 158-159)! Here he takes from Ray, p. 196, whose source is Pliny, 17. 44. Mather also quotes Galen in Latin on the minute parts of the bodies of insects. The classical reference is *De usu partium* (17. 1) but Mather draws it from Derham, p. 407 n. 11. Mather notes that Strabo offers an entertaining account of ant hills (p. 156), a reference which is perhaps ultimately dependent upon Strabo, *Geography* (2. 1, 9). In a discussion of locust-eaters in the East Indies, Mather writes about "the *Acridophagi*, mentioned by *Diodorus*, and by *Strabo*" (p. 162). These references are to *Diodorus Siculus*, 3. 29 and Strabo, 16. 4, 12.

In the chapter on Reptiles Mather describes Galen's account of mountebanks who stop the perforations of the teeth of poisonous vipers before they let spectators behold the vipers bite them (pp. 168-169). This is incorporated from Derham, p. [4]37 n. 8. A paragraph on the prodigious magnitude of some serpents includes many classical references. "Yea, *Suetonius* affirms, that one was exposed by *Augustus*, which was no less than fifty Cubits long. *Dio* comes up with him, and affirms, that in *Hetruria* there was one that was fourscore and five Foot long, which, after he had made fearful Devastations, was kill'd with a Thunderbolt. *Strabo* out-does him, and affirms, that in Coelo-Syria there had been one which was an hundred Foot long, and so thick, that a couple of Men on horseback, on each side of him, could not see one another. Yea, one that was an hundred and twenty Foot long, was kill'd near *Utica* by the Army of *Regulus*. Well might Austin say of these dreadful Animals, *Majora non sunt super Terram*" (p. 168).

This marvelous tale demonstrates wide knowledge of classical antiquity. Suetonius Tranquillus (c. A.D. 69-c. 140), born half a century after the death of Emperor Augustus, wrote on the topic mentioned in *The Lives of the Caesars*, 2. 43. Dio Cassius Cocceianus (c. A.D. 164-c.230) contains the account cited in his *Roman History*, 50. 8, 4. Etruria, an ancient country in central

Italy, comprises modern Tuscany and part of Umbria. Strabo's story is in his *Geography*, 16. 2, 17, and Coele-Syria is the ancient name for the Bekaa Valley in Lebanon. Marcus Atilius Regulus was a Roman general in the First Punic War, and Utica was an ancient city on the coast of North Africa, northwest of ancient Carthage or modern Tunis. The St. Augustine quotation comes from his *Exposition of Psalm 148* (Migne, *PL*, 37: col. 1943). Mather in all likelihood knows the authors mentioned, but he draws his account from Samuel Bochart, *Hierozoicon: sive bipertitum opus de animalibus sacrae Scripturae* (2 vols., London, 1663), 2:430-431.

As for the Fishes, their variety is very considerable. Pliny "reckons up" 176 kinds of them, and "our Christian *Pliny*"— Ray—raises the number many times. "If you'll believe Pliny and Company, *Vera est vulgi Opinio, Quicquid nascitur in parte Naturae ulla, et in Mari esse, praeterque multa quae nusquam alibi.*" Mather follows Francis Willughby, a seventeenth-century expert, in believing that Aristotle's division of the fishes into three kinds—cetacious, cartilaginous, and spinous—is the best (p. 173). Here the material on Pliny (9. 1) is from Derham, p. [4]40 n. 3; the information on Aristotle is from Willughby's *De historia piscium libri quatuor* (Oxford, 1686), bk. 1, which Mather may have used.

Additional classical references enable Mather to relate tall tales even while refuting them. Pliny mentions the *balaenae* of the Indian Sea which were 960 feet long and whales that were 600 feet long and 360 feet broad which came into a river of Arabia; Pliny also offers a reason why the largest animals are bred in the sea. But let what I give you of the 960 foot pass for a "*Plinyism,*" Mather writes, "and so what *Basil* in his *Hexaemeron* reports of Whales equal in bigness to the greatest Mountains, let the Censure of *Brierwood* pass upon it, as *an intolerable Hyperbole*: We will write more sober things." Mather passes by what Aelian affirms "of the Whale being five times beyond the largest Elephant." "*Dion*, a grave as well as an old Writer," reports "a *Whale* coming to Land out of the *German Ocean* sixty Foot in length, twenty in breadth" (pp. 176-177). This Pliny material (9. 2. 4, 6-7; 9. 1. 2) is from Derham, pp. [4]40-[4]41 n. 4. Basil the Great (330-379), who was abreast of the science of his time, wrote on whales in Homily 8 of the *Hexaemeron*. Claudius Aelianus (2d century A.D.) wrote *De natura animalium*, a miscellany on the peculiarity of animals in seventeen books. He discusses the size of elephants in 13. 8 and of whales in

16. 18. Dio Cassius recounted the large whale in his *Roman History* (54. 21, 2). Mather borrows all this material from Edward Brerewood (1565?-1613), professor of astronomy at Gresham College, who wrote *Enquiries Touching the Diversity of Languages, and Religions through the Cheife Parts of the World* (London, 1614), p. 109.

In the religious improvement of this essay, Mather writes: "I remember a *Crassus*, of whom 'tis reported, that he so tamed a *Fish* in his Pond, as to make him come to him at his calling him; verily, I shall have a Soul deserving *his Name*, and be more stupid than the *Fish*, if I do not hear the Calls which the Fish give to me to glorify the God that made them; and who has in their *Variety*, in their *Multitude*, in their *Structures*, their *Dispositions* and *Sagacities*, display'd his Glories" (p. 178). Marcus Licinius Crassus, a contemporary of Cicero who served in various public offices and in various ways attained influence, was best remembered for his wealth and greed; and maintenance of a piscina was a Roman status symbol. Aelian, *De nat. an.* 8. 4, is the ultimate source; perhaps Mather knows the ironic story told there from the original.

Consideration of Birds ought immediately to follow the Fishes, says Mather, "not only for the *Order* of their *Creation*, but also because as *Basil* notes, there is a Συγγένεια τοῖς πετομένοις πρὸς τὰ νῆκτα *Volantibus Affinitas cum Natantibus*" (p. 180). Surely Mather takes this from Alsted, p. 493, but the ultimate source is Basil, Homily 8, 2. Fin-toed birds are naturally directed to the water and fall to swimming there; thus ducklings, though hatched by a hen, go in water, though they have never seen it before, while the hen is in an agony to keep them out, "as Pliny expresses it, with *Lamenta circa Piscinae stagna, mergentibus se pullis, Natura duce*" (p. 184). This is from Ray, p. 147, and ultimately from Pliny, 10. 76.

"There is," Mather writes, "a considerable Observation of *Aristotle*, πτηνὸν μόνον οὐδὲν" (p. 184). The reason why birds have feet as well as wings is that there is not always sufficient food for them in the air, and without feet they could not perch on the trees. The writer's source is Ray, p. 181.

Mather's account of birds leads him to relate a story familiar to students of classical antiquity. "We celebrate the *Dove of Archytas*, whereof *Gellius* tells us, *Simulachrum Columbae e ligno ab Archyta, ratione quadam, disciplinaque mechanica factam, volasse*; the same whom we find celebrated by *Horace* for a noble *Geometrician*. This Dove surely had more Geometry in it than the πλαταγή, or *Childrens Rattle*, for which *Aristotle* celebrates him, as the Inventor of it" (p. 195). The classical sources are *The Attic Nights* of Aulus Gellius (10. 12), Horace, *Odes* (1. 2), and Aristotle's Politics (8. 6, 1340b 26-28). Mather takes over the tale from Derham, p. 317 n. 25. Mather then praises God who has with so much art contrived all the variety of birds, and with such perfection. "*Austin* says well, *Deus non solum Angelum et Hominem, sed nec exigui et contemptibilis animantis viscera, nec Avis pennulam, nec Herbae flosculum, sine suarum partium convenientia dereliquit*" (p. 195). This passage, from *De civitate dei*, (5. 11) Mather takes out of Derham, p. 396 n.

In the rhapsody that concludes this essay, Mather writes: "It was a celebrated Speech of the Philosopher, *Si Luscinia essem, ut Luscinia canerem*; I can *fly* much higher than they, and if I praise their Glorious Creator, I shall *sing* much *better* than they; *Homo sum, atque ut Homo canam colamque*" (p. 197). The unidentified spokesman here is Epictetus, the Greek slave who obtained his freedom and taught Stoic philosophy in Rome. Mather could have taken his information from Alsted, p. 472, or from the *Discourses* of Epictetus as reported by Arrian, 1. 16.

In the chapter on Quadrupeds, Galen, Aristotle, and Pliny are called upon about equally. Galen, an authoritative witness to design in nature, is cited on the strength of the lion, on the necks of animals being accommodated to their method of feeding, and on the kid of a goat (pp. 201, 205, 210). Galen reported that he took alive a kid out of the belly of a dam and brought it up; the embryo presently walked, as if he had heard, said Galen, that legs were given him for that purpose; then he smelled things set before him, and refusing them all supped only milk. But what Galen found most admirable was that the kid began to chew the cud, whereupon, said he, "*All that saw cried out with Admiration, being astonished at the natural Faculties of Animals.*" Mather takes the first two references from Derham, pp. 357 n. 9, 362; the last one from Ray, pp. 404-406.

Aristotle is mentioned on the location of the heart in man, on sea tortoises, and as the author of *De animalibus* (pp. 208, 213, 219). Mather takes the first reference from Derham, p. 365 n. 4; the second from Ray, p. 386. Pliny is mentioned on sea tortoises, on the legs of elephants being like pillars, and on the stomach of the camel (pp. 213, 201, 206). The first reference is from Ray, p. 386, and the others from Derham, pp. 354 n. 1, 363 n. 1. The necks of quadrupeds are commensurate to their legs, though this proportion is not kept in the elephant, who has a short neck. The excessive weight of his head and teeth would have been unsupportable. But his proboscis! "*Tully* takes notice, *Manus data Elephantis, quia propter Magnitudinem Corporis, difficiles aditus habebant ad Pastum*" (p. 205). This is from *De natura deorum*, 2. 47, 123, by way of Derham, p. 362 n. 1. In a discussion of cleverness in animals, Mather notes that many besides Plutarch have written *De sollertia animalium* (p. 213), and he recounts many interesting stories to illustrate his point. Plutarch's essay is in his *Moralia*; Mather apparently knows that Philo, Pliny, and Aelian also wrote on the subject.

Mather calls upon the Christian apologist Lactantius to censure men who do not learn from beasts the being and glory of God. "*Illos qui nullum omnino Deum esse dixerunt, non modo non Philosophos, sed ne Homines quidem fuisse dixerim; qui mutis simillimi, ex solo Corpore constiterunt, nihil videntes animo*" (p. 210). He quotes the passage (*The Divine Institutes*, 7. 9) from Derham, p. 371 n.

Mather's classical references on the horse, a "notable, docile, and tractable Animal," are a bit recondite. "Read *Solinus*, and see what Approaches the *Horse* makes to *Reason*! One would question which had most, *Caligula* or *Incitatus*" (p. 214). Gaius Julius Solinus wrote, probably soon after A.D. 200, *Collectanea rerum memorabilium*, a geographical summary of parts of the known world which contained stories about the cleverness of the horse. Caligula, the Roman emperor from A.D. 37 to 41, built a marble stable for his horse Incitatus. "There are antient Examples of other *Horses* besides *Bucephalus* and *Lethargus*," Mather adds, "that have been honour'd with stately *Funerals* and *Sepulchres* at their *Deaths*, as well as their Masters; yea, tho the Epitaph of *Adrian* be lost, his Horse's is preserved to this day" (p. 214). Bucephalus was the favorite horse of Alexander the Great. I have been unable to identify Lethargus. The Roman emperor Hadrian (A.D. 117-138) built a tomb with a stele and inscription for his favorite horse for the chase, Borysthenes. Dio's *Roman History* relates the story (69. 10). Mather probably takes most of this information from Edward Topsell, *The Historie of Foure-footed Beasts* (London, 1607), pp. 230-339 passim, but it is not all there.

Several animals yield man useful instructions, and Mather remembers an observation of Seneca which exemplifies a moral remark on the properties of some quadrupeds: "*Omnia quae Natura fera ac rabida sunt, consternantur ad Vana. Idem inquietas et stolidis Ingeniis evenit, rerum suspicione feriuntur*" (pp. 216-217). The passage is from Seneca the Younger, *On Anger*, 3. 30, 1-2.

In the essay on Man, by far the longest in the book, Cicero, Pliny, and Galen are the classical authorities most frequently cited, but some twenty-five additional ancients are named. "Father *Austin*," Mather writes, taxed the folly of those "who admired the *Wonders* in the other Parts of the Creation abroad, *et relinquunt seipsos, nec mirantur*, but see nothing in *themselves* to be *wondred* at" (p. 221). This quotes Augustine's *Confessions* (10. 8). The body of man is none other than "a Temple of GOD! A *Vitruvius* will teach us that the most exquisite and accurate Figure for a *Temple* will be found in a Conformity to an *Human Body*" (p. 222). The Roman architect Vitruvius Pollio (d. c. 25 B.C.) compares the human body to the perfect plan for a temple in *On Architecture* (3. 1).

According to Mather, "the *erect Posture* of Man, the *Os sublime*," is commodious for a "*rational Creature*" who must have dominion over those which are not erect. "*Tully* admires the *Providence of Nature*, as he calls it, adding the reason for it; *Sunt enim e Terra Homines, non ut Incolae atque Habitatores, sed quasi Spectatores superarum rerum, atque Coelestium, quarum Spectaculum ad nullum aliud Genus Animantium pertinet*." By this posture man has the use of his hands, "which, as Galen observes, are *Organa sapienti Animali convenientia*," and his eyes (p. 223). "*Os sublime*" is from Ovid, *Met.* (1. 85) by way of Derham, p. 324 n. 4. Mather is quoting *De natura deorum* (2. 16, 140) and *De usu partium* (1. 3), but he takes this material from Derham, p. 323 n. 3.

"No sign of *Chance* in the whole Structure of our Body," writes Mather, who proceeds to discuss the parts of the body and their location as evidences of design in nature. He quotes Cicero, cites Galen, and mentions Hippocrates in this capacity (pp. 225-227), taking all this from Derham, pp. 336 n. 1, 341 n. 5. A sympathy exists between the members of the body; "as *Pliny* notes, the *Face* in *Man* alone is the *Index of all the Passions*."

Such is the variety in the faces of man that, as Valerius Maximus observes, no two are alike. Had nature been a blind architect, men's faces might have been as similar as a hen's eggs. "It was one of *Pliny*'s Wonders, *In Facie Vultuque nostro, cum sint decem aut paulo plura membra, nullas duas in tot millibus Hominum indiscretas Effigies existere*" (pp. 227-229). Mather fabricates this from Derham, p. 346 (citing Pliny, 11. 51, 138), p. 347 (citing the Roman historian Valerius Maximus, 9. 14), and Ray, pp. 283-284 (citing Pliny, 7. 1, 8).

For authors in the physico-theological literary tradition down to Darwin, the eye afforded special evidence of design in nature, and Mather is no exception. "No rational Beholder can look upon the *Eye*," he writes, "without seeing Reason in the wondrous Workmanship thereof" (p. 235). He quotes Pliny (p. 235) and Cicero (p. 240) and cites Galen (pp. 235, 243) on the subject, taking this material from Derham and Ray. The ear is treated next. Pliny is cited on the virtue of ear-wax in curing the bites of men, scorpions, and serpents (p. 246), with Derham (p. 122 n. 13) as the source. The *membrana tympani* was noticed as long ago as Hippocrates' time, a detail available in Derham, p. 124 n. 17. As for sound, Alexander the Great reportedly had a "tube" which might be heard a hundred stadia (p. 249). The power of musical sounds over the spirits and bodies of man is very surprising. "What could the famous Timothy the Musician do upon Alexander" (p. 252)? The reference is probably from Derham, p. 135 n. 29. "*Ismenias* the *Theban*, by playing on the *Flute* or *Harp*, cured the *Sciatica*" (p. 252). Where Mather obtained this recondite detail I do not know.

In treating the nose, the tongue, and the sense of feeling, Mather quotes Cicero in Latin three times (all from *De natura deorum*, 2. 56, 141) and Pliny once (10. 90, 195), and mentions Theophrastus (pp. 253, 254, 255). The source is Derham, pp. 138 n. 2, 142 n. 3, and 145 n. 3. Galen is cited on the teeth (p. 255), an observation taken from Ray, p. 309.

The grand glory of the tongue is that it is the main instrument of speaking "What the Emperor *Justinian* himself asserts in his Rescripts;" Mather writes, "[*Vidimus venerabiles Viros, qui abscissis radicitus Linguis;*] that he himself saw *venerable Men*, who when their *Tongues* were cut out, at the very Root, yet continued plainly speaking the Truth of Christianity against the *Arians*; a Fact whereof many Witnesses are subpoena'd by *Cujacius*: it looks miraculous" (p. 259)! This wonderful tale is based on historical events. The Roman Empire included parts of Africa, but in 429 the Vandals under Gaiseric invaded and captured the fairest provinces, establishing their capital at Carthage. The Vandals treated the Libyans harshly during Gaiseric's reign of nearly forty years. The Arian Vandals persecuted orthodox Christians and imposed their faith on them, and this cruel policy continued during the reign of Honoric (477-484). Victor, bishop of Vita in Africa, left an eye-witness account of Vandal persecutions in these years. In Carthage, Victor reported, the Vandal king ordered the tongues and right hands of orthodox Christians "cut off at the very roote and stumpe: yet through the assistance of the holy Ghost, they so spake and speake still, as they did neuer before. If any man be incredulous, let him goe now to *Constantinople, and there shal he find Reparatus* a Sub-deacon, one of that company, speaking (and that eloquently) without any impediment. For which cause he is greatly reuerenced in the palace of the Emperor *Zeno*."[20]

The Vandal kings assured the peace of the Christians beginning in 496, but the Emperor Justinian (527-565) valued religious uniformity and decided to recover Africa nevertheless. The army was sent in 533, and Procopius of Caesarea, the historian of the reign of Justinian, went along as secretary to the commanding general. Procopius reports that Honoric forced Christians in Libya to change over to the Arian faith or suffer death, "and he also cut off the tongues of many from the very throat, who even up to my time were going about in Byzantium having their speech uninjured, and perceiving not the least effect from this punishment." Justinian or his lawyers knew these events well; Mather's Latin quotation is from the Code of Justinian (1. 27, 1).[21]

Mather cites Galen on the lungs, the arteries, and the muscles of the belly (pp. 263, 265, 273), drawing on Derham, p. 153 n. 8, Ray, p. 317, and Nehemiah Grew, *Cosmologia Sacra: Or a Discourse of the Universe as it is the Creature and Kingdom of God* (London, 1701), p. 27, respectively. He calls upon Galen, Cicero, and Aristotle to celebrate the hand and its uses (pp. 277-278).

Mather next considers the astonishing physical strength of some persons since the days of Samson and of Milo the Ox-carrier in the sixth century B.C. (pp. 279-280). Valerius Maximus and others cite examples. Mather then tells about such ancients as the "Tyrant *Maximus*" (actually Gaius Julius Verus Maximinus, who murdered and succeeded the Emperor Alexander Severus in A.D. 235), "*Marius*" (Caius Marius, a cutler, who in the time of Galienus was chosen emperor by the soldiers), and "*Salvius*" (Fufius Salvius, described by Pliny). Mather's source is Nathaniel Wanley, *The Wonders of the Little World: Or, A General History of Man* (London, 1678), pp. 38-39.

The Christian Philosopher comes finally to the soul of man. In introducing the subject, Mather calls on four ancient worthies—the "Pagan Orator"—i.e., Cicero—the poets Juvenal and Claudian, and Galen. The gist of their testimony, which is quoted in Latin, is that man's indwelling intelligence gives evidence of Divine Providence and that man's spirit alone remains when his body perishes (pp. 281-282). All of this material, which is based on *De natura deorum* (2. 58, 147), Juvenal's *Sat.* 15. 146-147, Claudian's *Panegyric on the Fourth Consulship of the Emperor Honorius* (234-235), and *De usu partium* (17. 1), is woven out of Derham, pp. 302-303 nn. 1-3.

The account continues by describing such "stupendous Faculties of the Soul" as wisdom, learning, and memory. The Jews tell us of a professor in their "Academy of *Sora*, who was called *Sagi Nahor*, or *Joseph of great Light*; he was *blind*, but it seems he had a Soul full of Knowledge" (pp. 282-285). The Academy of Sora in Babylon was founded in A.D. 219 and operated until the thirteenth century. "Sagi Nahor" is a Jewish euphemism for blind; its literal meaning is "abundant in light." Seneca the Elder's account of his own phenomenal memory and that of his companion Marcus Porcius Latro is mentioned, and Pliny's examples of the memories of Cyrus, Mithridates, and Carneades are rehearsed—the latter based on Derham, p. 303 n. 4.

The various inclinations of the soul are a wise provision of God that the business of the world may all be transacted: "*Diversis gaudet Natura ministris*" (p. 287). This Latin line is taken from Derham, p. 304 n. 5. "We find *Homer* sometimes admiring this Variety;" Mather adds, "and *Horace* entertains us with a

Sunt quos Curriculo,—which might have been extended to a Volume; for as one says, 'there may be found a *Sunt quos* for every thing under the Sun,'" (p. 287). On Homer, Mather follows Derham, p. 304, who quotes both the *Iliad* (13. 730-733) and the *Odyssey* (8. 167-168). Horace describes different walks of life, including his own as a poet, and writes: "Some there are whose one delight it is to gather Olympic dust upon the racing car" (*Odes*, 1.1). Much study is a weariness to the flesh, but there have been hard students other than Cato, "of whom Tully says, *Erat in eo inexhausta aviditas legendi, nec satiari poterat*" (p. 287). Cicero discussed Cato in *De finibus*, 3. 2, 7, but Mather follows Derham, p. 305 n. 6.

In treating man's inventions, Mather mentions Pliny on the Romans having a sun-dial but refuses to regard Boethius as the inventor of clock-work (pp. 289-290). Here Mather follows Derham, *The Artificial Clock-Maker: A Treatise of Watch and Clock Work* (London, 1700), p. 85, not realizing that Boethius did build a water clock and a sun dial.[22] The progress of invention leads Mather to optimism. If mathematics continues to improve in the future as in the past, "who can tell what Mankind may come to! We may believe, without having Seneca our Author for it, *Multa Venientis aevi populus ignota nobis sciet*" (p. 291). Here the author follows Ray, p. 201, quoting Seneca, *Natural Questions*, 7. 30, 5.

The union between soul and body, which for Mather consists in the conformity of our thoughts to our corporeal activity, is discussed in the last part of the treatise. Mather believes there is a Scale of Nature which passes "regularly and proportionably from a Stone to a Man"; several orders of animated body lie below intellect, and several orders of embodied intellect lie below pure Mind. The transition from human to perfect Mind is made by a gradual ascent; there may be angels whose faculties may be as much superior to man's as man's may be to those of a snail or a worm. "The highest Perfection that any *created Mind* can arise to, is that in the *Soul* of our admirable Saviour, which is indeed *embodied*; but it is the *Soul* of the *Man* who is personally united to the SON of GOD" (pp. 292-293).[23]

"*Aetheism,*" Mather concludes, "is now for ever chased and hissed out of the World." Having banished atheism, he proposes two "general Strokes of *Piety*." The first is that the works of God demonstrate his Power, Wisdom, and Goodness. The second is that the Christ of God must not be forgotten (pp. 294-297). After elaborating this theme, Mather writes, "It was an high Flight of *Origen*, who urges, that our *High-Priest's* having *tasted of Death*, ὑπὲρ παντός, FOR ALL, is to be extended even to the very *Stars*, which would otherwise have been *impure* in the sight of God; and thus are ALL THINGS restored to the *Kingdom* of the Father." The apostle Paul in Col. 1:19-20 may seem to favor this flight. If this be so, Mather affirms, then *"total Nature"* may be "sanctified to God that made it." Mather endorses the proposition that God created all things in the foreknowledge that the Son of God became a Man as well for this end as for ends more glorious, and without such an intuition He would not have made any thing which He has made (p. 300).

This part of Mather's treatise is very complicated, and the present essay permits only a brief sketch to help understand the views set forth. Origen (c. 185-c. 254), the Greek theologian, was the principal apologist of the early church. A prolific writer, his biblical exegesis and theological speculation were inseparable. The masterpiece among his commentaries was the *Commentary on the Gospel of John*, and here, in an allusion to Hebrews 2:9, he refers to Jesus "having tasted of death" (1. 40). Origen's most important theological work is *De principiis*, in which he advances the doctrine of the pre-existence of souls, rebirth, and universal salvation. His eschatology was based on belief in the justice and goodness of an omnipotent Creator and in the absolute free will of every rational being, including animated stars (*De principiis*, 1. 7). His doctrine of universal restoration was condemned as heretical by the Council of Alexandria in 400 and by the Fifth Oecumenical Council at Constantinople in 553. The Renaissance revived interest in Origen and stimulated fresh controversy over the doctrine of the ultimate salvation of everyone. George Rust, a member of the Cambridge Platonist School, defended Origen's opinions in *A Letter of Resolution Concerning Origen and the Chief of his Opinions* (London, 1661), and that book may have been known by Mather.[24]

The Son of God is the upholder of all things in the world, though man's sin has so perverted and rendered the world full of loathsome and hateful regions and "such *Scelerata Castra*" that the revenges of God would have long since rendered it a fiery oven if our blessed Jesus had not interceded for it (p. 301).

Suetonius had used this Latin label, the final classical reference in Mather's book, to describe the name given to the summer camp in which Drusus died (*Life of the Deified Claudius*, 1. 3).

As we have seen, Mather makes abundant use of classical and Christian antiquity in his treatise on Newtonian science. His greatest intellectual debt is to the Platonist-Augustinian tradition. According to Plato, nature is only half real, a system of symbols which reflect the non-sensible realities which lie beyond it. As Platonism spread, Plotinus in the early third century A.D. elaborated the philosophy of Plato as a basis for Hellenism in its struggle with Christianity. The Neo-Platonists devised the concept of the scale of emanations which connect the supreme Good with the whole hierarchy of its imperfect "images."[25]

Meanwhile, the Christian church became the heir of Platonic philosophy as Christian apologists appealed to Plato in their controversy with the gentiles. Origen extravagantly read the eschatology of Plato's myths into Christianity, while Augustine was instrumental in incorporating Platonism into the main current of Christian orthodoxy. The Augustinian doctrine derived from Plato and influenced by Neo-Platonism held that God is the author of both nature and Scripture. God reveals himself through the symbolism of nature, which fallen man can never adequately decipher, and through Scripture, which is infallible. The natural and the supernatural must be concordant. Through nature the invisible things of God are made known by things which are visible.

In addition to Plato and Augustine, Mather is indebted to many other classical authors, especially Pliny, Galen, Cicero, and Aristotle. Pliny provided comprehensive if often undiscriminating treatment of a wide variety of scientific topics. Galen and Cicero in their different ways emphasized the design argument and could readily be adapted to Christian purposes. Aristotle had been discovered and elevated to a position of highest authority in all branches of natural knowledge in the thirteenth century, and despite a revulsion against Aristotelian dogma during the Renaissance, Mather summons the Stagyrite as an expert witness.

The classics are both essential and peripheral to *The Christian Philosopher*. They are essential in that Mather's argument is based on the Platonic-Augustinian concept that the whole world is the temple of God and that there is no real distinction between the two symbolisms, the natural and the supernatural. Hence Mather can celebrate the exciting new discoveries in science and hail Sir Isaac Newton as "the *Perpetual Dictator* of the learned World" (p. 56) with no fear for the Christian faith. The classics are peripheral in that they are often a literary embellishment which does not affect the book's thesis. As embellishment, the classical references should be understood as part of the Renaissance tradition in which Mather had been educated and which was passing from the scene even as he wrote.

Mather borrows a large proportion of his classical references from intermediate sources, especially Derham, Ray, and Alsted. All authors borrow, but they acknowledge their debts in different ways. Though his Introduction alerts the reader, Mather borrows heavily, and largely without attribution. This practice, however unacceptable by modern standards, was common at the time. One must nevertheless know the classics to borrow from them confidently, and surely Mather knows the standard Latin authors and many others besides. Like many other learned persons at the time, he kept a commonplace book in which he regularly entered quotations and paraphrases from his readings, and his *Quotidiana* served as a source for his subsequent writing. Yet it seems clear that Mather found it easier to paraphrase and quote from contemporary authors—Derham's *Physico-Theology* was published only two years before Mather completed his manuscript—than from the classics themselves.

Wherever or however he obtained his information, Mather was certainly familiar with the scope of Greek and Latin literature. He exhibits wide-ranging knowledge with no evidence of taking it from a middleman in references to Fidentinus, Anaxagoras, Thales, Columella, salt, Cato, Crassus, clever animals, and Vitruvius. He draws on classical authors without naming them, as with Diogenes Laertius. And he is obviously well acquainted with the "anecdotal tradition" which circulated in all kinds of books, ancient, medieval, and early modern, which makes it almost impossible to discover the source of such tidbits as Ismenias' cure for sciatica.

In any event, Mather's content was more important than the sources he relied upon in writing his book. His purpose in *The Christian Philosopher* was to harmonize religion and the new science, and he skillfully used the literature of classical and Christian antiquity in producing one of the most important documents of early American intellectual history.

NOTES

I wish to express gratitude to the following for directing me to seven of Mather's classical references: Dr. Dorothy Schullian Adelmann of Cornell University, Mr. J. van Sint Feijth of the Thesaurus Linguae Augstinianae in Eindhoven, The Netherlands, and Professor Emeritus Luitpold Wallach of the University of Illinois. I also thank Mr. Randall Stewart, a graduate student in Classics and my Research Assistant, for help with some of the finer points of analysis. I gratefully acknowledge the helpful comments on a draft of this essay by Dr. Adelmann, Professors John J. Bateman and J. K. Newman of the University of Illinois, and Professor Meyer Reinhold of Boston University.

1. The best recent studies of Mather are Robert Middlekauff, *The Mathers: Three Generations of Puritan Intellectuals, 1596-1728* (New York, Oxford University Press, 1971) and David Levin, *Cotton Mather: The Young Life of the Lord's Remembrancer, 1663-1703* (Cambridge, Mass., Harvard University Press, 1978). Raymond P. Stearns, *Science in the British Colonies of America* (Urbana: University of Illinois Press, 1970), places Mather in a scientific context.

2. In this essay references to *The Christian Philosopher* will appear in the text immediately following the material paraphrased or quoted (as here). Mather is usually accurate in quoting his sources, though he changes case, alters syntax, and condenses to meet his stylistic needs. I have quoted Mather accurately without using *sic* to note lapses, but I have silently changed the ampersand to *et* and corrected obvious printer's and spelling errors. I have retained Mather's Greek diacritical marks (though many are erroneous).

3. Theodore Hornberger, "Notes on The Christian Philosopher," in Thomas J. Holmes, *Cotton Mather: A Bibliography of His Works*, 3 vols. (Cambridge, Mass., Harvard University Press, 1940), 1:135.

4. Middlekauff, *The Mathers*, pp. 302-304, and Stearns, *Science in the British Colonies*, pp. 403-405, 409, 424-426 may be taken as representative of authors who published on the subject from 1907 to 1972.

5. Cotton Mather, *Paterna: The Autobiography of Cotton Mather*, ed. Ronald A. Bosco (Delmar, N.Y., Scholars' Facsimiles and Reprints, 1976), 7; Cotton Mather, *Corderius Americanus: An Essay upon the Good Education of Children . . . . In a Funeral Sermon upon Mr. Ezekiel Cheever* (Boston, 1708), pp. 21-33. See also Robert Middlekauff, *Ancients and Axioms: Secondary Education in Eighteenth-Century New England* (New Haven, Yale University Press, 1963), pp. 53, 75-88.

6. Samuel E. Morison, *Harvard College in the Seventeenth Century*, 2 vols. (Cambridge, Mass., Harvard University Press, 1936), is authoritative; Levin, *Cotton Mather*, pp. 23, 25-26.

7. "Harvard College Records, Part III," Colonial Society of Massachusetts, *Collections*, 31 (1935), 329-339; Morison, *Harvard*, 1:200 (the quotation); Levin, *Cotton Mather*, pp. 42-48.

8. Mather, *Paterna*, p. 8; Morison, *Harvard*, 1:208-284 passim, 195-196.

9. Morison, *Harvard*, 1:292; Julius H. Tuttle, "The Libraries of the Mathers," *Proceedings of the American Antiquarian Society*, n.s. 20 (1911), 296-356.

10. Pliny the Elder, *Natural History*, Preface, 21. Hereafter, references to this work will appear in the text with only the author's name and location.

11. Charles E. Raven, *John Ray, Naturalist: His Life and Works*, 2d ed. (Cambridge, University Press, 1950), pp. 452-457, 466-467 (the quotations are at pp. 452, 467). Hereafter, references to Ray, *Wisdom*, will appear in the text with only the author's name and page. All references are to the fifth edition (1709).

12. Basil Willey, *The Eighteenth Century Background: Studies on the Idea of Nature in the Thought of the Period* (New York, Columbia University Press, 1940), pp. 39-42 (quotation at p. 39). On Ray and Derham see also Richard S. Westfall, *Science and Religion in Seventeenth-Century England* (New Haven, Yale University Press, 1958), pp. 62-69, 92-95, 127-130. Hereafter, references to Derham, *Physico-Theology*, will appear in the text with only the author's name and page.

13. For a brief modern treatment, see Frank E. Robbins, *The Hexaemeral Literature: A Study of the Greek and Latin Commentaries on Genesis* (Chicago, University of Chicago Press, 1912). For the larger context, see also Peter Brown, *The World of Late Antiquity: From Marcus Aurelius to Muhammad* (London, Thames and Hudson, 1971).

14. Cotton Mather, *Manuductio ad Ministerium: Directions for a Candidate of the Ministry* (Boston, 1726), p. 33. Hereafter, references to Alsted, *Theologia naturalis*, will appear in the text with only the author's name and page.

15. English translations of the dialogue called *Octavius* were published in 1636, 1682, 1695, and 1708, but Mather's quotation (of 17.6) follows none of these editions closely.

16. *Theophilus of Antioch: Ad Autolycum.* Text and Translation by Robert M. Grant (Oxford, At the Clarendon Press, 1970), 2.12. Theophilus says ten thousand mouths and tongues.

17. *The Posthumous Works of Robert Hooke* (London, 1705), p. 76.

18. The translation is from the Loeb edition.

19. M. Grieve, *A Modern Herbal*, 2 vols. ([1931] New York, Hafner Publishing Co., 1959), 2:701.

20. Victor, Bishop of Vita, *The Memorable and Tragical History of the Persecution in Africke, 1605* in *English Recusant Literature, 1558-1640*, ed. D.M. Rogers (Menston, Yorkshire, The Scolar Press, 1969), p. 102.

21. Procopius, *History of the Wars*, 3, 8. 4. The relevant portion of Justinian's Code merely says (in translation): "We saw venerable men who with difficulty related their sufferings, whose tongues had been cut out by the roots." See S. P. Scott, *The Civil Law: Including ... the Enactments of Justinian*, 17 vols. (Cincinnati, The Central Trust Co., 1932), 12:130.

22. Edmund Reiss, *Boethius* (Boston, Twayne Publishers, 1982), p. 25.

23. Belief in a Scale of Nature arose in antiquity and was a basic intellectual assumption in the early eighteenth century. The standard treatment is Arthur O. Lovejoy, *The Great Chain of Being: A Study of the History of an Idea* (Cambridge, Mass., Harvard University Press, 1936).

24. D. P. Walker, *The Decline of Hell: Seventeenth-Century Discussions of Eternal Torment* (Chicago, University of Chicago Press, 1964), pp. 3-23 passim; "Origen," in F. L. Cross and E. L. Livingstone, eds., *The Oxford Dictionary of the Christian Church*, 2d ed. (Oxford, Oxford University Press, 1974), pp. 1008-1010; H. Crouzel, "Origen and Origenism," in *New Catholic Encyclopedia* (1967), 10:767-774.

25. Alfred E. Taylor, *Platonism and Its Influence* (New York, Cooper Square Publishers, 1963), pp. 3-56 passim for this and the following paragraph. The strong influence of the Platonist-Augustinian tradition on American Puritanism is emphasized in Perry Miller, *The New England Mind*, 2 vols. (Cambridge, Mass., Harvard University Press, 1939-1953).

THEODOROS OF SAMOS:
AN ANCIENT GREEK ARTISTIC GENIUS

Raymond V. Schoder, S. J.

There are many scattered intriguing references among Greek authors to Theodoros of Samos as a famous pioneer in various areas of art in the Archaic Age. Most of these passages about him are collected in their Greek or Latin originals in Overbeck.[1] Some attention is paid him in the major surveys of Greek art and there is a summary of the data by Lippold in Pauly-Wissowa[2] and by Moreno in the *Enciclopedia dell'Arte Antica*.[3] Theodoros' achievements and artistic impact deserve fuller treatment—which this essay seeks to provide.

Since some of his works were made for Croesus (king of Lydia c. 560-546 B.C.) and Polykrates (tyrant of Samos c.540-522 B.C.), he was evidently active before and after the middle of the sixth century B.C., a period of great energy and development on cultural and political planes.

Diodorus[4] and Diogenes[5] call him the son of Rhoikos, a pioneer Samian architect and sculptor, as one of their sources, Hekataios of Abdera seems to have recorded. Diodorus says he was brother of Telekles. But Herodotus[6] states that he was son of Telekles, which seems the more reliable account. He further identifies Rhoikos as a Samian architect, son of Phileus.[7] Plato has Socrates list Theodoros along with the famous early sculptors Daidalos and Epeios.[8]

Some scholars, like Urlichs and Overbeck, postulate two artists called Theodoros, whom they distinguish as Elder and Younger; but others reject this solution to the problem of the long span of Theodoros' activity. Robertson straddles: "Theodoros (if he was indeed one) is a striking example of the way the arts, major and minor, mingle in archaic Greece."[9] It is best to consider him a single artist with long and diversified activity.

Theodoros is credited by the ancients with having invented several instruments and techniques which were taken up by later artists. This need not mean that he first conceived these devices and procedures; at least it involves his introducing them into Greek artistic practice, or notably improving on them. Pliny[10] states that Theodoros 'discovered' the *norma*, which is the T-square used in achieving accurate right angles (equivalent to Greek γνώμων); the *libella*: the plumb-line or level, consisting of a plummet and line attached to a frame to determine perpendicular and horizontal directions; the *tornus* or lathe; and the *clavis*—which seems to mean a builder's bar or lever, or perhaps wrench (like the French *clef*).

According to Pliny[11] some authorities held that modelling of clay (*plastice*) was first developed in Samos by Rhoikos and Theodoros, long before its appearance in Corinth, where others claimed that it had been invented by Boutades when he thought of filling in with clay an outline of a handsome youth's face which his daughter had drawn to aid her memory in his absence. Athenagoras[12] tells the same story and adds that the arts of clay modelling and statue-making were advanced by Daidalos and Theodoros "of Miletus"—which is an erroneous epithet. The 'invention' cannot have been of terracotta statuettes, which were already common in Greece by the eighth century B.C. It must refer to scale models in clay of statues to be made in bronze, or more likely the inner clay core, in the statue's basic pattern, around which a bronze figure could be cast. It was obviously a major step forward, for which Theodoros' pioneering genius is credited. Earlier bronze statues in Greece were either small, if solid, or made of sheets of bronze fastened around a wooden core (the hammered, *sphyrelaton* technique).[13] Pliny remarks[14] that once the new method was developed it became universal practice, so that no statue was made without a clay model, and adds "hence it is clear that this art of modelling clay is older than that of casting bronze."

Of special significance for all later bronze statuary is Theodoros' introduction of bronze casting on a large scale. Pausanias four time[15] credits Theodoros with this important contribution: "Theodoros of Samos ... first found how to melt iron and mould statues from it"; "the first to fuse bronze were the Samians Theodoros and Rhoikos"; "I showed earlier in my account that the Samians Rhoikos, son of Philaios, and Theodoros, son of Telekles, were the first to discover how to fuse bronze perfectly, and they were the first to cast it in a mould"; "the Samians Rhoikos, son of Philaios, and Theodoros, son of Telekles, first fused bronze and moulded statues from it."

This was no doubt the "lost-wax" technique, long in use in Egypt and the East, seemingly known in seventh century B.C. Greece, but not common until fully perfected by Theodoros and Rhoikos. It consisted of making a model of the planned statue in wood or clay, covering it with a thick layer of wax, enclosing this in a clay case, heating until the wax melted and ran out, and pouring molten bronze into the place of the wax, then removing the outer mould and (usually) the inner core and touching up the hollow bronze shell to final perfection.[16] Theodoros likely brought this technique back to Greece from Egypt, where he is reported to have gone with Telekles.[17]

Another technique which Theodoros adopted from Egyptian sculpture was that of pre-determined proportions of the figure. Diodorus' passage, just cited, records this borrowing of Egyptian procedure in a passage difficult to interpret: "The Egyptians state that the most renowned of old sculptors, Telekles and Theodoros, sons of Rhoikos, spent some time among them, and made for the people of Samos their ξόανον (wooden cult statue) of Pythian Apollo .... The Egyptian method of working is common there, but not among the Greeks. For the symmetrical proportions (συμμετρία) are judged not as they appear to the eye, as is the practice of the Greeks, but as soon as they lay out the stones and divide them up for working on, they establish a norm (ἀνάλογον) applicable from the smallest parts to the largest. They divide the scheme for the body into twenty-one sections plus one-fourth, in this way producing the whole symmetry of the body. Accordingly, when the artists agree among themselves on the size of the statue, they separate from one another and produce the various parts in the size agreed on in relation to all the parts in harmony—and this so accurately that their special way of working arouses amazement."

Diodorus goes on to say that Telekles and Theodoros made the Pythian Apollo statue for Samos by adopting the Egyptian procedure: "one half of the statue was made by Telekles in Samos, the other half by his brother Theodoros in Ephesus. When the two parts were put together, they fitted so perfectly that the work seemed to have been completely made by one person .... The statue is said to be in most ways very similar to the Egyptian style, with the hands stretched along the sides and the legs in the position of striding." In other words, this famous archaic statue was like the other early Greek standing male figures, stiffly formal, frontal, austere.[18] Whether Theodoros and Telekles made their statue in marble or bronze is not indicated, but Diodorus is clearly wrong in calling it a ξόανον, which is a technical designation of early wooden statues, usually for cult objects, rough and rudely shaped, keeping the over-all appearance of a tree trunk. The statue for Samos is at least evidence of Theodoros' activity in archaic Greek sculpture and of his contribution in advancing the technique and style.[19] Athenagoras also mentions the Apollo statue as a work of Theodoros and Telekles.[20]

A famous statue by Theodoros was his bronze self-portrait in Samos which Pliny admired. He says it was a marvellous likeness, executed with wonderful subtlety. In his right hand he held a file, in three fingers of his left hand he held a tiny four-horse chariot (*quadrigula*) so amazingly small that it was hidden, chariot and horses alike, under the wings of a fly made along with the statue.[21] Pliny adds that this tiny chariot with horses was later brought to Praeneste—presumably put on display there in the great temple of Fortune put up in the days of Sulla. Since Theodoros was renowned as a gem-engraver, some scholars assume that the quadriga was etched on a scarab-like small stone; but from the description in Pliny it seems rather to have been an independent three-dimensional marvel. Since portraiture, let alone self-portraiture, is not heard of otherwise in the early Archaic period, this report of Theodoros' work is another testimonial to his artistic inventiveness and originality.

An inscription found on the Acropolis at Athens, from a statue base, reads in Ionic characters: Θεό[δωρ]ος ἄγ[αλμα ἐποίησεν].[22] This may indicate some statue made by Theodoros and displayed on the Acropolis. But there is doubt among the experts in epigraphy whether the dating fits our Theodoros, as it may come from the early fifth century.

Theodoros was a notable pioneer also in architecture. He was associated with two of the colossal Ionic temples of the sixth century B.C., at Ephesus and Samos, among the very first to be built in stone in Greece. There had been from very early times on the important island of Samos a cult and sanctuary of Hera. Around the middle of the sixth century B.C. the earlier structures, which included the first clear example of a public stoa (roofed colonnade), were demolished and a vast new temple constructed, with a huge outdoor altar east of it. Herodotus says the first architect of the temple was the native Samian Rhoikos, son of Phileus.[23] Pliny adds Theodoros and Smilis as also its architects and calls it a 'labyrinth', locating it in one reference in Samos, in another in Lemnos.[24] The name is due to its resemblance to the great multi-columned hypostyle halls in Egypt, especially the famous 'Labyrinth' near Lake Moeris which both Herodotus and Strabo described[25]—Herodotus remarking that its vastness was beyond words "though the temples at Ephesus and Samos are remarkable." Pliny's reference to the "Lemnian labyrinth" is clearly an error, since he calls its architects "natives": Smilis, Rhoikos, and Theodoros—all Samians. Dinsmoor[26] shrewdly ascribes the error to Pliny confusing in his sources mention of ἐν λίμναις, a reference to the swampy area in which the Heraion in Samos was built. The new temple had 132 columns, a veritable 'labyrinth' of towering pillars, and was the pioneer instance of a double row of columns down the sides and triple rows across the front and back. Another innovation! Pliny notes that its column bases (he says 150 of them) were grooved by the lathe technique (which Theodoros had devised)—"the drums were raised in the workshop off the ground and balanced on wooden pivots so that they could be channelled as a boy turned them round and round."[27] Some of these column drums, reused in a later rebuilding of the temple after it burned down, have survived and demonstrate this lathe effect: deep horizontal grooves around both the concave lower portion and the higher convex part.[28] To the East of the temple Rhoikos constructed a huge new altar 120 ft. long, 54 wide. Of special interest is a treatise (now unfortunately lost) which Theodoros wrote describing and explaining the architectural details of the great temple—the first fully developed temple in the Ionic style. Vitruvius, the Roman architect, cites this 'book' by Theodoros, which is the earliest architectural treatise known from a Greek author.[29] It is possible that Theodoros was in charge of the rebuilding of the temple in the days of Polykrates, after it had burned down. It was the largest Greek temple anywhere.

When the temple of Artemis at Ephesus was rebuilt on a colossal scale, partly funded by King Croesus of Lydia, sometime after the mid-sixth century B.C., on designs of the architects Chersiphron of Crete and his son Metagenes, Theodoros, drawing on his experience at Samos, cleverly recommended that its foundations be bedded on layers of charcoal and wooly sheepskins to counteract the effect of the marshy ground chosen for it to protect it from earthquakes and landslides.[30] When finished, this temple became one of the wonders of the world.

Theodoros' wide-reaching fame gained him an invitation to come to Sparta and construct there a public assembly hall, known as Skias. Pausanias notes that "on the way out of the market place is what they call the Skias, where public assemblies are still held. They say that this Skias was the work of Theodoros the Samian, who discovered how to fuse iron and mould images from it. The Lacedemonians hung here on display the lute of Timotheus of Miletus . . . . Next to the Skias is a round building, in which are images of Olympian Zeus and Aphrodite."[31] Nothing of this building survives, and Pausanias' text does not solve several problems about its shape and material. The word σκιάς implies that the structure resembled a sun-shade of some kind, perhaps a long covered hall like a bower or arbor or some sort of canopy. Some interpret it as a rotunda, like a Mycenean tholos domed tomb, especially since the word σκιάς is used for the circular Tholos in the Agora at Athens.[32] But it is peculiar in that case that Pausanias goes on to describe as circular the building next to the Skias at Sparta, implying that it itself was not round. Because of the reference to Theodoros' discovery of smelting iron, it could be argued that the Skias was of metallic construction; but this is unlikely.

Besides his outstanding achievements in architecture and sculpture and new devices and procedures in their execution, Theodoros was famous throughout the Archaic Greek world for remarkable triumphs of metal-working. In narrating Croesus' many gifts to the sanctuary of Delphi, to conciliate Apollo and the Greeks, Herodotus describes two huge kraters (mixing-bowls) on display in the temple there: "he gave two very large kraters, one gold the other silver. The golden one used to stand on your right as you entered the temple, the silver one on your left. After the fire in the temple [548] they were moved—the golden one is now on display in the Treasury of the Klazomenians; it weighs eight and a half talents plus twelve mnas [sc. 522 pounds—over a quarter ton]. The silver one is now in the corner of the temple fore-court; it has a capacity of six hundred amphoras [=5400 gallons], as is known from its use by the Delphians for mixing wine for the festival of Theophania. The Delphians say that it is the work of Theodoros of Samos—and I believe it, for it is no ordinary piece, in my opinion."[33] This last remark reveals Herodotus' great admiration of Theodoros' artistic skill, which he had personally observed in many examples, unfortunately lost to us.

Athenaeus[34] reports that in the bed-chamber of the Great Kings of Persia was a krater all of gold, made by Theodoros of Samos.

Pausanias[35] says that the people of Lycia in southern Asia Minor claim that a bronze krater on display in the Apollo temple at Patara was dedicated by Telephus (son of Hercules and Auge) and made by Hephaestus! He rejects this boast on the score that "presumably they were not aware that it was the Samians Theodoros and Rhoikos who first fused bronze." This directly refutes the pretended antiquity of the krater; but it may also imply that it was the work of Theodoros, or at least worthy of him.

One of Theodoros' most widely admired products was the famous signet ring of Polykrates. Herodotus[36] tells the story delightfully: Polykrates, tyrant of Samos (540-522 B.C.) was so prosperous, famous, and successful at everything that his friend and ally, Amasis king of Egypt, was worried about his future, knowing that the gods in their jealousy of human happiness always arrange to bring such prosperity to ruin. So he wrote a letter to Polykrates, urging that to avoid such a certain reversal of fortune he temper his prosperity by some painful loss. He suggested that Polykrates throw away irrevocably something that he most prized, over whose loss he would grieve most bitterly. Polykrates saw the wisdom of this advice, and looking through his treasures for what he would miss most, came upon the signet ring made for him by Theodoros of Samos, son of Telekles. This was a precious emerald set in gold. So he took this far out to sea and threw it in, while his courtiers watched. He then went home and lamented over his lost treasure. A few days later a fisherman caught an exceptionally large and fine fish, and made a present of it to Polykrates. The cook discovered in the fish Polykrates' ring and brought it triumphantly to the dismayed prince, who saw in the event inevitable disaster looming for him. He reported this to Amasis, who broke off his treaty with Polykrates so that when the sure calamity befell him he would not have to grieve over him as a friend. Soon after, he was crucified by the Persians.

The story was retold by Strabo, Clement of Alexandria, and others.[37] Strabo says the ring was of precious stone, with an incised pattern (γλύμμα); Clement records that the design on the stone was of a musical lyre; Tzetzes states that the stone was a precious emerald, as does Pausanias, who says that Polykrates wore that ring more than any other and most gloried in it. Pliny reports that the stone was sardonyx, and was on display in Rome, in the Temple of Concord, set in a golden horn given by the Empress, but not shown in a prominent place [no doubt to protect it]; and he remarks that the engraved stone was still intact and undamaged in his time.[38]

Another marvel of delicate metal work was the famous golden Plane Tree and the golden Vine associated with it. Many ancient writers mention it with implication of its high artistic worth. Athenaeus[39] quotes Charys of Mytilene's account of Alexander the Great as reporting that in the bed-chamber of the Persian kings, hanging over the bed, was a golden Vine set with precious stones. And he cites Amyntas' description of it as having clusters of grapes made from precious stones, including emeralds, rubies, garnets. He says that the Persian kings often sat under this marvelous vine when giving official pronouncements and decision. Herodotus[40] relates that when Xerxes asked his officials who a certain very rich Lydian named Pythius was, he was told "he is the one who gave your father Darius the golden Plane Tree and the golden Vine, and he is still, we believe, the richest man in the world—after you." The wonderful creation had probably been made for Alyattes, from whom Pythius had received it. Pliny[41] also states that these "noble works, the golden Plane Tree and Vine were gifts to Darius," and says that they were among the vast loot in gold which Cyrus found when he conquered Asia. Himerius the sophist[42] explicitly says the golden Vine was the work of Theodoros of Samos, as also does Photius in his *Bibliotheca* (612-). Diodorus records that these precious objects were taken by Antigonos when he captured Susa, and melted down.[43] Several other writers also refer to this golden Vine or Plane Tree, which was evidently world-famous—a crown in Theodoros' artistic reputation.[44]

Pliny[45] names a Theodoros of Samos in his list of notable ancient painters whom he does not have space to treat in detail. But this is clearly not our Theodoros, as he is said to have been a disciple of Nikosthenes, who seems to belong to Hellenistic times, probably the third century B.C. Lippold[46] and Moreno[47] disassociate him from our Theodoros, as does Brunn in his discussion of the problem.[48] Perhaps there is a textual corruption in Pliny's statement, the Samius being a mis-reading for Sannus.

From this synthesis of the scattered and often discrepant data about Theodoros in ancient sources it is clear that he was a versatile and richly inventive artistic genius on many levels who merits wider notice and appreciation.

NOTES

1. J. Overbeck, *Die Antiken Schriftquellen zur Geschichte der Bildenden Künste bei den Griechen* (Leipzig, 1868; reissued 1959 by Georg Olms, Hildesheim). In these notes, the symbol # indicates the paragraph where the passage is found in Overbeck; '# part' indicates that only part of the original text is included in Overbeck. For the citations from Pliny, a handy guide is *The Elder Pliny's Chapters on the History of Art*, edited by K. Jex-Blake and E. Sellers in 1896, reissued with up-dated bibliography of Plinian scholarship 1896-1975 (by R. V. Schoder, SJ), which gives the Latin texts with facing translation and explanatory notes. Most of Overbeck's citations are given in English translation in J. J. Pollitt's *The Art of Greece 1400-31 B.C.* (New Jersey, Prentice-Hall, 1965).

2. Pauly, Wissowa, Kroll, al, *Real-Enzyklopädie der Klassischen Altertumswissenschaft* (Stuttgart, 1894—), vol. 5A, cols. 1917-1920 ("Theodoros 195").

3. Rome, Istituto della Enciclopedia Italiana, 1958 -. Vol. 7, pp. 811-812.

4. Diodorus Siculus, *Library of History* 1.98.5 (Overbeck # 269).

5. Diogenes Laertius, *Lives of the Philosophers* 2.103 (# 282).

6. *Histories* 3.41 (# 285).

7. *Ibid.* 3.60 (# 273).

8. *Ion* 533b.

9. Martin Robertson, *A History of Greek Art* (Cambridge University Press, 1975), vol. 1, p. 148.

10. *Natural History* 7, 198 (# 281).

11. *Ibid.* 35.152, 151 (# 262, 259).

12. *Legatio* 14.59 (# 261).

13. For description, see Robertson (above, n. 9), I.39.

14. *N.H.* 35.153.

15. *Description of Greece* 3.12.10; 9.41.1; 10.38.5; 8.14.8 (## 278, 276, 277, 275).

16. For the process, see G. M. Richter, *A Handbook of Greek Art* (London, Phaidon, sixth edition 1969), p. 55; and Robertson (above, n. 9), I.181.

17. Diodorus Siculus, *Library of History* 1.98 (# 279).

18. See examples in treatments of early Greek sculpture, e.g. Richter (above, n. 16), pp. 58-59.

19. There is an illustration of the Egyptian method of blocking a piece of marble with a grid of lines marking sections, in *The Encyclopedia of World Art* (New York, McGraw-Hill, 1961), vol. 4, plate 347.

20. *Legatio* 14.61 (# 280).

21. *N.H.* 34.83 (# 292).

22. I.G.[2] I.598.

23. *Histories* 3.60 (# 273).

24. *N.H.* 34.83; 36.90 (## 292, 283).

25. Herodotus, *Histories* 2.148; Strabo, *Geography* 17.37.

26. William B. Dinsmoor, *The Architecture of Ancient Greece* (London, Batsford, third edition 1950), p. 124, note 1.

27. *N.H.* 36.90 (# 293).

28. See illustration of such a column base in D. S. Robertson, *Greek and Roman Architecture* (Cambridge University Press, 1945), p. 97, fig. 44.

29. Vitruvius, *The Ten Books on Architecture* section 12 of Preface to Book 7 (# 274).

30. Pliny. *N.H.* 36.95-97; Diogenes Laertius, *Lives of Philosophers* 2.103.

31. *Description* 3.12.10-11 (# 278 part).

32. see data on the word in Liddell-Scott-Jones, *A Greek-English Lexicon* (Oxford, Clarendon Press, ninth edition 1940), p. 1610.

33. *Histories* 1.51 (# 284 part).

34. *Deipnosophists* 12, p. 514 (# 286).

35. *Description* 9.41.1 (# 276).

36. *Histories* 3.40-43 (# 285 part).

37. Stabo, *Geography* 14.1.16; Clement of Alexandria, *Paidagogos* 3.59; Tzetzes, *Chiliades* 7.210 (## 309-311); Pausanias, *Description* 8.14.8 (# 275).

38. *N.H.* 37.4, 8 (## 312, 313). This likely means that it was without engraved design. Because of this, and the specification of sardonyx, Fürtwangler thinks that this stone in Rome was not the famous signet, but perhaps some other that once belonged to Polykrates (*Die Antiken Gemmen*: Amsterdam, Hakkert, 1965, vol. 3, p. 81).

39. *Deipnosophists* 12, p. 514 (# 286).

40. *Histories* 7.27 (# 290).

41. *N.H.* 33.137 (# 289); 33.51 (# 288).

42. *Eclogae* 31.8 (# 287).

43. *Library of History* 19.48 (# 291 part).

44. Xenophon, *Hellenica* 7.1.38; Dio Chysostom, *Discourse* 57.12; Seneca, *Moral Epistles* 41.7.

45. *N.H.* 35.146 (# 2114).

46. In Pauly-Wissowa (above, n. 2) 5A col. 1920: Theodoros 200."

47. In *E.A.A* (above, n. 3). vol. 7, p. 813: "Theodoro 5."

48. Heinrich Brunn, *Geschichte der Griechischen Künstler* (Stuttgart, Neff, second edition 1889), vol. 2, p. 192.

THE GREEKS AND THEIR FEATS
Clarence A. Forbes

The lore that has descended to us from ancient Greece gives us glimpses of mighty muscle-men and of athletes who could throw their weights around. This begins at once in the earliest work of Greek literature, the *Iliad* of Homer. Homer, composing his poem in the eighth century, strove to portray the heroic age of the Trojan War, which took place five centuries earlier, in the thirteenth century. It is in the very nature of epic poetry, such as the *Iliad*, to glorify and idealize the past, and to magnify and exaggerate the exploits remembered from the brave days of old. The later epic poets simply imitated Homer and tried to outdo him in exaggeration. Let us see how this worked.

The chief hero of Troy in the Trojan War was Hector. At one point in the combat Hector successfully tried to break into the fortified ship-camp of the Greek invaders by hurling a huge stone against the ponderous, barred gate.[1] Homer says that the stone was so big that two men of his lifetime could have hardly lifted it up on a wagon. Later in the poem another leading Trojan hero, Aeneas, picked up a stone to throw at the Greek Achilles; and again Homer says that the stone was such a big thing that not even two men could pick it up—men of the sort that we get nowadays.[2]

The muscular feats narrated by Homer in the eighth century no longer seemed good enough in the third century. Jason, the principal hero in the tale of the Argonauts, as told in epic poetry by Apollonius Rhodius,[3] threw at the earth-born men a stone that *four* stalwart young men could not lift. The next famous epic, admittedly imitating both Homer and Apollonius, was written in Latin by Vergil; and here we find the native Italian hero, Turnus, picking up to throw at his enemy Aeneas a stone which *twelve* picked men could hardly lift, men of the sort that the earth produces nowadays.[4] Literary critics call this enhancement, i.e. an effort by a later poet to enhance and improve upon something written by an earlier poet. But instead of enhancement I should call it exaggeration run wild.

We should next give brief attention to Heracles, the god of Greek heavy athletes and strong men. Heracles was reputedly a human being who was later divinized, and in the days when he trod the earth with his twelve-inch feet his feats won him the fame of being the strongest man who ever lived. He it was who, a legend said, founded the Olympic Games in 776 B.C. and measured off the length of the Olympic stadium as exactly 600 feet by stepping off the desired footage, heel to toe, 600 footprints. Not only did he put his foot down with such lasting effect, but to give a sample of his prowess Heracles proceded to win two muscular events at the Olympics on a single day: wrestling and the pancratium. In a thousand years, until the Olympic Games were abolished, only seven persons were able to duplicate the Herculean feat of the double victory. These seven were called "the successors of Heracles" and they alone received the honorary epithet of *paradoxonikai*, "astounding victors." While Heracles is a mythical figure, his seven successors were historical persons.

Turning from the mythical Heracles, we fix our eyes on the historical Milo of Croton, a powerful wrestler of the sixth century B.C. Accord him a place in the Hall of Athletic Fame. He used to keep in training not by a daily dozen but by a daily seventeen pounds of meat and an equal poundage of bread, washed down by eight and a half quarts of wine. This reputed diet, aside from the wine, would have provided 50,000 calories a day. Modern Olympic athletes at their peak effort require about 8000 a day. It is permissible to believe that Milo did not eat six times as much as a champion athlete of today. All the while eating enthusiastically, Milo built up his strength by weight-lifting, and one must admire his ingenious scheme of steadily increasing the weight. First with an easy effort he lifted a young bull calf; then he proceeded to lift the same animal every day until it was full-grown. To convince any possible doubters, he stood in the stadium at Olympia, hoisted a four-year-old bull to his shoulders, carried it up and down the track, then killed it and ate it all up before the end of the day. Unbelievers call this a calf-and-bull story. But enormous Titormus, a huge shepherd of Aetolia, thought that he could compete with Milo, and demonstrated by eating an ox for breakfast. Fie on corn-flakes!

Milo's graduated exercises and heroic diet gave him the strength to win the victory in wrestling at the Olympics six consecutive times, over a period of twenty-four years of his life. He competed a seventh time, and was still so powerful that only by tactics of stalling did another man from Croton wrest the victory away from the mightiest wrestler of them all.

Milo used to like to amuse people by exhibitions of strength. The statues of Olympic victors, to be set up in the sacred enclosure near the stadium, were lifesize and made of bronze; when his own statue had been made Milo picked it up and carried it on his shoulders to the spot for its erection. He would hold a pomegranate in one hand so firmly that no one could get it away from him, but nevertheless without crushing it. He would stand on a greased discus and simply laugh at persons who ran at him like battering rams and tried to dislodge him from his perch. He would tie a cord tightly around his head and then hold his breath until the veins in his head swelled and broke the cord. Keeping his elbow tight against his side, he would hold out his right hand vertically and defy any one to move his little finger.

Mighty Milo came to a sad end. Near Croton he happened to see a tree-trunk that had been partly split open by wedges, and the wedges had been left in the cleft. He proudly undertook with the strength of his bare hands to finish splitting open the log, and strained until the wedges came loose and fell out. Then the fissure closed up on his fingers and held him a prisoner. The wolves came and ate him. I think that I shall never see an athlete stronger than a tree.

The lasting fame of Milo has stemmed from his feat of lifting and carrying the bull. Even Shakespeare knows of "bull-bearing Milo" (*Troilus and Cressida II*, iii, 248). Can we find any American imitators? An unsigned editorial paragraph in the *Nation* for 1931[5] told of a Tennessee farmer who read about Milo and decided to emulate him. Beginning with a small calf which rapidly picked up weight, the farmer daily picked up the calf's weight until it was an 800-pound yearling. And the name of the farmer? H. E. Man. Surely there are countless he-men in Tennessee, but the census-taker did not find this one. The editor of the *Nation* had a favorite athletic sport: pulling his readers' legs. Let us try again, with a look at *Time* for December 17, 1945, where a picture on page 70 eliminates the credibility gap. In honor of Borden's milk and its radio program, *County Fair*, a high-school boy named Allen La Fever daily hoisted a Jersey calf with the bucolic name of Phoebe (a perfect lady, observe; no bull) from the day she weighed 75 pounds until the day when she weighed 161. A good enough performance for a high-school boy; but when pretty Phoebe was fully grown there was no Milo in her life—only milk. By hefting the heifer Mr. La Fever merited a No-bull Prize.

When Greek civilization and Greek athletics were both in their prime, the sixth and fifth centuries B.C., athletes and strong men liked to display their strength by weight-lifting. One day the athlete Milo encountered the shepherd Titormus in the countryside of Aetolia. The two fell into an argument about which was the stronger. Taking Milo down to the river, Titormus showed him a weighty problem in the shape of a boulder. Milo tugged and shoved but could hardly budge it. Brushing him aside, Titormus picked up the boulder, hoisted it on his shoulders, carried it for sixteen yards, and then threw it away. Just to show that this did not exhaust his strength, he then caught a wild bull by the hind leg with his left hand and another with his right and held them both so that they were unable to escape.

We are not told the weight of the boulder lifted by Titormus. But Greek inscriptions in archaic lettering of the sixth century B.C. give us exact data on the prowess of two strong men who are otherwise unknown. At Olympia in the museum there is a block of red sandstone which weighs 288 pounds; on the stone one reads impressive words in Greek: "Bybon with one hand threw me over his head." Now such a weight, it if is on a balanced barbell gripped with two hands, can indeed by lifted: for example, the American Olympic medalist Paul Anderson has lifted 408 3/4 pounds (in a jerk) and the Russian Yuri Vlassov has lifted 435 1/4 pounds (in a press). But Bybon, whoever he was, could never have lifted with one hand a rough stone of 288 pounds. We may doubt whether there ever was such a person as Bybon, unknown as he is from any source except the inscription on the stone. The inscription may have been the work of some satirist who wished to make fun of the braggadocio of strong men. I commend the full discussion by the Welsh scholar H. A. Harris, who examined the stone carefully at Olympia and concluded that the inscription on it is merely a satiric hit.[6]

Now for the other strong man and his stone. On the volcanic island of Thera, now called Santorin, there is an egg-shaped mass of black volcanic rock weighting 480 kilos or 1056 pounds. The inscription on it in archaic and irregular letters says: "Eumastas the son of Critobulus lifted me from the ground." May we suppose that under optimum conditions Eumastas lifted the stone an inch or less? Gardiner: "To lift such a weight from the ground, though possible, is quite a good performance." Gentle reader, please try it yourself.

We should mention also a third stone which purportedly was lifted, but the inscription on it for technical reasons has been declared a forgery by four scholars with such impressive names as Fränkel, Weinreich, Herzog, and Hiller von Gärtringen. The stone is a real one, weighing 735 pounds. It was found in Epidaurus, near the temple and health-center of that city. The inscription[7] on it said: "Hermodicus of Lampsacus, paralytic. Asclepius healed him in temple-sleep and told him to go out and bring into the temple the biggest stone he could. He brought the one now lying in front of the shrine." Professor Rudolf Herzog, a close student of ancient miracles, states that on the Greek island of Cos he saw a gigantic workman pick up a piece of marble weighing about 278 pounds and carry it 100 yards. But can a man be a paralytic one day and a weight-lifter capable of carrying 735 pounds the next day? Professor Herzog sadly denies it. "If the report of the miracle, to doubt which there is no a priori reason, points to a stone really lying in front of the abaton before 300 B.C, then his stone was later replaced by a heavier one provided with the inscription, perhaps in order to magnify the miracle or perhaps because the original stone was lost." And now goodbye to the brawny weight-lifters.

The Greeks were good swimmers, and knowledge of swimming was universal among them. A Greek proverb for total ignorance said laconically; "Can't swim; can't read." Travelers know of the skillful work of the sponge-divers in modern Greece, and diving for practical purposes was certainly known in ancient days. Story-telling Herodotus gives us an account of the man whom he calls the best diver in the time of the Persian War, 480 B.C. Scyllias (also spelled Scyllis or Scyllus) desired to desert from the Persian fleet to the fleet of his Greek fellow-countrymen. "I marvel if what is told is true," says Herodotus; but the report was that Scyllias dove into the sea and swam underwater for eighty stades until he reached Artemisium, where the Greek fleet lay at anchor. Now eighty stades is about nine miles. "Some things resembling lies are told about this man," say Herodotus, "and in my opinion he went to Artemisium in a boat." (8.8) We may agree with Herodotus that here the sober truth received a little festive embroidery. Looking for sobriety in the Greek geographer Pausanias we discover that Scyllias was a real person, a frogman, and a hero honored by a statue in the holy city of Delphi. He had taught his daughter Hydna the art of deep diving; and during a storm the two of them dove under the Persian fleet, loosened the anchor ropes, and thus caused the fleet to suffer severely in the storm just before the naval battle of Artemisium. Far from under-valuing this underwater exploit, the admiring Greeks embellished it with an addition of a nine-mile underwater swim.

As I describe the athletic feats of the Greeks, and seem to pay no attention to Greek women, I fear that my female readers will accuse me of being a male chauvinist pig. Let me hasten to defend myself by saying that the male chauvinist pigs were the Greeks, who, with a few exceptions, excluded women from athletics. In one Greek city, however, the famous city of Sparta, all the girls were enrolled in a program of energetic physical education. Looking anxiously in the direction of Sparta, we are relieved to find one record of a woman's athletic feat unrecorded by Guinness. An exercise of Spartan girls, as we know from an Athenian comedy, was to jump nimbly in the air and quickly kick the buttocks with both heels. That such a feat can be done is shown by logic, if one simply reasons a posteriori. Men do push-ups; Spartan women did kick-ups. One Spartan woman established a record: she jumped and kicked her buttocks with her heels one thousand times in succession.[8] This feat was recorded on her tombstone, even if it has escaped the notice of Guinness.

Lady readers, I hope you get a kick out of this story. Also I invite all of my readers to notice that classical scholars, when they do research, insist on getting to the very bottom of the subject.

Recorded feats of Greek runners must necessarily deal with distance, not with speed. The Greeks had no accurate devices for measuring time; the sand-glass, the water-clock (clepsydra), and the sundial are all too clumsy and inaccurate for timing a sprint. Runners in the athletic meets competed against each other, not against a record; and therefore the Greeks did not try to determine who was the "world's fastest human." In celebrating "swift-footed" Achilles as the chief hero of the Trojan War, Homer was suitably vague about the swiftness of Achilles' feet.

Lacking the telegraph and telephone, the Greeks were dependent on couriers for the swift transmission of messages. The Greek name for a courier was *hemerodromos*, a "day-runner," for these couriers were not mounted and often ran all day long. Most famous of such couriers was the Athenian Philippides, whose exploit of 490 B.C. is celebrated by Herodotus (6.105f). The Athenians, needing military assistance just before the battle of Marathon, sent Philippides to implore help from the Spartans. The distance from Athens to Sparta by road and path is estimated at 130 miles. As for the timing, all we know is that Philippides arrived in Sparta on the day after he left Athens. If we suppose that he ran 65 miles the first day, had a night's sleep, and ran 65 more miles the second day, the feat is credible as well as creditable. Not worthy of attention is the late Greek story, unknown to Herodotus, that Philippides made the first "Marathon run" from Marathon to Athens (26 miles) to bring the news of victory over the Persians, and that he dramatically fell dead as soon as he had shouted the news. All this may be read in Browning's poem *Pheidippides*, but the reader of Browning should be warned that the courier spelled his name Philippides and that he never made a Marathon run.

After Philippides the most famous Greek courier was Philonides, in the service of Alexander the Great. The best run of Philonides is mentioned twice by Pliny the Elder (2.181 and 7.84) and once by Solinus (1.98), a late writer heavily dependent on Pliny. The run was from the city of Sicyon in the eastern Peloponnesus to the city of Elis, near Olympia, in the west. One passage of Pliny (2.181) spells out the record run in words, not in

Roman numerals, as 1200 stades in nine day-light hours. Pliny's wording here appears to be a translation from a Greek source, since he gave the measurement in Greek stades, not in Roman miles, and since in the time of Alexander the Great or only a very little earlier the Greeks began to adopt the Roman division of the day into hours. The other passage of Pliny (7.84) uses Roman numerals, and states the distance as MCCCV (1305) stades; but the passage of Solinus, verbally dependent on the second passage of Pliny, gives the distance in words, not in numerals, as 1200 stades. All classical scholars are painfully aware that the copyists of manuscripts made many errors in copying Roman numerals. Perhaps, therefore, Pliny did not contradict himself in the two passages, since Solinus seems to have derived the number 1200 from the second passage, where our available manuscripts of Pliny give 1305. Let us work with the number 1200; 1200 stades would be about 136 miles.

We know something of the famous Philonides not only from a Roman source, Pliny, but also from the Greek geographer Pausanias (6.16.5) and three Greek inscriptions. Although we have no statement that Philonides was an Olympic victor, Pausanias saw a statue of him at Olympia. Now nearly all the forest of statues which once populated Olympia have disappeared, but the German excavators found two copies of the inscription whereby Philonides, courier of King Alexander, dedicated his statue to Olympian Zeus.[9] The third inscription, found in 1954, is a broken stele, partially recording an honorific decree for the Cretan Philonides.[10] The findplace of the inscription was Aigion, a small city in the extreme north of the Peloponnesus, between but not directly between Sicyon and Elis. The only plausible reason for honoring Philonides in Aigion would be that he passed through this city in running from Sicyon to Elis. At a much later time, when Greece had long been under Roman sway, a Roman itinerary led from Sicyon via Aigion and Patras to Elis, about 940 stades.[11] This distance is considerably short of the 1200 stades mentioned by Pliny, and here we need to be reminded that the Romans aimed to make their roads straight, short, and businesslike. The roads and footpaths available in the time of Alexander the Great were crooked and casual. Bilinski, after studying the topography and roads of the Peloponnesus with the help of modern guide-books and road maps, chose two probable routes from Sicyon to Elis via Aigion and found that each measured 210 kilometers or 1145 stades. Now we have come close to the 1200 stades, obviously a round number, reported by Pliny.

Is it possible for a human being to run 136 miles, 1200 stades, in a nine-hour day? First we recall that the Greeks and Romans interpreted an hour as one-twelfth of the daylight, and at the time of the summer solstice this could be as much as 74 minutes; thus nine ancient hours could mean a little over eleven sixty-minute hours. Next we recall that native runners of the Tarahumara Indian tribe of Mexico can run 168 miles in a day without stopping. V. Silberer[12] reports a run of 124 miles in seventeen hours. Allowing for some exaggeration regarding the distance, it seems possible that Philonides ran from Sicyon to Elis, rather less than 136 miles, in one long day.

Other accounts from Greece lend support to the feat of Philonides. Pliny (7.84) says that a Spartan courier named Anystis duplicated the feat of Philonides in running from Sicyon to Elis. Plutarch (*Aristides* 20.4.5) declared that Euchidas in one day ran from Plataea to Delphi and return, the total distance being 1000 stades, again a round number, approximately 113 miles.

Those who have been lured by the lore of Greek athletics will expect the present paper to rehearse and discuss the famous feat of Phaÿllus. The Greek city of Croton in Southern Italy was a notable mother of athletes, of whom the greatest were Milo in the sixth century and Phaÿllus in the fifth. The historian Herodotus (8.47) briefly records that when Greece stood in danger from the Persians in 480 B.C. no Greek colony in Italy except Croton came to the aid of the motherland. At the glorious and decisive naval battle of Salamis, one ship, outfitted at the expense of Phaÿllus and manned by men of Croton, helped to defeat the Persians. Prior to the year of the battle, Phaÿllus was a recognized athlete and Panhellenic victor, having won in the Pythian Games at Delphi two victories in the pentathlon and one in the stade-race. Later in the fifth century Athenians in the theatre were expected to understand allusions to Phaÿllus as a proverbially fast runner.[13] But the lasting fame of Phaÿllus was as a pentathlete and was enshrined in a two-line Greek epigram, known from sundry sources.[14] I translate literally: "Phaÿllus leaped five more than fifty feet, and hurled the discus five less than a hundred feet." About the discus-throw of ninety-five feet no one is disposed to argue, since the Greek discus varied in weight from three to nine pounds, if made of metal, and up to fifteen pounds or more, if made of stone. A good athlete could surely hurl a not-too-heavy discus ninety-five feet. But the very idea that a man could jump more than half as far as he could throw a discus has caused some raised eyebrows. Now if one feat attributed to Phaÿllus in the brief epigram is reasonably possible, the other one should be equally so. There is a little corroboration in the proverb πηδᾶν ὕπερ τὰ ἐσκαμμένα "to jump beyond a pit," a proverb cited and explained by Zenobius, collector of proverbs in the second century of our era. Zenobius says: "Phaÿllus threw the discus and jumped the farthest. Once he jumped onto the hard ground beyond the fifty-foot pit; hence the proverb."

In considering Phaÿllus' leap some have recalled a casual remark by Aristotle:[15] "Pentathletes jump further when holding *halteres* than they do without them." The word *halteres*, often translated as "jumping weights," signifies stone weights which Greek jumpers held in their hands. Modern experimentation tends to corroborate Aristotle's remark, but the added distance covered by a jumper holding weights is not great; so that a single jump of fifty-five feet is still far beyond the bounds of possibility.

Now it was long suspected by several scholars that the jump in the Greek pentathlon was a triple jump, but this was vigorously denied by E. Norman Gardiner, the chief British authority on Greek athletics.[16] In Austria, however, there was a scholar who knew Greek athletics as well as Gardiner did. This was Julius Jüthner of Innsbruck. In 1935 Professor Jüthner published his discovery of a decisive passage in a late Greek commentator on Aristotle. Themistius,[17] the commentator, was interested in problems of space and motion, and his remark about the pentathlon was dropped casually. He said: "The jumpers in the pentathlon do not move continuously, since they leave out some part of the space in which they move." Now the motion of a modern long-jumper is continuous, as any observer knows. But in modern Greece the hop, hop, and jump is familiar; and in such a performance the motion is not continuous, and the total distance covered could be fifty or fifty-five feet. The world's record for this sort of triple jump is held by Jozef Schmidt of Poland (1960), and at 55 feet, 10 1/4 inches it slightly betters the jump of Phaÿllus. Jüthner concluded, and here he won the agreement of Walter Woodburn Hyde of Pennsylvania, that the jump in the Greek pentathlon was a hop, hop, and jump, and that in this sort of triple jump Phaÿllus did indeed cover fifty-five feet.[18]

We are not told that the jump of Phaÿllus was the best ever made by a Greek. It became famous through the cleverly worded epigram, and perhaps other meritorious feats of jumping were forgotten through lack of publicity. But we do have a sober prose statement, in the *Record of the Olympics* by Sextus Julius Africanus (third century A.D.), of a fifty-two foot jump by Chionis of Sparta. Chionis won the stade-race in the twenty-ninth Olympic, 664 B.C., and Africanus implies that his jump was made at the same Olympics, almost two centuries before the time of Phaÿllus.

Africanus did not break out into a poetic paean on the jump of Chionis, nor did he suggest that it was prodigious. Chionis' hop, hop, and jump was nearly as good as that of Phaÿllus, but it was not enshrined in poetry and therefore went unhonored as well as unsung. Greek literature and documents provide us with no other statements about the distance covered by jumpers. The jumps of Chionis and Phaÿllus are possible and plausible, and all doubts should now be laid to rest.

The Greeks were a healthy race who believed in well-proportioned bodies and saw no reason to endeavor to develop a special breed of muscle-men. Since the Greeks had the habit of not keeping records of time and distance at the Panhellenic Games or at any athletic games, and indeed had no timepiece except for the awkward and inaccurate waterclock, we necessarily lack reliable information on prodigious achievements by athletes in regulated competition. No one asks us to believe the exaggerations of the poets. Heracles was divine or semi-divine, and his exploits belong in Greek mythology, not in sober and truthful history. The feat of Phaÿllus in jumping is credible if it is properly understood as a triple jump. The excellent feats of professional couriers in long-distance running are inaccurately recorded but nevertheless are physically possible and are paralleled by similar feats of hardy tribesmen in our own century. Finally we must reckon with the tendency of athletes to draw the long bow and to enlarge upon their own achievements. When a Greek athlete opened his mouth, he put his feats in it.

NOTES

1. *Iliad* 12.445-462.

2. *Iliad* 20. 285-287.

3. *Arg.* 3.1365-7

4. *Aeneid* 12.8796-902

5. Vol. 133, p. 295.

6. *Sport in Greece and Rome*, 142-6.

7. *Inscriptiones Graecae IV* (2nd ed.) no. 121, lines 107-110 (ca. 420 B.C.).

8. Pollux, *Onomasticon* 4.102.

9. Dittenberger and Purgold, *Inschriften von Olympia* (1896) nos. 276-277; also in M.N. Tod, *A Selection of Historical Inscriptions* (Oxford 1948) vol. 2, no. 188.

10. J. Bingen, "Inscriptions d'Achaie: 19. Décret pour le Crétois Philonidas," *Bulletin de Correspondance Hellénique* 78(1954) 407-409. See the careful study by the Polish historian of ancient sport, Bronislaw Biliński, "L'hémerodrome Philonidès, son record et la nouvelle inscription d'Aigion," *Eos* 50 (1959-60) 69-80.

11. K. Miller, *Itineraria Romana* (Stuttgart 1916), p. 551.

12. *Handbuch der Athletik* (1900) pp. 89ff.

13. Aristophanes *Acharnians* 214; *Wasps* 1206.

14. Th. Preger, *Inscriptiones Graecae Metricae* (Leipzig 1891) no. 142.

15. Aristot. *De motu animalium* 3.

16. *U.A.S.F.*, 308f.

17. Themistius, *Comm. in Aristot. Graeca* V 2, p. 172 lines 26 ff. ed. Schenkl; J. Jüthner, "Zur Geschichte der griechischen Wettkämpfe," *Wiener Studien* 53(1935) 68-79.

18. W. W. Hyde, "The pentathlum jump," *Amer. Journ. of Philology* 59(1938) 405-417.

ACTS OF THE APOSTLES 26:4-5: ARE ALL THE TRANSLATIONS WRONG?*

John Francis Latimer

During the year 1978 I wrote the first draft of a paper entitled, "Born Again In the New Testament: A Study In Translation."[1] Catalyst for the study was the continuing national publicity given to that phrase after its initial use by former President Carter in the presidential campaign of 1976-1977. Since the media applied it to situations and circumstances that were nonreligious in nature and in some instances in very poor taste if not downright sacrilegious, I thought it would be interesting to write a paper showing how absurd and inappropriate such misapplications were as compared with legitimate and serious usage.

With that purpose in mind, the obvious starting point, to provide a suitable background for the paper, was location of passages in the New Testament where the English phrase, "born again," occurs. The one passage familiar to me from childhood was in the third chapter of the Gospel of John, which contains the well known account of the brief conversation between Jesus and a prominent Pharisee named Nicodemus. I quote from the King James version, beginning with verse 2, Nicodemus speaking: ". . . Rabbi, we know that thou art a teacher come from God: for no man can do these miracles that thou doest, except God be with him. (3) Jesus . . . said unto him, Verily, verily, I say unto thee, Except a man be *born again*, he cannot see the kingdom of God. ." After a question by the puzzled Nicodemus, Jesus concluded his explanation of the matter by expressing the same thought in a more emphatic but generalized way, in verse 7: "Marvel not that I said unto thee, *Ye* must be born again." By using the plural "Ye," he made it clear that the admonition had universal application.

In each of these two verses a marginal note gave "from above" as an alternate translation for "again." A check with several other leading English versions showed some rather startling variations: "born anew," "born over again," "born all over again from above," (once), and "begotten from above." (once).[2]

That the same adverb in Greek—ἄνωθεν—could have two such widely different *basic* meanings as "again" and "from above" seems strange enough, but to have such a possibility in the same context seems stranger still.[3] It also illustrates one of the problems facing translators, and the fact that an English concordance of the Bible would not be a safe source for locating all occurrences of a given word or phrase. Such a source could only be a Greek concordance. Fortunately I have one and it has been indispensible in this study.[4]

Somewhat to my surprise, the two Greek words translated "born again," etc., occur together only in John 3:3 and 7, cited above. As might be expected, the verb—γεννάω—occurs numerous times, but the adverb only eleven times outside of the passage in John. In five passages it has the unmistakable meaning "from above";[5] in three, "from the top."[6] In the remaining three, one need not concern us here.[7] Of the other two, the passage in Acts 26:4-5 is the *genesis*, so to speak, of this paper. In it, and in Luke 1:3, the adverb ἄνωθεν is used in a new context, the context of time.

Before quoting the passage from Acts and examining the various ways it has been translated, some information about Paul will help in understanding the reasons for the difficulties translators have had with it over the centuries.

As Paul himself tells us, he was born in Tarsus, in the southeastern part of the Roman province of Cilicia. He was therefore a Roman citizen by birth, a fact of some importance at a critical time in his life, and which, ironically enough, probably led to his death in Rome.[8] There are no details about his early life except that he left Tarsus for Jerusalem, studied under Gamaliel, the most distinguished teacher of Jewish law at the time,[9] became a zealous persecutor of Christians,[10] was converted to Christianity in a very dramatic manner,[11] and soon began a missionary life that made him the leading exponent and proponent of the Christian faith in the Mediterranean world. During the next twenty-five or so years—the chronology is uncertain—he was in Jerusalem a number of times.[12] On what turned out to be his last visit he was attacked by a Jewish mob enraged because of his preaching. A Roman centurion sent soldiers to rescue him, and at a hearing before the high priest, Ananias, Paul was accused of profaning the temple, of being an agitator among Jews everywhere, a leader of the sect of Nazarenes, and of preaching resurrection of the body. This last charge was the cause of serious dissension between the Pharisees who believed in the doctrine, and the Sadducees who did not. After his acquittal, when he was about to be released, Paul learned of a plot to kill him. The Roman centurion sent him under heavy guard to Caesarea, headquarters of Antonius Felix, Roman governor of Judaea.[13] About two years later, around A.D. 58-60, Porcius Festus was sent by Rome to succeed Felix. After a brief visit to Jerusalem to talk with officials about Paul, he came back to Caesarea with some Jewish elders and their official spokesman. After they had brought their charges at a formal hearing, Festus asked if he would go to Jerusalem for a trial over which he would preside. Paul spurned the idea and said he appealed to Rome. "You have appealed to Caesar," Festus said, "to Caesar you will go." But before arrangements for the journey could be completed, Herod Agrippa II, King of Ituraea, a small district northeast of the Sea of Galilee, arrived with his sister Bernice, to pay his respects to Festus. After he had learned about Paul and his appeal to Caesar, he expressed an interest in hearing his defense. Arrangements were made, Paul was brought in, still in chains, and Agrippa gave him permission to speak.[14]

Paul began by expressing his pleasure at being able to make his defense in the presence of King Agrippa, "Especially," he said, "because I know that you are an expert in all the customs and controversial issues among the Jews" (Acts 26:2-3). And then come the two verses with which this paper is primarily concerned. They are quoted first in Greek and then in Latin. For the convenience of those whose Greek may be a trifle rusty, the Greek is transliterated, and each word numbered. To show the relationship between the Latin and the Greek, the corresponding Latin words are also numbered, and the same pattern is followed in the English translations.[15]

```
        1    2    2     3     4   5    6      7    8    9
(4) Τὴν μὲν οὖν βίωσίν μου ἐκ νεότητος τὴν ἀπ' ἀρχῆς
    Ten men oun biosin mou ek neotetos ten ap' arches
         10    11 12  13    14  15 16         17       18
    γενομένην ἐν τῷ ἔθνει μου ἔν τε 'Ιεροσολύμοις ἴσασι
    genomenen en to ethnei mou en te Hierosolumois isasi
      19        20              21        22    23    24
    πάντες 'Ιουδαῖοι, (5) προγινώσκοντές με ἄνωθεν, ἐὰν
    pantes Ioudaioi proginoskontes me anothen ean
       25       26         27   28        29         30          31
    θέλωσι μαρτυρεῖν, ὅτι κατὰ τὴν ἀκριβεστάτην αἵρεσιν
    thelosi marturein hoti kata ten akribestaten hairesin
     32      33           34        35       36
    τῆς ἡμετέρας θρησκείας ἔζησα Φαρισαῖος.
    tes hemeteras threskeias edzesa Pharisaios.
```

```
           2       3      4    5      6        7    8    9    10
(4) Et quidem vitam meam a iuventute, quae ab initio fuit
    11  13   14  15      17             18       19      20
    in gente mea in Hierosolymis, noverunt omnes Iudaei,
        21       22 23   23     24    25         26
(5) praescientes me ab initio, si velint testimonium
        26          27        28           30          31
    perhibere, quoniam secundum certissimam sectam
      33      34         35      36
    nostrae religionis vixi Pharisaeus.
```

Despite their differences in vocabulary and grammar, these two passages have two similar characteristics. As the numerical sequence shows, their word order is remarkably similar. In word count the Greek has 37 against Latin's 34. A comparison of numbers shows the reason. Greek has five occurrences of the definite article (Nos. 1, 7, 12, 29, 32), and a conjunction (No. 16) which Latin does not have. It also has two particles (No. 2) in place of Latin's one. Latin begins with a conjunction which Greek does not match, a verb-object combination (No. 26) against Greek's verb which does not require an object to complete its meaning, and a preposition (No. 23) which Greek does not need. If Latin had a conjunction connecting the two prepositional phrases, Nos. 11-14 and 15-17, as Greek does (No. 16), translation of the two passages would be exactly the same except possibly for a slight difference in the translation of No. 30.

Despite the collection and collation of numerous manuscripts and papyri in the last hundred years, the texts of these two verses, Greek and Latin, vary very little from the texts which Tyndale and other Biblical scholars of the sixteenth and early seventeenth century had at their disposal. The *apparatus critici* of modern editions bear this out, and the English translations offer supplementary evidence should it be needed.[16]

In all likelihood translators used manuscripts in both languages, if they were available, and printed texts of the Latin Vulgate after 1456, and of the Greek text, after 1516, the date of Erasmus' edition, the first one ever printed. In the case of Tyndale's English translation of 1534, for example, it is known that he used the Greek text of Erasmus, the Latin Vulgate, and Martin Luther's German translation of Erasmus.[17] All of these may have played a part in subsequent English translations, together with Tyndale's version, for a number of years.

The Greek text of Erasmus went through five editions. The fourth and fifth editions of 1527 and 1535, became the basis for the third edition of a Greek text by Robert Stephanus (1503-1559), published in 1550. It was the first edition to have a critical apparatus. A revision of this in 1551 was the first edition with numbered verses. These last two editions were used by the translators of the Geneva New Testament published in 1557, and were used by Théodore de Bèze (Beza 1519-1605) in preparing two of his editions in 1588-89 and 1598, which were used by the translators of the King James version in 1611. A 1565 edition of Beza was printed in 1624 by the two Elzevirs, Bonaventure (1583-1652) and Abraham (1592-1652). The second edition, published in 1633, contains these words in the preface: "You [the reader] therefore have the text which is now received by all, in which we give nothing changed or corrupted." Two of the words in the Latin original of this sentence, *textum receptum*, in the nominative form, *Textus Receptus*, have been used ever since to designate the Greek text in the Elzevir edition of 1633. "It lies at the basis of the King James version and of all the principal

Protestant translations in the languages of Europe prior to 1881."[18]

The English translations used in this study are divided into three groups on the basis of one common characteristic for each group. Those in Group A do not have the translation of the conjunction, No. 16 in the Greek text, which is not found in the Latin text. The omission of the conjunction is one of the characteristics of the *Textus Receptus* in this particular passage in Acts. No text of the Vulgate, so far as I have been able to determine, has ever included it. In each translation the English of ἄνωθεν (No. 23) is underscored for easy reference.[19]

A. English Translations without the conjunction (No. 16) in verse 4.

(1) William Tyndale: 1534. Reprinted in 1938.

(4) "My lyvinge of a childe, which was at the first amonge
    4   3   5 - 6   7   10 8 - 9   11
myne owne nacion at Ierusalem knowe all the Iewes (5)
       14   13 15   17   18 19   20
which knew me *from the beginninge*, yf they would
  21   22   23   24   25
testifie it. For after the most straytest secte of our laye,
  26   28   30   30   31   33 34
lyved I a pharissye.
  35   36

(2) Bishop Cramner: The Great Bible: 1539 or 1540

(4) "My lyuinge that I haue led of a chylde (which was at
    4   3   5 - 6   7   10 8
the first amonge myne owne nacion at Ierusalem)
 -   9   11   14   13   15   17
knowe all the Iewes, (5) which knewe me *from the*
 18   19   20   21   22   23
begynninge, yf they wolde testifie. For after the most
              24   25   26   28   30
straytest secte of our religion I lyued a Pharisey."
  30   31   33   34   35   36

(3) The Geneva Bible: 1560. (The Bible of Shakespeare and Puritans). Facsimile Reprint, University of Wisconsin Press, 1969.

(4) "As touching my life from my childhode and what it
       4   3   5   -   6   7
was from the beginning among mine owne nation at
 10   8   9   11   14   13   15
Jerusalem know all the Iewes, (5) which knew me
   17   18   19   20   21   22
heretofore (if they wolde testifie) that after the most
    23   24   25   26   27   28   30
straite sect of our religion I liued a Pharise."
 30   31   33   34   35   36

(4) Rheims-Douai Version by Roman Catholic scholars: 1582.
(4) "And my life truly from my youth, which was from the
        4   3   2   5   6   10   8
beginning in my nation in Hierusalem, al the Iewes
    9   11 14   13   15   17   19 20
doe know: knowing me before *from the beginning*, (if
  18   21   22   21   23   24
they wil give testimonie) that according to the most
        25   26   26   27   28   29
sure secte of our religion I liued a Pharisee."
 30   31   33   34   35   36

(5) The King James Version: 1611. Reprinted many times.
(4) "My manner of life from my youth, which was at first
       4   3   5   5   6   10 8 9
among mine own nation at Jeresalem, know all the
  11   14   13   15   17   18   19
Jews; (5) Which knew me *from the beginning*, if they
 20   21   22   23   24
would testify, that after the most straitest sect of our
  25   26   27   28   29   30   31 33
religion, I lived a Pharisee."
   34   35   36

(6) The Englishman's Greek Testament.n.d. Stephens Greek text of 1550.

(4) "My manner of life then from youth, which from [its]
     4   3   3   2   5   6   7   8
commencement was among my nation in Jerusalem,
     9   10   11   14   13   17   18
know all the Jews, (5) who knew me before *from the*
  18   19   20   21   22   21   23
first, if they would bear witness, that according to the
  23   24   25   26   26   27   28   29
strictest sect of our religion, I lived a Pharisee."
   30   31   33   34   35   36

In all of these versions, except No. 3, the adverb (No. 23) is rendered "from the beginning," or its equivalent, "from the first." It repeats the idea expressed in the prepositional phrase (Nos. 8-9): "at the first," "from the beginning," "from [its] commencement." The two phrases therefore are synonomous expressions or parallel in meaning. Since the adverb (No. 23) modifies the Greek participle (No. 21), which really means "know before," the translation "heretofore" by No. 3. may be an attempt to express the meaning of "before" and "from the beginning" with one word. Nos. 4 and 6 are the only translations that bring out the full meaning of No. 21.

The translation of Nos. 7-10 could be based on either the Greek or Latin text for all six versions. In versions (1), (2), (3), (5), (6), however, the translation of No. 21 by a relative clause was probably based on the Latin text of Erasmus (see Note 20) rather than the Greek or Vulgate texts on page 4, in both of which No. 21 is a participle. Only version No. 4 translates No. 21 as a participle, and only it and version No. 6 bring out the full meaning of No. 21: "to know before." Erasmus brings out the meaning by using the adverb *prius*, meaning "before," with the simple verb *nosco* instead of the Vulgate's *praescio*.

Nos. 1 and 2 end an English sentence with No. 26, and make the noun clause, introduced by the conjunction (No. 27), into a complete sentence, in violation of Latin (or Greek) syntax. The other four construe the clause as the object of No. 21. That seems to be the usual interpretation, but one, as we shall see later, with which I disagree.

A relative clause, "that I have led," in the Great Bible (No. 2), is not found in any of the other five versions. It is almost certainly a translation from the Latin text of Erasmus: "Itaque vitam quidem meam, *quam egi* ab adolescentia, ..."[20]

Although the English in Nos. 1, 2, and 3 is obviously a product of its period, there is only one word whose meaning might not be immediately clear: the word "laye" in the last line of No. 1. According to the *OED* s.v. "lay," it means "law," and this translation of Acts 26: 5 is given as the reference.[21] In this context and in view of the translation, "religion" (No. 34) in the other five versions, Tyndale's rendition is provocative and unique among the nineteen translations.

As we come now to our next group of translations, it will be interesting to see to what extent modern scholarship has contributed to the increased understanding and interpretation of our two verses.

B. *English Translations without the pronoun* με *(No. 22) in verse 5.*

(1) Edgar J. Goodspeed: 1946: Based primarily on the text of Westcott and Hort.

    (4) "The way I lived from my youth up, spending my early
          1   3   3   5   —   6   10   8   —
    life among my own nation and at Jerusalem, is well
    9   11   14   14   13   16   17   18
    known to all Jews, (5) for they have known *from the*
    18   19   20   21   21   23
    first, if they are willing to give evidence, that I was a
    24   25   26   27
    Pharisee and my life was that of the strictest sect of our
    36   35   35   35   30   31   33
    religion."
    34

(2) The Revised Standard Version (RSV) 1952: An eclectic Greek text.

    (4) "My manner of life from my youth, spent from the be-
      4   3   3   3   5   —   6   10   7   —
    ginning among my own nation and at Jerusalem, is
      8   11   14   13   16 15   17

known by all the Jews. (5) They have known *for a long*
   18   19   20   21   21   21   23
time, if they are willing to testify, that according to the
  24   25   26   27   28   29
strictest party of our religion I have lived as a Pharisee."
   30   31   33   34   35   36

(3) Lake-Cadbury: 1933: Probably based primarily on Westcott and Hort.

    (4) "All the Jews know the life which from the beginning I
        19   20   18   1   4   7   8   —   9
led from my youth in my nation and in Jerusalem, (5) for
10   5   6   11 14   13   16 15   17
they have known *for a long time,* if they are willing to
   21   21   21   23   24   25   26
bear witness, that according to the strictest party of our
    26   27   28   29   30   31   33
rite I lived as a Pharisee."
34   35   36

(4) The Anchor Bible: The Book of Acts. Based on the Greek text of E. Nestle and K. Aland: 1963.

    (4) "As to my way of life, which was spent from my earliest
                  4   3   3   3   7   10   5 - 6 - 8
years among my own people and in Jerusalem, (5) all
-9   11   14   13   16 15   17   19
the Jews have known *for a long time*—if they will
  20   21   23   24   25
admit it—that as a Pharisee I lived in accordance with
-26   27   35   28
the strictest sect within our religion."
 29   30   31   33   34

(5) Richmond Lattimore[22]: 1982: Based on text of Westcott and Hort.

    (4) "All Jews know about my life, from youth onward,
       19   20   18   4   3   5   6
both in my own country and in Jerusalem, (5) and they
     11 14   13   16 15   17
have known *from the past,* if they will admit it, that I
   21   21   23   24   25   26   27

lived according to the strictest sect in our religion, as a
  35   28   29   30   31   33   34
Pharisee."
36

Although the Greek texts used in these five versions may differ slightly from the one on page 4, they all include translation of the conjunction (No. 16) in verse 4. They all translate the circumstantial participle (no. 21) by a finite verb in an independent clause, which is grammatically wrong, as I shall show later. That translation leads to two other errors: the treatment of the pronoun (No. 22) as a proleptic accusative,[23] and of the noun clause, introduced by the conjunction (No. 27), as the object of the participle (No. 21). No version gives the full meaning of the compound verb (No. 21): "to know before," and only Goodspeed (No. 1) fails to give a new translation to the adverb (No. 23).

In contrast to those in Section A, these translations vary somewhat in their treatment of the prepositional phrase (Nos. 8-9) in verse 4 and of the adverb (No. 23) in verse 5. Although Jerome quotes the Greek words in his Commentary, and says that they mean the same thing: "from the beginning," and emphasize the phrase (Nos. 5-6): "from my youth," no translation apparently agrees with that interpretation.[24] Erasmus, whether because of Jerome's influence or his own judgement, translates the two Greek expressions by the same Latin phrase, *ab initio*, which is also the Vulgate's rendition.[25] Such parallelism is not found in any of these five versions. One translates the adverb, "from the first," three "for a long time," and one "from the past." The first edition of *A&G* (1957) could have been consulted only by Nos. 4 and 5, but one of its predecessors, the revision of Edwin Preuschen's Greek-German lexicon of 1910, by Walter Bauer, in 1928, may have been of help to the other three. It was the first to contain considerable material from the papyri. It was revised in 1937.[26]

C. *English Translation with the Conjunction (No. 16) and the Pronoun (No. 22).*

(1) The American Standard Version of the New Testament: 1900.

    (4) "My manner of life then from my youth up, which was
         4   3   -   3   2   5   6   7   10

from the beginning among mine own nation and at
    8   9   11   14   13   16 15
Jerusalem, know all the Jews; (5) having knowledge of
     17   18 19   20   21   21
me *from the first*, if they be willing to testify, that after
 22   23   24   25   26   27   28
the straitest sect of our religion I lived a Pharisee."
 29 .   30   31   33   34   35   36

(2) James Moffatt: 1919. Based on the Greek text of Hermann von Soden: (1913).

    (4) "How I lived from my youth up among my own nation
           3   3   5   4   6   11   14
and in Jerusalem, all that early career of mine, is
 16 15   17
known to all the Jews. (5) They know me *of old*. They
 18   19   20   21   22 23
know, if they chose to admit it, that as a Pharisee I lived
     24   25   26   27   36   35
by the principles of the strictest party in our religion."
 28   29   30   31   33   34

(3) A Revision of the Challoner-Rheims Version (Catholic): (1941).

    (4) "My life, then, from my youth up, the early part of
      4   3   2   5   6
which was spent among mine own nation and at
                10   11   14   13   16 15
Jerusalem, all the Jews know; (5) for they have *long*
    17   19   20   18   23
known me, if only they were willing to give evidence,
 21   22 24   25   25   26   26
that according to the strictest sect of our religion I lived
 27   28   30   31   33   34   35
a Pharisee."
  36

N.B.: Since no Vulgate edition has the conjunction (No. 16) in verse 4, it is clear that a Greek text was also consulted, as was stated in the brief statement on the title page.

ACTS 26: 4-5

(4) Ronald Knox: 1945: Based primarily on the Vulgate but with some readings from Greek texts.

(4) "What my life was like when boyhood was over, spent
                         4   3   10
from the first among my own people and in Jerusalem,
  8   –   9   11   14   13   16 15   17
all the Jews know. (5) Their *earliest memory* of me,
19   29   18   23   22
would they but admit it, is of one who lived according
                                      35   28
to the strictest tradition of observance we have, a
           30
Pharisee."
36

(5) The New English Bible: The New Testament: 1970: Based on an eclectic Greek text edited by R. V. G. Tasker, 1964.

(4) "My life from my youth up, the life I led from the be-
    4   3   5   6   7   10   8   –
ginning among my people and in Jerusalem, is
  8   11   14   13   16 15   17
familiar to all Jews. (5) Indeed they have known me
  18   19   20   21   22
long enough and could testify, if they only would, that
    23   26   24   25   27
I belonged to the strictest group in our religion: I lived
           29   30   31   33   34   35
as a Pharisee."
36

(6) The Jerusalem Bible: The New Testament: 1969: Based on an eclectic Greek text.

(4) "My manner of life from my youth, a life spent from the
    4   3   3   3   5   6   7   10   8
beginning among my own people and in Jerusalem, is
    9   11   14   13   16 15   17
common knowledge among the Jews. (5) They have
       18   20
known me *for a long time* and could testify, if they
  21   22   23   26   24

would, that I followed the strictest party of our religion
     25   27   30   31   33   34
and lived as a Pharisee."
      35   36

(7) The New American Bible: The New Testament: 1970: Based primarily on the text of Nestle-Aland (1963), with some readings from the text of Aland, Black, Metzger, Wikgren: 1966.

    (4) "The way I have lived since my youth, and the life I
            1   3   3   3   6   7
have led among my own people from the beginning
  10   11   14   13   8   9
and later at Jerusalem, is well known to all Jews. (5)
 16   15   17   18   19 20
They have been acquanted with me *for a long time* and
    21   21   22   23
can testify, if they wish, to my life lived as a Pharisee,
 26 24   25   35   36
the strictest sect of our religion."
     30   31   33   34

(8) The New International Version of the New Testament: 1974: Based on an eclectic Greek text.

    (4) "The Jews all know the way I have lived ever since I
           20 19   18   3   3   3   5
was a child, from the beginning of my life in my own
  6   8   9   14
country, and also in Jerusalem. (5) They have known
  13   16   15   17   21   21
me *for a long time* and can testify, if they are willing,
22   23   26 24   25 25
that according to the strictest sect of our religion, I
 27   28   29   30   31   33   34
lived as a Pharisee."
  35   36

Since comments made on the translations in Sections A and B apply in most respects to those in Section C, we can now summarize, with some additional comments, the relationship between the translations and the Greek and Latin texts. Perhaps this can best be done in lexical and grammatical categories with appropriate headings. Subtopics can easily be identified by letters and numbers in the three Sections and numbers that correspond with those used to relate the translations to the Greek and Latin texts.

It is not possible to tell to what extent, if any, a given translation is influenced by its predecessors. There are some words and phrases of high frequency that would be translated very much the same in version after version. Those that occur infrequently and then in different contexts are the ones that vary somewhat in translation and at times result in paraphrase from an effort to be different. In our two verses the Greek words with which we are particularly concerned are Nos. 6, 16, 21, 22, 23; in Latin, only 21 and 22.

I. Meaning of the adverb (No. 23):

Since the translations in Section A were based on the Latin rather than the Greek text, except for No. 6, the prepositional phrase in Latin had only one basic meaning: "from the beginning," or "from the first." By the time No. 6 was published, probably sometime between 1870 and 1900, the Greek-English lexicons of Robinson, Urwick, and Thayer were available,[27] all of which gave those meanings for the adverb in the context of time. One of them might have been the source for Section B.(1) and C.(1). All the other versions in Sections B and C translate it "for a long time," or some variation of that phrase.[28]

As pointed out on page 11 above, evidence from papyri became available in printed form in 1928. The fact that ἄνωθεν in some contexts could mean "for a long time," however, does not mean that it must have that meaning in our passage. But even here it would make perfectly good sense but for a lack of parallelism with the prepositional phrase (Nos. 8-9) in verse 4. If Paul had wanted to say that the Jews had known him for a long time, with no thought of parallelism or of chiasmus,[29] he could have done so easily enough. If the adverb expressed extent of time, is it reasonable or logical to believe that both Jerome and Erasmus would have translated it with an ablatival phrase? It does not seem so to me. For translation of the adverb in the Modern Greek New Testament, see Appendix A-1, and comment under No. 6.

II. Construction of the participle (No. 21):

All the lexicons cited in this study give "to know before" as the basic meaning of the verb προγινώσκω, with the meaning "to have foreknowledge," in certain contexts, which do not apply to our passage. The Vulgate has *praescio*, with the same meanings. Erasmus uses the verb *nosco*, which means "to know," with the adverb *prius*, which means "before." Only two versions, however, Nos. A.(4) and (6), bring out the full meaning of the verb. Perhaps the feeling was that with the adverb the meaning of the simple verb was enough. If a person somewhat advanced in age had been known "from the beginning" or "for a long time," it would be reasonable and logical to think that he had been known "before" the circumstances under which he was speaking had taken place.

But the real problem with the participle is not so much its finer meaning but its construction and therefore the way it should be translated in English. The grammatical ground rules are quite explicit. For the present case only two need to be mentioned. (1) When the participle is used with a definite article in Greek, as in Nos. 7 and 10 in verse 4, the idiomatic translation calls for a relative clause and a finite verb.[30] When the participle modifies a noun or pronoun, it may be translated as a subordinate clause introduced by a conjunction or by a relative pronoun. The latter is the situation in this passage.[31] In Section A, the translations by a relative clause may have been influenced by the Latin text of Erasmus, who used a relative pronoun with a finite verb. Translation by a participle, as in A.(4) and C.(1), is not idiomatic English, and translation by a finite verb in an independent clause, as in all the other versions, is grammatically incorrect.

One other helpful ground rule should be mentioned. A present participle in Greek ordinarily denotes the same time as the main verb. By the marvelous virtuosity of Greek idiom and grammar, however, it may indicate action antecedent to the time of the main verb.[32] This is an important point to be kept in mind for the proper translation of No. 21. The translations in which it was treated as a finite verb in an independent clause, had it in the right tense but with the wrong construction. Even Greek grammar has limits to its flexibility.

III. Construction of the personal pronoun (No. 22).

In both the Greek and the Latin texts it is the object of the participle (No. 21) and is so construed in Sections A and C. In Section B, however, as pointed out in the comments, it is considered a proleptic accusative and may therefore be omitted in English translation.[33] This construction would be permissible if the participle (No. 21) were a finite form, which obviously it is not. Accordingly, all of the translations in Section B are wrong on that score. One, No. 4, carries the infraction a few steps further. It omits the only main verb (No. 18) in the two verses and its object (No. 3) becomes part of a prepositional phrase. The subject (No. 20) of the main verb becomes the subject of the participle (No. 21) converted into a finite verb, with No. 22 treated as a proleptic accusative and the noun clause (Nos. 27-36) as its object. The result is a rather smooth English sentence which bears little resemblance to the Greek and hardly qualifies even as a paraphrase.

IV. Construction of the conditional sentence.

In Greek such a sentence is composed of two parts: a *protasis*, composed of a conjunction meaning "if," introducing a finite verb, and a conclusion, called an *apodosis*, which must contain a finite verb.[34] A participle may function as a protasis, but never as an apodosis. In our passage Nos. 24-26 form the protasis. The apodosis is formed, not by the participle (No. 21), as is done in many of the English translations, but by No. 18, the only finite verb in an independent clause in the two verses.[34] The relative clauses in the translations of Section A cannot function as an apodosis; neither can the finite verbs used to translate the participle (No. 21) in Sections B and C.

In this connection, the translations in C.(5) through (8) form the conditional sentence in rather startling fashion: Nos. 24-25 form the protasis and No. 26, which is a complementary infinitive to No. 25, forms the apodosis—an almost incredible misconstruing of the Greek!

V. Construction of the noun clause (Nos. 27-36):

In translations A.(1) and (2) a complete sentence ends with No. 26. The noun clause (Nos. 27-36) then is translated as a complete sentence in itself. Apparently the model for this construction, interestingly enough, is Luther's translation of Erasmus' Latin text.[35] No other translation in the three groups follows this sentence pattern. They all, with the exception of C.(5)-(8), discussed in the last paragraph, make the noun clause (Nos. 27-36) the object of the participle (No. 21) converted into a finite verb in an independent clause.

This completes the detailed examination of nineteen different English translations of Acts 26:4-5, covering a span of exactly four hundred and fifty years. Since I have come to the reluctant and somewhat surprising conclusion that not a single version translates the Greek (or the Latin) correctly, I am venturing to suggest a new translation, the ultimate focal point and *raison d'être* of this paper.

Once more we find ourselves in the audience chamber of Porcius Festus, Roman governor Judaea, with headquarters at Caesarea. With him are King Herod Agrippa II, his sister Bernice, high ranking government officials and local dignitaries. After Paul had been given permission to speak and had paid his respects to King Herod, the second and third words in the Greek text, which the Grammars call "resumptive particles," suggest that Luke left out a few of Paul's remarks because they were similar to some he had recorded earlier, and began this part of the record with verse 4, when Paul says:

"So then, all Jews who have known me before
    2   2   19 20   21   22 21
from the beginning, (if they are willing to testify),
     23   24   25 25   26
know my way of life from my youth, (which was spent
 18   4   3 3   3   5.   6   7   10 10
from the beginning in my country and in Jerusalem),
 8   9   11 14   13   16 15   17
that in accord with the strictest sect of our religion I
 27   28   29   30   31   33   34
lived as a Pharisee."
 35   36

Since some editions of the Latin Vulgate (and of the *Textus Receptus*) inclose Nos. 24-26 in parentheses, I have done the same. For the sake of clarification, I have also inclosed Nos. 7-17. If the sentence is read without the words in parentheses, the combination of logic and grammar, which led me to this translation, will become perfectly clear. Logic suggests that only those Jews who had known (No. 21) Paul before from the beginning (No. 23) could have known (No. 18) his way of life from his youth, that he lived as a Pharisee. There is still only one main verb (No. 18). It has two objects, the noun (No. 3) and the noun clause (Nos. 27-36) in apposition with it. The participle (No. 21) is attributive and translated as a relative clause. The conditional clause (No. 24-26) forms the protasis to the apodosis (No. 18) in a condition of the present general type.

Ever since I made the first draft of this translation, a few years before the date of this paper, I have been hoping to find support for it in the version of some well known Biblical scholar. To my great pleasure, I believe that has happened. Here is the translation of this very passage, numbered like the other passages and with the translation of ἄνωθεν underscored:

"For alle iewis that bifor knewen me *fro the bigynnyng*
    2   19   20   21   21   21   22   23
knowe my liif fro the yungthe (that from the
  18   4   3   5   6   7   8   —
begynnyng was in my folk in ierusalem if thei wolen
     9   10 11 14 13 15   17   24 25   25
bere witnessyneg:) that bi the most certeyn secte of oure
  26   26   27 28   30   30   31 33
religioun, I lyued a farise."
     34   35   36

Although the original is Latin rather than Greek, and therefore without the conjunction (No. 16), the grammatical construction is essentially the same as in my version. There is a slight difference between the two, however, in emphasis and meaning. Logically, it seems to me, the "if" clause (Nos. 24-26) should follow No. 23, as it does in the original, and not No. 17, as in the version just quoted. If I am right, then my version may well be the first entirely correct translation of the passage ever made.

The translation from which this passage is taken has been atributed to John Wycliffe (ca. 1320-1384). It is not certain, however, how much of it is his and how much is the work of his close associates, Nicholas Hereford and John Purvey. The first version is dated about 1382 and its revision in 1395. These two verses, not numbered because that convenience did not take place until 1551, are from the English Hexapla (see Appendix A.1) and may be from the revision.

At any rate, if I may put it so, I count myself fortunate to be in such distinguished company, and gladly yield priority of translation to the famous Lollard minister and reformer.

Epilogue

In writing this paper, the first draft of which was finished in 1978, I have examined many English versions of the New Testament which have not been included in the detailed analyses or in the bibiliography. The nineteen selected for study seemed to be representative of the larger group. In analyzing each translation I have tried to be as objective as possible, with the use of such scholarly helps as were available. In the final analysis, however, I had to rely on my own judgment. That judgment in each case, as must be obvious, was based on a minuscule portion—two verses—of an entire version of the New Testament. And Aristotle's dictum,[36] "One swallow does not make a spring,"—*mutatis mutandis*—most certainly applies. The judgment made on two verses in no way applies to the edition as a whole.

Despite a wide variation in the translations studied, all but two of the nineteen—B.(5) in 1982 and C.(8) in 1974—followed the Greek and Latin word order rather closely, as did Tyndale, and those two changed the order only in verse four. To follow word order in this way, if it does not play too freely with English idiom, as these generally do not, can be a real service to those who might want to compare a translation with the original. There is a danger, however, that following a pattern may tend to perpetuation of an error. The grammatical errors that Tyndale (A.1) made in his translation of the passage, to the best of my knowledge have never been corrected in later translations. I am wondering if that would still be true if Biblical translators had made more use of the Wycliffite version. This is a matter that seems to me might well be explored by future translators of the world's most translated book.

APPENDIX A:
ENGLISH TRANSLATIONS OF THE NEW TESTAMENT

1. *The English Hexapla.* Exhibiting the Six Important English Translations of the New Testament Scripture. The Original Greek Text after Schalz. Preceded by a Historical Account of the English Translations. London: Samuel Bagster & Sons, 1841. [Translations by: John Wicliff (c. 1320-1384), William Tyndale (c. 1492-1536), The Great Bible (1539 or 1540), the Geneva Bible (1560), The Rheims-Douai New Testament (1582), The Authorized Bible (1611)].

2. James Moffatt. *The New Testament.* A New Translation, 1913. Reprinted in New York: Association Press, 1919. Based on the Greek text of Von Soden, 1913.

3. *The New Testament of Our Lord and Savior Jesus Christ.* Translated from the Latin Vulgate. A Revision of the Challoner-Rheims Version. Edited by Catholic Scholars Under the Patronage of the Episcopal Committee of the Confraternity of Christian Doctrine. Paterson, New Jersey: St. Anthony Guild Press, 1941.

4. Ronald Knox. *The New Testament of Our Lord and Savior Jesus Christ.* Newly Translated from the Vulgate Latin at the Request of their Lordships, the Archbishops and Bishops of England and Wales. New York: Sheed & Ward, 1945.

5. Edgar J. Goodspeed. *The Complete Bible—An American Translation* (with J. M. P. Smith who translated the Old Testament). The University of Chicago Press, 1939.

6. *The Holy Bible. Revised Standard Version.* New York: Thomas Nelson & Sons, 1952. *The New Testament* in 1946.

7. *The New English Bible. With the Apocrypha.* Oxford University Press. Cambridge University Press, 1970.

8. *The New Testament of Our Lord and Savior Jesus Christ.* Revised Standard Version. Catholic Edition. Translated from the Greek. Being the Version set forth A.D. 1611. Revised A.D. 1881 and A.D. 1901. Compared with the most ancient Authorities and Revised A.D. 1946. Prepared by the Catholic Biblical Association of Great Britain. Thomas Nelson & Sons, 1965. Not included in analysis.

9. *The New Testament of the Jerusalem Bible.* Reader's Edition. Garden City, New York: Doubleday and Company, Inc., 1969.

10. *The New American Bible.* Translated from the Original Languages with Critical use of All Ancient Sources by Members of the Catholic Bibilical Association of America. New York: P. J. Kennedy & Sons. London: Collier-Macmillan Limited, 1970.

11. *The New International Version of the New Testament.* Grand Rapids, Michigan: Zondervan Bible Publishers, 1974. Eclectic Greek Text.

12. *The Anchor Bible. The Acts of the Apostles.* Introduction, Translation and Notes by Johannes Munck. Revised by William Albright and C. S. Mann. Garden City, New York: Doubleday & Co., 1967.

13. Richmond Lattimore. *Acts and Letters of the Apostles.* New York: Farrar, Straus, Giroux, 1982.

APPENDIX A-1:
TRANSLATIONS IN GERMAN, FRENCH, ITALIAN, MODERN GREEK AND RUSSIAN

In the hope of getting some new insight into the Greek and Latin texts of our passage, with the help of my wife in French and a friend in Russian, I examined the translations listed below. They were all interesting but not helpful in any significant way.

1. *The Hexaglot Bible; Comprising the Holy Scriptures of the Old and New Testaments in the Original Tongues; Together with the Septuagint, The Syriac (of the New Testament), The Vulgate, The Authorized English, and German, and the Most Approved French Versions.* Edited by the Rev. Edward Riches De Levante, Assisted by Competent Biblical Scholars. In Six Volumes. Vol. VI. The Acts of the Apostles, etc. New York: Funk and Wagnalls Company, 1901.

2. *Das Neue Testament unsers Herrn und Heilandes Jesu Christi, nach der deutschen Übersetzung D. Martin Luthers.* Durchgesehene Ausgabe mit dem von der deutschen evangelischen Kirchenkonferenz genehmigten Text. Berlin, 1912.

3. *La Bible. Nouveau Testament. Introduction par Jean Grosjean et Michel Léturmy.* Textes Traduite, Présentés et Annotés par Jean Grosjean avec la collaboration de Paul Gros. Gallimard 1971.

4. *Il Nuovo Testamento Del Nostro Signore E Salvatore Gesù Cristo.* Roma: Deposito Di Sacre Scritture. n.d.

5. *The Complete Bible in Russian.* Published by the United Biblical Society. New York, Geneva, London. n.d. (I have no Russina type.)

6. Η ΚΑΙΝΗ ΔΙΑΘΗΚΗ ΤΟΥ ΚΥΡΙΟΥ ΚΑΙ ΣΩΤΗΡΟΣ ΗΜΩΝ ΙΗΣΟΥ ΧΡΙΣΤΟΥ ΤΟ ΘΕΙΟΝ ΑΡΧΕΤΥΠΟΝ ΚΑΙ Η ΑΥΤΟΥ ΜΕΤΑΦΡΑΣΙΣ ΕΙΣ ΤΗΝ ΚΟΙΝΗΝ ΔΙΑΛΕΚΤΟΝ ΒΙΒΛΙΚΗ ΕΤΑΙΡΕΙΑ ΕΝ ΛΟΝΔΙΝΩ 1952.

   It is interesting to note that all of the texts, except No. 3, omitted the conjunction τε in verse 4, and that the Modern Greek text had ἐξ ἀρχῆς as the translation of ἄνωθεν in verse 5. The translation of verse 5 in the Russian text shows a rather surprising variation: "They know me from long ago, if they would wish to bear witness, that I lived as a Pharisee strictly obeying the teaching of our faith."

And both German texts had a thought-provoking translation of θρησκείας in verse 5: "Gottesdienstes."

APPENDIX B:
GREEK AND LATIN TEXTS OF THE NEW TESTAMENT

Erasmi Opera Omnia. Volumina XI. Vol. VI. *Novum Testamentum.* Graece et Latine. Ed. Iohannes Clericus. Leiden, 1703-06. Abbr. *Erasmus.*

2. *The Vulgate New Testament.* With the Douay Version of 1582 in Parallel Columns. London: Samuel Bagster and Sons, 1872.

3. Η ΚΑΙΝΗ ΔΙΑΘΗΚΗ. *The New Testament,* Collated with the Most Approved Manuscripts; With Select English Notes in English, Critical and Explanatory; And References to those Authors who have best illustrated the Sacred Writings. To which are added A Catalogue of the principal Editions of the Greek Testament; and A List of the most esteemed Commentators and Critics. By E. Harwood, D. D. Vol. I. London: Printed by J. D. Cornish, M.DCC.LXXVI.

4. Η ΚΑΙΝΗ ΔΙΑΘΗΚΗ. *Novum Testamentum/* Juxta Exemplar Johannis Millii Accuratissime Impressum/ Editio Prima Americana/ Wigorniae, Massachusettensi:/ Excudebat Isaias Thomas, Jun./ Singulatim et Numerose Eo Vendita Officinae Suae/ April—1800. [Edited by Caleb Alexander].*

5. *The New Testament in the Original Greek.* The Text Revised by Brooke Foss Westcott and Fenton John Anthony Hort. New York: The Macmillan Company, 1937. (Original publication in 1881.) Abbr. *W&H.*

6. Η ΚΑΙΝΗ ΔΙΑΘΗΚΗ. Text with Critical Apparatus. London: British and Foreign Bible Society, 1923. (A reprint of the text prepared by Eberhard Nestle, and published in England in 1904 from the 4th edition.)

7. *Novum Testamentum Graece et Latine.* Utrumque textum cum apparatu critico imprimendum curavit D. Eberhard Nestle novis curis elaboravit D. Erwin Nestle. Editio sexta decima. For the American Bible Society, New York. Published by Privileg. Württ, Bibelanstalt, Stuttgart, 1954.

8. *Novum Testamentum Graece et Latine.* Apparatu Critico Instructum Edidit Augustinus Merk S. J. Editio Octava. Roma: Sumptibus Pontificii Instituti Biblici, 1957. Abbr. *Merk.*

9. *The Greek New Testament.* Being the text translated/ in the New English Bible, 1961. Edited with Introduction,/ Textual Notes and Appendix. By R. V. G. Tasker. London: Oxford University Press/ Cambridge University Press, 1964.

10. *The Greek New Testament.* Edited by Kurt Aland, Matthew Black, Bruce M. Metzger, Allen Wikgren. United Bible Societies. Printed by Württemberg Bible Society, Stuttgart, West Germany, 1966. *ABMW* = abbreviation.

* The first Greek New Testament published in the United States.

11. *Biblia Sacra Iuxta Vulgatam Clementiam.* Nova Editio. Logicis Partitionibus Aliisque Subsidiis Ornata/ R. P. Alberto Colunga, O. P. et Dr. Laurentio Turrado. Iterata Editio. Biblioteca de Autores Cristianos. Matriti MCMLIII.

12. *The Englishman's Greek New Testament;* Giving the Greek Text of Stephens 1550, withe the Various Readings of . . . Elzevir 1624, et al. Third Edition, London.

13. *The Greek New Testament According to the Majority Text.* Edited by Zane C. Hodges, Arthur L. Farstad. Nashville-Camden, New York: Thomas Nelson Publishers, 1982. (It is interesting to note that the conjunction is omitted in Acts 26:4).

APPENDIX C:
COMMENTARIES, LEXICONS, AND VOCABULARIES

1. *The Jerome Biblical Commentary.* Edited by Raymond E. Brown, Joseph A. Fitzmyer, Ronald E. Murphy. Volume I: The Old Testament. Volume II: The New Testament and Special Articles. Acts of the Apostles by Richard J. Dillon and Joseph A. Fitzmyer. Englewood Cliffs, New Jersey: Prentice Hall, Inc. 1968.

2. *The Expositor's Greek Textament.* Edited by W. Robertson Nicoll. Five Volumes. Volume II: *The Acts of the Apostles.* By R. J. Knowling. [The volume also contains *St. Paul's Epistle to the Romans,* by James Denny, and *St. Paul's First Epistle to the Corinthians,* by G. G. Findlay]. New York: Dodd, Mead and Co., 1900.

3. *The Beginnings of Christianity.* Part I. *The Acts of the Apostles.* Edited by U. J. Foakes Jackson and Kirsopp Lake. Vol. IV: English Translation and Commentary by K. Lake and Henry J. Cadbury. London: Macmillan and Co., 1923.

4. *Harper's New Testament Commentaries.* General Editor: Henry Chadwick. *A Commentary on the Acts of the Apostles.* Charles S. C. Williams. New York: Harper & Brothers, 1957. [In England: *Black's New Testament Commentaries*].

5. *A Greek and English Lexicon of the New Testament.* A New Edition by Edward Robinson, New York: Harper & Brothers, Publishers, 1879.

6. *Biblico-Theological Lexicon of New Testament Greek.* By Hermann Cremer. Third English Edition. Translated from the German of the Second Edition, with Additional Matter and Corrections by the Author, by William Urwick. Edinburgh: T. & T. Clark, 1880.

7. *A Greek-English Lexicon of the New Testament.* Being Grimm's Wilke's Clavis Novi Testamenti by Joseph Henry Thayer. New York: Harper & Brothers, 1887.

8. *Greek-English Lexicon to the New Testament.* By W. J. Hickie. New York: The Macmillan Company, 1937. Bound with the *Greek New Testament,* by Westcott and Hort.

9. *Handbook to the Grammar of the Greek Testament.* Together with Complete Vocabulary and an Examination of the Chief New Testament Synonyms. By the Late Rev. Samuel G. Green. New Impression: Revised. New York, Chicago, Toronto: Fleming H. Revell Company. n.d. but after 1912.

10. *A New Greek-English Lexicon to the New Testament.* Supplemented by a Chapter Elucidating the Synonyms of the New Testament with a Complete Index to the Synonyms. By the Late George Ricker Berry. Chicago: Wilcox & Follett Company, 1952.

11. *A Greek-English Lexicon of the New Testament and Other Early Christian Literature.* A Translation and adaptation of Walter Bauer's Griechisch-Deutsches Wörterbuch zu den Schriften des Neuen Testaments und der übrigen urchristlichen Literatur. Fourth Revised and Augmented Edition, 1952. By William F. Arndt and F. Wilbur Gingrich. Chicago: The University of Chicago Press. Cambridge: At the University Press, 1957. *A & G* = abbreviation.

12. *The Theological Dictionary of the New Testament.* Edited by Gerhard Kittel. Translated by Geoffrey W. Bromley. Grand Rapids, Michigan: William B. Eerdmanns Publishing Company, Vol. I, 1964. Third Printing, 1968.

13. *An Introduction to the Revised Standard Version of the New Testament.* By Members of the Revision Committee: Luther A. Weigle, Chairman. The International Council of Religious Education, 1946.

APPENDIX D:
GREEK GRAMMARS AND OTHER REFERENCE BOOKS

1. *A Grammar of the Greek New Testament in the Light of Historical Research.* By A. T. Robertson. Hodder & Stoughton, New York: George H. Doran Company, 1914, *ATR* = abbreviation.

2. *Allen and Greenough's New Latin Grammar.* Edited by J. B. Greenough et al. Ginn and Company, 1931. *Al & Gr* = abbreviation.

3. *Greek Grammar.* By William Watson Goodwin. Revised by Charles Burton Gulick. Ginn and Company, 1930. *G&G* = abbreviation.

4. *A Greek Grammar of the New Testament and Other Early Christian Literature.* A Revision of F. Blass and A. Debrunner "*Grammatik des neutestamentlichen Griechisch,*" incorporating supplementary notes by A. Debrunner. Translated and edited by Robert W. Funk. The University of Chicago Press, Chicago & London. The University of Toronto Press, Toronto. Second Impression 1962. *Funk* = abbreviation.

5. *A Concordance to the Greek Testament* According to the Texts of Westcott and Hort, Tischendorf, and the English Revisers. Edited by W. F. Moulton and A. S. Geden. Second Edition. Edinburgh: T. & T. Clark. Reprinted, 1906. *M & G* = abbreviation.

6. *An Idiom-Book of New Testament Greek*. By C. F. D. Moule. Second Edition. Cambridge: At the University Press, 1959.

7. *Dictionary of the Bible*. Edited by James Hastings. Revised Edition by Frederick C. Grant and H. H. Rowley. New York: Charles Scribner's Sons, 1963. *Hastings* = abbreviation.

8. *The English New Testament from Tyndale to the Revised Standard Version*. By Luther A. Weigle. Nashville: Abingdon-Cokesbury Press, 1949.

9. *The Bible in English 1525-1611*. By Craig R. Thompson. Washington, D. C. The Folger Shakespeare Library, 1958.

10. *Who Then Is Paul?* By Hubert Rex Johnson. Washington, D.C.: University Press of America, 1981. *Johnson* = abbreviation.

11. *Companion to the Greek Testament and English Version*. By Philip Schaff. New York: Harper & Brothers, 1883. *Schaff* = abbreviation.

12. *The Text of the New Testament*. Its Transmission, Corruption, and Restoration. By Bruce M. Metzger. New York and London: Oxford University Press, 1964.

NOTES

* This paper is an enlarged version of one part of the paper mentioned in the opening sentence on the first page. For help in its preparation, I am most grateful to Dr. Bruce M. Metzger, the George L. Collard Professor of New Testament Language and Literature, Princeton Theological Seminary; Dr. Edgar C. Reinke, Professor Emeritus of Classics, Valparaiso University; and Dr. Craig R. Thompson, Professor Emeritus of English, University of Pennsylvania. Needless to say, however, they are not to be held responsible for any errors of commission or omission that may be found therein.

1. It is hoped that a revision of the paper will be ready for publication in the not too distant future.

2. See Appendix A and B.12 for a list of English versions used in this study.

3. *A&G*, s.v. ἄνωθεν says that with γεννηθῆναι it "is purposely ambiguous" in this context, "and means both 'born from above' and 'born again.' " I think that both translations are wrong and give reasons for that opinion in the larger paper mentioned above. *A&G* (Appendix C.11).

4. *Moulton and Geden* (Appendix D.5).

5. John 3:31; 19:11; James 1:17; 3:15, 17.

6. Matthew 27:51, Mark 15:38, John 19:23.

7. Galatians 4:9. It will be discussed, along with the others, in the longer paper.

8. Acts 21:39; 22:3, 25, 29; 23:11; 25:11-12; 27:24; 28:14-16.

9. Acts 5:34-39; 22:3. For additional information about Gamaliel, see *Hastings* (Appendix D.7), s.v. Gamaliel. For an interesting account of Paul's life during his early life in Tarsus and as a student in Jerusalem, see Hubert Rex Johnson: *Who Then Is Paul?* (Appendix D.10), Chapters 1-3.

10. Acts 8:1-3; 9:1-2; 22:4-5; 26:9-12. Paul did not speak of "persecuting Christians," but of "persecuting this Way unto death, by binding and handing over into prison both men and women."

11. Acts 22:6-11 and 26:12-18. Paul never referred to himself as a Christian but as one who "worshipped the God of our Fathers according to the Way which people call a sect." Acts 24:14. The first occurrence of the word "Christian" is found in Acts 11:26: "... it happened that in Antioch the disciples were first called Christians." The second occurrence of the word in Acts (26:28) has been translated in different ways because of variations in the text. I venture a translation based on the text of *ABMW* and *W&H*: Agrippa to Paul at the close of the latter's defense: "In a short time," or "With little effort you are trying to make a Christian of me by persuasion."

12. Acts 9:10 through Chapter 24. Although the chronology is uncertain, see the article on Paul in *Hastings* (Appendix D.7), pp. 731-736, and the convenient outline in *Johnson* (Appendix D.10), pp. xiv-xv, with Biblical references. Also Chapters 5-13.

13. Acts 21:17 through Chapter 24. *Johnson*: Chapter 14.

14. Acts 25-26. *Johnson*: Chapter 15.

15. The Greek text is that of *W&H* and *ABMW* (Appendix B.5 and 10); the Latin that of the Vulgate as printed in *Merk* (Appendix B.8). In reading the tranliterated Greek words, the letter "e" in English is short when it comes under its "look-alike" in Greek; otherwise it has the sound of "e" in "prey." The English letters "ai", "ei", "oi", and "ou" are pronounced as dipthongs. The English letter "o" is long when it falls under the Greek letter "omega," otherwise it is short. The accents on the Greek words indicate the syllable to be stressed in English.

16. For the development of the most important texts, see Bruce M. Metzger: *The Text of the New Testament* (Appendix D.12), Chapters III and IV. Philip Schaff: *A Companion to the Greek Testament and the English Version* (Appendix D.11), Chapter 6. *Hastings*: s.v. "Text of the New Testament," but particularly Sect.1, pp. 979-980 and Sects. 34-40, pp. 989-991. For a list of all texts consulted, see Appendix B and C.2.

17. *Hastings*, s.v. English Versions, Sect. 15, p. 253; Craig R. Thompson: *The Bible in English* (Appendix D.9), pp. 5-6.

18. *Metzger*, p. 106. For a comprehensive account of the *Textus Receptus*, see Metzger, Chapter III. See also *Schaff*, pp. 225-249.

19. For a brief account of "The Bible in English, 1525-1611," see the Folger Booklet by Craig R. Thompson (Appendix D.9). For an extensive account of English versions from Wycliffe to the Revision of the King James in 1881, see *Schaff* (Appendix D.11), pp. 299-494. For an account covering the period from Wycliffe (1380) to 1961, see *Hastings*, s.v. English Versions, pp. 249-260. For an account of "The English New Testament from Tyndale [1534] to the Revised Standard Version [1946], see the volume of that title by Luther A. Weigle (Appendix D.8). For "An Introduction to the Revised Standard Version of the New Testament," see the Pamphlet of that title, edited by Luther A. Weigle (Appendix C.13).

20. Since the Latin translation by Erasmus differs in several respects from the text of the Vulgate as given on p. 4 above, it will be quoted in full to give the complete context:

(4) "Itaque vitam quidem meam, quam egi ab adolescentia, quae ab
       2   3   2   4   5   6   7   8
initio fuit in gente mea Hierosolymis, noverunt omnes Judaei, (5)
 9   10 11 13   14   17   18   19   20
Qui prius noverant me *ab initio*, si velint testimonium ferre, quod
21   21   21   22   23   24   25   26   26   27
secundam exquisitissimam sectam nostrae religionis vixerim
   28   30   31   33   34   35
Pharisaeus."
36

(4) And so my life indeed, which I spent from youth, which from the beginning was in my nation in Jerusalem, all Jews know, (5) Who knew me before *from the beginning*, if they are willing to bear testimony, that according to the strictest sect of our religion I lived as a Pharisee.

The numbers correspond to those in the text on p. 4.

21. *The Compact Edition of the Oxford English Dictionary*. Two Volumes. Oxford: At the Clarendon Press, 1971. Vol.I: s.v. Lay sb.³ Col. 1, p. 1584.

22. This construction may occur when the object (No. 22) of the verb (No. 21) is the subject of the following subordinate clause. *Funk* (Appendix D.4)

Sect. 476, p. 252. See *ATR* (Appendix D.1), p. 488, who calls the construction "The Accusative by Antiptosis." *AL&GR* (Appendix D.2), Sect. 576, call the construction," Accusative of Anticipation," and confines its use to Indirect Questions. The late Professor Paul Shorey used to call it the "I-know-thee-who-thou-art" construction from the passage in Mark 1:24 or Luke 4:34. All five translations in Section B translate the participle (No. 21) as if it were a main verb, and presumably on that basis consider the personal pronoun (No. 22) as a proleptic accusative which may then be left out of the translation. Such an interpretation is not in accord with the principles of grammar just quoted.

23. *Jerome* (Appendix C.1), p. 210, Sect. 109:4-8.

24. *Erasmus* (Appendix B.1), p. 532, Note 2.

25. *A&G* (Appendix C.11), p.v.

26. Of these only the participle (No. 21) and the adverb (No. 23) are of concern in this paper.

27. See Appendix C. 5, 6, 7 respectively.

28. *A&G* (Appendix C.11), s.v. ἄνωθεν gives "for a long time" as its meaning with the participle (No. 21). But s.v. προγινώσκω (No. 21) it gives the meaning of the adverb as "from time past." Although the adverb may have either of those meanings in certain contexts, that does not necessarily mean that it has either meaning in our passage. *Urwick* (Appendix C.6), s.v. ἄνωθεν gives "from of old" as a possible meaning, but specifically cites our passage for the meaning, "from the beginning." That does not mean that *his* interpretation is correct, but that meaning does form a parallelism with the prepositional phrase (Nos. 8-9), which I believe is an important consideration in this passage.

29. Luke obviously had some feeling for style, as shown by the first four verses in his Gospel. Whether he or Paul is responsible for the choice of words and constructions in our passage is probably a moot question. At any rate, in our two verses No. 3 occurs only here in the New Testament. Nos. 6 and 34 occur only four times each, and No. 21 only five times. Is it entirely accidental that in the parallelism mentioned so often, a prepositional phrase, Nos. 8-9, followed by a participle, No. 10, is paired with a participle, No. 21, followed by an adverb, No. 23, to form the familiar rhetorical figure of *chiasmus*? Wasn't this the writer's way of calling attention to the close relationship between these two parallel expressions? It seems so to me. Furthermore, the writer is careful to make the distinction between the verb (No. 18) that means to know something as a fact and the one (No. 21) that is generally used of knowing a person. In the former he uses a classical form, the only time, as it happens, that it is found in the New Testament. Could this be his way of emphasizing the only main verb in the sentence?

In the Vulgate, however, the verb *noverunt* (No. 18), from the verb *nosco*, obviously a cognate of the Greek verb (No. 21), is used of "knowing something as a fact," and the verb *praescientes* (No. 21) is used of "knowing a person." This is just the opposite of their usual distinction in Latin and rather strange in this context, because there is a Latin verb, *praenosco*, which is an exact counter-part of No. 21 in the Greek passage. Erasmus (Note 20) used the verb *nosco* in Nos. 18 and 21.

Of the modern language translations cited in Appendix A-1, only the Russian used the same verb for Nos. 18 and 21.

30. *Funk* (Appendix D.4), Sects. 411, 412, p. 212. *ATR* (Appendix D.1), pp. 764-4.c.

31. *Funk* 412, p. 212. *ATR* 1105-1106.

32. *Funk*: Sect. 339(3), pp. 174-175. *ATR*: p. 892(e).

33. See Note 22 above.

34. The condition is in the form of a present general, with ἐάν (No. 24) introducing the protasis, and No. 18 forming the apodosis. *Funk*: 371(4). *ATR* pp. 1016, 1019. G&G 1403a.

35. *Luther* (Appendix A-1:2. For the sake of comparison the passage is quoted in full.

(4) "Zwar mein Leben von Jugend auf, wie das von Anfang unter meinem
          2   4   3   5   6   7 8   9   11
Volke zu Jerusalem zugebracht ist, wissen alle Juden, (5) Die mich
  13   15   17   10   18   19   20   21 22
vorhin gekannt haben, wenn sie wollten bezeugen. Denn ich bin ein
   21   21   24   25   26   35
Pharisäer gewesen, welche ist die strengste Secte unsers
   36   35   29   30   31   33
Gottesdienstes."
    34

(4) Indeed my life from youth up, how it from the beginning among this

people at Jerusalem was spent, all Jews know, who have known me

before, if they willed to testify. For I have been a Pharisee, which is the

strictest sect of our divine service.

For the Latin text of Erasmus, see Note 20.

36. *Nichomachean Ethics* I.7.16 (1098 a 16).

CLASSICAL EDUCATION AND THE WESTERN TRADITION

Edgar C. Reinke

Articles have appeared in print of late that present sharply divergent views regarding the present state of our classical profession. On one side the charge is made that the day of substantial scholarship is now past, and that it is therefore its history, especially of its distinguished scholars in its Golden Age (1841-1931), upon which attention should now be focused.[1] The opposite argued view is that the fountain of traditional *Altertumswissenschaft* is not dried up at all but is in fact inexhaustible, ever beckoning the young classical genius to quaff freely from its eternally fresh waters.[2] Yet at least one classicist perceives a "disarray" in classical research, which he considers "a symptom of the ideological and spiritual malaise of our entire society in which established values have been dethroned but not replaced."[3]

At issue here again is the ever intriguing question: What is education? Historically true education has been liberal education, not "practical" training. Since it is liberal, education must therefore be worthy of the person who is free, free to develop innate talent to its maximum capacity in accordance with the established laws of an open, responsible society. It is thus the aim of this essay to define education in terms of the Graeco-Roman, Judaeo-Christian Western Tradition, the only tradition that has offered the individual the opportunity to realize potential ability and its rewards in an environment of liberty and freedom.[4]

Aristotle reasoned that, to be happy, one must be adequately furnished with material goods, not merely for a limited time, but for a complete lifetime.[5] He meant of course that money is an absolute necessity for living the "good life." But neither he nor any other Greek thinkers were misled into believing that external goods, the gifts of fortune, are an end in themselves. Unlimited wealth acquired for its own sake never appealed to their discerning judgment, to their doctrine of the mean, and Socrates declared that his wealth consisted, not in the number of his material possessions, but in the fewness of his wants.[6] And so in our search for a definition of education, education worthy of a person who is free, we must simultaneously find a satisfactory reply to the second query: What is the right life of the individual as a human being?

In our pre-occupation with nature and its products we have neglected the human being, the individuality of the person. The Greeks did not: the noblest of all investigations, declares Plato, is what man should be and what he should pursue.[7] To the Greeks the "Know thyself" emphasized by Socrates was more than a motto; it inspired the composition of Plato's *Republic*, stated by Rousseau to be "the best treatise on education in the world."[8]

Almost from the beginning of their history the Greeks adopted a reasoned view of life and not only desired but created a human ideal. And to this human ideal they gave the name ἀρετή, perhaps best translated as "excellence," though more often "moral excellence" or "virtue." However, the connotation of ἀρετή is not always the same in the progress of Greek thought. The Homeric hero, for example, possessed ἀρετή if he was brave and steadfast in battle. Thus, in the Trojan War, Odysseus gives up ease and security, Achilles sacrifices his life, Hector life, wife, and child, in an ardent devotion to the ideal of military courage. But other conceptions of ἀρετή are gradually developed by subsequent Greek authors until the culmination is reached in Plato, who with typical Greek love of order and symmetry assigns to ἀρετή a hierarchy of values:

> Now goods are of two kinds; there are human and there are divine goods, and the human hang upon the divine .... Of the lesser goods first is health, the second beauty, the third strength, ... and the fourth is wealth.

> ... For wisdom is chief and leader of the divine class of goods, and next follows temperance; and from the union of these two with courage springs justice, and fourth in the scale of virtues is courage.[9]

The Greeks accordingly formulated the idea of excellence in human existence which made life meaningful to them, whereas with us the disintegration of the historical Western ideal, a best in life, an ἀρετή, is largely responsible for the malady of our age, for its disorder and confusion. Since World War II, the majority of our society has been exchanging a foundation of faith and reason for the dimness of uncertain opinion. It is therefore submitted that the ἀρετή which the classical profession must again strive to attain as its highest ideal is tri-partite, comprised of a sound character, a disciplined mind, and a spirit dedicated to the service of humanity: *Aliis inserviendo consumor*.[10]

Surely as classicists we stand for character as well as scholarship, for neither without the other, but for the inter-play of both. History teaches inexorably that the conscience alone may not safely be followed without a dispassionate understanding of objective facts; for many a person has been led by an apparently good conscience to deeds resulting in ruin to himself and to his fellows. Yet knowledge without character, determined by the experience of the human race and the concept of the human being as a moral being, offers a panorama of possibilities suggestive of De Quincey's *On Murder as One of the Fine Arts* and tragically illustrated by two brilliant legal students at a large American university some sixty years ago.[11] As educated men and women we are therefore required in practice to be virtuous no less than intelligent and intelligent no more than virtuous.

But what about the development of character? True, the student who learns the ways of nature is likely to be strengthened in the qualities of sincerity and veracity. Do the natural sciences, however, yield further ethical instruction? The response must be in the negative, for the forces of nature are devoid of moral discrimination: rain falls on the just and the unjust alike; flood, tornado, and earthquake are no respecters of persons; lightning indeed is apt to strike the lofty spire of the church more readily than the hidden den of iniquity. In the realm of organic nature the wild animal seldom dies a natural death; it lives by hunting and is itself hunted. Yet as a basis of conduct the law of the survival of the fittest is repugnant to humanity. For the upbuilding of character we should do better, in secular studies, to turn to the masterpieces of Western literature, to literature particularly rich in moral content, the literature that had its inception along the shores of the Aegaean and beside the bank of the Tiber, although the modern literatures derived from Greece and Rome would serve our purpose too.

For who, in a study of the lyric poet Horace, if at all sensitive to beauty of thought and of language, would fail to be affected by the moral earnestness of that matchless phrasemaker? *Aurea mediocritas* ("The Golden Mean"); *Integer vitae scelerisque purus* ("A life unsullied and devoid of guilt"); *Aequam memento rebus in arduis servare mentem* ("Remember to preserve a calm mind in time of stress"); *Vis consili expers mole ruit sua* ("Power bereft of wisdom collapses of its own weight").[12] These and numerous other such felicitous dicta of that artist of life not only provide pleasure and enhance the aesthetic sensibilities, but also quicken ethical and moral consciousness. And in classical epic and dramatic poetry ethical distinctions are clarified through analysis of concepts, characters, and situations, whereby we are inspired, usually subconsciously and unobtrusively, to right conduct through admiration and imitation of the noble thoughts and deeds, or through disapproval and avoidance of their opposites, in the heroic personages made known to us therein. What a fine opportunity we have for laying the foundation of correct moral judgment in following the acts and analyzing the words and deeds of Virgil's Aeneas and Dido, or, in the drama, of Sophocles' Antigone, or Euripides' Alcestis or Medea! We may occasionally err in our interpretation of their conduct, because of an incomplete understanding of the ancient point of view; nor, to be sure, may we always be able to accept this view as valid; yet, by subjecting to critical examination the motives of a character of heroic stature on the level of action far removed from modern conditions and prejudices, we are acquiring a training of highest ethical value. And the more intensive such sympathetic study of the literary masterpieces becomes, the more powerful the impressions that the chief actors leave on the youthful mind. It matters little whether the details are forgotten. What does matter is the lasting ennobling of the character:

Much lost I, something stayed behind,
A snatch may be of ancient song;
Some breathings of a deathless mind,
Some love of truth, some hate of wrong.[13]

The first obligation of a college of liberal arts is to teach its students how to think, to develop their powers of analysis, so that they learn how to reason with clarity, logic, and conviction. Though our nutritive and sensitive functions, as we are reminded, again by Aristotle, are shared with plants and animals, it is the priceless endowment of the intellect, he emphasizes, that lends to human life its unique character and meaning.[14] Genuine education must consequently be based on a serious, consecutive, and progressive pursuit of intellectual studies that are definite, teachable, and generally hard.[15] This is the course that is to be followed, if the student wishes to be able to "see life steadily and see it whole,"[16] to "see things as they are,"[17] not superficially in masses, but accurately in detail. Having learned how to think and reason, the students so prepared will understand their own language and be able to express themselves intelligently therein; they will also have gained an insight into one or more basic civilizations, preferably in the original language; and by having cultivated their historical, constructive imagination, they will now be able to exercise sounder judgment and be in a position to interpret more correctly the current scene of life, of which they are a part.

Such severe intellectual discipline will not deny the importance of bodily health and relaxation from toil: Apollo too with his lyre sometimes wakes the slumbering Muse and does not always bend his bow.[18] The Greeks moreover were splendid athletes as well as original thinkers, while the Roman maxim, "A sound mind in a sound body," is as valid today as it was at the time when it was coined.[19] Nevertheless, even under the most favorable conditions we cannot expect the ordinary students to become scholars. For their ability may not be high enough for successful scholarship, their diligence may be unequal to its maintenance, and their daily tasks may interfere much with its constant practice and pursuit. Also the restlessness of the age has resulted in a general revolt against discipline and hard work, in the impatience of all serious pre-vocational study, and the demand for quick, even instant utilitarian results, in other words for the fast dollar. We are reminded here of the withering remark of Samuel Johnson relative to the uninitiated: "Sir, your levellers wish to level *down* as far as themselves; but they cannot bear levelling *up* to themselves."[20] Though the exaltation of mediocrity is evident everywhere in our society, the sober fact of the matter is that a people in its culture, in its statesmanship, in its higher occupations and professional careers, if it would survive, must by applied, intelligent study of the humanities relate itself to its roots, to the greatest achievements of its past, in order to draw salutary lessons and rational guidance for the present and future. Obviously no one is expected to be born with the genius of John Stuart Mill, who was introduced to Greek at the early age of three, or of Wilamowitz or Jebb or Gildersleeve or Paul Shorey.[21] Yet inherently the student of today is certainly as gifted as any of the past. What is needed, to ensure the gratifying rewards of success, is dogged persistence, unflagging zeal, and consistent effort: *Studendum vero semper et ubique.*[22] Let there furthermore be instilled a veritable passion for knowledge, an infectious enthusiasm for teaching and learning, so that our students too may exclaim in similar vein with Matthew Arnold:

> Rigorous teachers seized my youth,
> And trained my mind, and roused its fire,
> Showed me the high, white star of Truth,
> There bade me gaze, and there aspire.[23]

With character and intellect should be associated a magnanimous and noble spirit. As examples the Greeks, who believed that life is worth living already because it enabled them to contemplate the heavens and order of the universe, possessed the fresh vitality and joyous exuberance reflected in their spirit of inquiry and in all of their creative work. For they were firmly convinced that with the exception of death itself the secrets of the universe could be discovered if only they were sought. And they were the first to conceive the ideal of progress based on human effort and advancing knowledge. Thus the Parthenon on the Acropolis of Athens, standing calm and serene in the clear light of day beneath an azure sky, may be cited as the epitome of the Greek civic spirit and its glorious achievement. Whether seen from afar by the mariner at sea or by the pilgrim close at hand, the sheer beauty of this classic temple with its rational lines and harmonious proportions even now, after almost two and half millennia, thrills and exalts the viewer with reverential awe. This is why in one of his majestic odes Sophocles could cry in a burst of ecstasy: "Wonders are many, and none is more wonderful than man.... Cunning beyond fancy's dream is [his] fertile skill."[24]

But what was it that inspired Classical Humanism with its high ideals? Here is what Cicero has to say on this subject:

> All literature, all philosophy, all history, abounds with incentives to noble action.... How many pictures of high endeavor the great writers of Greece and Rome have drawn for our use, not only for our contemplation, but for our emulation. These I have held ever before my vision ... throughout my public career and have guided the workings of my mind and my soul by meditating upon patterns of excellence.[25]

When we turn from the reverence of the Greeks for the discoveries and inventions of man to their democratic spirit of fair play, we think at once of the grand oration of Athens' greatest statesman Pericles, delivered before the Athenian populace in its climactic age, and reported by the historian Thucydides, an oration that is still our best description of the democratic ideal, in which justice is secured for all and protection for the oppressed in accordance with the legislated laws, and in which talent in every branch of accomplishment is welcomed and honored, not for any reason of birth or wealth, but on grounds of excellence alone.[26]

Classical illustrations of altruism in the individual may be marshaled before the reader too. Here are a few: Trojan Axylus, respected and beloved, who dwelled alongside of the public road and at his open door welcomed all comers;[27] the aged country couple Philemon and Baucis, piously serving to Zeus, himself the god of hospitality, incognito with Hermes, their plain fare in their humble cottage;[28] Queen Dido, magnanimously offering to share her rule and city of Carthage with Aeneas and his shipwrecked Trojans, in words that recall the memorable line: *Non ignara mali miseris succurrere disco* ("Not unacquainted with misery I learn to come to the aid of the miserable");[29] Herodes Atticus, who devoted his enormous wealth largely to amazing benefactions and to buildings like the Odeon, still extant and in use at the foot of the Athenian Acropolis.[30] Then there is Pliny the Younger, the philanthropist who helped found the first school at his native town of Como, beautifully situated on the shore of Lago di Como in the Italian Alps. As an inducement, Pliny promised to match any sum of money collected by the town's fathers for the construction and maintenance of their educational institution: "Be encouraged by my generosity," were his words of exhortation, "since I desire that my own contribution be as large as possible."[31] Thus it was the humane Pliny who initiated the current practice of matching gifts as a method of raising funds for colleges and universities. Most impressive of all, however, is Aeschylus' Prometheus, that gigantic benefactor of helpless, primitive man, who poignantly presented him, groping in the dark, with the boon of fire, taught him the art of reading, of medicine and divination, and showed him the use of metals, of animals for transportation, and of the sailing vessel. All this he is described by the Greek dramatist as having accomplished in the face of seemingly insurmountable obstacles and with severe suffering to himself, in a universe that was hostile.[32] So overwhelmed were Beethoven and Shelley by the indomitable spirit of this Titan of Titans, soaring like Jove's eagle with steady eyes against the sun, that they were impelled, Beethoven to compose his powerful *Prometheus Overture,* Shelley his stirring poem, the *Prometheus Unbound.*[33]

Let us now trace the history of the classical curriculum itself. All-around education (ἐγκύκλιος παιδεία) was practiced initially by Isocrates at his school of Greek rhetoric in Athens and first designated by Cicero in his *De oratore* as *artes liberales.* It was then adopted by Quintilian in his education of the orator, and through him general education was spread through all parts of the Roman Empire, lasting almost until its fall.[34] In Quintilian's discipline St. Augustine and other early Church Fathers were educated and later Ausonius of Bordeaux and Sidonius of Lyons; sacred and profane studies combined in a mixed curriculum were intended to enable priests and monks to read theological and philosophic Latin and laymen to become civil and legal administrators. After this curriculum had been revived by Cassiodorus at his *Vivarium* in South Italy, then by Isidore of Seville, and thereafter by the Venerable Bede at Jarrow and Alcuin at York, it was transferred by Charlemagne to his palace school at Aachen on the European continent.[35]

Still later, at Paris and mediaeval universities elsewhere, under the influence of Martianus Capella's fifth-century allegorical poem on the marriage of Eloquence and Philology,[36] the seven *artes liberales* were established as the *trivium* and *quadrivium* that led to the bachelor's and master's degrees. And perhaps mainly because of its moral and ethical principles classical study received its support not only from the Church, but also from the government and public as well: "*Verbum caro factum,* The Word made flesh, the humanization of divinity.... Thus," exclaims McDonald of Ohio State University, "the classical concepts of the wholeness and self-sufficiency of man was joined with the Judaic concept of the absolute sovereignty of God."[37] This was the introduction of the Judaeo-Christian, Graeco-Roman Western Tradition.

Then in 1526 at Wittenberg the ἐγκύκλιος παιδεία, borrowed by Melanchthon from Quintilian, whom Melanchthon and Luther admired, became the University's new curriculum.[38] And when twelve years later at Strassburg Johannes Sturm as Headmaster opened the doors of the first German *Gymnasium,* "the strange but effective *sponsalia* finally blossomed into the wedded union of Christian Humanism." Subsequently the Jesuits adopted a classical curriculum in Messina, Sicily, and John Calvin at Geneva, Switzerland, and in the late 1500's Eton and Winchester founded classical schools in Anglican England.[39]

The aim of this Christian Humanism was to develop the *vir bonus vivendi peritus* ("the good man skilled in living").[40] Of the veritable legion of Renaissance authors and scholars trained in the classics were the Italian humanists Bocaccio and Petrarch, the French Ronsard, and the Dutch Erasmus, to name a few prominent examples. And for several centuries thereafter education based on Greek and Latin studies combined with Christian principles produced also the large majority of leaders in Europe who entered government, the professions, and occupations in business and trade.[41] It was "Christian Humanism" furthermore on which Harvard College and King's College (Columbia University) were founded, and at Oxford until 1852 membership in the Church of England was a requirement for the bachelor's degree.[42]

"Christian Humanism" has ideally endeavored to attain the score and more of secular values and objectives associated with classical education[43] One of its studies is Roman Stoicism, which reaches its culmination in Seneca, in whose cosmopolitan outlook there is recognized in each human being, despite weaknesses, some spark of an all-pervading divine essence; patience, kindliness, true humanity are the results of such a creed.[44] And Seneca too, together with Cicero and Roman jurists, was instrumental in formulating the Law of Nature as the basis of human rights, considered in 1776 in the Declaration of Independence as an equal partner of Divine Law and Christian Gospel.[45]

It is this opportunity of comparing and contrasting classical ideals with the teachings and tenets of the Bible, whether consciously or subconsciously, directly or indirectly, that is of inestimable value to Christian classicists. Though they are deeply impressed by Plato's exposition of his *Republic's* four cardinal virtues, courage and self-restraint and wisdom and justice, yet in striving for their attainment they will be inspired not so much by the logic of Plato as the exhortations of Christ. Plato's idea of deity moreover may be regarded as both noble and sublime, but Plato, the Christian classicist would point out, did not know the God of Revelation. Nor was religion as such the life blood of Greece as it has been of Palestine: the Greeks commenced with man and concluded with deity; the Christian man and woman believe that they know God through His revealed Word, which teaches them who they are and how to live their lives.

In its injunctions the Word directs the human race to become masters of the Universe (Gen. 1.26), which would include the discovery of its laws. Yet the Apostle Saint Paul, who was educated in Greek and Greek philosophy, utters this warning: "Though I have the gift of prophecy, and understand all mysteries, and all knowledge, and ... have not charity, I am nothing" (1 Cor. 13.2). Thereby this first Christian classicist, who does not disavow the life of the mind, yet subordinates the highest reason to the more elevated spirit of love and so places the loftiest human ideal, raised to an ineffable Christian ἀγάπη, within the reach of every human being, the uneducated and illiterate, as well as the poet and philosopher.

From the beginning of recorded history it has been the hope of immortality that, for the majority of the human race, seems to have given to human existence its ultimate meaning and validity; the wish, if not even the yearning, for immortality appears to be innate in mortals. In the *Phaedo* Plato, for example, believes that he has rationally demonstrated the immortality of the soul, and in the same dialogue Socrates says of his willingness to accept its argument: "The risk is at least beautiful."[46] In his essay *On Old Age* Cicero likewise looks forward to a future life "on yonder shore" and does not desire his belief to be wrested from him as long as he lived.[47] To Keats Lucretius becomes actually the Anti-Lucretius when he sees Lucretius "half in love with easeful Death."[48] Nevertheless, in general to the Greeks and Romans the significance of immortality was at most the remembrance of their worth in time to come. *Noblesse oblige*: Cicero knew this and sublimely gave up his life for his country; but it was his self-glorification that spurred the humanist to his supreme sacrifice. In true humility the Christian dedicates life, not to personal glory, but to the glory of God.

Homo sum; humani nil a me alienum puto ("I am a human being; I regard nothing pertaining to a human being as foreign to me").[49] Shall the complete human being, as Karl Weintraub has posited, be an egalitarian aristocrat?[50] Cicero can certainly be classified as a democratic aristocrat, as Karl Büchner has characterized him.[51] Emerson in fact declared that in every society the dominant element will always be an elite.[52] And in a syndicated newspaper column George Will, a former professor and son of a former professor, when deploring the licentious excesses of a growing number of teachers and students within and without the classroom, wrote several months ago:

> The world is divided, by no means evenly, between those who believe, as I do, that the proper aim of education is primarily to put something—learning—*into* students, and others who believe that the primary aim of education is to let something—"feelings," or "the self," or "authenticity," or something—*out* of students. If the task is "putting in," putting in a legacy of learning refined over the centuries, the legacy must be sifted and selected from. That is an aristocratic task; it is the business of intellectual authority, not political democracy.[53]

Of the fifty-five members of the American Constitutional Convention of 1787, a wise elite which Bancroft called the most sacred brotherhood of legislators in the history of the world,[54] the orator Curtis points out that thirty-three were college graduates, and that the eight leading spokesmen of the great debate were all college men.[55] To Jefferson the delegates were "demigods."[56] Many of them were well-read in classical literature, some at first hand.[57] Moreover, at least fifty of the fifty-five Framers of the Constitution were "orthodox members of one of the established Christian communions."[58] Though John Adams was a Stoic Unitarian and Jefferson an Epicurean Deist, both remained loyal to a "non-liturgical Christianity."[59] And though Aristotle, Polybius, and Cicero influenced the framing of the American Constitution, its Framers founded their document on Biblical principles: the State, if it would fare well, must rely for its support on morality and religion, in its administration by its officers and in the lives of its citizens.[60] And in his Presidential Farewell Address, delivered before the people on September 17, 1796, George Washington, who despite his limited, elementary education had presided as chairman over the Constitutional Convention, spoke these wise words:

> Of all the dispositions and habits which lead to political prosperity, Religion and Morality are indispensable supports.... The mere Politician, equally with the pious man, ought to respect and cherish them.... Let it simply be asked where is the security for property, for reputation, for life, if the sense of religious obligation *desert* the oaths, which are the instruments of investigation in the Courts of Justice? ... Whatever may be conceded to the influence of refined education on minds of peculiar structure; reason and experience both forbid us to expect that national morality can prevail in exclusion of religious principle.[61]

Included in the magnificent legacy bequeathed to us by the Western Tradition are the towering giants of our discipline's Golden Age (1841-1931). To these great scholars, European and British and American, we as their beneficiaries owe an enormous debt that can scarcely ever be discharged. Surely, if Thomas Jefferson was entitled with pardonable exaggeration to extol the delegates of the Constitutional Convention as "demigods," the same appellative might justly be bestowed upon the many Homeric heroes of our profession in its most flourishing era. What an inspiring sight, were we to behold their portraits adorning the walls of an international classical Hall of Fame! Several of these stalwarts were mentioned earlier in this paper. Lists of prominent classicists with biographical data may be perused in histories of classical scholarship.[62] To Paul Shorey, a mentor of the present writer, we shall now direct our attention as felicitously illustrative of the highest classical scholarship produced by the Western Tradition.

Throughout his long professional career of almost fifty years, first at Bryn Mawr College (1885-92), then at the University of Chicago as a charter member of its Faculty (1892-1934), Paul Shorey devoted most of his amazingly versatile scholarship to Athens' greatest philosopher Plato. So highly in fact did Mr. Shorey esteem Plato that already in his doctoral dissertation he argued Plato's infallibility: *Plato nunquam errat.*[63] Mr. Shorey's deep and abiding influence furthermore extended not only to his devoted students in the classroom, but also to readers of his numerous publications and to large audiences at lectures delivered by him in this country and abroad. In a biographical appreciation of Mr. Shorey one of his early students, Emily James Putnam, points out that to each issue of *Classical Philology*, of which he was editor for twenty-five years (1909-34), Mr. Shorey contributed "an article, a note, a text criticism, or a review," and in commenting on his beliefs she says she is "inclined to think that Shorey was a unitarian professionally, confessionally (by heredity at least), and passionally."[64]

"There are more things in heaven and earth, Horatio, than are dreamt of in your philosophy."[65] In the chapter titled "Platonism and Christ," a chapter of his last volume, published posthumously, Mr. Shorey expresses his view of ultimate reality. Here are a few of his statements concerned with this subject: "The immortality of the soul as an article of faith and hope, a sanction of moral law, an inspiration of poets, will be treated lightly by no student of humanity."[66] "If there is something more than mechanism, if there is a possibility of a purpose in the universe, if there is something more than a harmony of the elements or a nervous system in the mind and soul of man, that something more, however little we may know of it, opens up infinite possibilities for religious aspirations and hope. Without it there is nothing."[67] "For both Plato and Christ, conduct, in Matthew Arnold's phrase, is three-fourths of life, not to say nine-tenths. ... 'What shall it profit a man to gain the whole world and lose his own soul?' (Matt. 16.26; Luke 9.25)."[68] The acutely stated abstractions of Plato, Mr. Shorey adds, have their appeal to the intellectuals and aristocrats; the change of heart exhorted in the Sermon on the Mount and the "beauty and unity of Jesus' life" assured the ultimate triumph of Christianity.[69]

By 1914, however, the year of the outbreak of World War I, not only had the centuries-long reign of Quintilian waned, but the churches themselves were turning away from their classical curriculum and thereby severing the one remaining bond of European unity. The significance of this retreat was perceived by Hilaire Belloc in his terse observation: "Europe is the faith, and the faith is Europe, and the decline of the faith is the decline of Europe."[70]

Not surprisingly therefore the Carnegie Commission on Higher Education several years ago attributed the present floundering of education in the United States to an inability to define its goals.[71] And even more recently the Dean of the Faculty of Arts and Sciences at Harvard University bluntly asserted that "at the moment, to be an educated man or woman doesn't mean anything. ... The world has become a Tower of Babel."[72] If the "disarray" and "spiritual malaise" said to be affecting our classical profession is to disappear, a renewed, strong commitment to our classical roots would be imperative. Our primary objective clearly must again become the classical aim of the Renaissance, the development of the *vir bonus vivendi peritus*; around this priority all our other objectives must continually revolve. And what is more, the churches would be required to resume their historic association with classical studies by restoring their abandoned curriculum of the sacred and the profane through a re-emphasis of Latin and Greek. It would not be convincing to object that, since history does not repeat itself, a return to the past would be impossible. For who can deny that the world of today has indeed been witnessing a return to the past, tragically however to the dark age of barbarism?[73] Let us then hasten to wend our way back up the steep path that leads to the pure waters of Castalia, to the endless fount on Parnassus, ever drawing on its wisdom conjoined with the ethereal Beatitudes of the Sermon on the Mount, together becoming once again the two pillars of Western Civilization.

Get all you can out of life by putting all you can into life, if you would live the full life and be happy. *Beatus ille*[74] who embraces the timeless ideals of the Western Tradition, of Athens and Jerusalem, and as classicist in the development of character, mind, and spirit, of the *vir bonus vivendi peritus*, happily reflects their guiding light in both teaching and research.

NOTES

1. William M. Calder III, "Research Opportunities in the Modern History of Classical Scholarship," *CW* 74 (Feb. 1981): 241-51.

2. Rick M. Newton, "A Reply to William M. Calder III," *ibid.*, 75 (Nov.-Dec. 1981): 120f.; John F. Callahan *et. al.*, "A Reply to William M. Calder, Bis," *ibid.*, pp. 121f.

3. Dana Ferrin Sutton, "A Modern Proposal," *ibid.* (Mch.-Apr. 1982), pp. 249f. For other Notes on this controversy see *ibid.*, pp. 248f., 249, and *ibid.* (July-Aug., 1982), pp. 362f., 363f., and 364-66, at which last point the Editor announces that he "will close publication of this issue."

4. "The only freedom which deserves the name is that of pursuing our own good in our own way, so long as we do not attempt to deprive others of theirs or impede their efforts to obtain it," John Stuart Mill, *On Liberty*, in *Great Books of the Western World*, ed. Robert Maynard Hutchins *et al.*, 54 vols. (Chicago, 1952), 43:273.

5. Arist. *Eth. Nic.* 1177 a, 1178, 1098.

6. Xen. *Mem.* A 6.10.

7. Pl. *Leg.* 716 c.

8. In Pl. *Phaedr.* 229 cd, Socrates says that all his leisure is devoted to the Delphic inscription γνῶθι σαυτόν, which bade him to know himself. On Jean Jacques Rousseau's appraisal of the *Republic* see his *Émile, ou de l'Éducation*, new ed. (Paris, 1762), p. 6.

9. Pl. *Leg.* 631 (tr. Jowett).

10. Motto of Beta Phi Mu, chapter of the International Library Science Honor Society.

11. Thomas De Quincey, *On Murder Considered as One of the Fine Arts*, in his *Collected Writings*, ed. David Masson, 14 vols. (Edinburgh, 1889-90; repr. New York, 1968), 13:9-124. It would be too painful to elaborate on the illustration.

12. Hor. *Carm.* 2.10.5, 1.22.1, 2.3.1f., 3.4.65, respectively; unless stated otherwise, translations in this essay are the author's, Biblical citations being from the Authorized Version of 1611.

13. William (Johnson) Cory, *Ionica*, 2 vols. in 1; vol. 1 (London, 1858 and 1877); vol. 2 (privately printed, 1877), "A Retrospect of School Life," (unnumbered) lines 5-8 of stanza 4 (pagination lacking).

14. Arist. *De an.* 432.

15. T. S. Eliot, "Modern Education and the Classics," *Essays Ancient and Modern* (New York, 1936), pp. 169-85.

16. Matthew Arnold in his description of Sophocles, "To a Friend," *Poems*, in his *Works*, 15 vols. (London, 1903-4), 1:40.

17. James Russell Lowell, *Works*, Standard Library Edition, 11 vols. (Boston, 1890-99), 10:97.

18. Hor. *Carm.* 2.10.19f.

19. "Mens sana in corpore sano," Juv. 10.356.

20. James Boswell, *Life of Samuel Johnson*, in *Great Books of the Western World*, vol. 44 (21 July, 1763), p. 127.

21. John Stuart Mill, *Autobiography*, 2d ed. (London, 1873), p. 5. Ulrich von Wilamowitz-Moellendorf (1848-1931), Sir Richard Claverhouse Jebb (1841-1905), Basil Lanneau Gildersleeve (1831-1924), and Paul Shorey (1857-1934), outstanding classical scholars.

22. Quint. *Inst.* 10.7.27.

23. "Stanzas from the Grande Chartreuse," (1855), *The Poems of Matthew Arnold*, ed. A. T. Quiller-Couch (London, 1926), p. 272; cf. Pl. *Resp.* 401 cd, for Socrates' beautiful vision of the youths who have completed his strenuous educational program.

24. Soph. *Ant.* 332ff. (tr. Jebb); but in Sophocles' apostrophe of man in *OT* 1186f. the poet is pessimistic: "Races of mortal man/ Whose life is but a span,/ I count ye but the shadow of a shade" (Loeb tr.).

25. Cic. *Arch.* 44 (Loeb tr.). In Republican Rome the *imagines* or busts of their ancestors were shown to children, who were taught to read the inscriptions recounting their exploits, *Oxford Companion to Classical Literature*, ed. Paul Harvey (Oxford, 1937), p. 154.

26. Thuc. 2.35-46. It should be borne in mind, however, that democracy at Athens was limited to its citizens, to the exclusion of foreigners and slaves.

27. Hom. *Il.* 6.15-18.

28. Ov. *Met.* 8.618ff.

29. Virg. *Aen.* 1.630.

30. Glenn Warren Bowersock, *Greek Sophists in the Roman Empire* (Oxford, 1969), ch. 7.

31. Pliny *Ep.* 4.13.

32. Aesch. *PV* 436-506.

33. Ludwig van Beethoven (1770-1827), German composer; biography by Martin Cooper (1970). Percy Bysshe Shelley (1792-1822), English poet; biography by J. O. Fuller (1969).

34. Quint. *Inst.* 1.10.1; Aubrey Gwynn, *Roman Education from Cicero to Quintilian* (New York, 1926; repr. 1966), pp. 85 and 244.

35. William F. McDonald, "Classicism, Christianity, and Humanism," *The Endless Fountain*, ed. Mark Morford (Columbus, O., 1972), pp. 42-44.

36. George Kennedy, *Classical Rhetoric and Its Christian and Secular Tradition from Ancient to Modern Times* (Chapel Hill, N. C., 1980), pp. 175-77.

37. McDonald, *loc. cit.*, pp. 29f.

38. Walter Friedensburg, ed., *Urkundenbuch der Universität Wittenberg*, Part 1, 1502-1611 (Magdeburg, 1926): 146f. When Luther entered the Erfurt monastery in 1505, he demonstrated an early affection for the classics in carrying a copy of Virgil and Plautus under an arm; Martin Luther, *Werke: Tischreden*, 6 vols. (Weimar, 1912-21), 1:44, no. 116. On Luther's esteem for the functional and liberalizing study of Greek and Latin, *Werke: Briefwechsel* (Weimar, 1930-), vol. 3, p. 512, no. 596; *Werke*, vol. 15, pp. 27-53; see also Ernest G. Sihler, "Luther and the Classics," *Four Hundred Years* . . . , ed. W. H. T. Dau (St. Louis, Mo., 1916), pp. 240-54.

39. McDonald, *loc. cit.*, pp. 31f.

40. McDonald, *ibid.*, p. 47.

41. George Kennedy, *Quintilian* (New York, 1969), pp. 140f.

42. On the Wall in Harvard Yard a still distinct inscription cites the two objectives of the founders of Harvard College (1636): "After God had carried us safe to *New England*, and wee had builded our houses, provided necessaries for our liveli-hood, rear'd convenient places for Gods worship and setled the Civill Government; One of the next things we longed for, and looked after was to advance *Learning* and perpetuate it to Posterity; dreading to leave an illiterate Ministry to the Churches, when our present Ministers shall lie in the Dust." Cited and quoted by Frank Getlein, "The Flowering of New England Culture Was Off to an Early Start," *The Smithsonian* 13 (June 1982): 110. On the history of Harvard University see Samuel E. Morison, *The Founding of Harvard College* (Cambridge, Mass., 1935); on Columbia, *University on the Heights*, ed. Wesley First (Garden City, New York, 1969); on Oxford, Charles E. Mallett, *History of the University of Oxford*, 3 vols. (New York, 1924-27; repr. 1968).

43. William H. Woodward defines "Christian Humanism" as "the interaction between classical culture and Christianity," in a person of "literary and specifically classical cultivation," *Desiderius Erasmus concerning the Aim and Method of Education* (New York, 1904), repr. (1964) with a Foreword by Craig R. Thompson, p. xiii; this definition is applied to the Christian classicist in the present essay. The fullest list and best discussion of classical values and objectives are still to be found in *The Classical Investigation*, Conducted by the Advisory Committee of the American Classical League (Princeton, N. J., 1924).

44. Anna Lydia Motto, "Seneca as *amicus humani generis*," *Seneca* (New York, 1973), pp. 55-64.

45. Richard M. Gummere, *The American Colonial Mind and the Classical Tradition* (Cambridge, Mass., 1963), pp. 3f. However, there were Framers of the United States Constitution who viewed the theory of natural rights as dubious; M. E. Bradford, *A Worthy Company: Brief Lives of the Framers of the United States Constitution* (Marlborough, N. H., 1982), pp. ix, 21, 27, 31, 83, 90, 92, 178, 197.

46. Pl. *Phd.* 114 d.

47. Cic. *Sen.* 32.82-85.

48. John Keats, with reference to Lucr. 3.977, "Ode to a Nightingale," *Poetical Works*, ed. H. Buxton Forman (New York, 1895), pp. 293f.; but cf. George Hadzits, *Lucretius and His Influence* (New York, 1935; repr. 1963), p. 101; John W. Duff, *Literary History of Rome to the Close of the Golden Age* (New York, 1932), p. 286.

49. Ter. *Haut.* 77; it may be pointed out, however, that in this much quoted line the character who utters these words is attempting to justify his activity as a busybody, not as a man devoted to the study and welfare of humanity.

50. Karl J. Weintraub, "Noblesse in an Egalitarian World," *University of Chicago Magazine* 66 (1973): 12-15.

51. Karl Büchner, *Cicero: Bestand und Wandel seiner geistigen Welt* (Heidelberg, 1964), reviewed in *CJ* 61 (Dec. 1965): 129-31.

52. Ralph Waldo Emerson, *Complete Works*, ed. Edward Waldo Emerson, Centenary Edition, 12 vols. (Boston, 1903-4), 3:129.

53. As printed in the Orlando, Fla., *Sentinel* for Thursday, May 27, 1982, A-19. George Will is here citing an illustration of what is popularly being called "Secular Humanism." Historically, however, Humanism, by which is meant in the first instance Classical Humanism, has never sanctioned license; on the contrary, with its ideals it has preached the elevation of the human being. What is increasingly being witnessed in permissive society is not Humanism at all, but its exact opposite, Hominism namely, the nihilistic philosophy of the complete degradation of the human being.

54. George Bancroft, *History of the United States*, 6 vols., rev. ed. (New York, 1891), 6:441, "The American constitution is the most wonderful work ever struck off at a given time by the brain and purpose of man."

55. George William Curtis, *Orations and Addresses*, ed. Charles E. Norton, 3 vols. (New York, 1893-94), 1:325, where Bancroft's statement cited in the preceding note is included.

56. Thomas Jefferson, *Papers*, ed. Julian P. Boyd (Princeton, N. J., 1950-), vol. 12, p. 69, in a letter to John Adams, Aug. 30, 1787.

57. Gummere, *op. cit.*, p. 174.

58. Bradford, *op. cit.*, p. viii.

59. Gummere, *op. cit.*, p. 191; see also John Adams, *Works*, ed. Charles Francis Adams, 10 vols. (Boston, 1850-56), 3:484.

60. Bradford, *op. cit.*, p. ix; Gummere, *op. cit.*, p. 178.

61. George Washington, "Farewell Address," with an Introduction by James Thorpe (San Marino, Cal., 1972), pp. 18f.

62. For chronological lists of scholars with biographical data, John Edwin Sandys, *History of Classical Scholarship*, 3 vols. (New York, 1903-8; repr. 1967), vol. 3, *The Eighteenth Century in Germany, and the Nineteenth Century in Europe and the United States of America*; see also Harry Thurston Peck, *History of Classical Philology* (New York, 1911). These volumes, however, extend only as far as the close of the nineteenth century.

63. Paul Shorey, *De Platonis idearum doctrina atque mentis humanae notionibus commentatio* (Munich, 1884), p. 58, where the author pays tribute Plato: "cui soli omnium qui unquam fuerunt philosophorum contigit nunquam errare," with the added qualification, however, "Haec nimio fortasse erga Platonem studio atque amore dixi, ut lectori qui praecedentia neglexerit λαβήν dem." See too the recent translation of Mr. Shorey's Dissertation, with the Latin and English texts on facing pages, rendered by R. S. Hawtrey, *Plato's Theory of Forms and on the Concepts of the Human Mind*, with a Preface by Rosamond Kent Sprague, vol. 2, no. 1 (Spring 1982) of *Ancient Philosophy* (Pittsburgh, Pa., New Image Press, 1982), p. 58. Mr. Shorey's view of Plato's infallibility seems to be discerned in his later *Unity of Plato's Thought* (Chicago, 1904) and climactic volume, *What Plato Said* (Chicago, 1933).

64. Emily James Putnam, "Paul Shorey," *Atlantic Monthly* 161 (Jan.-June 1938): 799. A biography of Mr. Shorey and bibliography of his publications are presently being prepared by John F. Latimer, Professor Emeritus of Classical Languages at George Washington University. (Paul Shorey was regularly addressed by both Faculty and students at the University of Chicago as "Mr." Shorey. After World War I, during his last decade, his classical colleagues, all solid scholars, were in alphabetical order: Charles Henry Beeson, Robert Johnson Bonner, Carl Darling Buck, Gordon

Jennings Laing, Jakob Aall Ottesen Larsen, Henry Washington Prescott, Gertrude Elizabeth Smith, Berthold Louis Ullman. Gertrude Smith was addressed as "Miss" Smith, the others as "Mr." It was assumed that they all possessed the earned Ph. D. To apply the title "Doctor" or even "Professor" this thoroughly professional, superb staff would have regarded as the badge of a fresh-water college.)

65. William Shakespeare, *Hamlet*, act 1, sc. 5, lines 166f. Thus the Stratford Bard is not likely to have agreed with the young men who founded Phi Beta Kappa at the College of William and Mary on Dec. 5, 1776, that philosophy in itself is sufficient as pilot of life; Shakespeare would have made room for the Ten Commandments too.

66. Paul Shorey, *Platonism, Ancient and Modern* (Berkeley, Cal., 1938), p. 67.

67. *Ibid.*, p. 63. The theory of evolution Mr. Shorey labeled "ridiculous," Emily James Putnam, *loc. cit.*, p. 796.

68. Paul Shorey, *Platonism, Ancient and Modern*, p. 72.

69. *Ibid.*, p. 87.

70. As cited by McDonald, *loc. cit.*, p. 49; cf. Hilaire Belloc, *The Elements of the Great War* (New York, 1915), and his *The Crisis of Civilization* (New York, 1937).

71. As reported to the Faculty of Valparaiso University, Indiana, by its President, Dr. Albert G. Huegli.

72. Otto Friedrich, "Five Ways to Wisdom," *Time*, September 27, 1982, p. 70. Cf. Allan Bloom, "Our Listless Universities," *National Review* 34 (Dec. 10, 1982): 1537ff.; Mr. Bloom is a professor of the Committee on Social Thought and of the College at the University of Chicago.

73. When standards are steadily lowered, ultimately there are no remaining standards at all, and the absence of standards is the road to barbarism, to chaos and anarchy.

74. Hor. *Ep.* 2.1.

LOGOS, *MYTHOS* and *URDUMMHEIT*

Jeremiah Reedy

I set out in this essay to explore certain generalizations that have been made about the "world view of the Greeks" and that of ancient Israel, *e.g.* that Greek thought is abstract and static while that of Israel is concrete and dynamic. These generalizations turned out, however, to be the same ones that have been made about the Apollonian and the Dionysian or about *logos* and *mythos*, to use the terms used by the Greeks themselves. While pondering these dichotomies and the relationship between them, I learned of the claim that "Myths mediate contradictions." It became obvious that what was needed was a myth or theory that would resolve the contradictions between *logos* and *mythos* and everything they stand for. This realization led to a number of thoughts about *logos* and the origin of philosophy. At the same time it seemed a good idea to say something about the principle of contradiction before discussing mediation. The essay thus developed forwards and backwards from a central insight. I apologize for the fact that the result reads more like an outline for a book than a conventional essay. There is also a certain unfinished nature to what I have to say, but that is as it should be since no one will ever utter the final word on these subjects. In spite of these reservations I believe the essay contains a number of insights which are worth sharing. I have not found, for instance, in the literature on myth any attempts to determine the relationship between the principle of contradiction and the *coincidentia oppositorum*. Grace Beede will recognize here questions and themes which we discussed when I was a student of hers thirty years ago and a colleague twenty years ago.

Contradiction

The most certain of all principles is the principle of contradictions. According to it, "Being is not non-being." In logic it is stated less abstractedly: "Nothing can have contradictory predicates attributed to it." In ontology it is put this way: "Nothing can possess contradictory objective notes." In plain English: "Nothing can have mutually exclusive characteristics." Plato has Socrates express it this way:

> It is clear that the same thing cannot act in two opposite ways or be in two opposite states at the same time, with respect to the same part of itself, and in relation to the same object. So if we find such contradictory actions or states among the elements concerned, we shall know that more than one must have been involved.

After considering possible objections, he continues:

> No objection of that sort, then, will disconcert us or make us believe that the same thing can ever act or be acted upon in two opposite ways, or be two opposite things, at the same time, in respect of the same part of itself, and in relation to the same object.[1]

In the *Metaphysics* Aristotle writes, "It is impossible that the same [attribute] should at the same time belong and not belong to the same thing under the same respect; this, indeed, is the most certain of all principles."[2] The interested reader can find in the *Encyclopedia of Philosophy* a proof of this principle by a contemporary philosopher.[3]

There is also the principle of identity (Being is being; everything is what it is.) and the principle of excluded middle according to which something either is or is not, and there are no other possibilities. During periods of scepticism and confusion these principles are something a person can cling to. They seem to be immutable, absolute and necessary as well as being irrefragable, irrefutable and indubitable. They provide a sure point of departure for all of our knowing.

Not everyone, however, agrees. We are constantly being told that we in the West think in either/or categories because of the structure of our language or because of the influence of the archfiend Aristotle or for some other flimsy reason. *Zen and the Art of Motorcycle Maintenance*[4] comes to mind as well as *The Making of the Counter Culture*[5] and the works of Korzybski, the founder of what is called "general semantics."[6] These authors along with many others like to think that if Chinese had been Aristotle's native language instead of Greek, his logic would have been totally different, and so would have been the history of Western civilization. For a number of years, on the other hand, I have argued that every utterance however brief in whatever language, spoken in whatever society, be it primitive, archaic, underdeveloped, developing, advanced or whatever, uses the principle of contradiction and is, therefore, an affirmation of it. Even those who say it is false, I have argued, implicitly affirm it since they mean that at the same time and in the same sense it is not also true. Attempts to disprove the principle of contradiction are, as a contemporary French philosopher put it, "autophagic," *i.e.* they self-destruct.[7] Looking at it in another way, if one says *e.g.* that Socrates is alive and not alive at the same time and in the same respect, one predicate cancels the other and no assertion has been made.

Myths Mediate Contradictions

The French anthropologist Lucien Lévy-Bruhl (1857-1939), among others, thought that there had been a pre-logical stage in the evolution of human consciousness. For him "savages," as he called them, were half-witted or better dim-witted and lived like the Cimmerians of Homer's *Odyssey* (XI.13) in perpetual fog and mist.[8] The Germans coined a wonderful word to translate this *mentalité primitive*: *Urdummheit*—"primordial stupidity." The contemporary French thinker Claude Lévi-Strauss, on the other hand, has spent his life refuting the theory of his compatriot Lévy-Bruhl, and according to most authorities, *e.g.* G. S. Kirk, he has succeeded.[9]

Lévi-Strauss thinks that myths mediate contradictions; that they, in other words, attempt to resolve contradictions which trouble people consciously or unconsciously. "Mythical thought always progresses from the awareness of oppositions toward their resolutions," he writes.[10] The Oedipus myth, to give only one example, mediates between the belief that, on the other hand, man is autochthonous (*i.e.* born of the earth) and, on the other hand, the knowledge "that human beings are actually born from the union of man and woman."[11] According to this claim, then, all myths grapple with contradictions such as nature/culture, inside/outside, man's ways/animals's ways, life/death and so forth. It also follows, according to structuralists, that all humans think alive—not only all who are on earth today, but also all humans going back in history as far as we can go. The human mind seems to work like a binary computer, as Kirk puts it, sorting things into pairs of opposites.[12] According to Michael Lane, ". . . there is in man an innate, genetically transmitted and determined mechanism that acts as a structuring force" inclining us to dichotomize, and this belief is attributed not only to Lévi-Strauss but to Chomsky, Piaget, Roman Jakobsen and Francois Jacob, a biologist.[13] "The human espirit is structurally similar at every period and in every kind of society."[14] Reason is everywhere the same. Logic does not differ from society to society; it, like mathematics, is supracultural. "We are all brothers and sisters" say the structuralists, to which I add "We are all also Aristoteleans." I reason this way: All human societies have myths, all myths mediate contradictions, *ergo*, all humans are puzzled by contradictions (*i.e.* know and use, at least implicitly, the principle of contradiction which involves the other two first principles of Aristotelean logic.) But someone may say "mediate" means "to be in the middle," and if myths mediate contradictions, then this disproves the principle of excluded middle, and traditional logic is dethroned at last. But to this objection, Aristotle would say, "Wait a minute. Myths are products of the imagination; the things they speak of do not really exist. Between what is and what is not, there can't be anything. That's why we call these stories myths."

From the assertion, then, that myths mediate contradictions, I conclude that all humans, even the most primitive, are operating with the first principles of logic enunciated by Aristotle and rediscovered by Lévi-Strauss. All are bothered by contradictions; all are puzzled ultimately by the same thing that puzzled Wittgenstein and Heidegger and puzzles all of us from time to time: "How extraordinary that everything should exist!" "How odd that there should be anything; at times it seems that there might have been nothing." Why being and not not-being? All ask the ontological question.

Athens and Jerusalem

Modern scholars have offered a number of generalizations about the "world view of Greeks" over against that of ancient Israel.[15] It has been said, for instance, that for the Greeks ultimate reality was static whereas Israel had a dynamic world view, that Greek thought is abstract while that of Israel is concrete, that time for the Greeks was cyclical, for Israel, linear, and so forth. Now, while I have reservations about these for many reasons (*e.g.* in Greek thought one can find both the static and the dynamic and the abstract and the concrete) these pairs interest me greatly, and I have begun to see them as parts of larger patterns. (Diagram I contains a list of 37 such pairs, only a few of which I shall discuss here. Appendix I contains still more which I have included for comparison.) It seems, for example, that in philosophy itself there are two traditions. There are those who claim that *being* is ultimate and those who say *becoming* or change or process is.[16] In the *Theaetetus* Plato calls the first group the "faction of the whole"—τοῦ ὅλου στασιῶται and the champion of becoming he called οἱ ῥέοντες, "the flowing ones," translated by A. E. Taylor as "men of the flux" and by Jowett as "the river gods." Parmenides is the example *par excellence* of the first group; Heraclitus of the second.

DIAGRAM I

Being	Becoming
Apollo	Dionysus
1. abstract	concrete
2. τοῦ ὅλου στασιῶται (Apollonians)	οἱ ῥέοντες (Dionysians)
3. substance ontology	event ontology
4. Parmenides, Plato, Aristotle	Heraclitus, A. N. Whitehead, Kierkegaard, Sartre, Camus
5. static	dynamic
6. synchronic	diachronic

7. Athens | Jerusalem
8. definitions | narratives
9. *logos* | *mythos*
10. philosophy | poetry
11. timeless truths | history
12. absolutists | relativists
13. stasis | ecstasy
14. *physis* (= raw = nature) | *nomos* (=cooked, =culture)
15. either/or | both/and
16. "lumpers" | "splitters"
17. synthesis | diastasis
18. cognitive | affective
19. knowledge | faith & opinion
20. intellect (intellectualists) | will (voluntarists)
21. ignorance | sin
22. animus | anima
23. classicism | romanticism
24. noun | verb
25. nomothetic | idiographic
26. seeing | hearing
27. contemplative life | active life
28. *l'attitude totalisante* | atomistic[18]
29. discursive | non-discursive
30. theory | method
31. homogeneity | specification[19]
32. rationalism | empiricism
33. matter | energy
34. formalists | intuitionists (Mathematics)[20]
35. insecurity | boredom
36. unity (& rest) | plurality (& motion) (Aristotle)[21]
37. Lévi-Strauss, Jung | Freud[22]

I am going to call those on the left Apollonians and those on the right Dionysians. The Apollonians have a substance ontology, the Dionysians an event ontology. Apollonians love definitions for definitions capture verbally the essences of things. Dionysians despise definitions; they prefer aphorisms, stories, novels, plays, journals—narratives of any sort. After all, it takes a running account to deal with a running reality. The first love of Apollonians is *logos*, rational analysis, rational discourse, reason; the Dionysians love myths. Apollonians seek timeless truths such as "being is being" or "the whole is equal to the sum of its parts;" Dionysians scoff at such things as either trivial or meaningless. Plato speaks of the ancient war between philosophy and poetry.[23] The majority of philosophers certainly belong in the left-hand column, and all poets belong in the right-hand one. I put classicism in the left column and romanticism in the right. Classicism extols decorum, regularity and clarity; the romantic is enamored of license, irregularity, novelty and what is indistinct, suggestive, emotive, associative. Classicists see unity everywhere and try to promote it; they are socio-centered, advocates of community; whereas the romantics are strongly individualistic. They see diversity everywhere.

Stephen Toulmin, a distinguished philosopher from the University of Chicago, in a lecture (as yet unpublished) entitled "The Two Cultures Twenty-five Years Later" argued, *inter alia*, that there have always been two cultures, and beginning with the 17th century, he traced the history of the conflict to the present. There have always been, according to him, those who are interested in the universal, the abstract, the objective, and the absolute, on the one hand, and on the other those who are interested in the particular, the unique, the concrete, the subjective and the relative. This is true not only in the intellectual life in general, but in each particular field. He used anthropolgy as an example. There you have, for instance, Lévi-Strauss, as already indicated, who is concerned with universal rational structures, allegedly found at all times and in all places, whereas the anthropologist Duane Metzger felt called to describe in the greatest detail the classification of fire wood among one small group living in Mexico. (It would not be difficult to think of examples of these intellectual types from our own fields.)

Toulmin could have, however, begun his history of the two cultures much earlier. He could have started with Plato, as I indicated, or he could have begun in the Middle Ages. Then there was a great controversy between the champions of the contemplative life and those of the active life.[24] The former argued that one could serve God and humankind best by withdrawing from the world to a convent or monastery and spending one's days in prayer, meditation, mortification of the flesh and self-denial. On the other hand were those who thought Christians should devote their lives to performing the corporal works of mercy: feeding the hungry, clothing the naked, giving alms to the poor, burying the dead. Each faction supported its position with quotations from Sacred Scripture and the fathers of the church.

On a more abstract level medieval philosophers and theologians argued about the relative roles of the intellect and will. The intellectualists such as Aquinas claimed that the intellect was superior to the will, pointing out that people cannot desire what they do not know and that, therefore, the will is dependant upon the intellect (*Nil volitum nisi prius intellectum.*) Voluntarists such as Duns Scotus argued the reverse; it is the will that directs the attention of the intellect to this or that and consequently the intellect is subservient to the will. The relative role of intellect and will in God was even the subject of debate.

The list of dichotomies of the sort I am discussing could be extended almost indefinitely. We could discuss the cognitive and affective domains, rationalism and empiricism, bees and spiders (used by Jonathan Swift in *The Battle of the Books*). In mathematics there are formalists and intuitionists, and among biologists, if what my students tells me is correct, there are "lumpers" and "splitters." Some people see what is common and abstract; others focus on the concrete differences. In *The Myth of the State* Cassirer quotes Kant who made this same point in *The Critique of Pure Reason*: ". . . there are two groups of scholars and scientists. The one is following the principle of 'homogeneity'; the other the principle of 'specification.' The first endeavors to reduce the most disparate phenomena to a common denominator whereas the other refuses to accept this pretended unity or similarity. Instead of emphasizing the common features it is always looking for the differences."[25]

Let me sum this up in terms resurrected by contemporary sociologists—"nomothetic" and "idiographic." According to them, in every group there will be, on the one hand, those who want to do things rationally and logically, who think that *discipline* is the answer to all problems, who want to define everything explicitly and with the greatest clarity; and there will be, on the other hand, those who want immediate gratification, who think that *freedom* is the answer. These latter prefer ambiguity and uncertainty; they despise definitions and restrictions and are inclined to leave things vague and fuzzy. Of course, in each camp there is a spectrum and some moderate nomothetic Apollonians approach the position of the moderate idiographic Dionysians and *vice versa*.

Digression on the Meaning of Logos *and on the Difference Between First Awareness and Second Awareness*

According to Guthrie, in the fifth century B.C. and earlier *logos* had the following meanings:[26]

1.) Anything said or "written," *e.g.* a story, narrative, speech or conversation.
2.) Worth, esteem, reputation, fame.
3.) Thought or reasoning (from the notion of conversing with one's self).
4.) Cause, reason, argument.
5.) The truth of a matter, *e.g.* the real *logos*.
6.) Measure, due measure.
7.) Relation, proportion.
8.) General principle or rule.
9.) The faculty of reason. *Logos* is what distinguishes man from other animals.
10.) Definition or formula expressing the essential nature of anything.
11.) Miscellaneous.

In this paper I use *logos* in sense #9, *viz.* the faculty of reason, the ability to think logically and analytically. The first and third meanings may at times by relevant also since they are closely related. Number nine is the faculty, three the process and one the product.

Consider the following quotations:

> But in the understanding of recent philosophical thought, man's psychic life, however, exhibits a peculiar character which animals do not appear even in part to share. For man is the being who is present to himself. This presence of his being to himself is called consciousness.
>
> ... the nature of [human] consciousness, and man's radical distinction from the animal, would be

mistakenly expressed in the formula "Man not only knows, but knows that he knows." For the point is not that man, who can know beings other than himself, can also be an object of knowledge for himself. It is not that man can "reflect," that is, make his own (previous) act of knowledge the object of a (new) act of knowledge, and thus know that he is a knower. The point is that in the very act of knowing on object (whether a being other than himself, or the being which is himself) he becomes present to himself. Man does not require a further act of re-flection in order to be conscious. From the outset of consciousness he is *already* present to his own being. The animal's being, on the other hand, is neither in a first or in a reflective act present to itself . . .[27]

Dewart has very neatly made a distinction which I think is crucial for this discussion, *viz.* that between first awareness and second awareness. By the former I mean what Dewart calls "being present" to one's self, *i.e.* being conscious.[28] By second awareness I mean reflexion, *i.e.* "bending back" thought upon thought or upon one's existence. A human can go through a day driving a car, working, eating, conversing, playing the piano, *etc.*—carrying out many complex tasks without reflecting on what he is doing. In the evening one can sit down and reflect on the day's activities and discover that all day one was "present to himself" although he did not advert to it. This is the difference between first awareness and second awareness, the latter of which has also often been described as "introspection." I believe that Julian Jaynes in his *Origin of Consciousness in the Breakdown of the Bicameral Mind*[29] is discussing the origin of first awareness and that Snell, for the most part, is discussing the evolution of second awareness although neither author uses this terminology.[30] I am interested in the differences between *mythos*, *logos*, and second awareness; and so was Cornford and Burnett and Zeller and everyone else who has written about *logos* and *mythos* although to date no one has distinguished carefully between *logos* (logical thought) which may be concrete or abstract and second awareness (reflective, introspective thought) which is always abstract and which is philosophical thought. *Mythos* and *logos* may exist with or without first awareness, but obviously second awareness is impossible without first awareness. Second awareness made possible the "birth of philosophy," and, although there was clearly a pre-philosophical stage in the evolution of human consciousness, there never was a pre-logical one, *logos* being precisely what distinguished the first humans from their non-human ancestors. Jaynes has raised an entirely new question.

Solution to the Problem of Relationship Between the "Opposites" in Diagram I

There seems to be universal agreement that in humans there are two realms or domains, *logos* and *mythos*. In the first, the first principle is the principle of contradiction which says that opposites can never be united. In the other, the *mythos* domain, opposites are always united and the "first principle" is the *coincidentia oppositorum*, the unity of opposites. If myths mediate contradictions, then they always assert the unity of opposites, *i.e.* that truth is contradictory (not merely paradoxical because paradoxes can be resolved, but contradictions can't). But one wants to know which of these principles is true. Which obtains outside the mind, in extramental reality? Does reality have a rational structure and do the rules of logic correspond to the laws of nature or is there no such correspondence? If we choose the principle of contradiction, then the unity of opposites is incoherent nonsense, but if we choose the *coincidentia oppositorum*, then we can have both. It can unite itself to its opposite. This is the only case where the antithesis can also be the synthesis, and Heraclitus was right! There is change, but there is also the *logos*. Either/or and both/and are mediated by both/and, and this is an adumbration of the solution to the problem of the relationship between the Apollonian and the Dionysian.

The schema in Diagram I has the *imprimatur* of a distinguished philosopher; it is, he said, basically sound, and he wanted to add to the list. But reflection upon the relationship between *logos* and *mythos* has convinced me that revision is necessary. The reason is simple: being and becoming are not polar opposites. The opposite of being is non-being, and becoming mediates between being and non-being. Research reveals that Plato discussing becoming said this rather explicitly in the *Republic*: "Now if there is something so constituted that it both is and is not, will it not lie between the purely real and the utterly real?"[31] Becoming is, as it were, a mixture of being and non-being. Becoming is a process in which some things seem to pop into existence while others lapse into non-being. One thinks of the green apple that becomes red.[32] Having realized the true relationship between being, becoming and non-being, we need a new diagram; see Diagram II.

DIAGRAM II

```
                    Becoming
          Being  /            \  Non-being
```

	Being	Becoming	Non-being
Symbols	Apollo	Dionysus (god of suprarational)	Hades (or Dionysus god of irrational)
Modes of thought	logos	mythos	Urdummheit
Ontology	substance	event	nihilism
Representative figures	Parmenides	Heraclitus	Gorgias, Cratylus
Types of truth	absolute truth	relative truth	absolute error
Certitude	knowledge	faith/opinion	ignorance
Art	classicism	romanticism	theater of absurd
Physics	matter	energy	antimatter or nothingness
Ancient atomism	atoms	motion	void
Sociologist	nomothetic	idiographic	anarchist
Jung	animus	anima	?

Almost everything in the right hand column of Diagram I must now be moved to the middle, but let us put the irrational on the right and the supra-rational in the middle. *Mythos* lies between *logos* and *Urdummheit*. Between yes and no, myth stands as a "maybe." Not only does each myth mediate a contradiction, but mythopoesis is an expression of becoming and mediates the ultimate contradiction, that between being and non-being, between life and death, between *eros* and *thanatos*.[33] Everyone has forgotten about non-being and nihilism. In philosophy as in everything else, things come in threes, not twos. As George Steiner says in *After Babel*, "when analyzing complex structures, human thought favors triads."[34] There is matter, energy and anti-matter; atoms, motion and void; Mother Earth, *Eros* and Father Sky. In other words, we do appear to sort things into pairs of opposites and then seek a third thing, a *tertium quid*, that will bridge the gap. Here is the ontological foundation for all of these triads: something either is or it isn't (being and non-being). If it is, it either changes or it doesn't. This gives us static being, non-being and becoming as ultimate categories, and there do not appear to be others.

Jerusalem stands for faith, and faith like Plato's "opinion" lies between knowledge and ignorance, at least as far as certitude is concerned. Everything else in the middle is also a "mixture" of opposites. The static is somehow contained in the dynamic, the abstract in the concrete, nature in culture, the synchronic in the diachronic, theory in method, and a responsible active life supposed prior contemplation or else it will be just meaningless activity. The empiricist is a rationalist but doesn't know it and so forth. Implicit in *mythos* from the very beginning was *logos*.

I believe that Nietzche went through a reasoning process similar to the one described in the last few pages. Kaufmann explains it this way:

> They [Hegel and Nietzche] assumed the metaphysical inquiry has not been pushed to the limits as long as a thinker is confronted with two or more principles. Ultimately, any duality has to be explained in terms of a single force.[35]

> Both thinkers [Hegel and Nietzche] postulated a single basic force whose very essence is to manifest itself in diverse ways and to create multiplicity—not *ex nihilo*, but out of itself.[36]

The "Dionysian" of the *Götzen-Dämmerung* is no longer that of *The Birth of Tragedy*. In his early work, Nietzsche tended toward a dualistic metaphysics, and the Dionysian was conceived as a flood of passion to which the Apollinian principle of individuation might give form. In the "dithyrambs" of *Zarathrustra* this opposition of the two gods was repudiated, and the will to power was proclaimed as the one and only basic force of the universe. This fundamental principle, which Nietzsche still called "Dionysian" is actually a union of Dionysus and Apollo: a creative striving which gives form to itself.[37]

Dionysus has become "Lord of the Universe"—he has succeeded Zeus as, according to Detienne, some Orphics taught he would.[38] And how appropriate that Dionysus and Apollo should have shared the shrine at Delphi! Dionysus, the incarnation of the *coincidentia oppositorum* unites himself to his opposite Apollo. The significance of this is that *logos* and *mythos*, reason and faith, philosophy and revelation, Athens and Jerusalem are not mutually exclusive; they are complementary, and one can embrace both parts of each pair without contradiction. I conclude by stating seven theses which I trust will make my point clearer.

Conclusion

Thesis I. Logos was abstracted (*i.e.* "pulled away," separated, extracted, differentiated) from *mythos* by the Greeks in the sixth century B. C. It is convenient to think of Thales as the first philosopher (and scientist) although as Simplicius says "he had many predecessors, as also Theophrastus thinks, but so far surpassed them as to blot out all who came before him."[39] Appendix II below lists some differences between myth and philosophy; Appendix III gives factors which no doubt contributed to the birth of philosophy in Miletus in the 6th century. Space does not allow us to discuss either subject here since our task is to try to understand what the phrase "the birth of philosophy" means. Snell speaks of the "Discovery of the Mind,"[40] Kirk of the transition from "mythopoeic to rational modes of thought,"[41] Frankfort of the "emancipation of thought from myth,"[42] Detienne of "the lofty path from natural to philosophical consciousness,"[43] Lloyd of "informal logic," "archaic logic," and "formal logic,"[44] and Lévi-Strauss of the *"bouleversement"* (=overthrow) of mythic consciousness.[45] Clearly there is a consensus that there was a "change of mind" in ancient Greece!

LOGOS, MYTHOS, AND URDUMMHEIT

If, as Ruesch and Kees think, "man thinks simultaneously in two different ways,"[46] philosophy was born when humans learned to inhibit, at least for a time, the non-discursive, intuitive mode and think only in a discursive way. Hence, as Snell has emphasized, *logos* was not invented; it was discovered. It had been present from the beginning implicitly and in germ just as North America existed before Columbus discovered it.[47] Putting it another way, philosophy was born when men identified the first principles of *logos*, the principles of contradiction, identity and excluded middle and rejected the *coincidentia oppositorum* of *mythos*, and this is precisely what Vernant says:

> La naissance de la philosophie apparaît donc solidaire de deux grandes transformations mentales: une pensée positive, excluant toute forme de surnaturel et rejetant l'assimilation implicite établie par le mythe entre phénomènes physiques et agents divins; une pensée abstraite dépouillant la réalité de cette puissance de changement que lui pretait le mythe, et récusant l'antique image de l'union des opposés au profit d'une formulation catégorique du principe d'identité.[48]

The discovery of grammar provides a model although I readily admit that this analogy, like all analogies, "limps." (*Omne simile clauditat*.) Just as people spoke languages for thousands (millions?) of years in the "pre-grammatical" age without realizing or reflecting upon the fact that their language had a structure and rules that governed, *e.g.* the use of cases, tenses, voices, *etc.*, so people in the pre-philosophical period thought and thought logically (in a concrete way) although they did not reflect on what they were doing. Once the first grammarians made explicit the rules that had been implicit from the birth of language and developed a vocabulary for discussing the structure of language (nominative case, passive voice, *etc.*) everyone endowed with sufficient intelligence began to be able to think about language and to discuss grammar. The rules of grammar must have been identified by comparing a large number of examples and abstracting from them what was common while ignoring the accidental differences. So too, once the first philosophers had begun to think abstractly and reflectively and had begun to look for the "one" behind the "many" and developed a vocabulary for discussing and thinking about such things, then others learned quickly to do likewise. As Leslie Dewart puts it:

> ... growth in consciousness typically comports the experience of knowing clearly now that which, as we "come to think of it," we had been aware of all along, even before we "reflected" on it, and yet had somehow managed not to notice. Consciousness develops as we become conscious of that which, in a sense, we already were conscious of.[49]

It seems to me that one should not underestimate the importance of developing a vocabulary for thinking and discussing abstract concepts, and Snell has rightly stressed the important role played by the definite article in Greek. The existence of the definite article made it possible to make abstract nouns from adjectives and verbs (the hot, the dry, seeing, hearing) and these substantives "in the field of philosophy and science serve as the stable objects of our thinking."[50]

Finally, if there is any truth in Jaynes' theory (and I think it must be taken seriously), we understand why it took so long for humans to develop the ability to think abstractly and reflectively: second awareness is impossible without first awareness. These developments are perhaps paralleled by the conquest of the Titans, the birth of Dionysus, the birth of Apollo, and the synthesis of the Apollonian and the Dionysian in Dionysus.

Thesis II. There was at least one significant change in consciousness in ancient Greece, and it made both philosophy and science possible. Philosophy *stricte dicta* apparently spread from Greece elsewhere; it does not seem to have evolved independently in other places.[51]

Thesis III. It is silly to lament the loss of mythic consciousness, especially if Jaynes is correct since for thousands of centuries people would have lived like ants (or robots) with no inner life and no ability to consciously enjoy life. We (and society) are better off with two modes of thought. The question, I suppose, is has thinking rationally and abstractly impaired our (*i.e.* Western man's) ability to think intuitively. I say, even if it has, the loss is worth it.

Thesis IV. One should not deplore reasoning with dichotomies; there is apparently no other way to reason.

Thesis V. In a sense Apollo (*i.e.* the Apollonian) was the "late comer" to Greek (and human) thought, not Dionysus. ". . . Dionysus himself lived in Delphi with Apollo . . . not only did he enjoy equal rights but was the actual lord of the sacred place. One could even maintain that Dionysus had been in Delphi earlier than Apollo."[52]

Thesis VI. All real problems are dilemmas. All real problems involve mutually exclusive concepts or courses of action. If they are not mutually exclusive, there is no real problem.

Thesis VII. Not only do myths mediate contradictions, theories of all sorts do too and so do philosophies and theologies and scientific hypotheses. Lévi-Strauss' own theory was developed to resolve the problem that results from the fact that the content of myth seems arbitrary and contingent, on the other hand, and yet, on the other hand, there are striking similarities in myths from various parts of the world.[53] One could go through the history of western philosophy, beginning with Thales and the problem of the one and the many, and show that each philosopher developed his or her system to resolve a dilemma. In theology, too, all the controversies have dealt with reason and faith, free will and God's foreknowledge, *homoiousia* or *homoousia*, infant baptism vs. baptism of adults and so forth. In science we are told that Einstein was searching for a "general field theory" which would resolve the contradiction between the theory of relativity and that of quantum mechanics.[54]

Let me conclude with what may be a surprise ending. Being by definition refers to everything that is; but if becoming exists, and it surely does, it must be included within being. A "mixture of being and non-being" will not be less real than "pure being" since non-being neither adds nor subtracts anything. The notion that becoming exists apart from being is, therefore, a myth; it is held between being and non-being by will and imagination. The conclusion is inescapable: There will be an end to time, and Dionysus must die.

APPENDIX I

Table of Oppositions of the Pythagoreans

1. limit, unlimited
2. odd, even
3. one, plurality
4. right, left
5. square, oblong
6. good, bad
7. male, female
8. resting, moving
9. straight, curved
10. light, darkness

Of these, numbers 1, 3, 7 and 8 clearly fit into my scheme; further study would be required to explain the others which appear *prima facie* to be based on Pythagorean "value judgments."[55]

Yin	Yang[56]
shady side of house	sunny side of house
darkness	daylight
cold	warmth
female	male
night	day
moon	sun
earth	heavens
west	east
north	south
soft	hard
heavy	light
weak	strong
behind	in front
below	above
right	left
death	life
common	noble
sorrow	joy
poverty	wealth
misery	honor
ignominy	celebrity
rejection	love
loss	profit

A "Potpourri of Dichotomies"[57]

Suggested by

C. S. Smith	atomistic	gross
Price	analytic or reductionist	synthetic or concrete
Wilder	numerical	geometric
Head	symbolic or systematic	perceptual or non-verbal
Goldstein	abstract	concrete
Reusch	digital or discursive	analogic or eidetic
Bateson & Jackson	digital	analogic
J. Z. Young	abstract	map-like
Pribram	digital	analogic
W. James	differential	existential
Spearman	education of relations	education of correlates
Hodges	directed	free or unordered
Freud	secondary process	primary process
Pavlov	second signalling	first signalling
Sechenow (Luria)	successive	simultaneous
Lévi-Strauss	positive	mythic
Bruner	rational	metaphoric
Akhilinanda	Buddhi	Manas
Radhakrishnan	rational	integral

APPENDIX II

SOME DIFFERENCES BETWEEN MYTH AND PHILOSOPHY:

Myth	Philosophy
Found in traditional societies	Found in non-traditional ones[58]
Has I/thou relation with nature	I/it relation[59]
Looks to supernatural for explanations	World to be understood in its own terms. Rejected supernatural (to an extent)[60]

Asserts unity of opposites	Contradictions cannot be true simultaneously
Emotional associations	Logical consistency becomes a virtue[61]
Appeals to emotion and reason	Appeals to reason only
Fantastic & poetical	"Factual gains upper hand over fantastic"[62]
Personifications	Concepts
Involves majority	Only a minority involved
Stories with plots	Arguments, definitions, hypotheses
Myths, like dreams, occur without control of will.	Involves disciplined search for truth[63]
Found in oral societies	Found in literate societies[64]
Myths have special visual (pictorial) quality.	Works with concepts
Myths are accepted uncritically	Allegedly provable; philosophy initiates a continuing dialogue. Progress results.[65]
Concrete and specific	Abstract and general
"extrospective"	introspective
diachronic	synchronic
Provide *exempla* for behavior[66]	Ethics

La naissance de la philosophie apparait donc solidaire de deux grandes transformations mentales: une pensée

APPENDIX III
"WHY MILETUS?"

Factors which may have contributed to the emergence of philosophy in Miletus in the sixth century B.C.

1. Prosperity, materialism and leisure
2. Curiosity and wonder
3. Freedom of thought and expression
4. Contact with other societies revealed the "relativity of religious representations." (Consider Xenophanes.)

LOGOS, MYTHOS, AND URDUMMHEIT

5. Landscape, sea, quality of light[67]
6. Disenchantment with Olympian gods. Pessimism.
7. Urban society. Alienation from nature.
8. Presocratic thought not exegetical.[68]
9. The invention of writing.

NOTES

1. Plato, *Republic*, trans. by F. Cornford (New York: Oxford U. Press, 1957) pp. 132-133.

2. J. A. Smith and W. D. Ross, eds. *The Works of Aristotle*, Vol. VIII *Metaphsics* (Oxford: Clarendon Press, 1908) Bk. IV, Chapter iii.

3. S. Körner, "Laws of Thought," *The Encyclopedia of Philosophy* (New York: Macmillan, 1967) Vol. IV, p. 416.

4. Robert M. Pirsig (New York: Wm. Morrow & Co., 1974).

5. Theodore Roszak (Garden City: Doubleday, 1969) Chapters VII & VIII.

6. See esp. *Science and Sanity, An Introduction to Non-aristotelean Systems and General Semantics* (Lakeville, Conn.: Institute of General Semantics, 1958).

7. J. Maritain, *Distinguish to Unite* (New York: Scribner's, 1959).

8. *How Natives Think*, trans. L. A. Claire (London, 1926); *Primitive Mentality*, trans. by L. A. Claire (London, 1923) and *passim* in G. S. Kirk's works on myth.

9. G. S. Kirk, *Nature of Greek Myths* (Baltimore: Penguin Books, 1974) pp. 42, 74 and *Myth, Its Meaning and Functions* (Cambridge: University Press, 1971) p. 246.

10. As quoted in Kirk, *Myth*, p. 44.

11. Claude Lévi-Strauss, "The Structural Study of Myth," in *Myth: A Symposium*, ed. by Thomas Sebeok (Philadelphia: American Folklore Society, 1955) p. 92.

12. Kirk, *Nature of Greek Myths*, p. 81.

13. Michael Lane, *Introduction to Structuralism* (New York: Basic Books, 1970) p. 15.

14. Kirk, *Nature of Greek Myths*, p. 81.

15. See for example James Muilenburg, *The Way of Israel* (New York: Harper & Row, 1961) and Thorlief Boman, *Hebrew Thought Compared with Greek* (New York: Norton & Co., 1960).

16. On the meaning of being and becoming, see the relevant articles in the *Encyclopedia of Philosophy* or J. Macquarrie, *Principles of Christian Theology* (New York: Scribner, 1966) p. 111.

17. Plato, *Theaetetus* 179d in the *Works of Plato*, ed. by I. Edman (New York: Modern Library, 1928) p. 531 ff.

18. Lane, pp. 34-35.

19. See below note 25.

20. Wm. Barrett, *The Illusions of Technique* (Garden City: Anchor Press) p. 89.

21. *Metaphysics*, Book IV, Chapter II.

22. Charles Segal, "Pentheus on the Couch and on the Grid: Psychological and Structuralist Readings of Greek Tragedy," *The Classical World*, Vol. 73, 3 (November 1978) pp. 129 ff.

23. *Republic*, Bk. Ten 607b (Cornford p. 339). For a discussion of this "longstanding quarrel" see W. Kaufmann, *Tragedy and Philosophy* (New York: Doubleday, 1968) Chap. I.

24. Cuthbert Butler, *Western Mysticism* (New York: Harper & Row, 1966) p. 155 ff.

25. E. Cassirer, *The Myth of the State* (New Haven: Yale Univ. Press, 1969) p. 6.

26. W. K. G. Guthrie, *A History of Greek Philosophy* (Cambridge: Univ. Press, 1967) p. 420.

27. L. Dewart, *The Future of Belief* (New York: Herder & Herder, 1966) pp. 80-81.

28. Consciousness, according to Bernard Lonergan, means the "awareness immanent in cognitional acts." *Insight* (New York: Harper & Row, 1978) p. 320.

29. (Boston: Houghton Mifflin, 1976).

30. *The Discovery of the Mind*, trans. by T. Rosenmeyer (New York: Harper & Row, 1960).

31. *Republic* 477 (Cornford p. 184); see also Macquarrie, p. 111.

32. Kerenyi says that same thing about life: "Thus, death and the destruction of life would be a part of life itself." *Dionysus, Archetypal Image of Indestructible Life* (Princeton Univ. Press, 1976) p. 204. See also *Phaedo* 70d where Socrates argues that as a general principle "opposites come to be out of opposites" (faster from slower, waking from sleep, greater from less, etc.) and W. Otto, *Dionysus, Myth and Cult* (Bloomington; Indiana U. Press, 1965) pp. 189-190.

LOGOS, MYTHOS, AND URDUMMHEIT

33. For an assertion of the unity of *eros* and *thanatos* see Norman O. Brown, *Life Against Death* (Middletown: Wesleyan U. Press, 1959).

34. George Steiner, *After Babel* (London: Oxford U. Press, 1975) p. 253.

35. Walter Kaufmann, *Nietzsche* (New York: Meridian, 1956) p. 206.

36. *ibid.* p. 207.

37. *ibid.* p. 245. Parmenides may have reasoned in somewhat the same way since he set out to speak of two ways and spoke of three.

38. Marcel Detienne, *Dionysos Slain* (Baltimore: Johns Hopkins Press, 1979) p. 88.

39. Kirk & Raven, *The Presocratic Philosophers* (Cambridge: Univ. Press, 1957) p. 84.

40. The subtitle of his book is *The Greek Origins of European Thought*.

41. *Myth*, p. 238.

42. Henri Frankfort *et al.*, *Before Philosophy* (Baltimore: Penguin Books, 1967) p. 237.

43. *op. cit.* p. ix.

44. G. Lloyd, *Polarity and Analogy: Two Types of Argumentation in Early Greek Thought* (Cambridge: Univ. Press, 1966) p. 3.

45. As quoted by Detienne, p. 1 and Kirk, *Myth*, p. 238.

46. Robert Ornstein, *The Nature of Human Consciousness* (W. H. Freeman, 1968) p. 121.

47. Snell, p. viii.

48. Jean Pierre Vernant, *Mythe et pensée chez les Grecs* (Paris: François Maspero, 1971) p. 106.

49. *The Future of Belief*, p. 84.

50. p. 229.

51. "No other people—not the Chinese, not the Hindus—produced *theoretical* science, and its discovery or invention by the Greeks has been what has distinguished Western civilization from the other civilizations of the globe." W. Barrett, *Irrational Man* (Garden City: Doubleday, 1958) p. 64.

52. Otto, p. 203.

53. "The Structural Study of Myth" p. 83.

54. *Time Magazine*, September 10, 1979, p. 42.

55. Lloyd, p. 16.

56. Lloyd, p. 35.
57. Ornstein, p. 119.
58. Kirk, *Nature of Greek Myths*, p. 27.
59. Frankfort, Chapter I.
60. Vernant, p. 106.
61. Kirk, *op. cit.* p. 278.
62. Kirk, *op. cit.* p. 278.
63. Kirk, *op. cit.* p. 282.
64. Kirk, *op. cit.* p. 278.
65. Frankfort, p. 251.
66. Kirk, *op. cit.* pp. 108, 289-93, 301.
67. C. M. Bowra, *The Greek Experience* (New York: New American Library, 1957) p. 23.
68. W. Kaufmann, *Philosophic Classics* (Englewood Cliffs: Prentice-Hall, Inc., 1968) p. 1.

NOTES ON CONTRIBUTORS

Daniel L. Arnaud is currently on the staff of Groton School, Groton, Massachusetts. A graduate of Groton and Carleton College, he received the M.A. from the University of South Dakota and the Ph.D. from Stanford. Before returning to Groton, he taught at Lawrence University, Appleton, Wisconsin, was Executive Director of the Thomas J. Watson Foundation, Vice President of the Salzburg Seminar and Managing Director of Earthwatch Expeditions.

Herbert W. Benario, Professor of Classics at Emory University, has been president of the Classical Association of the Middle West and South and the Vergilian Society of America. He has published a translation of *Tacitus Agricola, Germany, Dialogue on Orators* (1967) and is the author of *An Introduction to Tacitus* (1975), *A Commentary on the Vita Hadriani in the Historia Augusta* (1980), and *Tacitus Annals 11 and 12* (1983). He was a Fellow of the American Council of Learned Societies in 1978 and the recipient of an OVATIO from CAMWS in 1979.

Carrie Cowherd received her A.B. from Indiana University and her M.A. and Ph.D. from the University of Chicago. From 1967 to 1970 she taught at the University of South Dakota with Grace Beede who showed, by her example, what a teacher should be and do. Subsequently, she taught at the University of Wisconsin-Milwaukee. She is now at Howard University, where she is Director of the Humanities Program and Director of the Honors Program, in addition to her position in Classics. Current interests include Persius, Euripides, and Aristophanes.

Gertrude C. Drake was graduated from Cornell University in 1930 specializing in English and classics. She obtained the degree of M.A. from Chicago University in 1931. She studied Chaucer with John Manly, Shakespeare under Professor Baskerville, and Roman comedy under Henry W. Prescott. Her doctorate, obtained from Cornell in 1939, was directed by Lane Cooper, Harry Caplan, and James Hutton. Her latest position was Professor of the Humanities at Southern Illinois University at Edwardsville. She retired in 1977.

Gerald F. Else (1908-1982) was born in Redfield, South Dakota. He received his A.B., M.A. and Ph.D. from Harvard where he taught from 1935 to 1943. As Captain, U.S.M.C.R., 1943-45, he served with the Office of Strategic Services in Washington, D.C., Egypt, Greece, Italy and Liberia. He was chairman of the Department of Classics, State University of Iowa from 1945 until 1957 and of the University of Michigan's Classics Department from 1957 until his retirement in 1976. One of this country's most distinguished classicists, Dr. Else was President of the Classical Association of the Middle West and South (1955-56) and of the American Philological Association (1964). He was a Fulbright Senior Research Scholar at the American Academy in Rome, a Fellow of the American Academy of Arts and Sciences, a Senior Fellow of the Center for Hellenic Studies, Washington, D.C., and a member of the National Council on the Humanities. From 1969-76 he directed the Center for the Coordination of Ancient and Modern Studies at the University of Michigan. Among the many honors he received were honorary degrees from the University of South Dakota (1975) and the University of Nebraska (1976). He is the author of numerous articles and monographs and two seminal works: *Aristotle's Poetics: The Argument* and *The Origin* and *Early Form of Greek Tragedy*.

Born in New England in the first year of this century, **Clarence Allen Forbes** was educated by omnivorous reading and by slow degrees (from Bates College and the University of Illinois). After teaching the classics for fifty-three years at one college and seven universities, he was in 1971 put out to pasture, where he grazes unobtrusively on the meadows of asphodel.

Brent M. Froberg, Associate Professor of Classics at the University of South Dakota, succeeded Grace Beede and served as chairman of the Department of Classics from 1970, the year of Dr. Beede's retirement from classroom teaching, until 1981. Professor Froberg who holds B.A. and M.A. degrees in Classics from Indiana University and a Ph.D. degree in Classics from The Ohio State University, taught for one year (1968-69) in the Classics

Department of The University of Tennessee and is currently executive secretary of Eta Sigma Phi, National Honorary Classical Fraternity.

Dionysios A. Kounas, a native of Sioux City, Iowa, matriculated in 1959 at the University of South Dakota where he majored in History, Classical Greek, and Political Science with Honors Curriculum Minors. He achieved numerous academic distinctions and was graduated *cum laude* in 1963. As a Woodrow Wilson Fellow, he entered graduate study at the University of Illinois and with the aid of a University of Illinois Fellowship, he completed the M.A. degree in Classical Greek and Ancient History in the summer of 1964. Two years later he successfully completed the preliminary doctoral examinations and became the recipient of a Woodrow Wilson Ph.D. Dissertation Fellowship for 1966-67. His Ph.D. in Ancient Greek History and Classical Greek was awarded in 1969. Since 1967, he has taught numerous courses in these areas at the University of Kansas, where he currently holds the position of Associate Professor of Greek History. Professor Kounas has journeyed to Greece many times and in 1973 spent six months there researching as a N.E.H. Younger Humanist Fellow. He has also presented a number of papers at conferences and is author of several works. His two most noted publications are his editions of *Pericles Son of Athens* and *The Silver Mines of Laurion*.

John Francis Latimer was born in Clinton, Mississippi in 1903. He received the B.A. (1922) and Litt.D. (1964) from Mississippi College, the Master's from the University of Chicago (1926), and the Ph.D. from Yale (1929). Before coming to The George Washington University in 1936, he had been a high school teacher-coach and principal, an instructor at Vanderbilt, a Master at the Taft School in Watertown, Conn., an assistant professor at Knox College, and an associate professor at Drury College. Before retiring as Professor Emeritus of Classics from George Washington in 1973, in addition to teaching and chairing the department, he had served as assistant and associate Dean of Faculties, Director of Foreign Student Affairs, and for sixteen years as University Marshal. Currently he is president of the Society of the Emeriti at the University.

He is a member of the AIA and life member of APA. He was president of the CAAS (1955-57), and president (1960-66) and Executive Secretary (1966-73) of the American Classical League. He has published numerous papers in classical periodicals and is the author of *What's Happened to Our High Schools?* (1958) and editor of a reprinted edition of *A Life of George Washington in Latin Prose, A Grammatical and Historical Commentary*, and, with 29 colleagues, of *A Composite Translation*, all published in 1976.

A naval officer in World War II, he served on board the heavy cruiser Quincy (Battleship X) in the Atlantic and Pacific Fleets, rising to the rank of Commander, and is now Captain USNR (Ret.) He and his wife, the former Helen Blundon, make their home in Washington.

Richard Luman, a native of Ottumwa, Iowa, earned the B.A., M.A. and Ph.D. degrees from the State University of Iowa. He did post-doctoral work at Harvard, Yale and in the Vatican Library. Professor Luman has taught at U.S.D., the University of Chicago and Haverford College where he is currently Associate Professor of Religion. He has held visiting professorships at Princeton Theological Seminary, St. Joseph's College and Columbia University. Author of over 200 book reviews, Richard Luman is widely known in this country and Europe as an authority on life and culture in the Middle Ages. Among his special interests is medieval Icelandic literature.

Jeremiah Reedy, a native of South Dakota, grew up in Vermillion, graduating from Vermillion High School in 1952. After earning his bachelor's degree in Italy, he was awarded an M.A. from the University of South Dakota (1960) and an M.A. (1964) and Ph.D. (1968) from the University of Michigan. He taught classics at the University of South Dakota with Grace Beede from 1959 to 1962 and from 1964 to 1966. Since 1968 he has been a member of the faculty of Macalester College in St. Paul, Minnesota where he is Professor of Classics, Chairman of the Department and Coordinator of the Humanities Program.

Among his publications are *Boccacio, In Defense of Poetry, Articulating the Ineffable: Approaches to the Teaching of Humanities*, and articles in various classical journals. His interests include classical linguistics, Greek philosophy, and the relationship between Greek thought and Christianity. Professor Reedy has been a student, colleague, neighbor and life-long friend and admirer of Grace Beede.

A graduate of the Chicago Latin School, **Edgar Reinke** earned the baccalaureate and doctoral degrees in Greek and Latin at the University of Chicago and the master's degree in librarianship at the University of Minnesota. From 1937 to 42 and 1946 to 49 he taught at Alabama State College for Women, Montevallo. During World War II he served in the European Military of the United States as bilingual translator and cryptanalyst. From 1949 to his retirement in 1975 he taught as Professor of Classical Languages at Valparaiso University, Indiana. He now resides in Florida. Professor Reinke is the author of two volumes and a number of professional articles and reviews.

Raymond V. Schoder, S.J. is Professor Emeritus of Classical Studies at Loyola University, Chicago, where he has taught graduate courses in Greek and Latin literature and Classical Art and Archaeology since 1951. He earned his Ph.D. in Classical Studies from St. Louis University (1944) and the S.T.L. degree in theology from West Baden Pontifical University. After entering the Society of Jesus in 1933, he was ordained in 1947. Father Schoder travelled extensively abroad through most of the ancient classical world and took over 17,000 color slides for use in teaching, lecturing and publications. His books include: *A Reading Course in Homeric Greek*, *Masterpieces of Greek Art*, *Ancient Greece from the Air* and *Landscape and Inscape* (photos of places and things in the poems of G.M. Hopkins), and he is author of nearly 200 articles for classical and other journals. His photos have been used in 250 books to illustrate history, art and archaeology. He has lectured widely for the A.I.A. at colleges, universities and academic groups in the U.S. and in Athens, Rome, London, Leiden, Ankara, Istanbul, Tokyo, Bonn and Rio de Janeiro. Father Schoder served many times as director of summer programs in classical archaeology in the Cumae area and in Sicily and Rome for the Vergilian Society.

Winton U. Solberg was born and reared in Aberdeen, South Dakota. He earned a bachelor's degree with high honors at the University of South Dakota, concentrating in History and in Political Science. Immediately upon graduation he entered the U.S. Army for over three years, during which time he served as an infantry officer in combat in Germany for seven months. He earned a Ph.D. in American History from Harvard University, and taught at the U.S. Military Academy at West Point, Yale University, and Macalester College in St. Paul, Minnesota, before joining the faculty at the University of Illinois. He has also been a Fulbright professor in Bologna, Italy (1967-68) and at Moscow University in the Soviet Union (1978), and in 1981 was a Visiting Professor at Konan University in Kobe, Japan. A specialist in American Intellectual and Cultural History, Professor Solberg is the author of *The Federal Convention and the Formation of the American Union*; *The University of Illinois, 1867-1894: An Intellectual and Cultural History*; and *Redeem the Time: The Puritan Sabbath in Early America*. He and his wife, the parents of three children, live in Urbana, Illinois.

Judith Lynn Sebesta is currently Professor of Classics at the University of South Dakota. She is the author of *Carl Orff Carmina Burana Cantiones Profanae: Original Text with Introduction, Facing Vocabularies and Study Materials* (Lawall Publications, 1983) for intermediate Latin classes. Her other interests include methodology, computer assisted instruction and the late Roman poet Claudian.

James E. Spaulding, following graduate studies at the *Institut universitaire de hautes études internationales* and Stetson University, received his Ph.D. in medieval history from Duke University. Since 1967, he has been a member of the History Department of the University of South Dakota. Author of a basic text on numismatics and articles and papers on numismatic art and the application of numismatic evidence to historical studies, he is currently completing a book-length work on the theory and practice of numismatic portraiture.

CARMINA BURANA

A TEXTBOOK BY **JUDITH LYNN SEBESTA**

ORIGINAL LATIN POEMS • FACING VOCABULARY • ESSAYS • ILLUSTRATIONS

ENGLISH TRANSLATION BY JEFFREY M. DUBAN

REVISED EDITION $8.50. Exam. Copy $5.75

This Textbook contains the 24 *Carmina Burana* Latin songs arranged by Carl Orff, also facing vocabulary and essays by Judith Sebesta, and an English Translation by Jeffrey M. Duban.

This textbook is recommended for classroom use as a delightful and educational supplement for your daily Latin fare (spend just five minutes a class with this textbook and one of the recordings).

Orff's musical arrangement is easily available on cassettes, LP records, and laser disks. In 1983, Ray Manzarek (formerly of The Doors) came out with a rock arrangement, available on cassettes.

Buy this textbook from us, Orff's or Manzarek's recordings from your records store.

SING IT, READ IT, ROCK TO IT

Then watch Latin come alive — unbelievably more than ever — in your classroom and in the showers.

> My general reaction is one of enthusiasm that this text (*Carmina Burana: Cantiones Profanae*), so ripe for intermediate level use, has received such careful attention (by Sebesta). The introductory material deals with the questions one would expect such material to address and does it with sensitivity both to the poetry and to the needs of the prospective student audience. I would welcome an opportunity to use this in an intermediate level course at my own university.
>
> (Edward V. George, University of Texas)

BOLCHAZY-CARDUCCI PUBLISHERS
8 SOUTH MICHIGAN AVENUE
CHICAGO, ILLINOIS 60603